Job and Work ANALYSIS

Second Edition

Job *and* Work
ANALYSIS

Methods, Research, and Applications for Human Resource Management

Michael T. Brannick
University of South Florida

Edward L. Levine
University of South Florida

Frederick P. Morgeson
Michigan State University

SAGE Publications
Los Angeles ▪ London ▪ New Delhi ▪ Singapore

For information:

Sage Publications, Inc.
2455 Teller Road
Thousand Oaks, California 91320
E-mail: order@sagepub.com

Sage Publications Ltd.
1 Oliver's Yard
55 City Road
London EC1Y 1SP
United Kingdom

Sage Publications India Pvt. Ltd.
B-42, Panchsheel Enclave
Post Box 4109
New Delhi 110 017 India

Printed in the United States of America on acid-free paper

Library of Congress Cataloging-in-Publication Data

Brannick, Michael T.
Job and work analysis : methods, research, and applications for human resource
management. / Michael T. Brannick, Edward L. Levine, Frederick P. Morgeson. —
2nd ed.
    p. cm.
Rev. ed. of: Job analysis / Michael T. Brannick, Edward L. Levine. 2002.
Includes bibliographical references and index.
ISBN-13: 978-1-4129-3746-7 (cloth)
    1. Job analysis I. Levine, Edward L. II. Morgeson, Frederick P.
III. Brannick, Michael T. Job analysis. IV. Title.
HF5549.5.J6B65 2007
658.3′06—dc22

2006033698

14 15 16 17 18 10 9 8 7 6 5 4

Acquiring Editor:	Cheri Dellelo
Editorial Assistant:	Anna Mesick
Production Editor:	Sanford Robinson
Copy Editor:	Pam Suwinsky
Typesetter:	C&M Digitals (P) Ltd.
Cover Designer:	Candice Harman

Contents

Preface

Job analysis provides useful tools for those working in human resource management, human factors, and industrial and organizational psychology. Others, such as industrial engineers, have also used these tools. Although job analysis has been with us since the dawn of scientific management, it still provides valuable guidance for those who wish to develop new programs or improve existing ones that enhance the contributions of people in organizations. Such programs can help people work smarter, improve hiring and training, make jobs safer, provide a more satisfying work environment, and even allow some of us to make money watching other people work (the last item is one of our favorites). Once you have read this book, you too will be convinced of the value of job analysis.

Who Will Benefit From This Book?

This book is intended mainly for undergraduate and graduate students in classes covering human resources management, including classes in job analysis, industrial psychology, organizational behavior, and more specific classes in areas such as personnel selection, training, and compensation. The book can stand on its own or be used with another text that covers the class content. Professionals in a variety of areas, especially human resources or personnel, may find the book useful. It should be particularly helpful to those new to the human resources function in companies and in government. But even experienced professionals may find a new wrinkle or two.

Purpose

In this book, we describe several methods for discovering, understanding, and describing the nature of work and applying the results of job analysis to problems arising in the management of people at work. We have made judgment calls about what to include and exclude among the many methods and applications available. Methods that are commonly used in industrial engineering for applications such as work scheduling are given minimal attention. However, we feel that the most important and commonly used methods in human resource management are treated in enough detail that you, the reader, should become familiar with their value and uses. We show in detail some of the marriages between job analysis methods and purposes. We have discovered from teaching job analysis that such marriages are central to understanding its value. Finally, we have incorporated some practical suggestions for doing job analysis based on research and on our own experience. In many places throughout the book, we cross-reference other chapters that are relevant to the topic at hand. Thus, the instructor may choose to assign chapters in an order different from that in the book, and professionals may access those chapters that meet their immediate needs.

A Note on Voice

At various points in the book, we report experiences that one or the other of us has had in job analysis or human resources practice more generally. In such instances, we say "we" rather than distinguish who did what among the authors, for it tends to distract the reader from the point. We often address the reader directly to avoid passive voice.

Acknowledgments

We thank the Sage editorial staff, especially Jim Brace-Thompson, and freelance copy editor Pam Suwinsky for their help with the manuscript; and several reviewers who have either taught with the first edition of this book, carefully read the revised manuscript, or both, for their thoughtful and helpful comments. We also owe a great debt to those who contributed to the current state of our knowledge and skill. Ronald Ash, PhD, and Juan I. Sanchez, PhD, collaborated with us in past research and have been instrumental to our own development. Many others have helped educate us, and more important, advanced the field. They and their work are referred to often in the chapters that follow. A special note of thanks goes to Dr. Ren Nygren at DDI, and Dr. Carol Jenkins at Bigby-Havis for supplying a great deal of useful information on new developments in competency modeling. Also deserving our gratitude are Drs. Dave Thomsen, Alan Mead, and Lyle Leritz at the Economic Research Institute for their updates on the PAQ and the DOT.

1

Introduction

Job analysis and work analysis cover a host of activities, all of which are directed toward discovering, understanding, and describing what people do at work. Although work analysis is the more inclusive term, covering analysis of team functioning, work processes and systems as well as jobs, we bow to tradition and use most often the term *job analysis* in this book. Job analysis and work analysis are important because they form the basis for the solution of virtually every human resource problem. Such problems can be illustrated by a couple of chats we had recently.

Robert Hart (not his real name) is vice president of human resources for InDigital (not the real name of the company, either), a rapidly growing supplier of computer hardware to computer retailers. InDigital uses a test as part of the hiring process for the job of senior sales associate. The test indicates whether sales associates have the knowledge needed to do the job. The test has items about computer hardware, such as what a hard drive is, and items about operating the sales computer system, such as what screen to use to place an order. As a government contractor, InDigital must obey laws that apply to companies receiving federal money. Recently, InDigital was audited by the U.S. Office of Federal Contract Compliance Programs, which enforces laws about equal employment opportunity. The Office of Federal Contract Compliance Programs auditor said to Robert, "Tell me about this *test* you are using for promotion." Robert said, "Oh, that's not a *test*. It's just a little *screen*, you know." It probably will not surprise you to know that the auditor was not satisfied by Hart's attempt to get off the hook. Hart then called us and asked for some help in showing whether the test is a solid indicator of sales knowledge, as required by the Office of Federal Contract Compliance Programs.

Karen Shartle is the owner of Clear Vision, a retailer that produces eyeglasses and contact lenses for customers in about an hour. Karen has three stores, each of which has an optometrist or two on staff, some lab workers, and some salespeople who help clients decide what glasses to buy. Karen called for help with her pay rates. She is having trouble attracting and keeping staff in her stores, and she thinks that her pay scale for the jobs in her stores may be out of line with the pay scales used by others in this industry.

The solution to both of these problems begins with job analysis. Before we can determine how well the test works or what is the proper pay for a job, we need to know what the job is. For the testing problem, we then need to know what knowledge is required to perform the job successfully. For the compensation problem, we need to know the pay of other similar jobs. And for other problems, we need to know special aspects of jobs or of people. In subsequent chapters, we detail several methods for conducting a job analysis to solve problems like these. In the remainder of this chapter, we will (1) present an overview of the book, (2) identify the uses of job analysis, (3) define key terms, (4) describe the major building blocks of job analysis methods, and (5) present a couple of examples of job analysis projects we have completed to whet your appetite for what is to come.

Overview of the Book

As we just noted, Chapter 1 includes definitions and a brief coverage of the uses of job analysis. This chapter is intended to show the practical importance of the material covered in the subsequent chapters. The next four chapters describe the most important techniques of job analysis, with emphasis on those methods that can be used for more than one purpose. Chapter 2 focuses on work-oriented methods, that is, methods that center on what gets done. For example, in the job of auto mechanic, a work-oriented method would focus on tasks such as adjusting brakes. Chapter 3 focuses on worker-oriented methods, that is, methods that center on how the worker does the work. For example, in the job of mechanic, the analysis might focus on the knowledge or judgment used to select the proper tool for the job. Chapter 4 focuses on hybrid methods, that is, those methods that try to gather work- and worker-oriented information simultaneously. Chapter 5 focuses on techniques used to analyze managerial jobs and methods for analyzing the jobs of teams.

Chapter 6 covers job analysis and the law. We mention the most important statutes and describe their implications for conducting job analysis in such a way as to keep out of legal trouble.

The next two chapters describe applications of job analysis. We focus on how best to "marry" the purpose and method (shotgun marriages are not included); we also describe and critique research literature that is relevant for each of the topics. Chapter 7 covers several common human resource applications, including job descriptions, performance appraisal, compensation, and job design. Chapter 8 covers topics most dear to the heart of many an industrial psychologist, namely, staffing and training. Please bear in mind that job analysis is a tool to help us achieve goals in the areas named, not an end in itself. A theme that comes up over and over again is that the purpose we have in mind, and our limits in terms of money and time, will dictate the type of job analysis we do.

The final two chapters cover two rather different topics. In Chapter 9, we discuss doing a job analysis study. We offer a theoretical rationale and practical advice about planning and organizing a job analysis study and collecting and analyzing data. Although such information can be found in other texts, it is not usually found in a single, handy place (if we do say so ourselves), nor is it usually organized with practice in mind, as it is here. Chapter 10, the final chapter, focuses on the future of job analysis.

We have also prepared a small Web site to give supplemental materials that you might find useful. To see it, set your browser to http://jobandworkanalysis .com.

The Uses of Job Analysis

Job analysis is used for a large number of purposes. Several authors have developed lists of such uses, including Ash (1988), Ash and Levine (1980), McCormick (1979), Prien and Ronan (1971), and Zerga (1943). Our list follows but updates that of Ash (1988) and Ash and Levine (1980). The list covers purposes of interest to organizations as they manage their workforces.

1. *Job description.* A job description is a brief written description of work—it's a snapshot intended to communicate the essence of the job. A job description usually contains identifiers (job title plus other classifying information), a summary (mission or objective statement), and duties and tasks (what gets done), and it may contain other information such as reporting relations, accountability, and minimum qualifications. Among other things, job descriptions are important for communicating the nature of the job to someone who doesn't already know what the job is.

2. *Job classification.* Job classification is the process of placing one or more jobs into a cluster or family of similar jobs (for example, because of its requirements, a job is classified, say, as a Programmer Analyst III). The family may be based on lines of authority, duties, and responsibilities of the work or behavioral requirements of the job. Job classification can be important for setting pay rates and selecting employees.

3. *Job evaluation.* Job evaluation is the process of establishing the worth of jobs to an employer. Employers want the pay for various jobs to match their value

in relation to one another within the company and to stack up well against pay rates offered by other companies. By maintaining fair pay, job evaluation helps to attract and retain people.

4. *Job, team, and system design and redesign.* Job design is the process of bundling tasks or clusters of tasks into a collective called a job. Job design is necessary whenever a new job is created. Team design is the process of bundling tasks or clusters of tasks for a team of workers as opposed to individuals. Systems design overlaps with team design but also attends to assigning tasks to equipment and people in the system. Job, team, and system redesign is the sorting of tasks to replace old jobs and functions with new ones. Job redesign is often part of an effort to increase work efficiency. It may also be conducted to increase employee satisfaction, motivation, safety, or product quality. In today's dynamic business climate, many jobs are being redesigned almost on a daily basis.

5. *Human resource requirements and specifications.* Human resource requirements refer to human attributes necessary or desirable for performing the job. Such attributes are often thought of as knowledge, skills, abilities, or other characteristics (KSAOs). For example, an accounting job might require skill in using a 10-key adding machine (or keyboard). Job specifications refer to minimum qualifications or experience that employers require for the job (for example, a college degree in engineering, 6 months of experience as a cashier). These specifications can be used to inform job applicants and staff charged with screening applicants about the standards the applicants must meet.

6. *Performance appraisal.* Performance appraisal is the process of evaluating the job performance of individuals (and now teams) who have been working for some period. Usually, performance appraisals are completed by management and used to help make decisions about raises and promotions and to give workers feedback about their performance. They are sometimes used as motivational tools. Because of equal employment opportunity laws, it has become increasingly important to tie performance appraisals to important tasks and work behaviors required by the job.

7. *Training.* Much of what workers need to know, think, or do to perform successfully on the job is learned after they are hired. Training is the process by which such learning takes place. Job analysis informs the development of training by identifying the key KSAOs job incumbents need to perform the tasks of a job. Once it is clear what KSAOs job incumbents still need to develop, appropriate training can be designed.

8. *Worker mobility.* People move into and out of jobs, and sometimes occupations. It is generally in everyone's best interest that people and jobs fit together well. Career counseling provides individuals with information about jobs and about themselves that is intended to promote beneficial worker mobility. Some organizations provide formal career ladders or paths that are intended to foster skill development and occupational success for individuals.

9. *Workforce planning.* Workforce planning is essentially the flip side of worker mobility. Organizations want to plan for jobs that will need to be filled and to

be confident that qualified applicants will be available to fill them. Job analysis can indicate the KSAOs needed to be successful in a particular job. Organizations can then design selection and training programs to ensure that applicants will possess the needed KSAOs.

10. *Efficiency.* Improving efficiency at work includes things such as shortening the work process or making it easier to do, for example, (1) reducing the number of physical movements in a repetitive task, (2) developing work aids (perhaps a checklist giving all the needed steps for completing a job), or (3) designing better tools (such as a shovel of a certain size).

11. *Safety.* Job analysis can identify specific behaviors and working conditions that increase the chances of accidents and injury. Improving safety can involve changes in the work process, the development of work aids and tools, or changes in the work context (work environment).

12. *Legal and quasi-legal requirements.* Several different laws apply to conditions of employment, including hiring, training, paying, promoting, and firing employees. Several governmental agencies are charged with enforcing such laws. The agencies include, among others, the Equal Employment Opportunity Commission (EEOC), the Office of Federal Contract Compliance Programs (OFCCP), and the Occupational Safety and Health Administration (OSHA). Each agency has sets of guidelines intended to help employers to comply with employment laws. Job analysis is used to describe jobs and worker qualities so that interested parties can determine whether employment practices serve to improve productivity and efficiency and do not unlawfully discriminate against people.

Some might argue that our list of purposes is not complete, that there are other purposes to be served by job analysis. Well, yes, such purposes include quality of work life, stress management, and finding employment for the hardcore unemployed. Some might choose test development as a category. Or we might have added a "miscellaneous" category, except we wanted to avoid 13 purposes. For the sake of harmony, let's assume that the list is reasonably but not totally complete.

Actually, the major category missing from our list is what might be called "societal purposes" for job analysis, purposes that extend beyond the boundaries of any single organization. Some examples include *vocational guidance,* where school-based counselors or counselors in private practice help people find occupations that match their aptitudes and interests; *labor market data,* where job information is used as a basis to report unemployment rates or rates of creation of new jobs; and *skills transferability,* where rehabilitation counselors help disabled or displaced employees move from one type of job or occupation to another. Such are topics for other books.

The 12 purposes in our list are not necessarily exclusive of one another. For example, job classification and job evaluation both can affect pay rates. Changing a job through job design most likely will create a need for training and could change the job requirements and performance appraisal techniques. A single job analysis may be conducted to accomplish several purposes at once. Most of the job analysis techniques described in this book are intended to serve multiple purposes. The take-home message of this section of the chapter has been that job analysis helps to solve practical problems at work and forms the foundation for virtually every human resource management system.

Definitions

Various authors use terms such as *job, position,* and *task* to mean different things. It is important to define terms so that we can communicate effectively. Our scheme is to define a job by approaching it from both ends of the work content spectrum, both the very broad and the very narrow. We begin by working from the very broad end of the spectrum. At the broadest level, we have the entire world of work. This includes all jobs and, because it fails to make distinctions among them, isn't very useful in practical work. Immediately below this level is the *branch.* An example of a branch of the world of work is the public safety branch, which encompasses all those jobs whose content deals with such duties as law enforcement, security, and firefighting and with the effects of natural disasters. The world of work can be divided into about a dozen branches. Each branch can be further divided into about a dozen *groups.* An example of a group within the public safety branch would be law enforcement jobs. Proceeding downward toward our target concept of the job, we can divide groups into a set of *series.* The sworn law enforcement officer series, for example, would include police officer, detective, police sergeant, lieutenant, captain, and major.

Finally, we arrive at the term *job.* An example of a job in the sworn law enforcement officer series might be police officer. A job refers to the work content performed by a group of people with similar work, such as the work described by the title "police officer." The definition of the term *job* is still a bit vague at this point. We will return to it after building up toward the job from the smallest pieces of work content.

The smallest unit of work that can be identified as having a clear beginning, middle, and end is called an *element.* An example from the police officer job would be dialing the telephone. Another way to think about an element is that any smaller unit of work content would require descriptions of physical motions or sensory processes. For example, to dial the phone, you have to pick up the handset and punch in a series of numbers. Reaching for the phone, grasping it, moving it toward the ear, listening for the dial tone, and so forth are all considered here to be physical motions or sensory processes rather than elements of work content.

The next larger unit of work is called an *activity.* Activities are clusters or groups of elements directed at fulfilling a work requirement. A police officer uses the telephone on many occasions as part of the activity "Answering calls related to landlord-tenant disputes." When a job is analyzed down to the level of activities, you might expect to find more than a hundred activities in a typical job and several hundred activities in more complex jobs.

Tasks are collections of activities that are directed toward the achievement of specific job objectives. An example of a task for police officers might be "Talks to conflicting parties to settle disturbances." A thorough job analysis for a typical job will usually produce from 30 to 100 tasks. Tasks have a clear beginning, middle, and end. The end of the task is linked directly to the goals of the job. In the previous example, one of the goals of the job is to settle conflicts.

The next larger unit is the *duty.* This is a collection of tasks all directed at general goals of a job. For police officers, a duty might be "Vice activities," which would include apprehending drug users and sellers, answering calls related to gambling and pornography, and so forth. A thorough job analysis might produce 5 to 12 duties for a typical job.

A *position* is a set of duties, tasks, activities, and elements able to be performed by a single worker. In our terminology, each employed person has a position rather than a job. The *job* is defined as a collection of related positions that are all similar enough in terms of the work performed or in the goals that they serve for the organization so that everybody in the organization agrees to call the positions by the same job title. A recap of the definitions of terms is provided in Table 1.1, using another facet of police work.

We can think of job analysis using a short definition or a long definition. First, the short definition: *Job analysis* refers to the process of discovery of the nature of a job. This is the essential feature of job analysis, and is easy to

Table 1.1   Examples of Defined Terms

Term	Example
Branch	Public safety
Group	Law enforcement
Series	Sworn law enforcement officers
Job	Police officer
Position	Janet O'Mally, Police Officer, District A
Duty	Traffic enforcement
Task	Issue tickets to violators
Activity	Pull motorist over
Element	Switch on siren and lights

remember. However, it isn't as sharp a definition as we would like. Three additional features help shore up our definition. First, to qualify as a job analysis, a systematic procedure is necessary. The procedure involves a number of steps that are specified in advance by the particular method chosen by the *job analyst*, that is, the person analyzing the job. Second, the discovery must proceed by breaking the job up into smaller units. The units could be duties, tasks, activities, or elements. On the other hand, the units might be rather different entities, such as requirements for visual tracking, problem solving, or grasping long-handled tools. Third, the job analysis must result in some written product, either on paper or in electronic form. The job analysis can result in any number of different products, such as a job description, a list of tasks, or a job specification.

To be valuable, a job analysis must be systematic, careful, and thorough. Now, the long definition: *Job analysis* is the systematic process of discovery of the nature of a job by dividing it into smaller units, where the process results in one or more written products with the goal of describing what is done in the job or what capabilities are needed to effectively perform the job.

You may be worried about the distinctions among the levels of the spectrum of work. "How can I tell an activity from a task from a duty?" "Well," we respond, "don't worry; be happy." It turns out that the level (broad to narrow) will depend on what you are doing with the information and that this will tend to be clear when you start the project. For example, if you are doing job evaluation, you will want a few broad descriptions of work, but if you are developing off-the-job training, you will want very specific, step-by-step descriptions (maybe even elements). So bottom line, worry about getting the information to serve the purpose for which you are doing the job analysis rather than making fine discriminations among terms.

Building Blocks of Job Analysis Methods

Job analysis methods are made up of a large number of building blocks, but these all fall into four categories:

1. Kinds of job *data* collected

2. Methods of *gathering* data

3. *Sources* of job information

4. Units of *analysis*—what gets analyzed, including the level of detail

At this point, you might be thinking, "At last! Just what I always wanted to know!" On the other hand, you might be thinking, "Why have we got another list in this chapter?" To be an effective job analyst, you have to know what you are doing, and that means making lots of choices about the methods you use. To make informed choices about the methods, you first need to know what the choices are. The choices are what this list is about. It may help to think about the choice you would have to make to analyze a specific job (perhaps a job you might want someday) while reading through the building blocks. We describe each component of a job analysis method in some detail.

KINDS OF JOB DATA COLLECTED: DESCRIPTORS

Designers of job analysis methods usually have some purpose in mind for their method, and they design it so that the kinds of data collected will serve that purpose. For example, those who want to develop tests for selecting new employees will typically collect data about employee characteristics, such as abilities or skills. The following list runs from more general kinds of data to more specific kinds of data and is aimed at the study of jobs performed by individuals rather than work teams.

1. *Organizational philosophy and structure.* This type of data reflects the way that a job fits into the organization and its mission. For example, if we analyze the job of prison guard or correctional officer, we will try to determine whether management views the job as serving a rehabilitative function or a custodial function. We can expect a correctional officer who is viewed as a rehabilitator to spend more time with inmates, to interact more pleasantly with them, and to offer counseling on a variety of issues. The correctional officer who is a custodian is more likely to watch rather than interact with inmates, to speak curtly and formally to them, and to refer requests for advice and help to workers designated as counselors.
    The organizational structure refers mainly to an organizational chart. This type of information reveals what the relationships among jobs are and the nature of the supervisor/subordinate reporting relationships. A chart showing that electricians have apprentices reporting to them suggests immediately that at least a part of the electrician's job consists of training activities.

2. *Licensing and other government-mandated requirements.* These requirements may influence a job's content directly or may place limitations on the type of person who may hold the job. For example, in health service organizations, there are a number of professional jobs that may require suitably licensed or certified practitioners, the prime one among them being the physician. Water and wastewater treatment plant operator in water and sewage treatment facilities is another example of a job that requires a state license. Such licensing requirements may foster studying, training, and other activities in the job so that the worker may acquire and retain the license.

3. *Responsibilities.* Information about responsibilities tells us what types and levels of authority and accountability a jobholder has. For example, when

analyzing the job of bank manager, it may be helpful for a job analyst to know whether a manager can approve loans, and if so, how large the amounts of the loans may be.

4. *Professional standards.* Workers who consider themselves to be professionals usually form professional associations (for example, the Society for Industrial and Organizational Psychology, the American Medical Association, or even the National Federation of Associations, which is dedicated to the spirit of joining). These in turn are likely to establish standards of conduct that affect the performance of a job. For example, psychologists who use or develop tests in their jobs are guided by the testing standards of the American Psychological Association. A professional psychologist who is involved in testing clients, applicants, and employees must adhere to these standards or risk censure and expulsion from the association.

5. *Job context.* Information about job context deals with the environment that surrounds the job. Is the work conducted in a hot or a cold climate? Indoors or outdoors? In a dangerous setting or a safe one? Are workers crowded together or separate? Are workers paid by the piece or by the week? Are workers on rotating shifts or standard work schedules? All these and other questions provide an understanding of the setting within which job activities take place.

6. *Products and services.* Information on the products and services produced by the worker in a job is often critical for insight into the nature of the work. Take the activity of throwing pots (making ceramics). If we can see the bowls, pots, coffee cups, and other products produced by the potter, we would learn quite a bit about the nature of the activity (turning, pinching, glazing, firing, and so on). Notice that most of this stuff is perfectly round. But, is there something different about the handle of the coffee cup? Or consider a chiropractor. We would learn a great deal about the job by watching a chiropractor apply forces of various kinds to patients' backs. What about the use of hands, machines, and other devices?

7. *Machines, tools, equipment, work aids, and checklists.* Some jobs rely heavily on machines, tools, and equipment. Skilled craft jobs such as plumber and electrician are key examples. A full understanding of these jobs would be impossible without an inventory of the tools, machines, and equipment used in the job. We once reviewed applications for the job of printer. Under the description of duties, the applicants listed only the brands and model numbers of the printing machinery they operated. Some jobs are named for the machine, such as "forklift operator." Work aids and checklists refer to guides for the worker that tell what sequence of steps must be carried out to complete a task. A pilot must follow a rather extensive checklist before takeoff to ensure that the plane is safe and ready. Such work aids are treasure troves of information for the job analyst.

8. *Work performance indicators.* Information on work performance might include the length of time it takes to complete a task, standards on quality of performance required, and standards that specify the manner in which activities may be carried out. There is some overlap here with professional standards, except

that work performance standards are set by companies, factories, or public agencies themselves, not by professions. Organizations may establish such standards to show what constitutes a fair day's work, or what amount of scrap or waste can be tolerated.

9. *Personal job demands.* Information on personal job demands might touch on physical demands. For example, an analyst might need to know if the job requires climbing, bending, crouching, or lifting heavy objects. In addition, a job analyst might explore the physical costs to the worker in terms of fatigue, consumption of a certain amount of oxygen, and enduring the stress of heat, cold, or gravity. The job of astronaut is one for which these types of data are critical. Likewise, the job analyst might need to know about social and psychological demands. Does the job call for unusual work schedules, intense periods of concentration, or long periods of time when a worker must remain alert but nothing happens? A police officer's job is a case where these kinds of job aspects are important.

10. *Elemental motions.* For certain jobs in which many complicated maneuvers are made very quickly, such as a professional football player, the analyst may have to pay attention to the individual elements that make up these maneuvers. Otherwise, the analyst would not understand tasks like blocking or tackling. Assembly jobs are another example.

11. *Worker activities.* This kind of information attempts to look at the job from inside the worker looking out. As a result, it focuses on the worker's mind, senses, and ways of responding to situational demands. Thus, making decisions, interpreting visual information, solving a work problem, planning a correct response, and making the response all fall under this category of data. Viewing jobs in this way, job analysts can analyze many different kinds of jobs into a common set of worker activities. Recently worker emotions have become a focus of interest, and indicate what kind of emotional responses and displays the worker is expected to engage in. Some refer to this as "emotional labor."

12. *Work activities.* Unlike *worker* activities, data on *work* activities come from a vantage point outside the worker and are based on the observable behaviors of the worker. Thus, fixing a flat tire, typing a report, and giving aspirin to a patient are examples of the kinds of data we get when we focus on work activities.

13. *Worker characteristic requirements.* What are the skills, abilities, knowledge, attitudes, values, and personality traits needed to perform a job? Does the job require people who are extroverted, methodical, expert in a computer language, or proficient in dancing? This type of data is what we are after when we study a job's worker characteristic requirements. For activities such as employee selection and training, this type of information is usually critical.

14. *Future changes.* A careful job analysis may consider changes to the mission or goals of the work and also changes to the tasks, particularly through changes in the machines, tools, equipment, and work aids. For many jobs, new technology is being introduced that changes the nature of the tasks to be

performed. Depending on the purpose of the job analysis, the changes may be quite significant. For example, if the main part of the job is operating a complex piece of machinery and the whole interface between the person and the machine will be changing in 6 months, it makes little sense to devise an extensive training program for the current machine. Instead, it might make more sense to devise training for the new machine.

15. *Critical incidents.* Critical incidents are short stories about particular instances of either outstanding or poor performance. Each must include the conditions and the problem faced by a worker, what the worker did, and the outcome. A critical incident of outstanding performance for the job of first-line supervisor in an electric power plant might be, "The supervisor smelled a poisonous gas. He immediately donned a gas mask and evacuated the area. Then he spotted the source of trouble, shut down the equipment, tagged it, and had a mechanic repair it. Before shutdown he notified the operator to get another unit in service so the supply of electricity was not interrupted."

Table 1.2 lists each of the kinds of data that an analyst might collect and examples of most kinds of data taken from the job of a police officer. In particular situations and to accomplish the purposes of a job analysis, the list of descriptors may need to be expanded or refined. For example Morgeson, Delaney-Klinger, and Hemingway (2005) found that role breadth was importantly implicated in job performance. They defined this variable as the sheer number of tasks incumbents claim to perform. The greater the number, the better was the performance in their study. In the context of teams and team training, Levine and Baker (1990) added such descriptors as team mission. The Occupational Information Network (O*NET) is designed to serve society at large and so has a much more elaborate set of descriptors than the list presented here. Chapter 4 covers the O*NET system in detail.

METHODS OF DATA COLLECTION

Having selected the types of data you want, you now have to figure out the ways to gather it. The list that follows covers the methods that job analysts use for data collection.

1. *Observing.* A job analyst may learn a good deal about a job simply by observing and recording what a worker does. Naturalistic observation occurs when the analyst's presence has little or no effect on the worker's behavior. This can be achieved by conducting observations over a long enough period of time that the worker no longer pays any attention to the analyst. Or the analyst may observe more actively by asking questions about particular behaviors as they occur. An example of the latter approach is the ride-along process when a police officer's job is being analyzed. The police officer typically explains the reasons for certain actions and responds to questions posed about work behaviors by the job analyst during an 8-hour shift in a patrol car.

Table 1.2   Examples of Descriptors

Descriptor	Example for the Job of Police Officer
Organization philosophy and structure	To protect and serve the public; paramilitary structure; reports to sergeant
Licensing and other government-mandated requirements	Certification as a peace officer by the State Police Officer Standards and Training Board
Responsibilities	Decides when to use deadly force
Job context	Physical danger; work on holidays; may involve working around horrible smells (for example, arresting an advanced alcoholic); rotating shifts
Products and services	Enforces traffic laws; assists stranded motorists
Machines, tools, work aids, and equipment	Computer, flash light, handcuffs, "Miranda" card, patrol car, regulation firearms; computer terminal
Work performance indicators	Arrest records
Personal job demands	Periods of inactivity followed by exertion; may involve climbing, sprinting, crouching, and so on; long periods of driving and sitting in patrol car
Elemental motions	Applying a choke hold
Worker activities	Decide whether vehicle registration has expired
Work activities	Write traffic ticket
Worker trait requirements	Honesty; drug avoidance
Critical incidents	Although off duty, Officer Brandon noticed two motorists who were about to come to blows over a parking space. She stopped them from shouting at one another and got them to choose the winner by flipping a coin. The winner parked and the loser drove away without further argument.

The willingness to get out in the field with a worker often has a side benefit over and above the gaining of familiarity with the job. When observation is part of the analysis, the job analyst often gains increased acceptance and increased credibility among workers and supervisors in the organization. Martinko (1988) offered some helpful hints about how to observe employees working. Capturing a representative sample of work activity during periods of observation is critical.

2. *Interviewing individuals.* In this method, the job analyst asks questions of jobholders and supervisors about a job under study. The interviews are typically based on what took place during some period of time, such as the previous day, week, or month. Carefully planned and structured interviews will typically work best.

3. *Group interviews.* A group of knowledgeable workers and supervisors may be assembled for the purpose of discussing a job. Group interviews offer the advantage of making more efficient use of the analyst's time. Also, fewer burdens are placed on the analyst when it comes to integrating the information that might be gathered in a series of individual interviews.

4. *Technical conference.* A technical conference involves meeting one or more experts to better understand the reasons for the existence of a job. For example, for a sewage processing technician job, a staff chemist might be interviewed to better understand how sewage is purified. This allows the analyst to understand the functions of the technician's equipment.

5. *Questionnaires.* Questionnaires may be considered self-administered interviews that are typically very carefully structured and pretested. Often the items on a questionnaire are tasks or activities, and workers are asked to evaluate the tasks on one or more different scales. One such scale might be how difficult each task is to perform.

6. *Diaries.* The diary is a method in which incumbents write down periodically the activities they have been engaged in at a particular time. Diary keeping may require that workers make an entry each time they switch tasks. Still another approach to diary keeping may involve making entries every half-hour to indicate what the worker has done during the preceding half-hour. Typically, diaries are kept over a 2- to 3-week period.

7. *Equipment-based methods.* Sometimes a job analyst may collect data about jobs by using equipment of some sort. Most commonly, the equipment might consist of a recording device such as a camera, videotape recorder, or audio-tape recorder. If the nature of the data to be collected bears on the physical demands on a worker, then measuring devices such as electrocardiograms might be used.

8. *Reviewing records.* A job analyst will often find a great deal of useful information in company records. Previous job performance appraisal material, position descriptions, accident reports, correspondence that is issued by a worker, and examples of other work products contained in records are illustrations of the kinds of things a job analyst might look for.

9. *Reviewing literature.* A job analyst may consult reports and books produced inside a particular organization or outside of it. The inside materials might include training manuals, training materials, checklists, and user manuals. Materials from outside the organization might include books about particular occupations, job analysis studies conducted in other settings that are summarized in report form, previous job descriptions, or published job analysis databases.

10. *Studying equipment design specifications.* Where a job is heavily dependent on equipment or machinery, a job analyst may learn a great deal about the job by studying material such as blueprints or schematic drawings. These may provide insight into how the worker must interact with the particular piece of equipment.

11. *Doing the work.* Although rarely done in practice, analysts may sometimes decide to learn about the job under analysis by actually doing it. This approach is usually limited to simple jobs, and where errors in performance are not highly critical. Thus, an analyst would not want to engage in the work of a brain surgeon but might serve as a baker's assistant or a trucker's helper. However, not all such projects are dull. We know of one analyst who learned to fly an airplane as part of a job analysis project.

SOURCES OF JOB ANALYSIS DATA

Because the sources of data are, with only a few exceptions, indicated by method of data collection, we merely list them here. Where the connection is not obvious, we offer a few words of explanation. Sources that may supply job analysis data include the following:

1. The job analyst

2. The jobholder's immediate supervisor

3. A high-level executive or manager

4. The jobholder

5. A technical expert such as a chemist or college professor

6. An organizational training specialist

7. Clients or customers

8. Other organizational units

9. Written documents (for example, records, equipment specifications)

10. Previous job analyses

Two members of the list probably need a bit of explanation. Clients or customers offer a special perspective on how a job should be done. Their information may help to establish standards of performance or to suggest tasks that need to be done but are not currently being done by a worker. In this age of concern about customer service and customer satisfaction, the customer is more and more frequently used. Including clients may also serve a political purpose. We recently involved community members in the analysis of police officer jobs in part to show community involvement in the job analysis and also to increase community acceptance of the resulting job description. Organizational units that interact with the unit where a job being analyzed is situated may be quite helpful in clarifying how the job fits into the total organizational scheme. For example, we might ask employees in the human resources department of a company how they work with the research and development department. Other organizational units may be internal customers of the job where clients are external customers of the job.

UNITS OF ANALYSIS

When designing the job analysis method, we have decided to collect certain kinds of data, to collect it by means of a particular method, and to enlist the aid of specific sources for our data. Now we need to attend to the issue of how we will summarize, analyze, and report the data. We describe here nine methods of data analysis and reporting. Some of the data analytic strategies overlap with the kinds of job data collected, discussed earlier. This is because the kind of job data collected may not necessarily be the end product we desire. For example, we may collect work activities, but we may analyze the activities by listing the worker characteristics needed to perform the activities. Or we may collect information on duties and tasks, but group them into job dimensions. For example, duties and tasks related to assigning work to others, evaluating others, and assisting others' progress may be grouped into a job dimension called "leadership."

1. *Duties.* We may collect a host of different kinds of job data from numerous different sources by various means and summarize it by describing the dozen or so major duties performed by people in a particular job. Because statements of duties capture a great deal of information about a job in a relatively few words, the use of duties as a mode of analysis may be helpful for such functions as job evaluation and classification or creation of job families. An example of a duty might be "Preparing and managing a budget."

2. *Tasks.* Rather than analyze at the level of duties, we may decide to summarize our data in the form of tasks. Tasks may lend themselves to a variety of applications where the need for a relatively comprehensive picture of the job exists. Employee selection is one such application. We might be able to transform one or more tasks directly into a work sample test, in which applicants are scored on their ability to perform important parts of the job.

3. *Activities.* Activities often serve as the items in questionnaires that are sent to incumbents and their supervisors for completion. They are quite efficient in this role, and the job analyst may be content to report them in the form of activities, rather than combining the data into tasks or duties.

4. *Elemental motions.* Job analysts who are concerned about the most efficient ways to do physical work usually will summarize their data in the form of elemental motions. Such detailed information may prove helpful in designing work and in teaching new workers how to accomplish a task. We once toured a friend's bakery. During the tour, he asked for help in making rolls, and he demonstrated how to shape the rolls by hand. His movements were quick and sure and inevitably resulted in a near perfect roll. After several attempts, we gave up because we just could not make a good-looking roll. But if we had had a slow-motion video to watch with stop action and a list of elements, we might have been more successful.

5. *Job dimensions.* We may take a variety of job analysis data and summarize the data in the form of basic job dimensions. These are different from duties because they focus on the workers' sensory and mental processes as well as the workers' modes of response. Examples of job dimensions are "Organization of work," "Planning," and "Decision making." The *Position Analysis Questionnaire* method of job analysis (described in Chapter 3) relies on job dimensions that have been derived from careful research. These job dimensions are groupings or clusters of the worker activities we described under the heading "Kinds of Job Data Collected." Other systems of job analysis also deal with job dimensions. In the *Threshold Traits Analysis System* (see Chapter 3), two out of a larger number of job dimensions are "Vigilance and attention" and "Application of information and skill."

6. *Worker characteristic requirements.* Sometimes a job analyst may be content to analyze and summarize job data in the form of worker characteristic requirements. Some methods of job analysis have predetermined listings of characteristic requirements. Two examples of such methods are (1) *threshold traits analysis,* which uses 33 worker traits, such as "creativity" and "oral expression," and (2) *task analysis* as conducted by the U.S. Department of Labor, which uses a fairly comprehensive list of worker attributes including cognitive abilities, interests, and temperaments. Other methods of job analysis rely on listings of worker characteristic requirements that are developed for particular jobs. The *job element method* (see Chapter 3) focuses only on worker characteristic requirements and generally yields a listing of 50 or more types of knowledge, skill, ability, and other characteristics that a worker must possess to do the job under analysis.

7. *Scales applied to units of work.* Some job analysts may not be content to list all the tasks or duties or activities or dimensions of a job. Rather, they go further and apply a number of scales to the activities, tasks, or duties they choose. Such scales allow analysts to make judgments about a number of things. For example, the use of such scales may indicate how difficult or important a task is for a job relative to other tasks. Scales may also be used to indicate the extent to

which particular tasks involve certain kinds of interactions with data, people, or things. The data, people, and things scales are part of the job analysis method called *functional job analysis*, which is described in Chapter 2. Scales may also be devised for particular applications. For example, if an analyst is interested in building a training program, he or she may develop a scale to assess how difficult a task is to learn.

8. *Scales applied to worker characteristic requirements.* Just as scales may be applied to units of work, so may they be applied to worker characteristics. For example, a selection specialist may wish to know which among a large number of job-related abilities are the most important ones to measure. The job element method of job analysis includes scales to measure whether particular abilities or skills can distinguish between superior and average workers, and such scales help determine what abilities are most important. Some scales try to gauge the extent to which characteristics are needed to carry out tasks. Information about closely linked task-trait combinations can be useful for designing a training program.

9. *Qualitative versus quantitative analysis.* Last but not least in this list is the extent to which each job analyst relies on narrative descriptions of what has been found rather than statistical analysis of numbers derived from scales. As job analysis becomes more and more scientific, there seems to be more reliance on numbers. But qualitative descriptions still have their place in such documents as job descriptions.

SUMMARY OF THE BUILDING BLOCKS

Table 1.3 provides a checklist of each of the four kinds of descriptors and their elements. This could come in handy if you are either planning a job analysis or reviewing one.

A Couple of Job Analysis Projects

You want to get your hands in to see how things work, do you? Okay, here are a couple of examples of how we went about analyzing jobs in two different organizations. These examples illustrate the four building blocks we described in this chapter. They also anticipate some aspects of Chapter 9, where we get into the nitty-gritty of actually conducting a job analysis.

EXAMPLE 1: EVALUATION OF AN ELECTRICAL TRANSMISSION AND DISTRIBUTION TRAINING PROGRAM

We were asked to evaluate the effectiveness of a training program used for the lineman job at a medium-sized electric utility company. The training

Table 1.3   Summary of Building Blocks

Descriptor	Method of Data Collection
1. Organization philosophy and structure	1. Observing
2. Licensing and other government-mandated requirements	2. Interviewing individuals
3. Responsibilities	3. Interviewing groups
4. Professional standards	4. Technical conferences
5. Job context	5. Questionnaires
6. Products and services	6. Diaries
7. Machines, tools, work aids, and checklists	7. Equipment-based methods
8. Work performance indicators	8. Reviewing records
9. Personal job demands	9. Reviewing literature
10. Elemental motions	10. Studying equipment design specifications
11. Worker activities	11. Doing the work
12. Work activities	
13. Worker trait requirements	
14. Future changes	
15. Critical incidents	

Sources of Job Analysis Data	Units of Analysis
1. Job analyst	1. Duties
2. Job holder's supervisor	2. Tasks
3. High-level executive	3. Activities
4. Job holder	4. Elemental motions
5. Technical expert	5. Job dimensions
6. Organizational training specialist	6. Worker characteristic requirements
7. Clients or customers	7. Scales applied to units of work
8. Other organizational units	8. Scales applied to worker characteristic requirements
9. Written documents (for example, records, equipment specifications)	9. Qualitative versus quantitative considerations
10. Previous job analyses	

program offered 242 separate modules, which were part of a multiyear apprenticeship program for these hardy, brave souls who keep the electricity flowing even during stormy and windy conditions. As part of this effort, we wanted to provide evidence of the validity of the program by *showing how the training content compared with job requirements.* This purpose drove our choice of methods to use. Know your purpose! This is key to all that follows.

Company management hired us. To kick off the project, we met with Transmission and Distribution (T&D) training staff to introduce the project and to find out if they had any issues needing attention. (As an aside for all you future consultants, you depend upon the people in the company to achieve your goals. Win them over up-front by inviting them to be part of the process.) We thought that tasks (see Chapters 2 and 4 for more about tasks) and knowledges, skills, abilities, and other personal characteristics (see Chapters 3 and 4 for more about KSAOs) would be just the thing to focus on. The tasks and KSAOs correspond to the descriptors 12 and 13 in the list shown in "Kinds of Job Data Collected" earlier in the chapter. As an alert reader, you have doubtless anticipated something about the units of analysis to be used as well.

Luckily we had access to a previously compiled list of 385 tasks (for example, install automatic dead-ends on wire) and 34 KSAOs developed after hiring on with the company (for example, ability to rig headlines, slings, and come-alongs). Companies keep this sort of information if they think it will come in handy, and in a training department, it typically does. Check out our list of "Sources of Information," items 9 and 10.

We assembled a group of job experts, including linemen, supervisors, a T&D trainer and a planner analyst. This group had a collective 154 years of experience. If you jump back to our list of sources of information, you may notice that items 2, 4, 5, and 6 apply, though not in that order. We leave the proper ordering and the popping of aspirin as exercises for the reader. Back to our story. We first met the group to explain that we wanted them to review and revise the tasks, KSAOs, and ratings of their relative importance. We gave them complete lists to study and analyze on their own. The group reconvened 3 weeks later, and made changes to ratings of 14 tasks, deleted six, split a few into two, and changed the step in the apprentice progression in which 27 tasks would first be done. Eight KSAOs were re-ranked in importance. You have doubtless noticed that we mentioned having our experts review ratings of tasks and of KSAOs. Check out items 7 and 8 in our list of units of analysis.

We then reviewed the modules against the tasks and found that 359 of 385 (93 percent) were covered by the 242 modules, while 27 of the 34 KSAOs (79 percent) were developed by the training modules. These data were entered into a report and to us represented solid evidence of the content validity of the training. Here we are, back at the original purpose of the study. We hope that you can see some kind of logic to our choices for the project, mainly that what we did seems to be relevant to the purpose and outcome of the study. Let us try another example in which, you, the alert reader, will pick out the purpose of the study, descriptors of job data, methods of data collection, sources of job analysis data, and units of analysis.

EXAMPLE 2: JOB ANALYSIS FOR
DEVELOPING MINIMUM QUALIFICATIONS

Here's another, different example that is all about selection of staff rather than training. As part of a long-running court case on equal employment opportunity, a large hospital delivering mental health services to in-patients and outpatients faced a problem with the minimum qualifications (MQs) it was using to screen people for a large variety of jobs. Minimum qualifications are typically statements of education, training, and work experience that people must have to be considered for a job. An example for a professor would be a PhD degree in some specialty and 2 years of postdoctoral experience. The court case had found some indication that MQs for a bunch of jobs had an adverse effect on the job chances of members of a certain minority group. The court turned to us to establish whether the MQs were valid in screening out those who were not qualified for the jobs they applied for, which would justify the use of these MQs even though they had an adverse effect on job chances of the plaintiffs. We found that there was really no accepted method for developing and validating MQs, and so with the help of staff at the hospital and the state human resources department we invented one that the court accepted. Here's how it works. We will illustrate with one of the jobs from the bunch where the MQs were in question, namely—pharmacy technician (PT).

Of course we held meetings with key staff to kick the project off. We had our purpose specified as developing valid MQs for this job. The original MQs for PT were, "Two years of experience in assisting a registered pharmacist in the compounding and dispensing of prescriptions."

As with our first example, we decided that our stated purpose could be best accomplished by using tasks and KSAs (not O's because O's involve things like personality and you can't tell about personality from a job application), but with a twist. We first developed full lists of tasks and KSAs with the aid of panels of six to nine job experts—one panel for tasks and one for KSAs. But rather than using the full list of tasks and KSAs as a basis for developing and validating MQs, we wanted to split out a smaller number of these that were suited for distinguishing between those who are just barely acceptable for a job and those who are not. This is, after all, what MQs are designed to do. So in a fit of ingenuity (we book authors like to flatter ourselves) we created scales that the experts could use to identify those particular tasks and KSAs. For the tasks, we asked experts to tell us whether even barely acceptable employees should be able to perform the task being rated (Yes or No). For KSAs, we asked experts to tell us whether even barely acceptable employees must possess the level or amount of this KSA to do the job (Yes or No). An example of a task that survived the cut was, "Check patient records to determine drug allergies and interactions." A KSA that made it through was, "Ability to communicate orally with pharmacists/other health care professionals." Notice that the experts said that even barely acceptable beginning pharmacy techs would have both these qualities.

From this more select list of tasks and KSAs, human resource specialists could do research to find out what kinds of training, education, and work experience would provide the capacity to carry out the tasks or develop the KSAs needed for even a barely acceptable worker. They then formulated what we called "MQ profiles" that another panel of experts rated in terms of whether each of the profiles provided the prospective employee with what is needed to perform at a barely acceptable level on each task and KSA in the select lists. For PT, six different profiles survived this rating process. So now there would be six ways for people to qualify, not just the one way based on the original MQs. Two of the profiles included, "Eighteen months of experience assisting a pharmacist in a *non-hospital* setting. Such duties must include maintaining patient medication records, setting up, packaging and labeling medication doses; and maintaining inventories of drugs and supplies," and, "Completion of a Hospital Pharmacy Technician program accredited by the American Society of Hospital Pharmacists." Clearly the new MQs allow for more ways to qualify, and shorten the time requirements, thus enhancing the job chances of all applicants including those in the plaintiff's group. The findings for PT and numerous other jobs were fully documented in technical reports filed with the court.

Those interested readers who want a more complete version of the MQ example can access the paper by Levine, Maye, Ulm, and Gordon (1997). (This is not to imply that all you readers are not utterly fascinated by this example. We know there are other legitimate demands on your time.) A more recent take on job analysis for MQ development can be found in the paper by Buster, Roth, and Bobko (2005).

Chapter Summary

This chapter has fulfilled four primary goals. First, we have argued that job analysis is important because it forms the basis of solutions to many practical problems. Second, we provided an overview of the book. Third, we offered definitions of several terms used in job analysis, especially the job. Fourth, we presented descriptions of the building blocks of all job analysis methods. Finally we presented a couple of examples of projects that indicate how job analysis helped accomplish important objectives. Now that you have gained familiarity with the basic aspects, you are ready to move ahead with your exploration of the exciting world of job analysis.

2

Work-Oriented Methods

This chapter and the three that follow focus on methods of job analysis that are primarily applicable to purposes pursued by human resource specialists and industrial/organizational psychologists. Some methods, such as time-and-motion study, should be of interest to industrial engineers or engineering psychologists. Within this context, we have selected methods for closer review based on our judgment about their extent of use for more than one purpose. The reader should be aware that there are a large number of methods available, and not all of them can be covered in detail within a textbook. For information on other methods we cannot cover here due to space limitations, an excellent source is the *Job Analysis Handbook,* edited by Gael, Cornelius, Levine, and Salvendy (1988). Some of the information in this chapter is practical, how-to-do-it material. If you need more than what is here, jump to the second half of Chapter 9, where we provide additional practical details.

The focus of this chapter is on work-oriented methods, that is, methods that concentrate primarily on what the worker does, including tasks, tools, machines, and work context. Other methods focus on attributes of the worker needed to successfully accomplish the work, such as strength, mental computation, or the knowledge of real estate law. Such methods are known as *worker-oriented methods,* and these are the focus of Chapter 3. Some methods attempt to gather extensive information about the work and the worker simultaneously. Such methods are called *hybrid methods,* and these are described in Chapter 4. Chapter 5 is reserved for methods for analyzing the work of managers and teams. To some extent, our placement of methods into chapters is as much a matter of convenience as of real distinction among methods. We discuss functional job analysis in the chapter on work-oriented methods, for example, but we could have placed it just as easily into the hybrid chapter. Therefore, it is more accurate to think about work and worker orientations as matters of emphasis or degree rather than all or none.

Four general types of work-oriented job analysis are described in this chapter. We call the first, general kind of job analysis *time-and-motion* study (see Amrine, Ritchey, & Hulley, 1975; Davis et al., 2004; International Labour Organization, 1992; Mundel & Danner, 1994). Time-and-motion study refers to a large number of specialized techniques usually aimed at improving the effectiveness or efficiency of work. The second general area is *functional job analysis* (FJA). FJA is broken into two closely related methods, the U.S. Department of Labor (DOL) method, described in the *Handbook for Analyzing Jobs* (U.S. Department of Labor, 1972), and Fine's FJA, described in Fine and Cronshaw (1999). The third type of work-oriented method of job analysis is the *task inventory*. Two related versions of the task inventory are described: the *Comprehensive Occupational Data Analysis Program* (Christal & Weissmuller, 1977) and the *Work Performance Survey System* (Gael, 1983). The fourth method is known as the *critical incident technique* (Bownas & Bernardin, 1988; Flanagan, 1954).

The primary function of work-oriented job analysis methods is to allow the job analyst to understand what the worker does in the job and to document and communicate that understanding. The four kinds of job analysis methods differ in how they achieve that purpose. The methods also differ in their suitability for other purposes, such as specifying content for training, writing job descriptions, and so forth.

Time-and-Motion Study

Time-and-motion study evolved primarily from industrial engineering rather than from industrial psychology. Pioneers in this field included Frederick Taylor and Frank and Lillian Gilbreth, who studied, among other things, bricklayers and physically disabled workers. The primary goal of time-and-motion study is to improve effectiveness or efficiency of job performance, although it has also been used for other purposes, including the design of training programs and inferring the human abilities necessary for completing tasks. It is most often used in manufacturing and construction industries.

Time-and-motion study encompasses a large number of techniques. The particular technique chosen for a study will depend on the purpose of the analysis. For clarity of presentation, we distinguish between time study and motion study. Although time study and motion study often use identical techniques, they are usually aimed at different targets.

Time study is directed mainly toward discovering the time taken to complete a given task or the time allocated to different tasks that comprise a job. Time to complete a task is often used to set standard times for task completion, for example, how long it should take to drill a hole in a certain piece of metal with a drill press or to sew a zipper into a garment with a sewing machine. When time allocation across tasks is the primary focus, the main purpose may be either to describe the amount of time on various tasks for staffing purposes (for example, job applicants can be told that for the majority of their time on this job they will be discussing manuscripts with authors over the phone) or as a preliminary step. If the preliminary step shows particular tasks to be the most time consuming, those tasks will be good candidates for redesign to improve efficiency.

In motion study, the main effort goes into discovering the sequence of steps (often body motions) used in completing a task. A bricklayer, for example, moves mortar from a palette to the bricks already in place using a trowel and spreads the mortar so as to hold the brick. The bricklayer then places the brick on the mortar, taps the brick in place, and removes excess mortar with the trowel.

Effectiveness and efficiency are typically improved in time-and-motion study through a deliberate process of design that may include making the task easier for the worker by changing the process of work, the job context (for example, lighting), the materials input to the job, or the product output from the job. In bricklaying, for example, efficiency may be improved by minimizing the number of strokes of the trowel per brick and minimizing the distance that the brick must travel to be put into place. Although the savings in time for a single brick may be small, the savings in time to build a brick wall will be large.

TIME STUDY

Work Sampling

Work sampling is a method of gathering observations about one or more workers over time. A chart of all the activities (usually the tasks in the job plus reasons for not being on task) is drawn up before the study. For a professor's job, categories might include giving lectures, writing exams, grading papers, analyzing data, writing reports, and dozing at one's desk (just kidding on this last one). Over a period of time, frequencies of all the activities will be gathered; a typical study may include 2,000 observations over a 2-week period (Niebel, 1988), although there are methods for estimating the number of observations needed for a given degree of accuracy of the results (Mundel & Danner, 1994, pp. 126–129). At the end of the study, relative frequencies will be converted to percentages. Such percentages estimate the relative amounts of time that the worker spends on each category. Illustrations of observation forms for two such studies appear in Tables 2.1 and 2.2.

For most work sampling studies, an observer will be hired and trained to carry out the observations at random time intervals. This is not the only method of observation, however. Cameras have been used to take pictures or videotapes of worker behavior at random intervals. Such pictures are scored (that is, assigned to work activities) while viewing the pictures. Sometimes the

Table 2.1   Industrial Work Sample Summary

Machine	Cutting	Setup	Idle	Inspect	Misc	Total
20′ VBM	101	7	14	2	6	130
16′ VBM	102	34	14	15	0	165
16′ Planer	119	34	10	5	5	173
14′ Planer	140	8	5	7	2	162
72′ Lathe	99	13	12	7	3	134
Total	561	96	55	36	16	764
%	73.43	12.57	7.12	4.71	2.09	100

SOURCE: Adapted from Niebel, B. W. (1982). *Motion and Time Study,* p. 557. Homewood IL: Irwin. Reproduced with permission of the McGraw-Hill Companies.

Table 2.2   Work Sampling of Bank Tellers in a Branch

Observer: Murphy						
	Observation Times					
Employee	8:29	8:57	10:15	12:40	1:50	3:10
Ames	1	7	8	1	6	2
Bruk	2	1	2	5	2	1
Carter	Absent					
Hotelling	3	1	2	1	4	8
Jackson	2	3	2	4	1	2
Montgomery	1	1	2	1	4	4
Stahl	Absent			2	1	2

Categories: 1. Check cashing; 2. Depositing funds; 3. Instructions; 4. Money orders; 5. Calculating; 6. Act-to-act moves; 7. Balances; 8. Idle/waiting.

workers themselves keep track of their activities. Usually, a system such as a bell or a beeper is used to make sure that the incumbent writes down activities at randomly chosen times. Incumbents are probably not the best source of information if the study is to focus on time away from task.

Standard Setting

Work sampling can be used in setting standard times (expected performance task times for proficient workers). However, work sampling does not directly estimate the amount of time necessary for a qualified worker to accomplish a task successfully. Several other methods are useful in establishing an allowed time standard, that is, a specific time that should be used to accomplish a task when the task is being performed according to preferred procedures, the equipment is in good condition, and so forth. Before discussing such techniques, it is worth noting that setting time standards can be useful in promoting efficiency and effectiveness. Time standards are often used in incentive systems. If workers beat the standards, that is, work more quickly than expected, then they are paid extra for the surplus work. Time standards are also useful for comparing different methods of accomplishing a task. Other things being equal, the quickest way to complete the task is the best. Other engineering (plant operating) uses of time standards include estimating costs of labor and products, and balancing production lines and work crews (McCormick, 1979).

Stopwatch Time Study. With this technique, the job analyst watches incumbents perform the task and records how long it takes them to complete the task or portions of the task. Many repetitions of task completion are recorded, so that the analyst has a distribution of times for task completion at the end of the study. A measure of central tendency (mean, median, mode) will be taken as a representative time for task completion. The representative time will not by itself become the standard time. This is because the standard, or allotted, time also takes into account normal downtime, fatigue, and the observer's judgment of how fast the observed worker was working. The observer makes a judgment, called a *rating,* that is used to adjust the representative time upward or downward depending on how fast the observed worker appeared to be working relative to some standard. The standard time will be based on the representative time, the observer's rating, and allowances for downtime and unavoidable delays. Thus, standard time is what the company expects to see on average from a competent, conscientious worker.

Predetermined Time Systems. Other methods for setting standard times do not require observing an incumbent completing tasks. Various ways of synthesizing a task or job from prior information exist. In one such method, basic or elemental movements are treated as having known standard time values taken from prior research. The analyst needs only to know the basic or elemental steps used in task completion. Armed with such knowledge, the analyst looks up the time values of the elemental movements and adds them to find the standard value for the task.

Industry Standard Data. A closely related system uses standard time data from prior analyses of similar tasks, typically within an industry. For example, a woodworking machine shop has many machines used to shape and cut wood. From prior studies, many of the tasks may have known standard task times. When a new job comes along, the known standard task times can be used to synthesize the standard time for the new job, so long as it is composed of tasks that have already been analyzed. The difference between the predetermined time system and the industry standard system is that the predetermined time system uses elemental motions to synthesize the task, whereas the industry standard uses tasks or task elements to synthesize tasks and jobs.

MOTION STUDY

As with time study, *motion study* refers to a collection of techniques. In motion study, the techniques are used to examine how the work is completed with an eye toward improving effectiveness or efficiency. The general philosophy is that there is probably *one best way* to do the job given the current technology, and it is most likely to find or approximate this best way through a systematic, empirical (that is, scientific) approach rather than intuition. The one best way may have to be modified, however, in case of workers' disabilities.

Graphs and Flowcharts

Graphs and flowcharts are methods of externalizing a sequence of events. The events and their sequence can be examined with an eye toward changes that might make the work more efficient. Figure 2.1 represents two ways in which an orderly can bring hospital patients a meal.

In the original method, the orderly brings a serving table to the middle of the room, and then takes one trip from the table to each patient. In the improved method, the table moves around the room with the orderly, who takes meals to two patients at once. The improved method results in many fewer steps total to complete the job. Timely service to patients, meals at the right temperature, and wear and tear on the worker are all improved.

A flowchart showing essentially the same information as Figure 2.1 can be seen in Figure 2.2. Approximately the top third of the flowchart contains summary information. The bottom two thirds contain detailed descriptions of

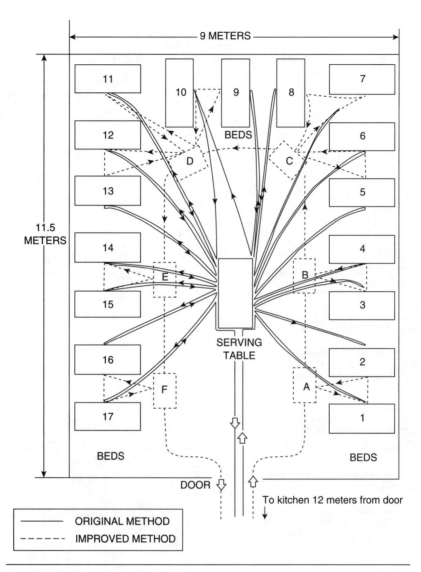

Figure 2.1   Sequence as a Graph

SOURCE: International Labour Office (1992). *Introduction to work study* (4th ed.) (p. 118). Geneva: Author. Copyright (c) 1992 International Labour Organization. Reprinted with permission.

serving dinner. The middle third contains the original method, and the bottom third contains the suggested improved method. A series of steps (tasks, motions) is listed under each method, one for each row. Columns are devoted to quantity, distance, time, symbol (more on this shortly), and remarks. Looking at the

FLOW PROCESS CHART	MAN TYPE			

CHART No. 7 SHEET No. 1 OF 1	S U M M A R Y			
Subject charted: *Hospital nurse*	ACTIVITY	PRESENT	PROPOSED	SAVING
	OPERATION O TRANSPORT ⇨	*34* *60*	*18* *72*	*16* *(–12)*
ACTIVITY: *Serve dinners to 17 patients*	DELAY ◻ INSPECTION ◻ STORAGE ▽	— — —	— — —	— — —
METHOD: PRESENT/PROPOSED	DISTANCE (m)	*436*	*197*	*239*
LOCATION: *Ward L*	TIME (man-h)	*39*	*28*	*11*
OPERATIVE (S): CLOCK No.	COST: LABOUR	— —	— —	— —
CHARTED BY: DATE:	MATERIAL (trolley)	—	*$24*	—
APPROVED BY: DATE: –	TOTAL (*Capital*)		*$24*	

DESCRIPTION ORIGINAL METHOD	QTY. (*plates*)	DISTANCE (m)	TIME (min)	SYMBOL O ⇨ ◻ ◻ ▽		REMARKS
Transports first course and plates –						Awkward load
* Kitchen to serving table on tray*	} 17	16	.50			
Places dishes and plates on table	17	—	.30			
Serves from three dishes to plate	—	—	.25			
Carries plate to bed 1 and returns	1	7.3	.25			
Serves	—	—	.25			
Carries plate to bed 2 and returns	1	6	.23			
Serves	—	—	.25			
* (Continues until all 17 beds are served.*						
* See figure 42 for distances)*						
Service completed, places dishes on						
* tray and returns to kitchen*	} —	16	.50			
Total distance and time, first cycle		122	10.71	17 20	— — —	
REPEATS CYCLE FOR SECOND COURSE		192	10.71	17 20	— — —	
Collects empty second course plates		52	2.0	— 20	— — —	
TOTAL		436	23.42	34 60		
IMPROVED METHOD						
Transports first course and plates –						Serving
* Kitchen in position A – trolley*	} 17	16	.50			trolley
Serves two plates	—	—	.40			
Carries two plates to bed 1; leaves one;		⎡1.5⎤				
* carries one plate from bed 1 to bed 2;*	} 2	⎨0.6⎬	.25			
* returns to position A*		⎣1.5⎦				
Pushes trolley to position B	—	3.0	.12			
Serves two plates	—	—	.40			
Carries two plates to bed 3; leaves one;		⎡1.5⎤				
* carries one plate from bed 3 to bed 4;*	} 2	⎨0.6⎬	.25			
* returns to position B*		⎣1.5⎦				
* (Continues unit all 17 beds are served. See*						
* figure 32 and note variation at bed 11)*						
Returns to kitchen with trolley	—	16	.50			
Total distance and time. First cycle	—	72.5	7.49	9 26		
REPEATS CYCLE FOR SECOND COURSE	—	72.5	7.49	9 26		
Collects empty second course plates	—	52	2.00	— 20		
TOTAL	—	197	16.98	18 72		

Figure 2.2   Flowchart

total time and distance for the first cycle shows how many meters were covered and how many minutes serving the first course took. Note that in the original method, the total distance for the first cycle was 436 meters and took 23.42 minutes. In the improved method, the total distance for the first cycle was 197 meters, and the total time was 16.98 minutes.

There are several standardized systems for creating flowcharts. The systems have symbols that denote different activities; one such system is shown in Figure 2.2, where a circle represents an operation and an arrow represents transporting something. The sequence of events is shown by a line made of connected dots shown under standard symbols in the center of Figure 2.2, and it is summarized at the top right of the flowchart. Flowcharts help show where an activity is repeated, when delays occur, and so forth. Such information is used with standard checklists to make design recommendations (for example, can delays be avoided, can repetitive actions be combined). Earlier writings suggested good design principles for motion, such as "The arms should move symmetrically" or "The feet should be given work that requires strength but little precision." Now, however, there are specialized checklists for a very large number of different circumstances (Mundel, 1988), so that it is not practical to illustrate them.

Micromotion Analysis

With flowcharts and diagrams, the analyst breaks the job or task into a sequence of steps, such as serve meals onto plates, take the plates to patients, and retrieve the plates after dinner. Micromotion analysis, on the other hand (no pun intended), starts with one of the steps and breaks it into elemental motions. For example, consider the orderly beginning to serve dinner. Motions would include grasping the lid of a container, moving the lid, placing the lid on the serving tray, letting go of the lid, moving the hand to a spoon, grasping the spoon, moving it to the mashed potatoes, and so on (we can only imagine the series of motions precipitated by one of the patients yelling, "Food fight!").

There is a standard set of terminology for describing elemental motions. Each element is called a *therblig* (Gilbreth *almost* spelled backward). Each therblig has a standard symbol and color used to chart the sequence of motions in a task, much as was shown in Figure 2.2. The names of a few therbligs and definitions are shown in Table 2.3. Micromotion study is particularly well suited to the analysis of tasks that take place at a workstation, such as assembling a ballpoint pen.

Recording Techniques

Time-and-motion study often uses film, video, and other recording technology to create records of how a task is completed. The way in which the technology is used depends on the time-and-motion study method chosen.

Table 2.3   Definitions of Therbligs

Name	Definition
Search	Occurs when hand or eyes are hunting or groping for something *Example:* Trying to find or pick a part from a pile
Select	Occurs when one object is being picked from among several *Example:* Locating a particular bolt from among several
Grasp	Consists of taking hold of an object *Example:* Closing the fingers around a pencil

In micromotion analysis, it is common to take slow-motion photography to make very precise estimates of the times of various motions. On the other hand, in work sampling and flowcharting, time-lapse photography may be used so that the analyst can see an hour's work go by in 4 minutes. Other recording devices are also used occasionally. For example, a dynamometer might be used to record the force (torque) applied by a drill press operator when drilling holes in metal. This would be done to find the best balance between speed of drilling and breaking of drill bits.

CRITICISM OF TIME-AND-MOTION STUDY

Time-and-motion study has been ridiculed for its excessive emphasis on efficiency. For example, one critic described what industrial engineers would say about a symphony:

> There seems to be too much repetition of some musical passages. Scores should be drastically pruned. No useful purpose is served by repeating on the horns a passage which has already been handled by the strings. It is estimated that if all redundant passages were eliminated the whole concert time of 2 hours could be reduced to 20 minutes. . . . In many cases the operators were using one hand for holding the instrument, whereas the use of a fixture would have rendered the idle hand available for other work. ("How to Be Efficient," 1959, pp. 454–455)

The industrial engineering approach was closely allied with the notion of "scientific management" during the first quarter of the 20th century. Frederick W. Taylor was able to save a steel company about $78,000 per year (big money back then; adjusted for inflation the amount is more than $1.5 million in today's dollars!) by designing shovels so that they all carried about 21.5 pounds of matter, whether it was ash, coal, or iron (Schultz & Schultz, 1990). Such increases in efficiency allowed companies to be much more profitable. Taylor advocated that management should share the increased profit with labor. Labor and the general public, however, believed that management would instead use increased productivity to hire fewer workers, and of course, management did so more than once.

Although the U.S. industry is increasingly service oriented rather than industrial, time study is still used for setting standards. When it is used for standards, however, there are tricky psychological aspects to consider. For example, workers may refuse to beat the standard because they believe that if they do, then management will revise the standard rather than pay the incentive. Workers often refer to people who set time standards as "quick checkers."

We also note that the criticism of time-and-motion study as being excessively concerned with efficiency is rather unfair because the techniques were designed to improve productivity. And we have seen an example of how a worker and the service he or she provides can improve. Time-and-motion study may also be useful in designing machines or robots to take over more dangerous and stressful tasks from people. We discuss other aspects of job design in Chapters 5 and 7, where we describe approaches that are designed to increase human comfort or interest in the work itself. In recent years, work design has expanded to cover work context and the connections between jobs (for example, Horgen, Joroff, Porter, & Schon, 1999; Parker & Wall, 1998). We describe some of this work in our chapter on job analysis for teams.

Functional Job Analysis

The U.S. Department of Labor is concerned with matching people to jobs throughout the U.S. economy. Consider for a moment the number of jobs involved and the even larger number of people to be matched to the available jobs. How would you proceed? It became clear to the DOL that in addition to all the administrative functions to be fulfilled, two types of information would be necessary to match people and jobs: (1) a description of the work and (2) a description of the worker qualifications necessary to successfully accomplish the job so that applicants could prepare for and apply for jobs.

Initial goals of the DOL approach included classifying job offers from employers into skill levels and classifying employees into groups matched with jobs. Later goals of the DOL included preparing materials for vocational counseling and for classifying jobs for worker mobility, that is, attempting to show which jobs workers can most easily move to given their present employment.

In the 1930s, when our parents and grandparents were working, there were numerous U.S. federal-state employment agencies entrusted with the mission to match people and jobs. Each agency would compile information about jobs using its own sources, create its own job titles with individual meanings, and assign workers to job opportunities. Because of a lack of common language, the employment agencies had trouble communicating with one another, and progress toward a truly national system of matching people to jobs was slow (Droege, 1988).

By the end of 1939, a group of energetic souls had analyzed and described about 54,000 jobs using a common system. The information was used to classify jobs into occupations and to provide brief summaries of each job. The results were published as thousands of occupations in the first *Dictionary of Occupational Titles* (*DOT;* U.S. DOL, 1939). The most recent edition of the *DOT* (a revision of the fourth edition) includes descriptions of both occupations (see Table 2.4 for sample descriptions) and worker characteristics believed necessary for success in each occupation.

The *DOT* has proved difficult to maintain and to update. An alternative approach called O*NET (described in Chapter 4) has been developed. The Department of Labor has stopped updating the *DOT* and has positioned O*NET as its replacement.

The job analysis procedure developed by the DOL was intended to be comprehensive (after all, it must handle all the jobs in the U.S. economy), standardized (to allow for communication among various agencies), and efficient. The procedure uses trained job analysts to interview and observe incumbents and to complete a standardized report. Detailed descriptions of how the DOL method is applied can be found in the *Handbook for Analyzing Jobs* (U.S. DOL, 1972). With the advent of O*NET, which stands for *Occupational Information Network,* this method has fallen into disuse, but its features remain important for job analysts to consider.

A FUNDAMENTAL DISTINCTION OF FJA: WHAT GETS DONE VERSUS WHAT THE WORKER DOES

When we think of jobs, we often think of the goals, aims, or responsibilities of the job rather than the steps required to accomplish them. Sample goals include a doctor curing illness, a bus driver moving people from place to place, and a professor publishing research reports. Unfortunately, the goals or aims are usually insufficient by themselves for creating products useful to other people. Such products might include a determination of what skills are needed for job incumbents to successfully accomplish a job, or the development of training programs for jobs. To build worker attribute lists or to develop training programs, statements of the steps used in accomplishing the goals of the job are needed. The bus driver, for example, does not pick people up and carry them on his or her back. Rather, the driver operates the bus by turning the

Table 2.4   Sample Job Descriptions from the *Dictionary of Occupational Titles*

022.061-010 CHEMIST (profess. & kin.)

Conducts research, analysis, synthesis, and experimentation on substances, for such purposes as product and process development and application, quantitative and qualitative analysis, and improvement of analytical methodologies: Devises new equipment, and develops formulas, processes, and methods for solution of technical problems. Analyzes organic and inorganic compounds to determine chemical and physical properties, utilizing such techniques as chromatography, spectroscopy, and spectrophotometry. Induces changes in composition of substances by introduction of heat, light, energy, and chemical catalysts. Conducts research on manufactured products to develop and improve products. Conducts research into composition, structure, properties, relationships, and reactions of matter. Confers with scientists and engineers regarding research, and prepares technical papers and reports. Prepares standards and specifications for processes, facilities, products, and tests.

153.287-010 HOOF AND SHOE INSPECTOR (amuse. & rec.)

Inspects hoofs and shoes (plates) of horses at racetrack to determine that hoofs have been trimmed to prevent stumbling during race and to detect loose or broken shoes; Records names of horse, owner, and RACEHORSE TRAINER and condition of horse's hoofs and shoes. Presents information to STEWARD, RACETRACK for further action. May remove and replace broken or cracked plates. May instruct handlers to secure plates or trim horse hoofs as required.

185.167-034 MANAGER, MERCHANDISE (retail trade; wholesale tr.)

Formulates merchandising policies and coordinates merchandising activities in wholesale or retail establishment: Determines mark-up and mark-down percentages necessary to ensure profit, based on estimated budget, profit goals, and average rate of stock turnover. Determines amount of merchandise to be stocked and directs buyers in purchase of supplies for resale. Consults with other personnel to plan sales promotion programs.

250.257-010 SALES AGENT, INSURANCE (insurance)

Sells insurance to new and current clients: Compiles lists of prospective clients to provide leads for additional business. Contacts prospective clients and explains features and merits of policies offered, recommending amount and type of coverage based on analysis of prospect's circumstances, and utilizing persuasive sales techniques. Calculates and quotes premium rates for recommended policies, using calculator and rate books. Calls on policyholders to deliver and explain policy, to suggest additions or changes in insurance program, or to make changes in beneficiaries. May collect premiums from policyholders and keep record of payments. Must hold license issued by state. May be designated according to type of insurance sold as Sales Agent, Casualty Insurance (insurance);

(Continued)

Table 2.4 (Continued)

Sales Agent, Fire Insurance (insurance); Sales Agent, Life Insurance (insurance); Sales Agent, Marine Insurance (insurance). May work independently selling variety of insurance, such as life, fire, casualty, and marine, for many companies and be designated Insurance Broker (insurance). May work independently selling for one company and be designated General Agent (insurance).

529.682-026 LOZENGE MAKER (sugar & conf.)

Operates machine that rolls dough into sheets, and embosses and cuts dough into candy lozenges: Positions and secures cutting and embossing dies in place, using wrench. Adjusts ram stroke of cutting die to synchronize it with speed of dough rollers and discharge conveyor. Turns handwheel to adjust clearance between rollers. Dumps lozenge dough into hopper and starts machine. Sprinkles cornstarch onto dough to prevent sticking to rollers and dies. Examines and weighs formed lozenges for conformity to size, shape, and weight specifications, and readjusts roller speed and clearance to meet product standards. May adjust printer bars on machines to print or emboss designs on lozenges before cutting.

712.687-022 GAS-MASK INSPECTOR (protective dev.)

Inspects assembled gas masks for conformity to specifications: Examines chemical containers, facepieces, straps, and rubber hoses for defects, such as blisters, tears, and faulty stitching. Tests masks for leakage around glass eyepieces, using suction-cup device. Tests chemical containers for content, and for leakage under pressure, using gauge. Tests absorbing quality of chemicals, using smoke meter.

SOURCE: U.S. Department of Labor, n.d. *Dictionary of Occupational Titles* (4th ed., revised).

steering wheel, depressing the accelerator and brake pedals, leaning on the horn, describing the ancestors of weaving drivers, and so forth. The professor doesn't publish articles, but rather collects data, analyzes them, and describes them in a particular format.

> The distinction between what gets done and what the worker does is important because people are more apt to agree about the human activity involved when the description is what the worker does (Fine, 1988). Consider the statement "Welds steel pipes." On the face of it, this appears to be fairly clear. However, we don't know exactly what the person is doing to accomplish the task. Several different kinds of welding techniques may be used. Or consider the following example: Determines the qualifications that employees must possess in order to fill vacant positions.

[versus]

Reviews/analyzes job description data (e.g., training manuals and performance requirements), drawing on experience and psychological background in order to determine employee qualifications for vacant positions. (Fine, 1988, p. 1027)

Note that in the second example, the actions of the worker are more clearly specified. Focusing properly on what the worker does versus what gets accomplished on the job is one of the more difficult things about doing work-oriented job analysis.

WORKER FUNCTIONS

FJA is based on the premise that whatever workers do, they do in relation to one of three aspects of work: data, people, or things. *Data* are abstractions or symbols. Examples of data are numbers, words, and blueprints. Thus, data are more inclusive in FJA than in common speech, where data commonly refer to numbers, but not other symbols. *People* in the FJA system correspond to what we ordinarily think of as people, but also to animals when they are attended to or treated as part of the work (for example, a veterinarian would be considered to be highly involved with people). *Things* are tangible, real objects, such as sacks of cement, blown glass figurines, or computers.

According to early writings on FJA, functions within data, people, and things could be arranged in a hierarchy of complexity from simple to complex. Hierarchies for the DOL FJA and Fine's FJA are illustrated in Table 2.5. For each system, the level of complexity is indicated by a numbering system to the left of the function. For the DOL system, larger numbers refer to less complex functions; for Fine's system, larger numbers refer to more complex functions. In Fine's system, different functions with the same number refer to functions at the same level of complexity. For example, coaching, persuading, and diverting are all at level 2 in Fine's complexity scale. The two systems show minor differences among the functions.

Table 2.6 lists some definitions and examples of selected levels for each of the three functions for both systems. Initially, functions were thought to be arranged so that the highest level of complexity for the job would summarize all the necessary information about the job with respect to functions with data, people, and things. This was because the functions were arranged so that more complex functions always included less complex functions. For example, if a job involved analyzing, then the job would also involve compiling, computing, copying, and comparing, but not coordinating or synthesizing. More recent writings admit that the hierarchical relationships are not exact (Droege, 1988; Harvey, 1991).

The *Handbook for Analyzing Jobs* (U.S. DOL, 1972) provides a report form (called a *schedule*) in which the analyst records the function(s) with which the

Table 2.5   Worker Function Hierarchies

Data	People	Things
Department of Labor (SOURCE: U.S. DOL *Handbook for Analyzing Jobs*).		
0 Synthesizing	0 Mentoring	0 Setting up
1 Coordinating	1 Negotiating	1 Precision working
2 Analyzing	2 Instructing	2 Operating, controlling
3 Compiling	3 Supervising	3 Driving, operating
4 Computing	4 Diverting	4 Manipulating
5 Copying	5 Persuading	5 Tending
6 Comparing	6 Speaking, signaling	6 Feeding, offbearing
	7 Serving	7 Handling
	8 Taking instructions, helping	
FJA (SOURCE: Fine & Cronshaw, 1999, p. 38).		
6 Synthesizing	8 Leading	4A Precision working
5A Innovating	7 Mentoring	4B Setting up
5B Coordinating	6 Negotiating	4C Operating-controlling
4 Analyzing	5 Supervising	3A Manipulating
3A Computing	4A Consulting	3B Operating-controlling I
3B Compiling	4B Instructing	3C Driving-controlling
2 Copying	4C Treating	3D Starting up
1 Comparing	3A Sourcing information	2A Machine tending I
	3B Persuading	2B Machine tending
	3C Coaching	1A Handling
	3D Diverting	1B Feeding-offbearing
	2 Exchanging information	
	1A Taking instructions-helping	
	1B Serving	

SOURCE: A portion of this table was reproduced from Fine, S. A., & Cronshaw, S. F. (1999). *Functional job analysis: A foundation for human resources management.* Mahwah, NJ: Erlbaum. Reprinted by permission.

incumbent has significant involvement and the level with which the incumbent functions in relation to data, people, and things. For example, a counselor in a high school might have significant involvement with data and people, but not things. The approximate levels for data, people, and things would be analyzing, persuading, and handling, respectively.

Table 2.6   Sample Definitions and Examples of Worker Functions

---

Department of Labor

Data Functions

Synthesizing: Integrating analyses of data to discover facts and/or develop knowledge concepts or interpretations
Example: Creates satirical or humorous cartoons based on personal interpretations of current news events

Analyzing: Examining and evaluating data. Presenting alternative actions in relation to the evaluation is frequently involved
Example: Evaluates student loan applications and determines eligibility based on need and academic standing

People Functions

Mentoring: Dealing with individuals in terms of their total personality in order to advise, counsel, and/or guide them with regard to problems that may be resolved by legal, scientific, clinical, spiritual, and/or other professional principles
Example: Provides treatment for individuals with mental and emotional disorders

Serving: Attending to the needs or requests of people or animals or the expressed or implicit wishes of people. Immediate response is involved
Example: Rents bicycles to patrons at beach, resort, or similar recreational facility

Things Functions

Driving-Operating: Starting, stopping, and controlling the actions of machines or equipment for which a course must be steered, or which must be guided, in order to fabricate, process, and/or move things or people
Example: Steers vessel over course indicated by electronic equipment, such as radio, fathometer, and land radar to transport passengers to fishing locations for catching fish and other marine life

Feeding-Offbearing: Inserting, throwing, dumping, or placing materials in or removing them from machines or equipment that are automatic or tended or operated by other workers
Example: Places eggs in holder that carries them into a machine that removes earth, straw, and other residue from egg surface prior to shipment

---

Fine's FJA

Data Functions

Synthesizing: Takes off in new directions on the basis of personal intuitions, feelings, and ideas (with or without regard for tradition, experience, and existing parameters) to conceive new approaches to or statement of problems

---

(Continued)

Table 2.6 (Continued)

Fine's FJA
and the development of system, operational, or aesthetic solutions or resolutions of them, typically outside of existing theoretical, stylistic, or organizational context Analyzing: Examines and evaluates data (about things, data, or people) with reference to the criteria, standards, and/or requirements of a particular discipline, art, technique, or craft to determine interaction effects (consequences) and to consider alternatives **People Functions** Leading: Sets forth/asserts a vision that has an impact upon and defines the mission, culture, and values of an organization; sets direction, time perspective, and organizational structure for achievement of goals and objectives; models behavior that inspires and motivates achievement (distinct from management) Exchanging Information: Talks to, converses with, and/or signals people to convey or obtain information, or to clarify and work out details of an assignment, within the framework of well-established procedures; for example, requests clarification of a verbal signal (in person or on radio) or hand signal **Things Functions** Driving, Controlling: Starts, stops, and controls (steers, guides) the actions of machines in two-dimensional spaces for which a course must be followed to move things or people. Actions regulating controls require continuous attention and readiness of response to traffic conditions

SOURCE: Adapted from U.S. Department of Labor (1972). *Handbook for analyzing jobs*, Washington, DC: U.S. Government Printing Office.

JOB ANALYSIS PROCEDURE

The DOL FJA relies on a trained job analyst to gather information and complete the job analysis schedule. The analyst prepares for the analysis by gathering existing information about the job, such as

- Books, periodicals, or other technical information available in libraries
- Process descriptions such as flowcharts and organizational charts
- Job descriptions and other technical documentation prepared by trade associations, trade unions, or professional societies
- Pamphlets, books, or other information prepared by various agencies of the government

Such preparation gives the analysts an initial idea about the nature and purpose of the job. It will also prove useful in talking with people who hold the job or supervise it because the analyst will already be familiar with some jargon and the basic tasks involved.

The DOL *Handbook's* preferred method of gathering information is the observation/interview. In this method, the analyst either (a) watches the worker do the work, and then interviews the worker, the immediate supervisor, or both, or (b) watches the worker and simultaneously interviews the worker about what is being done. In either case, the analyst is taking notes while the worker is working.

The observation/interview has the benefit of allowing the analyst to see how the job is actually performed and to let the analyst ask questions when he or she fails to understand some aspect of the work. Occasionally, the observation/ interview cannot be used because the management refuses to allow it (perhaps because of secrecy or danger), or because the job is composed of primarily unobservable tasks (that is, mental tasks such as planning). In such cases, the analyst must rely on interviews and other sources of job information.

Fine's current method of collecting data is to gather a panel of subject matter experts (job incumbents) who report how they complete their work (Fine & Cronshaw, 1999). The assumption is that incumbents know the job better than supervisors, engineers, or other technical experts (Fine & Cronshaw, 1999, pp. 67, 73). The role of the job analyst is to translate their sentences into statements that follow a grammar peculiar to this method of job analysis (discussed later). The analyst writes task statements describing how the work gets done in language understandable to the incumbents, and the analyst gives a form to incumbents asking whether the statements present an accurate and complete picture of the job.

DESCRIBING THE WORK

The DOL FJA has a specific procedure and even a special grammar for describing the work itself. For the work performed, the FJA structure is

- Worker functions (data, people, things)
- Work fields
- Methods verbs
- Machines, tools, equipment, and work aids
- Materials, products, subject matter, and services

The worker functions have already been described. The rest of the structure is described next, beginning with work fields. Table 2.7 shows an example of each of the structural elements and representative task statements.

Work Fields

Work fields are broad areas of work content used to classify all the jobs in the economy into a collection of 100 fields, each with a three-digit number. The jobs are classified according to (a) common tools, equipment, and so forth or (b) common economic purposes to be satisfied by jobs. In Table 2.7, the work field is painting, and the number is 262.

Table 2.7   FJA Grammar

PAINTING - 262

Creating and reproducing designs of lettering, or depicting ideas, using tools such as pencils, crayons, brushes, or spray guns. Distinguish from *Brushing-Spraying* and *Immersing-Coating* which are for the purpose of covering without producing designs or lettering.

Methods Verbs

Blanking Out	Lettering	Sketching	Tinting
Coloring	Rubbing	Spotting Out	Touching Up
Drawing	Shading	Spraying	Wiping
Inking			

Machines	*Tools*	*Equipment*	*Work Aids*
Lettering Machine	Air Brush	Camera	Canvas
Spray Machine	Burnishing Tools	Projectors	Charts
	Charcoal		Diagrams
	Handtools		India Ink
	Knives		Letters
	Pencils		Magnifying Glasses
	Pens		Oil Paints
	Spray Guns		Plastics
			Reducing Glasses
			Tempera
			Templates
			Water Colors

Paints landscapes, portraits, still life, abstract designs, or other compositions in oils, water colors, or tempera.

Draws cartoons for publication to depict news topics in satirical or humorous manner.

Devises layout, and paints letters and designs on wood or cardboard blank to make sign.

Paints designs on rug surfaces, using spray gun and stencils.

Paints or inks flower designs on enameled surface of jewelry or buttons, using brush or pen.

SOURCE: U.S. Department of Labor (1972). *Handbook for analyzing jobs,* pp. 139–140. Washington, DC: U.S. Government Printing Office.

Methods Verbs

Methods verbs serve to identify what the worker does. They show how the objectives in the work field are accomplished. Examples in Table 2.7 include coloring and sketching. The verbs listed under a given work field may not be an exhaustive list, but they are informative and provide at least a place to start the analysis.

Machines, Tools, Equipment, and Work Aids

Machines, tools, equipment, and work aids (MTEWA) are tangible objects used by the worker to accomplish work goals. Machines are mechanical devices that apply force. They are typically operated or driven (for example, drill presses, buses). Tools are manipulated to work on or move things, usually by hand (for example, chain saw, screwdrivers). Equipment covers two broad categories of devices. The first is devices that apply forces other than mechanical to objects. Such devices would include ovens and stills. The second category includes devices that generate power or communicate signals, such as switchboards, ammeters, and transmitters. Work aids are broader in concept here than in our definition from Chapter 1. They are used in support of machines and tools, but are not actually part of the work transformation (for example, clamps, vises). In our view, the precise distinctions among MTEWA are unimportant for conducting and communicating job analysis. MTEWA do have an important place in the construction of task statements, however, as discussed in our sections on sentence structure and Fine's method, which you will encounter if you keep reading.

Materials, Products, Subject Matter, and Services

Materials, products, subject matter, and services (MPSMS) are the work outputs, or immediate goals, of the job. Sample materials include clay, coal, and sand. Sample products include bread, light bulbs, and pastries. Sample subject matter includes horticulture, astronomy, and air traffic control. Sample services include retail trade, laundry, and mental health counseling. Again, precise distinctions among MPSMS are not nearly as important as is their place in constructing task statements.

SENTENCE STRUCTURE AND ANALYSIS

The DOL uses a particular grammar to write statements about tasks. Such a grammar is necessary because it results in standard, precise statements intended to apply across jobs and analysts. The structure of task statements is illustrated by several examples in Table 2.8. The statement always begins with a verb, which says what gets done. The subject (the worker) is implied rather than stated. The verb is usually followed by an immediate object (what is done to). Finally, an optional infinitive phrase follows. The phrase describes how the action is accomplished and/or why the action is accomplished. The infinitive phrase may contain two parts. The first part is an infinitive (or work field verb). The second part is the object of the infinitive (MPSMS).

In Table 2.8, in the first example, the action verb is *evaluates*, the immediate object is *ability . . . of animals*, the infinitive (work field) is *to train*, and the object of the infinitive is *animals*.

Table 2.8   Structure of Task Statements

Job Worker Situation: Trains wild animals such as lions, tigers, bears, and elephants to perform tricks for entertainment of audience at circus or other exhibition, evaluating ability, behavior, and performance of each animal. Originates acts based on performance of animals.

		Infinitive Phrase	
Verb	*Immediate Object*	*Infinitive*	*Object of Infinitive*
WORKER FUNCTION	MTEWA, DATA, PEOPLE	WORK FIELD	MPSMS
Evaluates	ability, behavior, and performance of animals	to train	animals
Trains	wild animals	to entertain	audience
Manipulates	objects	to train	animals

Job Worker Situation: Compares positive motion picture films with reference prints to detect irregularities in detail and color. Signals operator to project positive motion picture film on screens. Compares positive film with reference print for color density and picture definition. Rejects films having defects, such as blurs, scratches, and perforations.

		Infinitive Phrase	
Verb	*Immediate Object*	*Infinitive*	*Object of Infinitive*
WORKER FUNCTION	MTEWA, DATA, PEOPLE	WORK FIELD	MPSMS
Compares	positive motion picture films with reference prints	to detect	film defects
Signals	operator	to project	film
Handles	film and prints	to reject	defective film

SOURCE: U.S. Department of Labor (1972). *Handbook for analyzing jobs*, pp. 191, 194. Washington, DC: U.S. Government Printing Office.

OTHER CHARACTERISTICS OF THE DOL FJA

Although the primary focus of FJA is on tasks, FJA also provides substantial information about worker characteristics and working conditions. The DOL schedule (report form) used for reporting the job analysis contains ratings on worker traits required by the job in five areas. The areas are general educational development (evaluated not by years of schooling but by the kinds of tasks, such as advanced calculus); specific vocational preparation (the amount of training time for the job, ranging from a short demonstration to more than 10 years); aptitudes (including general intelligence, verbal aptitude, numerical aptitude, spatial aptitude, form perception, clerical perception, motor coordination, finger dexterity, manual dexterity, eye-hand-foot coordination, and color discrimination); temperaments (adaptability requirements made by the job, such as planning, interpreting feelings, influencing people, judgment, measurements, dealing with people beyond giving instructions, handling repetitive work, resistance to stress, attention to detail, and dealing with variety without loss of efficiency); and interests (preferences for dealing with certain types of activity, such as [1] things and objects versus communication of data, [2] business contact with people versus scientific and technical, [3] routine, concrete activity versus abstract or creative activity, [4] activity for the presumed good of people versus dealing with machines or processes, and [5] preference for prestige versus preference for tangible products). There are also ratings of physical demands and environmental conditions. The physical demands include muscular (motor) demands such as strength, climbing, stooping, and reaching. They also include sensory demands, such as hearing and seeing. Environmental conditions concern the relative amounts of time spent inside and outside; extreme cold and heat; wet and/or humid conditions; noise; vibration; various hazards such as mechanical, electrical, or explosives; and atmospheric conditions such as fumes, dust, gases, and poor ventilation. The characteristics evaluated by the analyst are fairly comprehensive.

You can see in Table 2.4 that each job description is preceded by a 9-digit Occupational Code Number supplied by the Department of Labor. The first three digits correspond to a grouping of type of work by the content of the work itself. For the chemist, the number 022 signifies that the work belongs to a specific type of Professional, Technical and Managerial Occupation. Jobs that are similar in the first three digits are thought to be similar to one another in content and relatively easy to transfer skills from one to another, that is, people qualified for one such job should be qualified for another such job. The middle three digits correspond to the job's functional relations to Data, People, and Things. For the chemist job, the numbers are 061, which correspond to Synthesizing, Speaking/Signaling, and Precision working, respectively. The final three digits serve to uniquely identify the particular job to separate it from others with the same first three digits.

Fine's FJA

The sentence structure advocated by Fine and Cronshaw (1999) is similar to that of the DOL method. The basic structure can be defined by a series of questions. The answers to the series of questions form a task statement, which is the heart of describing a job in FJA. The series of questions and answers is as follows:

- Who? (subject)
- Performs what actions? (action verbs)
- To whom or what? (object of verb)
- Upon what instructions or sources of information? (phrase)
- Using what tools, equipment, or work aids? (phrase)
- To produce/achieve what output? (in order to . . .) (Fine & Cronshaw, 1999, p. 50)

In addition to task statements, Fine's FJA also produces ratings on the three functions scales (data, people, and things). Additional scales include work involvement, reasoning development, mathematical development, and language development.

COMPARISON OF THE DOL FJA AND FINE'S FJA

Both systems appear useful in helping the job analyst understand, document, and communicate the behavioral content of a job, that is, how a worker achieves the goals inherent in the job. Fine's version contains elements lacking in the DOL method. First, Fine's FJA distinguishes not only the level of complexity of the function but also the orientation, or level of involvement with the function. Orientation refers to the percentage of a task occupied by a particular function. For example, if a social worker were explaining to a client why the client should dress appropriately for a job interview, the orientations might be 35 percent data, 60 percent people, and 5 percent things (Levine, 1983).

A second difference between the DOL FJA and Fine's FJA is that Fine's FJA uses ratings of complexity and orientation at the task level in addition to the job level of analysis. Focusing on the task rather than the job has advantages and disadvantages. An advantage of focusing on the job is that fewer judgments must be made. Only one rating of complexity for each function must be made. As the number of tasks increases, the number of judgments about complexity increases as well. On the other hand, tasks communicate work better than an overall summary of the job. Tasks vary in the level of complexity of functioning with data, people, and things. It is not clear how tasks that vary in complexity of functioning with data, people, and things should be combined into an overall job rating. Should the tasks' complexity be averaged? Should the task with the highest level of complexity be chosen to represent the job? Presumably, ratings of involvement and complexity at the task level would be more reliable across judges or raters than similar ratings at the job level.

The DOL version includes a number of worker attributes that are not included in analyzing the work in Fine's FJA, such as temperaments and environmental conditions. However, Fine's system does acknowledge the contribution of both worker and organizational variables to work efficiency, productivity, and worker growth.

RESEARCH ON FJA

Studies of the reliability of ratings used in the *DOT* showed mixed results (Cain & Green, 1983; Geyer, Hice, Hawk, Boese, & Brannon, 1989; Schmitt & Fine, 1983; Trattner, Fine, & Kubis, 1955). Cain and Green (1983) studied the reliability of 20 of the ratings commonly used in the *DOT.* They found that some aspects were rated more reliably than others. The ratings of involvement with data and people were highly reliable, but ratings of involvement with things were not. The involvement with things ratings were also more affected by specific job descriptions than were the data and people ratings. *DOT* ratings refer to occupations, that is, a collection of similar jobs. However, job analysts make their ratings on the basis of a single job, and the ratings in the *DOT* are the modal value of a sample of analysts' ratings. The study showed that ratings of data and people vary little from job to job within an occupation, but that ratings of involvement with things varied considerably across jobs within an occupation. Similar results were found by Trattner et al. (1955) for ratings of worker trait requirements, where intellectual and perceptual requirements were rated reliably, but physical ability requirements were not. Much of the evidence for the validity of a job analysis procedure rests on the method's usefulness in achieving the goals of the job analysis. For many applications of job analysis, the purpose of the analysis is to gather information used in making a decision. For example, job analysis may inform decisions about what traits or tests should be used to select employees from a group of applicants, or what the content of a training program should be. Thus, a key to the validity of a job analysis method is its usefulness. The *DOT* was designed to match people and jobs, and it was used by the federal and state governments for this purpose. The *DOT* and related publications are also used for other purposes, including job training programs, disability determination, rehabilitation counseling, and vocational and occupational education (Droege, 1988). The *DOT* provided a description of virtually all the jobs in the U.S. economy. The O*NET system was introduced to become the new standard for these purposes. More on this later.

Task Inventories

A task inventory is a listing of all the work activities performed to complete one or more jobs; each activity is commonly referred to as a *task*. Task inventories typically involve surveys of job experts, usually incumbents and their supervisors, who respond to the list of items in various ways, such as whether they carry out the activity as part of their job. The tasks in task inventories tend to be more narrowly defined than are tasks in FJA. In FJA, there tend to be about 5 to 10 tasks. In a typical task inventory, there may be more than 100 tasks. Two different examples of task inventories are shown in Tables 2.9 and 2.10. It is customary to organize groups of tasks under the goals or duties used in completing the job (Spector, Brannick, & Coovert, 1989). Often the tasks are listed alphabetically under "duty" so that it is easier to search for a specific task (this is helpful to tell whether a task has been omitted or to change a response to a task).

HISTORY

Terry and Evans (1973, cited in Gael, 1983) reported that the first use of the task inventory dates back to 1919, when the method was used to develop

Table 2.9 WPSS Example

	Difficulty
Listed below are tasks. Rate each task for difficulty based on the amount of skill needed to do the task satisfactorily.	1. Very much below average 2. Below average 3. Slightly below average 4. About average 5. Slightly above average 6. Above average 7. Very much above average
1. Assign personnel to installation or repair projects.	
2. Brief personnel on unit security or safety rules.	
3. Complete manhour accounting forms for work crews.	
4. Conduct supervisory orientation of newly assigned personnel.	

SOURCE: Adapted from Gael, S. (1983). *Job analysis: A guide to assessing work activities.* (p. 104). San Francisco: Jossey-Bass. Reprinted by permission of Jossey-Bass, Inc., an imprint of John Wiley & Sons, Inc.

Table 2.10   Task Inventory for a Drug Clerk in a Pharmacy (Partial listing of
"customer service" duty)

Task	"X" if Done	Time Spent	Difficulty to Learn
		1 = Small amount 2 = Less than average 4 = Above average 5 = Large amount	1 = One of the easiest 2 = Easier than most 3 = Average 4 = Harder than most 5 = One of the hardest
1. Answer customer questions about products and services			
2. Call patient about scrip not picked up after 7 days			
3. Make refunds			
4. Recommend products to customers			
5. Refer medical questions to pharmacist			
6. Ring up merchandise and prescriptions on register			

training for skilled trades. Task inventories were not widely used until the
1950s. The form of task inventory most commonly used today is largely attrib-
utable to the U.S. Air Force (USAF). The USAF was interested in finding or
developing a job analysis method that would provide a quantitative description
of the work, could be applied to both large and small samples, could be applied
directly to job incumbents rather than job analysts, and could be processed
electronically (Morsh, Madden, & Christal, 1961).

The result of the search was the general task inventory approach. During
the 1950s and 1960s, research and development by the USAF on how to collect
and analyze data from task inventories resulted in the Comprehensive
Occupational Data Analysis Program (CODAP), a computerized system for
collecting and analyzing task inventory data. Christal and Weissmuller (1988)
described some of the research in developing CODAP, and they warned that

modifying the way in which data are collected often results in degraded data. The Work Performance Survey System (WPSS) is a task inventory approach used in industry that descended directly from CODAP and the USAF. The WPSS was developed during the 1970s by American Telephone and Telegraph (AT&T), and documented by Gael (1983). The WPSS is similar in many ways to CODAP. Both systems are described and differences noted in what follows.

A task inventory is a survey that is presented to incumbents and supervisors to provide the data for the job analysis. The job analyst has three primary roles in the job analysis: designing the survey questionnaire, administering it to a sample of employees, and analyzing the results.

SURVEY DESIGN

Background Information

The questions in the survey (tasks) are typically written by job analysts. In developing the task statements, the job analyst will often use many sources of information, including the following:

- *Observation.* Often the analyst will observe the job being done. The incumbent or a supervisor may explain what is happening while the job is being performed. The observation also provides information about job context (for example, noise, temperature, lighting).
- *Background materials.* Written information such as job descriptions, training materials, and organizational charts are often used. Other material such as training films or tools and equipment may also be examined. Job descriptions typically outline the duties contained in the job. Training materials can help specify many tasks and jargon that are part of the job.
- *Interviews.* Job incumbents, supervisors, and training specialists will usually be interviewed to help describe tasks and to review task lists to ensure that the job is described completely.

Structure of Tasks

The structure of tasks used in a task inventory loosely follows that used in FJA. Typically, the first word is an action verb. The verb is followed by a direct object. Additional qualifying statements may be included that help define the task by showing how, when, or why the task is done. A range of tasks and styles is shown in Tables 2.9 and 2.10. The example "Make refunds" in Table 2.10 shows the bare-bones approach. On the other hand, the example "Call patient about scrip not picked up after 7 days" begins with an action verb and direct object, and then qualifies the reason for the call (failure to pick up a prescription) and the conditions under which to take action (7 days after the prescription has been filled but not picked up).

The task statements will be entered into a survey questionnaire and given to people who will respond to the statement in various ways, such as to say whether they do the task as part of their jobs. The tasks must be written in such a way as to be readily understood by the respondents. It is wise to consider the reading level of the respondents and to avoid unfamiliar abbreviations and jargon. It is permissible to use jargon that is readily understood by the respondents, however.

Determining the Appropriate Level of Specificity

Most jobs can be described in a paragraph of 10 sentences or less, or by a list of hundreds or even thousands of specific actions. One of the major difficulties of writing a task inventory is deciding how specific the task statements should be. Gael (1983) defined a task as "a discrete organized unit of work, with a definite beginning and end, performed by an individual to accomplish the goals of a job" (p. 9). A good task statement, then, should refer to activities that are followed to accomplish a goal. Task statements that refer to goals without referring to activities are too broad. For example, "Takes care of customers" states a general goal, but not the activities used to accomplish a goal. A rule of thumb to use in thinking about tasks is to consider whether the task can be broken into meaningful bits without referring to specific sequences of movement. For example, "Call customers to notify them that merchandise has arrived" is a medium-sized task. To break the task into smaller pieces, one would have to refer to picking up the phone, dialing the numbers, and so forth. In general, statements that refer to specific movements are too elemental to serve as good task statements.

The proper level of specificity in a task statement also depends on the purpose of the job analysis. If the main purpose of the analysis is performance appraisal, for example, the tasks can be written fairly broadly. If designing training programs is the primary objective, however, then tasks must be more specific. The purpose of the analysis is also important when deciding whether to include qualifying information beyond the action verb and direct object in the task statement. When designing training materials, for example, one will want to know whether a hole is dug with a shovel or a backhoe.

Selecting Response Options

All task inventories ask respondents one or more questions about the tasks in the inventory. All inquire in one way or another about the involvement of the incumbent with the task. The inventory may yield information about involvement by simply asking incumbents to check whether they do the task as part of their job, or it may request a judgment of the degree of involvement of the incumbent with the task, the time spent on the task, or the importance of the task to the job. A large number of other questions can also be asked of the respondent. Such questions include the consequence of error in task performance (that is, *criticality*, or the degree to which incorrect task performance results in negative consequences), the difficulty to learn the task, the ability of others to cover for the incumbent on the task, and even satisfaction with the task. WPSS inventories typically ask one or more of the following questions (Gael, 1983, p. 94):

1. How important or significant is each task to your job?
2. How much time do you spend on each task?
3. How frequently do you perform each task?
4. How difficult is it to perform each task?

Which (if any) of such scales should be used has been controversial, as has the meaning of responses to such scales. For interesting positions on the controversy, see Fine (1988) and Christal and Weissmuller (1988).

On the other hand, the way in which questions are put to respondents is potentially very important. If respondents do not understand what is meant by *criticality*, or if they do not agree with one another about its meaning, then the data may not serve their intended purpose. The available evidence about the reliability (subject matter expert [SME] agreement) comes from several sources (for example, Christal, 1971; Cornelius, Schmidt, & Carron, 1984; Manson, Levine, & Brannick, 2000; McCormick & Ammerman, 1960; Sanchez & Levine, 1989). Recently Dierdorff and Wilson (2003) cumulated the results of more than 100 studies and found that reliability of scales to rate tasks was .77, while for more general work activities it was .61. They found scales of frequency and importance were more reliable than scales of difficulty and time spent (.70 and .77 versus .63 and .66, respectively). Taken together, the research suggests that reliable estimates of task characteristics can be obtained with large samples. With small samples of incumbents, it is probably neither economical nor advisable to develop and administer the task inventory.

For companies and public agencies to reduce legal liability under U.S. law, some indication of task importance is likely to be necessary (Kleiman & Faley, 1985; Sanchez & Fraser, 1992). How best to measure task importance has also been a bit controversial (for example, Cascio & Ramos, 1986; Kane, Kingsbury, Colton, & Estes, 1989; Levine, 1983; Levine & Dickey, 1990; Sanchez & Fraser, 1992; Sanchez & Levine, 1989). There appear to be two potential options for assessing task importance. Sanchez and Levine (1989) suggested that a composite of criticality and difficulty to learn is the most appropriate choice for assessing task importance because it produces the most reliable ratings and requires only two items (that are likely candidates for inclusion anyway). On the other hand, Sanchez and Fraser (1992) found that overall judgments of importance were as reliable as composite measures, suggesting that a single rating of importance is sufficient.

Regardless of how importance is measured, we must note that the purpose of the job analysis should inform the choice of scale. In constructing a training program, for example, it is important to know whether most incumbents are actually performing a task. A task that is done by nearly everyone is a good candidate for training. On the other hand, one would probably also like to know how difficult a task is, and how serious a mistake on the task is likely to be. A task that is not difficult to learn and that does not have serious consequences of error is a good candidate for learning on the job. A task that is difficult to learn and has serious consequences of error is a good candidate for off-the-job training, or perhaps selection (no training or minimal training for the current company). Table 2.11 shows a list of questions by purposes. Note that some purposes require answers to more questions than others.

Demographic Data

It is common to ask for background information about the respondents as part of the survey. Common survey questions include experience in the job, location of the job (for example, geographical region, parent organization), age, sex, and so forth. Such information can be used to describe the sample of respondents, to show how well the sample of respondents represents the whole population of potential respondents, and to split or group the data for additional analysis. Such analyses might include whether different regions group tasks into jobs differently, or whether more experienced respondents spend more or less time on specific tasks than do less experienced respondents. In general, ratings are not markedly affected by incumbent demographics such as age (Spector et al., 1989), although there are instances where they have been. Education (Cornelius & Lyness, 1980) and job level (Smith & Hakel, 1979) have been shown to affect ratings; job level probably is associated with education. Incumbent job performance and tenure appear not to affect ratings (Conley & Sackett, 1987; Cornelius & Lyness, 1980; Schmitt & Cohen, 1989; Silverman, Wexley, & Johnson, 1984; Wexley & Silverman, 1978; for an exception, see Borman, Dorsey, & Ackerman, 1992). The source of job information (incumbent versus supervisor) also has been shown to affect ratings (Moore, 1976, cited in Gael, 1983). Given these findings, we generally recommend that large, representative samples of informants be used to make ratings of tasks. However, should circumstances require, technical panels of carefully selected job experts with broad experience in the job under study can provide ratings very similar to large samples of incumbents (Ash, Levine, Higbee, & Sistrunk, 1982).

Table 2.11   Matching Questions and Purposes in Task Inventories

Purposes	Questions					
	If Done	*Importance*	*Criticality*	*Difficulty*	*Time Spent*	*Frequency*
Describe jobs	X	X	X		X	X
Design/Redesign jobs	X	X	X	X	X	X
Match skill and job requirements	X			X		
Develop staffing and span of control requirements	X				X	X
Establish training requirements	X	X	X	X	X	X
Conduct operations reviews of actual versus desired task performance	X				X	
Compare jobs' similarities and differences	X	X	X		X	
Develop task-by-task performance evaluation	X	X	X			

SOURCE: Adapted from Gael, S. (1983). *Job analysis: A guide to assessing work activities.* (p. 95). San Francisco: Jossey-Bass. Reprinted by permission of Jossey-Bass, Inc., an imprint of John Wiley & Sons, Inc.

DATA ANALYSIS

Both CODAP and WPSS were designed for computerized data analysis. Computers are handy for compiling, listing, and analyzing large amounts of data. Both programs are capable of producing a wide variety of reports. The primary report is a list of tasks along with statistical summaries of the responses to the questions in the inventory. Portions of a sample WPSS output are shown in Table 2.12, which shows data about the job of the supervisor of people who maintain telephone poles and wiring.

In the output, tasks are listed as the first (leftmost) column, and each task is listed as a row. The second column is reserved for labels to identify the entries in the remaining columns. The columns to the right of the second column are for the total sample and for demographic groups. In the WPSS printout, an entire task listing is prepared separately for each task attribute, such as significance, criticality, and so forth. (Table 2.12 is prepared for responses to the significance item.) In Table 2.12, we can see that there were 113 job incumbents sampled from the entire company, and that five came from the C&P group and six came from the Illinois group. For each task, responses are summarized by the proportion who reported that they do the task, the mean response of those

Table 2.12   Sample WPSS Output

Statistics for Significance				
Significance		Company Total	C & P	Illinois
	N =	113	5	6
1. Analyze office costs/ expenses for budgeting purposes	PROP	0.97	1.00	0.83
	MEAN	3.67	3.40	2.80
	STD	1.71	0.89	1.79
2. Assign development of long- range force/training requirement	PROP	0.92	0.80	0.83
	MEAN	4.05	4.00	4.00
	STD	1.79	1.15	1.41
3. Determine personnel needs for a new project	PROP	0.90	1.00	0.83
	MEAN	3.59	5.00	2.80
	STD	1.71	2.00	2.05
4. Determine work flow and office design layout	PROP	0.92	0.60	0.83
	MEAN	3.38	4.33	3.00
	STD	1.77	1.53	2.12

SOURCE: Adapted from Gael, S. (1983). *Job analysis: A guide to assessing work activities.* (p. 129). San Francisco: Jossey-Bass. Reprinted by permission of Jossey-Bass, Inc., a subsidiary of John Wiley & Sons, Inc.

doing it, and the standard deviation of the responses (the computation of the mean and standard deviation are described in our chapter on doing job analysis). In Table 2.12, we can see that 97 percent of the respondents to the survey in the entire company reported that they analyzed office costs/expenses for budgeting purposes. The mean significance rating of the respondents was 3.67 overall, with a standard deviation of 1.71 (both on a 7-point scale; see Table 2.9, which illustrates the scale for difficulty). We can see that the company overall gave a mean of 3.67 for the significance of budgeting, but the Illinois group gave a lower mean of 2.80. Such an analysis allows one to see whether there is variability in task response by region, job experience, or sex, for example.

Both CODAP and WPSS have other programs for a variety of purposes. Such programs can be used to generate lists of tasks to be used in performance evaluation or to compare the content similarity of two different jobs, or as input to a clustering program to create job families. An extended description of how the data analysis matched the intended purpose of the job analysis is beyond the scope of this book. Such descriptions can be found in Gael (1983, for WPSS) and in Gambardella and Alvord (1980, for CODAP). A briefer description of the CODAP system is given in Christal and Weissmuller (1988). Now that computers are nearly ubiquitous, high-quality data analysis and word processing are readily available and the specific programs used by CODAP and WPSS are less important. Virtually anyone with experience in the common statistical packages can produce reports similar to those in CODAP or WPSS more quickly by using widely available programs than by learning CODAP or WPSS.

Critical Incident Technique

The critical incident technique was developed and used for several U.S. Army Air Force projects in World War II. Its first major presentation to those outside the military appeared in an article by Flanagan (1954). As described by Flanagan, the method requires SMEs to recall specific instances of worker behavior on the job. The behaviors should represent outstanding or unacceptable performance. Such behaviors are the critical incidents. As in FJA, there are rules or systems for writing critical incidents. Flanagan required three pieces of information to be included with each incident:

1. A statement of the context, that is, what led up to the behavior or the problem or opportunity confronting the worker

2. The employee behavior itself

3. The consequences of the behavior

Critical incidents must be written so that they communicate clearly to the eventual users of the information (typically, other job experts, such as supervisors, instructors, or selection specialists). Enough must be written about the context so that others can understand the background. The behavior itself must be written so that it is clear what the worker did. Inferences or statements about worker traits instead of behavioral descriptions are to be avoided. Table 2.13 shows examples of critical incidents that vary in the degree to which they follow the rules for writing such items.

In practice, it is often difficult to get SMEs to generate good critical incidents, at least initially. The phrase "critical incident" has connotations that bring to mind unbidden images of the nuclear disaster at Chernobyl. When explaining the method to SMEs, it is best to call the method something else, such as "behavioral examples." If the SME cannot generate examples, or the examples are not terribly useful ("came to work on time for 20 years"), it may be helpful to have the SME focus on the most successful person on the job and to describe what that person does that makes him or her successful. Alternatively, it may help to ask the person to list a few things that are essential

Table 2.13   Sample Critical Incidents

Poor	Better
The police officer reacted to a fire quickly, putting it out with a fire extinguisher. It could have caused considerable damage in the ensuing explosion, but the officer's action prevented injury or serious damage.	An engine fire started in a car at a gasoline pump in a gas station. The police officer was driving by on patrol, noticed the fire, stopped, and quickly extinguished the fire with the chemical extinguisher from her patrol car. Her quick action prevented a major fire and explosion.
The clerk showed good initiative in checking work.	The clerk noticed an item in a letter that didn't appear to be right, checked it, found it to be opposite to the intended meaning, and corrected it.
The department chair forgot things and made the students' lives more difficult.	The department chair forgot to assign an instructor for a class. At the first class meeting, there was no instructor present and the students could not verify whether they were enrolled.

SOURCE: Adapted in part from Bownas, D. A., & Bernardin, H. J. (1988). Critical incident technique. In S. Gael (Ed.), *The job analysis handbook for business, industry, and government* (Vol. 2, pp. 1120–1140). New York: Wiley. Reprinted by permission of John Wiley & Sons, Inc.

to successful performance, or to give the person a list of topics (for example, planning, leadership, initiative) and then to work from this list. It is often difficult to get people to describe the actual behavior and not inferences based on the behavior. If the SME says that the employee "showed good initiative," the SME must be asked what the person did that made him or her think that the employee showed good initiative.

Latham and Wexley (1993) suggested several practical tips in collecting critical incidents. First, SMEs should not be asked about their own performance because they tend to recall effective incidents more readily than ineffective incidents. The incidents recalled should have occurred in the past 6 to 12 months because longer memory may distort results and because the nature of the job may have changed. SMEs should generate positive incidents before negative incidents because if negative incidents are collected first, the SME may doubt the purpose of the data collection (perhaps a witch hunt).

TIPS FOR CAPTURING AND WRITING CRITICAL INCIDENTS

For writing a behavioral example:

1. Get the key circumstances or context of the behavior, such as "in the operating room, with the patient unconscious . . ." or "we were laying concrete for a sidewalk. . . ."

2. Get the behavior.
   a. Make it specific. Focus on one behavior for one incident rather than a series of behaviors. Rather than telling the entire story about how the concrete came to be faulty, tell us that the worker added too much water to the mixture.
   b. Focus on the behavior, not an inference about the qualities of the person. If the expert tells you that worker was creative, say, "Good, but what did the worker do that made you think that he or she was creative?" If the expert says that the surgeon was inattentive, you say, "What did the surgeon do that made you think so?"
   c. Was the behavior simply adequate, or was it particularly effective or ineffective?

3. Get the outcome. The outcome should be the direct result of the behavior in the context. The concrete failed to set properly, the patient had an adverse side effect, the solution to the problem resulted in a machine breaking less frequently, and so forth. The outcome will usually tell you whether the behavior was effective or ineffective.

For running a meeting of SMEs:

1. Avoid the term "critical incidents"; try "behavioral examples," or "work snapshots." Ask your SMEs to imagine that they could take a snapshot of a worker

doing something that would stand for the whole story, for example, pouring in water for the concrete story.

2. Start with the good examples.

3. Have SMEs imagine specific people and tell stories about them.

4. Make the stories job related.

5. Use dimensions or tasks as prompts if the SMEs are hesitant.

6. Sometimes we are concerned about the extent to which the target person was responsible for the outcome. This could be reported as a percentage, or as a description of the role of others or the context (for example, good or poor tools or equipment).

RESEARCH ON THE CRITICAL INCIDENT TECHNIQUE

Several studies have focused on generating critical incidents. It appears that it matters little whether incidents are collected in groups or individually (Wagner, 1951) and that minor changes in the wording of instruction to produce critical incidents has little effect (Finkle, 1950, cited in Bownas & Bernardin, 1988). On the other hand, the source of information (for example, incumbent, supervisor, or client) does appear to matter in terms of the kind of incidents written. Different sources attend to different aspects of performance (Borman & Vallon, 1974; Wagner, 1951).

Initial use of the critical incident technique simply called for generating lists of incidents through free recall. Job analysts or other SMEs could subsequently group the incidents into categories or dimensions that share a common thread of activity (for example, baking bread), human ability (for example, consideration of others' feelings), or equipment (for example, cockpit controls). Subsequent research suggests that giving writers dimensions prior to generating critical incidents is helpful. Writers given dimensions generate more incidents than writers not given dimensions, and there is no difference in quality between the groups (Bownas & Bernardin, 1988).

Critical incidents provide a richness of detail about actual work behaviors. They are frequently used in constructing forms used in performance appraisal (Bownas & Bernardin, 1988), and this method is a favorite one for this purpose (Levine, Ash, Hall, & Sistrunk, 1983). However, research evaluating the psychometric characteristics of performance appraisal forms has shown that forms based on critical incidents do not appear more reliable than simpler forms if proper attention is given to important dimensions of work performance (for example, Bernardin & Beatty, 1984; Landy & Farr, 1980; Schwab, Heneman, & DeCotiis, 1975). Results generally indicate that any carefully developed performance appraisal format will work about as well as any other, although a performance appraisal method called *behavioral observation scales,* which is based on critical incidents, has been quite successful in many instances (Latham & Wexley, 1977; see also Wiersma & Latham, 1986).

The critical incident technique has been used for purposes other than performance appraisal, such as identifying traits for selection (Dunnette, 1966), training needs assessment (Bownas & Bernardin, 1988), and training design (Gilbert, 1978). Flanagan (1954) described several studies that anticipate the results of the research included here, both about methods (different sources produced different incidents, minor wording changes in instruction do not matter) and about applications (selection and training).

Chapter Summary

In this chapter, four general approaches to analyzing the content of jobs (that is, what the worker does) were described: time-and-motion study, functional job analysis (FJA), task inventories, and the critical incident technique. All of the methods are applicable to more than one purpose.

Time-and-motion study was described as a collection of methods primarily used to improve the effectiveness and efficiency of task completion. Each of the techniques allows the analyst to gain information about the sequence of events and/or the time to complete elements of the work.

We described two variants of FJA, the Department of Labor method and Fine's FJA. Both of the methods share a focus on what the worker does in relation to data, people, and things. Both methods use a specific grammar to describe tasks. Fine's FJA extends the DOL method by including ratings of orientation toward, as well as complexity of involvement with, data, people, and things.

Tasks are central not only to FJA but to task inventories as well. The tasks in task inventories tend to be more finely detailed and numerous than those in FJA. The task inventory typically uses incumbents as sources of information where incumbents rate each task in a survey in terms of one or more features, such as time spent, difficulty to learn, and consequences of error. Designing a survey for a task inventory was described in some detail, including writing items, selecting response options, and choosing informants. Analyzing the data from the survey was also described. The general approach was illustrated by two computerized data collection and scoring programs, CODAP and WPSS.

Finally, the critical incident technique was described. The critical incident technique uses subject matter experts (SMEs) to generate specific behavioral examples that include a problem situation, what the worker did, and the results of that action. We reviewed approaches to collecting and analyzing the data and noted some of the applications of the critical incident technique. More detailed discussions of the applications of job analysis methods to specific problems can be found in Chapters 7 and 8.

3

Worker-Oriented Methods

In this chapter, we describe job analysis methods that focus on attributes or characteristics that people need to be able to complete their jobs successfully. One of the main uses of such information is to hire qualified people. Often the attributes refer to the person and might be considered psychological characteristics. For example, some characteristics are perceptual, such as use of color vision or sense of touch. Others refer to mental processes, such as arithmetic reasoning or speaking a foreign language. Still others refer to skill in using tools or equipment, such as a violin or a forklift. There is another class of attributes covered in worker-oriented methods that refers more to the context of work, and these are shorthand ways of saying that a person needs to have whatever is needed to cope with the job. For example, a person may need the ability to work alone or to work in noisy or dusty environments. Sometimes the abilities become more or less synonymous with the task, such as the ability to weld or to dance. In such cases, it is difficult to determine whether we are talking about the work or the worker. But in this chapter, the *intent* of the job analysis procedure is to describe jobs from the worker's point of view rather than the work itself.

In some ways, worker-oriented methods are the most "psychological" of the methods of job analysis. The psychology comes from attempting to determine what it takes to be good at a job. We are sometimes amazed at how skilled human performance can be. For example, we have been amazed watching a professional figure skater (that looks so effortless!), a guitar player knocking out a tasty riff (how does he do that?), or an astronomer pointing out features of some celestial object (how could she possibly know anything about a quasar?). What is it about these people that makes them so good at what they do? Of course, they have spent years practicing their specialty, but do they also possess something special, some needed capacity? On the other hand, are there some things that we are unlikely ever to be really be good at, regardless of the time spent? Could it be drawing, tennis, calculus, poetry, or playing the violin? One of us (Brannick) will never progress beyond drawing stick figures.

What does it take to be good at a job, and how do we find this out? That is the topic of this chapter. Job analysts have generally agreed to capture these human attributes by referring to KSAOs (knowledge, skill, ability, and other personal characteristics). There are several ways of defining these human attributes. One approach was offered by Levine (1983). We adapt those definitions here. *Knowledge* is the existence in memory of a retrievable set of technical facts, concepts, language, and procedures directly relevant to job performance. *Skill* is the developed or trained capacity to perform tasks that call for the use of tools, equipment, or machinery. *Abilities* involve the relatively enduring capacity to acquire skills or knowledge, and to carry out tasks at an acceptable level of proficiency where tools, equipment, and machinery are not major elements. Finally, *other personal characteristics* include job-relevant interests, preferences, temperament, and personality characteristics that indicate how well an employee is likely to perform on a routine, day-to-day basis or how an employee is likely to adjust to a job's working conditions. (If you casually drop the term "KSAOs" among job analysts they will immediately accept you into their secret society, even if you don't know the secret handshake.)

Several different techniques are described in this chapter. First, we describe the *job element method* (JEM). JEM is the earliest of the worker-oriented methods. It blurs the distinction between what gets done and what abilities are required to do the job. This method breaks a job down into pieces called *elements* (small surprise there) that are described in terms that job incumbents can easily understand. But note that these elements are very different from the elements we discussed in Chapter 2.

Next we turn to the *Position Analysis Questionnaire* (PAQ). The PAQ was developed with the notion that it should be applied to a wide variety of jobs. The PAQ was developed over years of study and has been applied to a very large number of jobs since its development. You might say that the PAQ is a famous name in the business of job analysis. The PAQ lists a large number of standard elements (for example, the job requires standing; it also uses the term *element* to mean something a bit different; here "element" is just an item to respond to) that the job analyst records on a specially designed form.

We then turn to other trait-based worker-oriented methods. We briefly describe three methods that focus on other standard lists of human abilities, the *Threshold Traits Analysis System* (TTAS), the *Ability Requirements Scales* (ARS), and the *Occupational Reinforcer Pattern* (ORP). The list of traits in the TTAS is global and comprehensive. The list is useful, among other things, for keeping you from overlooking something important. The abilities covered by the Ability Requirements Scales (see Table 3.6 later in the chapter for a sample of these) are each linked to one or more psychological tests. The Occupational Reinforcer Pattern characteristics are linked to human motives at work that can be used for vocational purposes. The other two methods in this section are noted for their attention to tools and equipment. The methods are the *AET*

(*Arbeitwissenschaftliches Erhebungsverfahren zur Tätigkeitsanalyse;* we will translate for you later so you can get this right on a TV quiz show) and the *Job Components Inventory* (JCI). The AET, which, as you may have guessed, was developed in Germany, looks at jobs from a human engineering standpoint and asks how the job might be done in such a way that it is more friendly to the worker. The Job Components Inventory lists 220 items related to tools and equipment.

Finally, we describe methods used in *cognitive task analysis.* Cognitive task analysis is the most recently developed of the worker-oriented techniques. Cognitive task analysis attempts to gain a better understanding of the mental processes and strategies that are used in completing the job. To do so, cognitive task analysis often focuses on the difference between novice and expert performance on the job.

The common thread through all the worker-oriented techniques is the focus on the qualities workers must have to be successful.

Job Element Method

JEM is probably the earliest of the worker-oriented job analysis approaches. It was developed in the 1950s by Ernest Primoff and associates in the U.S. Civil Service Commission (now the U.S. Office of Personnel Management, Office of Personnel Research and Development; see Primoff, 1957). JEM is the worker-oriented method that is most similar to the work-oriented methods. JEM focuses on work behaviors and the results of this behavior rather than more abstract characteristics. An *element* in JEM is a combination of behaviors and associated evidences. Elements are named through terms commonly used in the workplace rather than terms developed by psychologists. For example, "the behavior of acting in a dependable fashion, evidenced by punctuality, commendations for dependability and a record of doing exactly what is required by the job, is an element termed Reliability" (Primoff & Eyde, 1988, p. 807).

CONTENT OF ELEMENTS

Elements cover a broad range of behaviors, including cognitive, psychomotor, and work habits. Cognitive elements include such items as recognizing tools and their uses, reading blueprints, and computing means and standard deviations. The psychomotor elements include the ability to sense and perceive (for example, color vision) and to carry out simple to complex motor actions, such as operating an electric drill or a chisel or piloting a jet fighter. Work habits refer to collections of behaviors that are more motivational in character. According to Primoff and Eyde (1988), one of the advantages of JEM over more narrow task analytic approaches to job analysis is the

Table 3.1   Examples of Job Elements

Job	Element or Subelement
Office Manager	Ability to gain conformance Ability to apply procedures Ability to meet deadlines
Police Officer	Have good physical coordination No fear of firearms Ability to recall facts
Electrician	Understanding of theory and instruments Understand ammeter, ohmmeter, voltmeter Knowledge of shop math

SOURCE: Adapted from Primoff, E. S., & Eyde, L. D. (1988). Job element analysis. In S. Gael (Ed.), *The job analysis handbook for business, industry, and government* (Vol. II, pp. 807–824). New York: Wiley. Reprinted by permission of John Wiley & Sons, Inc.

use of work habits as elements. Work habits used as elements might include such items as willingness to take on extra work or willingness to make sure that the work is done perfectly, without error. Table 3.1 contains sample elements and subelements for several jobs.

Steps in the JEM

Here are the steps:

1. Gather elements from subject matter experts
2. Have the experts rate each element on four scales
   a. B
   b. S
   c. T
   d. P
3. Derive scale values from the expert ratings
4. Share derived ratings with experts
   a. TV
   b. IT
   c. TR
5. Use results in your application (for example, developing tests)

Each step is explained in detail next.

GATHERING INFORMATION FOR JEM

JEM is usually conducted by a professional analyst, who serves as the project leader, and a team of six subject matter experts (SMEs), who are usually incumbents and supervisors. There are typically two sessions that take 3 to 5 hours each. During the first session, SMEs brainstorm and rate a list of elements that the analyst compiles. The product of the session will be a list of job elements and ratings of them. The analyst will then retire to analyze the ratings and compile the results. After some work, the analyst will return to the SMEs for the second session, in which the results of the first session will be put to some particular purpose, such as developing a test, performance measure, or training program.

In the first session, the analyst will encourage the SMEs to be exhaustive in their list of elements. When the SMEs begin to tire, the analyst will ask such questions as:

- What else might a worker show that would prove he or she is superior?
- If you had to pick out one person to get a special bonus for outstanding work, what might you look for?
- What might make you want to fire someone?
- If a worker is weak, what might cause trouble? (Primoff & Eyde, 1988, p. 809)

When all of the elements have been listed, the analyst asks the SMEs to provide subelements. Subelements are specific behavioral examples that illustrate the meaning of the element. For example, in Table 3.1, under the electrician job, an example element was "Understanding of theory and instruments." This was illustrated and partially defined by the subelements "Understand ammeter, ohmmeter, voltmeter" and "Knowledge of shop math."

RATING SCALES

At this point, the analyst has compiled a series of statements (elements) that detail what a worker needs in order to do the job. The worker traits (knowledge, skills, abilities, and other characteristics) are behaviorally defined in terms that job experts understand. The next step in the job analysis is to collect ratings from the analysts on a series of four rating scales. The rating scales used by JEM are Barely Acceptable (B), Superior (S), Trouble Likely If Not Considered (T), and Practical (P). All scales are rated with a three-category response. The SME provides a 0 if the scale has some minimal value, a check (✓) if the scale applies somewhat, and a plus sign (+) if the item is highly applicable.

Barely Acceptable (B)

The rating for the B scale requires a judgment as to whether barely acceptable workers must possess an element to do the job. Barely acceptable workers are those who are just scraping by. If they were any worse, they would not be qualified to do the job. Barely acceptable workers must possess the most basic of skills; otherwise they would not be acceptable. If almost none of the barely acceptable workers have the element, the SME would give a 0. If some barely acceptable workers have the element, it would receive a ✓, and if all have it, it would receive a +. If we consider the element "breathing" for most jobs, all barely acceptable workers would have this element (otherwise they would probably not be able to work), so SMEs would assign a + to this element.

Superior (S)

The rating for the S scale asks SMEs to describe how useful the element is for distinguishing the superior worker (0 is *not useful,* ✓ is *valuable,* and + is *very important*). It might be helpful to think about things that might earn a worker some kind of award from his or her employer, for example. The point is not merely that the superior workers possess the characteristic but that, in addition, the characteristic distinguishes the superior worker from the other workers. For example, superior workers all breathe, but breathing would not result in an award for superior work (the SMEs would assign a 0 to this element). A police officer might receive an award for bravery, for example, when the officer risked his or her own life to save the life of a person in a burning building. If so, bravery (or conduct above and beyond the call of duty) might get a + for this element.

Trouble Likely If Not Considered (T)

The rating for the T scale asks SMEs to describe whether trouble is likely if the element is not included in an examination or screen for new hires (0 is *OK to ignore,* ✓ is *some trouble,* and + is *much trouble*). For example, breathing is safe to ignore. Although there most certainly would be problems on the job if one didn't breathe, this can be safely ignored because all the applicants can be assumed to breathe. It is not something we would test for. On the other hand, we would expect a great deal of trouble if a brain surgeon were unable to use surgical instruments such as scalpels and clamps deftly (causing SMEs to select + for this element). For another example, we might expect trouble for visually impaired operators of heavy equipment such as buses and aircraft.

Practical (P)

The rating for the P scale asks SMEs whether job applicants are likely to possess the element. If we select for the element, how many of our job openings can we fill? (0 is *almost no openings,* ✓ is *some openings,* and + is *all openings.*) Again, if we consider the element *breathing,* we would expect to fill all openings after requiring it and screening for it. On the other hand, if we require fluency in two foreign languages for grocery clerks, we are unlikely to fill any positions (at least in the United States).

DERIVED SCALES

The analyst will then take the SME responses and prepare them for the second session. The SME responses to the four scales are analyzed and combined in various ways (some rather complex) to make them more useful for human resources applications. Table 3.2 shows the results of one such analysis.

The first four columns refer to the scales completed by the SMEs, that is, Barely Acceptable, Superior, Trouble Likely, and Practical. The numbers in the columns are percentages of the maximum possible scale scores. For example, with six SMEs, the maximum possible points would be 12 (where $0 = 0$, $\checkmark = 1$, and $+ = 2$). If the sum of the SME points were 6, the percentage would be 50.

Total Value (TV)

The first derived scale is total value (TV). *Total value* refers to the value of the element in "differentiating abilities of applicants for a job" (Primoff & Eyde, 1988, p. 812). The scale is defined as $TV = (S—B–P) + (SP + T)$, which is not a blindingly obvious formula. So let's take it a little at a time to try to make sense of it. The first part of TV is $(S—B–P)$. The first term basically says, "Let's select employees using elements that are both (1) useful in spotting superior workers and (2) not found among most of the people in our workforce." The second part of the equation $(SP + T)$ also contains S and P, as did the first. This time, however, they are being multiplied rather than subtracted. The reason that S and P are multiplied in this part of the equation is so that if we cannot fill any of the positions if we select on the element $P = 0$, then the product SP will be zero, so the high standing on S will be discounted. This means that the total sum will be reduced so that we are less likely to select for something that we cannot find. We then add the value for T (Trouble Likely) because we want to select for troublesome elements if we can. So, taken as a whole, TV says something like this, "Let's select for elements that pick workers who will prove superior and reject workers who will prove to be problems. But let's not select for the elements if they are too common or too uncommon among workers." The TV scores are calculated as sums of points and then transformed so that their maximum value is 150. TV values greater than 100 are thought to be significant and are called *elements* in the JEM results.

Item Index (IT)

Item index (IT) refers to the extent to which a subelement is important in the content of a test. IT is computed by $IT = SP + T$, which is the second part

Table 3.2   Partial JEM Results for a Police Officer

Element	B	S	T	P	TV	IT	TR
Have good physical coordination (S)	60	63	79	92	55	65	46
Have no major physical incapacity (RS)	81	44	96	94	23	59	33
Ability to engage in weaponless physical contact (S)	68	68	80	87	55	66	49
No fear of firearms (S)	73	49	81	90	27	56	33
Ability to compare signatures	39	58	27	50	29	29	50
Ability to recover from glare of oncoming lights (S)	74	43	71	89	15	50	25
Have sufficient height to see over roofs of cars (SC)	92	30	71	95	14	43	6
Ability to work outdoors in bad weather for long periods (S)	72	53	67	92	26	54	29
No unusual vocal characteristics (lisp, high pitched)	66	37	62	94	4	44	19
Ability to change a car tire (SC)	94	23	57	95	32	33	4
Ability to determine reasonable grounds for arrest (TS)	60	89	48	44	56	42	88
Ability to function while in physical danger (E)	58	94	90	86	101	84	76
Have honesty (RS)	76	85	98	95	86	86	58
Possess good judgment (E)	46	96	86	93	111	88	75
Have good leadership ability (TS), (S)	25	92	53	71	90	62	86

SOURCE: Adapted from Primoff, E. S., & Eyde, L. D. (1988). Job element analysis. In S. Gael (Ed.), *The job analysis handbook for business, industry and government* (Vol. II, pp. 807–824). New York: Wiley. Reprinted by permission of John Wiley & Sons, Inc.

NOTE: In column heads, B, S, T and P are the four rating scales: B = Barely Acceptable, S = Superior, T = Trouble Likely If Not Considered; P = Practical, TV = Total Value; IT = Item Index; TR = Training Value

In parentheses, E = Element, S = Significant Subelement, RS = Rankable Screenout, TS = Training Subelement, SC = Screenout. You cannot obtain the tabled values of TV, IT, and TR in this table from the tabled values of B, S, T, and P because the resulting columns (TV, and so on) are rescaled after they are calculated. Items in the column headings are defined in the text.

of the TV computation. The numbers in the IT column are also percentages of the maximum possible score. Subelements with IT values greater than 50 can be used to rank applicants.

Training Value (TR)

Training value (TR) refers to the value of the element in training, amazingly enough. TR is computed by $TR = S + T + SP' - B$, where P' is the reverse of P, so that if all openings can be filled by applicants, then $P = 0$. This basically says that we would like to train people on skills that superior workers have and that will prove troublesome if absent ($S + T$). However, we only need to train employees on those skills that are not readily available in the labor pool ($SP' - B$).

ASSIGNING ELEMENTS TO CATEGORIES

Elements or subelements are determined by their profiles of scores as shown in Table 3.3.

During the second session, the analyst will share the results of the first session with the SMEs, as is shown in Table 3.3. The SMEs will make use of the information in such activities as designing tests. JEM is particularly useful in developing work sample tests for selection. For example, one screenout item in

Table 3.3   Categories of JEM Elements and Subelements

Category	Description
E	Element is marked when the TV is 100 or greater. (If E is marked, no other letter is marked.)
S	Significant subelement is marked when IT is 50 or greater.
TS	Training Subelement is marked when TR is 75 or greater.
SC	Screenout (minimum requirement) is marked if B and P are both at least 75 and T is 50 or greater.
RS	Rankable Screenout is marked if a subelement meets both the values for S (Significant subelement) and SC (Screenout). RS means that the subelement has a minimum value needed for the job, but above that level can also be used to rank job applicants.

SOURCE: Adapted from Primoff, E. S., & Eyde, L. D. (1988). Job element analysis. In S. Gael (Ed.), *The job analysis handbook for business, industry, and government* (Vol. II, pp. 807–824). New York: Wiley. Reprinted by permission of John Wiley & Sons, Inc.

Table 3.2 is "Have sufficient height to see over roofs of cars." It would be a simple matter to take a person into a parking lot and see whether he or she can see over the roofs of most cars. Of course, it might be simpler still to determine what minimum height is needed to see over the roofs of cars and then use a yardstick to measure job applicants for that minimum. (This element would cause some controversy in practice because it constitutes a height requirement that will exclude a disproportionate number of women. Is this item important enough to include in an expensive testing process?) For another example, another screenout item is "Ability to change a car tire," and this item might make a reasonable work sample test. Unfortunately, some elements do not easily result in work sample tests. Consider the rankable screenout item "Have honesty." It is not immediately clear to us how this should be tested. Should we check for lies on an application blank? Should we leave a wallet in the room with the applicants to see if they report it or pocket it? Should we ask them questions taken from social desirability scales, such as "Before voting, do you carefully check on all the candidates?" Answering "Always" to this question may indicate that a person is more interested in creating a favorable impression than in being honest.

JEM also provides for checks on the job analysis through the development of products that were the impetus for the analysis. For example, a test may be developed. If the test is not working properly, then the problematic aspect of the test may lead to another look at the job. For example, in a test of electricians, Primoff and Eyde (1988) noted that some electricians who were clearly not qualified were passing a portion of the exam. This caused the analysts to revisit the job, where they found that the better electricians could use and maintain specific electrical equipment. The test was modified to include this equipment, and the problem was solved. The unqualified electricians no longer passed the test. JEM can also be used to choose tests developed outside the current job and job analysis. We turn to this next.

RESEARCH ON JEM: THE J-COEFFICIENT

The J-coefficient (job coefficient) was developed by Primoff in the 1950s. Perhaps because most of Primoff's writings were published by the U.S. government rather than in the typical academic journals, his ideas were never widely adopted. However, his intuitions about the way job elements and tests are related turn out to have an elegant mathematical basis that few scholars have pursued. We present the basic ideas without the elegant mathematics (but we do, of course, provide references for those with a thirst for a deeper understanding of the issues).

Overall job performance represents a value to the organization that results from the incumbent's performance over some period of time on specific tasks. In the case of a police officer, for example, overall job performance might result from making arrests, driving safely, being a mentor to a new, junior officer, addressing elementary school children as part of a community relations program, and so forth. Alternatively, we might think of overall job performance as resulting from a series of job elements such as those collected during JEM (for example, recovering from the glare of oncoming lights, functioning well while in physical danger, behaving honestly). In other words, the job elements cause overall job performance. Some job elements may be more important than others, and the more important elements should be more highly correlated with overall job performance in a population of workers. If we were to correlate auto mechanics' overall job performance with various elements, we would expect to find that mechanical aptitude showed a higher correlation than did ability to function while in physical danger, for example.

In traditional test validation, some measure of overall job performance is correlated with a test (the resulting correlation is often called a *validity coefficient;* we cover correlations in Chapter 9, doing a job analysis). For example, supervisory ratings of overall job performance by mechanics might be correlated with test scores on a mechanical aptitude test. We would expect to see that better mechanics as indicated by their supervisors would also have the higher test scores. The J-coefficient is an estimate of the validity coefficient that would result if such a validation study were conducted. However, the J-coefficient is derived in part from human judgments rather than empirical comparisons of test scores and overall job performance.

To compute a J-coefficient, we need three pieces of information: (1) the correlations of job elements with overall job performance, (2) the correlations of tests with the job elements, and (3) the correlations of the job elements among themselves. Primoff advocated using SMEs to provide estimates of the correlations of the job elements with overall performance for any given job. The other values (correlations of tests with elements and of elements with elements) were to be developed over years of research and compiled into tables in which the accuracy would increase as evidence mounted across people and jobs. A computational example of a J-coefficient is shown in Trattner (1982). Given information about several tests, one can compute J-coefficients for each test and then choose the test with the largest coefficient.

Although Primoff suggested the use of judgment for element-job performance information and a more empirical approach for test-element relations, it is clearly possible to use humans to estimate test-element correlations and to compute empirical estimates of element-performance relations. Hamilton and Dickinson (1987) compared several different methods for generating the information needed for J-coefficients and found that several different methods provided comparable, consistent estimates of J-coefficients. Furthermore, they compared the J-coefficients to validity coefficients computed on the same sample and found close agreement between the two estimates, thus suggesting that human judges can provide data useful for predicting the validity of tests when traditional validation studies are not feasible.

REMARKS ON JEM

JEM is admittedly circular (and proudly so, we might add). For example, in a job element analysis, a sample ability is "Ability to disassemble an office desk." Note that such an ability is defined to be whatever is needed to complete the task successfully. There is no necessary reference to some other knowledge or ability that might explain task performance, such as knowledge of mechanical principles, knowledge of the use of tools, spatial reasoning, and so forth. JEM does not deny the existence of knowledge, skills, abilities, and other characteristics (and sometimes incorporates more abstract elements). However, rather than talking about such basic aspects of tasks, JEM often refers to broader and narrower collections of job-oriented behaviors. As Primoff and Eyde (1988) noted, "Tests and other products are *not* inferred from the job analysis, but *incorporate* the work example definitions of the subelements" (p. 815, italics in the original).

We find this to be a powerful argument when JEM is used to develop tests that are essentially work samples. Part of the reason for avoiding basic abilities such as perceptual speed or analytical reasoning is most likely the strong behaviorist tradition in psychology in the United States that lasted almost from the beginning of psychology until the 1970s. As much as humanly possible, behaviorists avoided talking about mental states and instead focused on observable behavior. Thus, the focus on work behavior as a worker-oriented approach is very satisfying to a behaviorist. In more recent years, psychology has become focused on cognitive process and states, turning away from the behaviorists' denial of the usefulness of mental states.

However, the argument that traits are not inferred is less compelling when JEM is used to select tests that have been constructed for other purposes. When picking tests off the shelf, JEM used a standard set of abilities and tests that had tabled relational values. (The tabled values indicate how closely tests and work elements are associated with one another.) Such a scheme does require job analysts to infer the degree to which such abstract abilities as perceptual speed and verbal reasoning are required by the job. Also, the emphasis on observable behaviors might lead to ignoring efficient, valid tests that could enhance the effectiveness of employee selection.

Let us briefly mention two other problems with JEM. First, there has been no solid evidence to show that the complex rating formulas are always necessary. Second, a heavy reliance on SME input from start to finish can lead to screening tools that can get you into some legal hot water. The height requirement we mentioned for the job of police officer is an example.

Despite its problems, JEM has had a huge impact on job analysis. Aspects of this approach have found their way into many other methods. And the terms *knowledge, skills, abilities,* and *other characteristics* have become part of the lingo of job analysts everywhere.

Position Analysis Questionnaire

DEVELOPMENT AND STRUCTURE OF THE PAQ

The PAQ was developed in the 1960s by Ernest McCormick (as well as his colleagues at Purdue University). It was designed around the well-known behaviorist formula S-O-R, where the organism (O) receives a stimulus (S) and makes a response (R). But the PAQ also notes that the environment and social setting play a role in job performance. Unlike JEM, the PAQ was designed so that the same elements apply to all jobs. Again, the term *element* has a different meaning across the two techniques.

Before 2004, the PAQ consisted of 194 items or elements. Of these, the first 187 concern either a human attribute (for example, color perception) or an aspect of the job requiring accommodation by the human (for example, the job makes use of written information, the jobholder experiences vibration). The last seven items (188–194) concern compensation (pay) for the job and are not considered here. The items are collected into six major divisions, which are listed in Table 3.4. Information input, for example, concerns what type of information the jobholder gets, and where and how he or she gets it. The major divisions are further divided into subdivisions called *sections* and *subsections*. Each section or subsection is composed of related items. Sample subdivisions and items are also listed in Table 3.4. In 2004, the PAQ was supplemented by job analysis questions used in U.S. Social Security disability determinations; new job analysis questions added by the August 23, 2004, amendment to the Fair Labor Standards Act (FLSA; the first major change since 1949); analysis questions long-believed to be required, such as "ability to sit/stand/shuffle"; education requirements; and certain stress-related questions. Exactly 300 items are now used.

The job analyst considers each item relative to the job under consideration and decides whether the item applies to the job. If the item does apply, then the analyst rates the job on the item. Although the PAQ is named for the term *position,* it is typically used to analyze the *job* as we have defined it. That is, the PAQ is usually used to analyze a group of related positions that are similar enough to be called a job and given a single title. (You have won our undying gratitude if you remembered this.) The analyst then records for each item his or her judgment about the item with regard to a rating scale developed for the PAQ. There are six different rating scales used in the PAQ. Only one rating scale applies to any given item. Each rating scale is illustrated in Table 3.5 along with sample items.

The PAQ manual notes that specially trained analysts, managers, and even incumbents can complete the PAQ. However, in most cases specially trained analysts should be used. We recommend that incumbents should not, if possible, complete the PAQ because it requires a high level of reading comprehension and many rather abstract judgments. Also, many of the PAQ scales will not

Table 3.4   Structure of the Position Analysis Questionnaire

Major Division	Subdivision	Illustrative Job Element
Information Input	Sources of job information Discrimination and perceptual activities	Use of written materials Estimating speed of moving objects
Mediation (Mental) Processes	Decision making and reasoning Information processing Use of stored information	Reasoning in problem solving Encoding/decoding Using mathematics
Work Output	Use of physical devices Integrative manual activities General body activities Manipulation/ coordination activities	Use of keyboard devices Handling objects/ materials Climbing Hand-arm manipulation
Interpersonal Activities	Communications Interpersonal relationships Personal contact Supervision and coordination	Instruction Serving/catering Personal contact with public customers Level of supervision received
Work Situation and Job Context	Physical working conditions Psychological and sociological aspects	Low temperature Civic obligations
Miscellaneous Aspects	Work schedule, method of pay, and apparel Job demands Responsibility	Irregular hours Specified (controlled) work pace Responsibility for safety of others

SOURCE: Adapted from McCormick, E. J., Jeanneret, P. R., & Mecham, R. C. (1989). *Position analysis questionnaire*. Logan, UT: PAQ Services, Inc. Reproduced by permission of PAQ Services Inc.

Table 3.5   Sample PAQ Scales and Items

Item Type	Sample Item
Extent of Use (U)	17. Touch (pressure, pain, temperature, moisture, etc.) (information input) N = Does not apply; 1 = Nominal/very infrequent; 2 = Occasional; 3 = Moderate; 4 = Considerable; 5 = Very substantial
Importance to the Job (I)	39. Analyzing information or data (for the purpose of identifying underlying principles or facts by breaking down information into component parts, for example, interpreting financial reports, diagnosing mechanical disorders or medical symptoms, etc.) (mental processes) 113. Executives/officials (corporation vice-presidents, government administrators, plant superintendents, etc.) (relationships with other persons) N = Does not apply; 1 = Very minor; 2 = Low; 3 = Average; 4 = High; 5 = Extreme
Special Codes (S)	46. Education (indicate using the code below, the level of knowledge typically acquired through formal education that is required to perform this job. Do not consider the type of knowledge typically acquired in technical or vocational school—see item 48) (mental processes) N = Does not apply; 1 = Less than that required for completion of high school curriculum; 2 = Level obtained by completion of high school curriculum; 3 = Level obtained by some college work; 4 = Level obtained by completion of usual college curriculum; 5 = Level obtained by completion of advanced curriculum (such as graduate school, medical school, law school, etc.)
Amount of Time (T)	89. Standing (do not include walking) (work output) N = Does not apply (or is very incidental); 1 = Under 1/10 of the time; 2 = Between 1/10 and 1/3 of the time; 3 = Between 1/3 and 2/3 of the time; 4 = Over 2/3 of the time; 5 = Almost continually
Possibility of Occurrence (P)	145. Temporary disability (temporary injuries or illnesses which prevent the worker from performing the job from one full day up to extended periods of time but which do not result in permanent disability or impairment) (job context) N = No possibility; 1 = Very limited; 2 = Limited; 3 = Moderate; 4 = Fairly high; 5 = High
Applicability (A)	154. Business suit or dress (expected to wear presentable clothing such as tie and jacket, street dress, etc., as customary in offices, stores, etc.) (other job characteristics) N = Does not apply; 1 = Does apply

SOURCE: Adapted from McCormick, E. J., Jeanneret, P. R., & Mecham, R. C. (1989). *Position analysis questionnaire*. Logan, UT: PAQ Services, Inc. Reproduced by permission of PAQ Services Inc.

apply for any given job, and this may be difficult for an incumbent to accept. Incumbents should usually not fill out the PAQ when job analysis is to be used for determining compensation.

In completing the PAQ, the trained analyst ordinarily first observes and then interviews several incumbents who are performing the job. Observing the job is very useful in understanding the job context (noise, vibration, heat, and so on). It is also a useful point of departure for the analyst to note what is not obvious from watching the job. For example, a person operating a machine may know what to do from looking at a dial, from a timed duration, or simply from listening to the sounds a machine is making. It may not be obvious to an observer just what cues the incumbent is using. After observing the job, the analyst interviews one jobholder after another to complete the items in the PAQ. In general, the analyst talks to the jobholder about the PAQ item and its relevance to the job. For most of the items, however, the job analyst actually decides on the appropriate rating. For a few items, such as time spent, the analyst may ask the jobholder for a rating.

PAQ RESULTS

The PAQ is scored by computer. The computer printout lists dimension scores and overall scores for the major PAQ divisions. In addition, the computer prints estimates of aptitude test scores, estimates of job evaluation points to be used for setting salaries, and FLSA analyses, the computer's analysis on whether or not the job is covered by the Fair Labor Standards Act (see Chapter 7 for a description of the FLSA).

The PAQ also provides more detailed information about each item (element) in the survey that shows how the current job compares to other jobs contained in the PAQ database. The PAQ database has a large number of jobs cutting across the whole economy. In general, the numbers show how much of the attribute the job requires relative to other jobs.

USES OF THE PAQ

The PAQ was designed to meet two primary objectives. The first was to develop a standardized approach to identifying the person requirements of jobs, thus eliminating the need for costly test validation studies for each job (at least this was the intent). The second purpose was to help organizations with job evaluation for compensation. Early research on the PAQ, therefore, concerned selection and job evaluation. However, other uses for the instrument were adopted, and the record of research has grown quite large. Today, a major use of the PAQ is for determining disability; it is used by many long-term disability insurance carriers.

RELIABILITY AND VALIDITY

Several studies have examined the reliability of PAQ ratings, and the results have been mixed (see Jones, Main, Butler, & Johnson, 1982; McCormick & Jeanneret, 1988; Smith & Hakel, 1979). Agreement among judges has typically been highest when the comparison is of scores across items for the same job and lowest when the comparison is across the same items between jobs. That is, judges tend to agree with one another when both are filling out the PAQ on the same job and we compare scores across items. Note that this does not tell us about how well the PAQ can distinguish among jobs. For that, we have to analyze multiple jobs. When we examine agreement across jobs, we find that the agreement is not as good. Studies have also examined the rate-rerate reliability of the PAQ. The resulting estimates are in the high .70s and .80s (McCormick & Jeanneret, 1988), which is satisfactory. McCormick and Jeanneret (1988) also noted that such stability estimates were obtained from trained job analysts as well as job incumbents and supervisors, although the incumbents and supervisors tend to give higher ratings. However, the same concerns about the meaning of reliability estimates (within versus between jobs) between judges also apply to rate-rerate estimates.

One line of research related to the validity of the PAQ concerns the relation of PAQ scale scores to salary data across jobs. Recall that one of the main purposes of the PAQ was to determine compensation. Differences in job requirements should be related to differences in pay, so that more demanding jobs should be more highly paid. Numerous studies of the PAQ have shown that scores derived from the PAQ predict well salary data across jobs and occupations, that is, salary data aggregated across positions (for example, McCormick, Jeanneret, & Mecham, 1972). Such results support the validity of the PAQ.

The PAQ was also intended to be useful in personnel selection. Research has shown that PAQ scales were related to incumbent mean scores on the General Aptitude Test Battery (GATB; U.S. Department of Labor, 1967) across 163 jobs (McCormick et al., 1972). Furthermore, the PAQ was able to show differences in validity, that is, the test-criterion correlation based on the job requirements. For example, when the PAQ's estimates of the need for cognitive ability in jobs increased, the validity of tests of cognitive ability increased (Gutenberg, Arvey, Osburn, & Jeanneret, 1983).

RESEARCH ON THE PAQ: COMMON KNOWLEDGE EFFECTS

The study we mentioned earlier by Smith and Hakel (1979) generated a lot of interest in the research community. What they did was to collect PAQ ratings on 25 jobs from five groups of people, namely, incumbents, supervisors, job analysts, undergraduate students given only a job title, and undergraduate students given a job title plus additional information about the nature of the job. In this study, students given only a job title were almost as reliable as professional job analysts. More remarkable were the correlations among the PAQ ratings when averaged within each group. All of the groups produced PAQ ratings that on average correlated in the .90s with the rest of the groups' averages, which indicates that the resulting PAQ profiles were virtually indistinguishable. This result generated a lot of interest because if students armed solely with job titles can produce the same PAQ profiles as professional analysts, then (among other things) the job security of the analysts is in question. How could this be? Does the PAQ only measure shared job stereotypes or do most people actually have a pretty good idea of the abilities needed to tackle lots of jobs?

Further evidence that analysts could produce reliable PAQ ratings from reduced information (that is, something less than observing and interviewing incumbents) was provided by Jones et al. (1982). Perhaps part of the problem is that the PAQ is not very sensitive to the amount of information available to the analyst; that is, it measures only large differences among jobs. If so, the PAQ could show the difference between, say, a professor of mathematics and a jet engine mechanic, but not between a professor of mathematics and a professor of geology. Indirect evidence in support of this position was given by Surette, Aamodt, and Johnson (1990), who asked students to analyze the job of college resident assistant.

Others, however, were quick to point out that perhaps the results in Smith and Hakel (1979) and Jones et al. (1982) were in some sense misleading. One thrust of the rebuttal concerns the DNA, or "does not apply," items found in the PAQ. If we score such items "zero" and include them in the reliability analysis, we find that the reliabilities are larger than if we exclude such items from the analysis. In other words, people who are not very familiar with the job may still know that some elements do not apply to the job. For example, we can guess that a taste tester makes little use of written sources of information on the job. On the other hand, most professors do make use of written information, but they do not use long-handled tools (except, perhaps, when disciplining unruly students). Evidence consistent with this position was provided by Harvey and Hayes (1986) and by DeNisi, Cornelius, and Blencoe (1987).

Others set about investigating the agreement among items that *do* apply in the PAQ (Cornelius, DeNisi, & Blencoe, 1984). It turns out that people given little job information do not agree well with one another or with experts about the degree to which the items that do apply are important to the job. For example, lay people may agree that a patrol officer makes use of written information, but may not agree about how frequently such information is used. Friedman and Harvey (1986) also found that more information given to analysts produced better agreement.

What are we to make of all this? First, people do have a general knowledge of the gross outlines of occupations that allows them to tell that some items are not likely to apply to a given job. The resulting PAQ profiles across jobs show more accuracy than one would expect, primarily because of the DNA items. On the other hand, to get high-quality PAQ profiles, the person who fills out the PAQ needs to be very familiar with the job and trained in completing the PAQ. In general, students armed solely with a job title are not likely to provide very accurate ratings.

RECENT PAQ DEVELOPMENTS

PAQ Services changed owners in 2004. There are several new developments as a result. PAQ Services is now managing what it calls the *enhanced Dictionary of Occupational Titles* (eDOT), which is intended to replace the Department of Labor's *DOT.* PAQ also manages the eDOT Skills Project, which updates the data in the eDOT, including adding new titles, such as Web designer, and archiving old titles that no longer exist in today's economy.

The PAQ has also incorporated new items of various sorts. Some new items concern regulations regarding the assessment of exemption status under the Fair Labor Standards Act. Historically, PAQ has provided an FLSA exemption prediction with all job analyses. To provide accurate status estimates under the new (2004) FLSA rules, PAQ incorporated FLSA items directly from the regulations. Other new item types include items related to professional and managerial work, the addition of Social Security Disability Assessment items, and other job analysis items to meet a wider variety of human resource (HR) needs.

PAQ Services provides support to instructors through products and services that can be used in the classroom, including free PAQ materials, scoring, reports, job analysis software, and HR courses. More information may be obtained on the PAQ Web site: www.paq.com.

REMARKS ON THE PAQ

The PAQ has been used extensively, often to solve problems related to personnel selection and job evaluation. As mentioned earlier, despite the PAQ's popularity and broad use, we do not recommend its completion by job incumbents who are not highly educated because the reading level of the PAQ is high, and many judgments called for are hard to make. We would also avoid having incumbents and supervisors complete the PAQ when it is used for determining compensation because both groups tend to provide higher ratings and mark more items as applying than do professional analysts. The PAQ is often not very informative about managerial jobs. We are pleased by several recent developments in the PAQ, especially with efforts to use electronic means to update a national database of job information.

The PAQ has many positive qualities to recommend it. It uses a common set of elements for all jobs. The common elements help make it useful for job evaluation and for forming job clusters or families. The PAQ is helpful in identifying knowledge, skills, and abilities and in defending the job-relatedness of tests. Also, it is an off-the-shelf method that is relatively quick and inexpensive to use. The PAQ is the first of several methods for estimating trait requirements for jobs; we briefly describe three of these next.

Other Trait-Based Worker-Oriented Measures

There are many other worker-oriented job analysis methods that are based on sets of human skills and abilities. Rather than describe each of those in detail, we briefly sketch a few selected systems. The interested reader can pursue any or all in more detail as the need arises and can explore other methods in addition to the ones described here.

THRESHOLD TRAITS ANALYSIS SYSTEM

The Threshold Traits Analysis System was developed in 1970 by Felix Lopez to provide a theoretically coherent, trait-oriented, multipurpose, and legally defensible method of job analysis (Lopez, 1988). The entire TTAS contains several different pieces. Some pieces are designed for describing traits for selection, some are designed for training, and some are designed for job description (although a TTAS can be used for other purposes as well, including job evaluation). However, the heart of the system is the threshold traits analysis (TTA), which is based on a standard set of 33 traits. TTAS traits are broadly classed into two sections, "can do" and "will do." The "can do" traits are described as abilities and contain the physical, mental, and learned traits. Under the physical area, for example, is the job function "physical exertion." Physical exertion includes the traits "strength" and "stamina." Strength is described as the ability to lift, push, or pull objects, and stamina is described as the ability to expend physical energy for long periods. For a second example, under the mental area a job function is "information processing." One of the information processing traits is "comprehension," which is described as the ability to understand spoken and written ideas.

The "will do" traits are described as attitudes and contain the motivational and social traits. Examples of motivational traits include "adaptability to change," "adaptability to repetition," and "dependability." Examples of social traits include "tolerance," "influence," and "cooperation." The 33 traits and their examples are designed for communication with analysts and users of the job analysis products. The traits can be further subdivided if necessary and lists of synonymous traits are provided in the manuals describing the system (Lopez, 1986).

ABILITY REQUIREMENTS SCALES

The ability requirements approach was developed by Ed Fleishman and his colleagues (for example, Fleishman, 1982; Fleishman & Mumford, 1988;

Fleishman & Quaintance, 1984). A comprehensive description of each ability and tests for each are described in Fleishman and Reilly (1992). A sample of these abilities is shown in Table 3.6. The Ability Requirements Scales are used to evaluate or judge the degree to which each of the generic human abilities is required by the job. Because each of these abilities is linked to one or more tests, results of the ARS job analysis may be used for selection. The generic nature of these abilities also lets us build job families, which are clusters of jobs that are similar in their required abilities.

OCCUPATIONAL REINFORCER PATTERN

The theory behind this method is based on how individuals differ in their needs (Borgen, 1988). For example, some people need more recognition than others do. Some people are not happy working alone, but others are. Some prefer to work in formal settings, whereas others prefer to work in casual settings, and so forth. The Occupational Reinforcer Pattern is an attempt to represent the

Table 3.6   Examples of Generic Human Abilities

Ability	Description
Cognitive Abilities	
Oral comprehension	Understand spoken words
Mathematical reasoning	Reason with mathematical symbols
Speed of closure	Combine bits into meaningful pattern
Spatial orientation	Tell where you are in relation to an object
Psychomotor Abilities	
Control precision	Operate a vehicle
Multilimb coordination	Coordinate movements of two or more limbs
Finger dexterity	Make skilled movements of the fingers
Speed-of-limb movement	Move limbs quickly
Physical Abilities	
Static strength	Exhibit push or pull strength
Dynamic flexibility	Repeatedly bend, stretch, and twist
Gross body equilibrium	Demonstrate balance
Stamina	Continue working over time
Sensory/Perceptual Abilities	
Night vision	See in the dark
Hearing sensitivity	Hear loudness and pitch
Speech recognition	Understand speech
Speech clarity	Speak clearly

ways in which jobs provide the things that people want or need. Thus, the ORP is intended to be useful for vocational guidance. There are associated tests of needs for individuals that can be used to suggest occupations that appear to be appropriate for an individual based on the similarity of the needs of the person to the rewards provided by the job. The traits used in ORP are shown in Table 3.7.

Table 3.7   Examples of Occupational Reinforcers

Reinforcer	Description
1. Ability utilization	Use your abilities
2. Activity	Keep busy all the time
3. Authority	Tell people what to do
4. Compensation	Fair pay
5. Creativity	Try out own ideas
6. Moral values	Avoid conflict between work and self
7. Security	Have steady employment
8. Social status	Job with prestige
9. Variety	Work changes frequently
10. Autonomy	Plan work with little supervision

METHODS WITH SUBSTANTIAL ATTENTION TO EQUIPMENT

We have not yet described worker-oriented approaches that emphasize equipment. Two such approaches are AET (for three long German words; Rohmert, 1988) and the Job Components Inventory (Banks, 1988).

AET

The AET (okay, you asked for it, *Arbeitwissenschaftliches Erhebungsverfahren zur Tätigkeitsanalyse*—as promised, the translation is "ergonomic task analysis data collection procedure") comes from an ergonomics perspective, which attempts to minimize human stress and strain while maximizing performance quality and quantity. The AET pays particular attention to the equipment used to complete the work and to the working conditions or environment. The AET is often used in redesigning work to make it less stressful to the workers.

Ergonomics is about designing things for human use. This is an exciting and rewarding field if you like doing things that have a beneficial impact on other people's lives. Just because someone is strong doesn't mean that he or she should spend all day lifting wheels from the ground onto automobile axles.

It might be possible to build a ramp so that the wheel rolls to the axle and saves the worker from repetitive back strain. Ergonomic design ranges from the simple to the complex—from hand tools such as screwdrivers to computer interfaces that can be programmed to fly a jet from Denver to Atlanta without further human input. It is also involved whenever we want to make accommodations for disabilities. We may change the job to eliminate a task that is difficult for an individual, or we may change the way in which the task is accomplished by providing a work aid or tools of some sort. If the job occasionally involves driving a car, for example, we might move that task to another person so that an otherwise qualified person could do the job. Or we might provide a magnifying glass and bright light for a worker who has poor vision.

Job Components Inventory

The Job Components Inventory (Banks, 1988; Banks & Miller, 1984) was developed in Britain to describe a wide range of entry-level jobs. The descriptors were to be useful in vocational guidance and training so that young people could understand what the jobs actually were and how to prepare for them. One part of the JCI covers 220 tools and pieces of equipment. Some types and examples are tools for marking or drawing (scribes, dividers); tools for measuring length, angles, size, or levels (micrometer, protractor); and tools for holding or securing objects (clamp, tweezers). Although the JCI was designed primarily for vocational guidance purposes, because of its emphasis on tools, it can be used as part of job analysis for many training programs.

Cognitive Task Analysis

Cognitive task analysis is a worker-oriented approach that differs in several ways from the other methods we discuss in this chapter. Cognitive task analysis is the most recently developed of the methods described in this chapter. Applications began in the 1990s. Cognitive task analysis has its roots in cognitive psychology and cognitive science. Cognitive science is something of a blend of cognitive psychology, computer science, engineering, and philosophy that aims to understand the mind by producing models of mental activity. Cognitive scientists have become very interested in expertise. To study expertise, they typically take a task into the laboratory and have novices and experts complete it. They infer the mental activities that experts use to complete tasks, including strategies, processes, knowledge, and so forth. They then usually write computer programs that are intended to imitate what experts do.

Also unlike most of the other worker-oriented methods, cognitive task analysis does not refer to a specific set of traits or elements used to understand the human abilities required by work. Rather, cognitive task analysis refers to a collection of different approaches or methods that are related by their common goal of understanding the mental activities used by experts in completing the task being analyzed.

Cognitive task analysis usually begins with the completion of a work-oriented job analysis method that describes in detail the job's duties and tasks. From the list of tasks, some tasks are chosen for further study by means of cognitive task analysis. Cognitive task analysis is often very expensive, time consuming, and difficult to apply (Seamster, Redding, & Kaempf, 1997). Therefore, for applied work, some subset of tasks is chosen for further study using some cognitive task analysis methods that are appropriate and feasible. Cognitive task analysis provides information about the mental processes used to complete the job that are often omitted from both work-based methods and trait-oriented worker-based methods. For example, a pilot must navigate to fly successfully. A task from a pilot's task inventory might read "Determine current location." A trait-based worker-oriented method might list knowledge of maps and compasses, visual acuity, and visualization ability. However, none of these methods is likely to point out that there may be several different ways in which to determine one's current location and that the difference between novices and experts may lie chiefly in knowing when the different methods are most appropriate.

Seamster et al. (1997) presented a comparison between work-oriented task analysis and cognitive task analysis, which is summarized in Table 3.8.

Table 3.8   Comparison of Work-Oriented Task Analysis and Cognitive Task Analysis

Work-Oriented Task Analysis	Cognitive Task Analysis
Emphasizes behavior	Emphasizes cognition
Analyzes target performance	Analyzes expertise and learning
Evaluates knowledge for each task separately	Evaluates the interrelations among knowledge elements
Segments tasks according to behaviors required	Segments tasks according to cognitive skills required
Representational skills are not addressed	Representational skills are addressed
Describes only one way to perform	Accounts for individual differences

SOURCE: Adapted from Seamster, T. L., Redding, R. E., & Kaempf, G. L. (1997). *Applied cognitive task analysis in aviation.* Brookfield, VT: Ashgate. Reproduced by permission of Ashgate Publishing.

TYPES OF KNOWLEDGE AND SKILL

The descriptors used in cognitive task analysis often refer to knowledge and skill. Different authors slice the pie somewhat differently. However, some terms are commonly used, and these are described next. *Declarative knowledge* is factual knowledge, often of the type that can be spoken or declared. Declarative knowledge is knowledge of *what*. For example, the name of the current president of the United States is a bit of declarative knowledge that you most likely possess. If you have been reading this chapter, you now have the names of several worker-oriented job analysis methods on the tip of your tongue, and these names are also bits of declarative knowledge. *Procedural knowledge* is knowledge of *how*. Procedural knowledge implies steps, techniques, or procedures in general. For example, you probably know how to drive a car and how to ride a bicycle. You may know how to drive a car with a stick shift, and the sequence of steps involved in shifting gears (grab the gear shift, depress the clutch, foot off the gas, shift the gear, release the clutch while applying foot to gas, release the gear shift). If you drive a stick shift car, it is probably much easier for you to actually shift gears than it is for you to explain to someone else how to do it. Some authors describe *generative knowledge*, which allows you to figure out what to do in a new problem situation. You use generative knowledge when you arrive in an airport you have never seen before. Such knowledge will help you locate your baggage and transportation to your final destination. A final type of knowledge described here is *self-knowledge*, which refers to knowledge about what you do and do not know, and what you can and cannot do. You probably have a well-developed idea of the sorts of problems you can solve confidently and those you would not attempt. For example, most of us can make simple household repairs such as changing a light bulb, some of us can rebuild a car engine, and most of us would not willingly attempt surgery on ourselves.

Cognitive task analysis sometimes makes the distinction between knowledge and skill (Seamster et al., 1997). Seamster et al. (1997) described knowledge as referring to information possessed by the jobholder, whereas skill refers to a process that uses information (they talk about procedural skills rather than procedural knowledge). They defined several types of skill, including automated skills, representational skills, and decision-making skills.

Automated skills are mental processes that are fast and effortless. For most adult Americans, driving an automobile has become an automated skill. When you first begin to drive, it is a very difficult task, and changing the radio station while driving can be a real challenge. As driving becomes automated, however, virtually no effort is needed to keep the car in the proper lane at the proper speed, and one not only can change the radio station without much trouble but also can carry on a conversation or think about something totally unrelated to driving (but not, apparently, use a cell phone).

Representational skills imply the use of mental models, that is, a mental representation of some device, process, or system. For example, you have some type of representation of a car and how it works in your head. Such a representation is very helpful if your car won't start. Representational skills are very important for any job involving mechanical devices. However, such skills are much more broadly applicable and are used whenever jobs involve real objects (for example, surgery, firefighting) or social systems (for example, how to secure resources to complete a project in a large corporation).

Decision-making skills are techniques such as rules of thumb, mental simulation, or other processes that allow experts to arrive at appropriate decisions quickly and accurately. You probably have developed some rules about how to respond when you are driving and you see a traffic light turn yellow. Depending on your speed and distance from the intersection, you will ignore the light, speed up, or prepare to stop. You may have already made a decision to stop or not before the light turns. This allows you to make the decision very quickly and with some accuracy.

The process of cognitive task analysis involves the discovery of how experts complete their jobs. The analyst will attempt to determine what cognitive knowledge and skill are used and how the expert employs them to achieve superior performance. The analysis will link the tasks to mental processes. DuBois, Shalin, Levi, and Borman (1995) suggested organizing the relations of tasks and mental processes by creating a matrix in which knowledge requirements (declarative, procedural, generative, self) are crossed with task types (for example, technical tasks, organizationwide tasks, teamwork, communication). The resulting matrix helps ensure that the analyst includes all relevant tasks and knowledge requirements.

COGNITIVE TASK ANALYSIS METHODS

Seamster et al. (1997) described five classes of methods of data collection and analysis.

1. *Interviewing methods.* The interview can be used to ask SMEs about mental processes that are used in routine task performance or in critical situations. Structured interview formats have been developed for this method. For example, a police officer might be asked, "What do you need to know to make an arrest that will stand up in court?"

2. *Team communication methods.* Teams that communicate extensively in the course of completing their work can be observed or recorded. The communications among the team members can be analyzed for evidence of mental processes. For example, a firefighter's assessment of the source of a fire might be established by the kinds of questions he or she poses to other members of the team.

3. *Diagramming methods.* Tasks can be represented by various diagrams such as path-goal diagrams, decision trees, or other charts that indicate the relations among concepts. For example, one could diagram the steps involved in troubleshooting a car that won't start (Is the key in the ignition? Is the car in gear?).

4. *Verbal report methods.* Often job experts are asked to "think aloud" while they are completing a task. Occasionally, the experts may be asked to report on their thoughts before or after doing the work. The verbal reports are analyzed to infer goals, strategies, or automated skills.

5. *Psychological scaling methods.* Job experts may be asked to sort, rank, or rate a series of objects. The resulting categories or ratings are then analyzed through scaling or clustering programs to provide a quantitative representation of the results. This usually results in a representation of the relations among a set of concepts. For example, a pilot might be given a set of 25 cards, each of which presents a problem that might be encountered during flight (for example, lost radio contact, engine failure, ill passenger). The pilot would be asked to sort the cards into piles that are similar to one another. Several pilots would be asked to complete the sorting task. One possible analysis would be to represent the similarity of the problems as a map in which similar problems are close to one another whereas less similar problems are farther from each other.

A SIMPLE EXAMPLE

Seamster et al. (1997) analyzed the job of screener, which is a security job at an airport. The screener looks at X-ray pictures of carry-on luggage that passengers are bringing with them as they board the aircraft. It is the screener's job to spot guns, explosives, and other dangerous objects in the X-rays or by manual search so that such objects do not board the planes in the hands of the passengers. In addition to being accurate in spotting dangerous objects, the screener also needs to move quickly so that lines at the security checkpoints do not become so long that passengers become overwhelmed by rage. (If you've done much flying, you know what we are talking about.)

The purpose of the analysis was to enhance training for the position. The analysts focused on the decisions made by the screener. The screener examines each bag and must take one of three actions: pass the bag, search the bag manually, or stop the bag, physically capturing it in the screening machine. The cognitive task analysis was designed to better understand the process that expert screeners use to decide the proper course of action for each bag.

Analysts interviewed screeners away from the security checkpoints. Screeners were asked to provide incidents that had tested their skills. The next step was to have screeners provide verbal protocols ("think aloud") during actual task performance at the security checkpoint. Screeners mentioned what they were looking at in each picture and how they decided what to do with each bag. The analysts also directly observed the work by standing behind the screeners as they worked. Analysts were allowed to ask questions, such as how they might hide a weapon in a briefcase that had just passed through the machine.

The cognitive task analysis resulted in a model of the screener's decision about each bag. The model can be represented as a series of steps. The screener looks at the X-ray and decides whether there is anything odd or dark (potentially of interest) in the bag. If there is not, then the bag is passed. If there is something of interest, the screener takes a closer look at it to determine what it is. If it is a threat, the screener will trap the object in the machine by stopping it. If the screener does not recognize the object as a threat, he or she will determine whether the object is large enough to conceal a threat. If it is, the screener will search the bag. If it is not, the screener will pass the bag.

The analysts concluded that one main difference between novice and expert screeners is the large "library" of stored images that experts have. This library allows experts to identify most of the things that they see in the X-ray pictures. (This is an automated skill that is virtually effortless for the expert screener.) Novices cannot identify many of the same objects, and they end up searching many more pieces of baggage than do the experts.

Cognitive task analysis can be used for several important purposes, including reducing human error, improving training, and increasing systems reliability. Errors might be reduced in several ways. For example, some jobs such as piloting an aircraft involve a very large amount of information that is displayed visually. If you've ever peeked into the cockpit of a commercial jet, you know what we mean. To help avoid missing crucial information (such as approaching a mountain at night), some information is displayed as auditory warnings ("pull up"). Or errors might be reduced by determining common mistakes in identifying cues. It is important in the military that soldiers can tell friend from foe (for example, tanks, aircraft) quickly and accurately through visual inspection, for example, and people can be trained to do so.

RELIABILITY AND VALIDITY

Because cognitive task analysis is not one but rather many different analyses, it is difficult to discuss reliability and validity as one would for a single procedure in which the steps and materials are set. However, Seamster et al. (1997) have noted that the results may vary depending on the method used and the particular experts studied. They noted that because cognitive task analysis focuses on experts, it is necessary to study actual experts during the study; that is, the SMEs selected for the study must be able to perform the job at consistently superior levels. They recommended using at least two different measures of expertise (for example, time in job, measures of superior performance, peer nominations) to choose the SMEs for the study. They did not provide a minimum number of SMEs to use in a given study. However, because cognitive task analysis allows for individual difference in performance, it is likely that the results will be influenced by the choice of SMEs for study and therefore that multiple SMEs be studied whenever this is feasible.

With regard to validation, very little has been published to date. We note here that as with any job analysis method, much of the validity resides in the usefulness of the technique for its intended purpose. To date, cognitive task analysis has been applied to training, systems design, and performance measurement with apparent success. Seamster et al. (1997) advised that conclusions from cognitive task analysis should always be based on two different methods of data collection. They further advised to use one method to develop models or hypotheses and then to select a second method that will provide the most efficient test of the hypotheses.

REMARKS ON COGNITIVE TASK ANALYSIS

At its best, cognitive task analysis provides unique information about mental processes at work. Cognitive task analysis illuminates how experts perform the job, and this can be useful for many applications, especially training. However, cognitive task analysis is also expensive and time consuming. Increased experience (dare we say expertise?) will help clarify the conditions under which the results of cognitive task analysis justify its expense.

Chapter Summary

We have described several worker-oriented methods of job analysis. We began with the job element method (JEM), which is the earliest method devised. JEM analyzes the job demands on the worker into pieces that jobholders understand to be the important elements of the work. Such elements are clearly related to work samples, which are in turn useful for such applications as selection, performance evaluation, and training. JEM can also be used to select tests that are not job samples or simulations with the use of the J-coefficient.

We next turned to the Position Analysis Questionnaire (PAQ), which is possibly the most widely used of the worker-oriented methods. The PAQ describes jobs in terms of about 300 standard requirements, such as use of pictorial materials, amount of planning, requirement for transcribing, use of mathematics, use of long-handled tools, operation of powered water vehicles, and exposure to vibration. The PAQ was developed for selection and job evaluation, but it has seen much wider application. The reliability of the PAQ's individual items appears rather low, but the reliability of the scale scores appears adequate. The PAQ may not be the best choice to analyze closely related but different jobs because of its generic elements. On the other hand, these generic elements permit us to do some things, such as cluster jobs into families, quite well.

In the Other Trait-Based Worker-Oriented Methods section, we described five other job analysis methods. Three of these were described in terms of lists of traits. Both the Threshold Traits and the Ability Requirements Scales offer extensive sets of human abilities linked to psychological tests, whereas Threshold Traits also include motivational and social job requirements. The Occupational Reinforcer Pattern shows a list of traits related to human motives at work. The other two methods were chosen for their serious treatment of tools and equipment at work. The AET was developed from an ergonomic approach that seeks to reduce the stress of job demands on people through proper job design, especially where people interact with machines and tools. The Job Components Inventory contains a section with 220 items relating to skills needed for using tools and equipment.

The final section of the chapter described cognitive task analysis, which is the newest of the worker-oriented approaches. Cognitive task analysis seeks to understand and describe the mental processes used by experts during job performance. Unlike the other methods in this chapter, cognitive task analysis is not a single approach with steps that can be articulated prior to the specific project. Rather, cognitive task analysis is a flexible set of tools, all of which have the same general aim. Cognitive task analysis generally starts with a behavioral, task-oriented job analysis and subsequently seeks to understand and represent the mental processes that experts use to perform the tasks of interest. Although it seems promising for such purposes as training, cognitive task analysis's value as a job analysis approach is still in the testing stage.

4

Hybrid Methods

In Chapter 2, we covered job analysis methods that are primarily concerned with tasks or the work itself. These focused on observable behaviors and outcomes of worker actions. An example of such a method is the task inventory. In Chapter 3, we covered methods that are primarily concerned with human information processing requirements or worker characteristics. An example of such a method is the Position Analysis Questionnaire. In this chapter, we describe methods that use multiple kinds of data by design. We call such methods *hybrid methods* because they are usually developed with an eye toward combining features of two or more of the job analysis methods. This chapter covers three such hybrid methods:

1. Combination job analysis method (C-JAM)

2. Multimethod Job Design Questionnaire (MJDQ)

3. Occupational Information Network (O*NET)

We describe each in turn. As we stated in Chapter 2, there is some wiggle room in our categorizing of methods in terms of whether they are work, worker, or hybrid methods. You can accuse us of fuzzy thinking if you wish. We won't complain.

And while we are at it, let us make another point about job analysis methods. As the analyst, you are not forced to choose a single method described in this book (or outside it, for that matter). You can choose more than one method, or you can choose pieces of various methods to suit your needs. The important thing is to keep in mind precisely what those needs are and to choose accordingly. (For more on this, see the beginning of Chapter 9 on choosing a job analysis method.) On the other hand, it is useful to study the methods as they exist so you will be familiar with them and can choose according to your needs. It might be useful to think of yourself as a chef in training at a culinary academy. At first, you learn the use of the tools of the trade and the classic recipes. As you gain skill, you create your own masterpieces.

Combination Job Analysis Method

The *combination job analysis method* (Levine, 1983) borrows a bit from those methods that focus on tasks, such as *functional job analysis* and the *Task Inventory/Comprehensive Occupational Data Analysis Program* (TI/CODAP). This gives us information about what gets done on the job and how, which is information that is essential for legal, quasi-legal, and other purposes. The method also borrows from the *job element method* so that information about the human attributes needed to perform the tasks is summarized. Information about human attributes is essential for purposes such as personnel selection. A few easily understood scales are also provided to allow for the determination of what tasks and what human attributes are most important in a particular job. In C-JAM, task statements are developed and the importance of the tasks is rated. Then the knowledge, skills, abilities, and other characteristics (KSAOs) needed to perform the tasks are developed and rated on their importance for job performance. (The section on C-JAM borrows heavily from Levine, 1983.)

TASK STATEMENTS

Tasks generally involve the change of, or an attempt at changing, some material, person, product, subject matter, or set of data from one form to another form. The change is attempted by means of a worker's efforts either applied directly or exerted through the use of particular tools, machinery, equipment, or work aids. The form in which tasks should be written is as follows:

1. There is an implied subject of the task sentence, namely, workers, employees, or managers. The implied subject is plural, not singular.

2. There is a verb that tells what function the employees are performing.

3. The object of the verb may be data, people, or machines, equipment, work aids, or tools.

4. There is a phrase starting with the word *to* or the words *in order to* that gives the purpose of the workers' activity.

(Okay, this should look kind of familiar. If not, you might want to grab a cup of coffee and review functional job analysis in Chapter 2.) At times, tasks may be written in a shortened form. For example, the phrase that gives the purpose of an action may be left off if the purpose is obvious or well known to the users of the job analysis study. Or the tool used for the task may be excluded, if it is obvious from the action verb.

Here are some examples of task statements:

1. For personnel testing specialists:
   a. Write multiple-choice test items for particular jobs to evaluate applicant qualifications.
   b. Ask/answer questions and provide information to applicants to resolve applicant appeals/complaints about test scores.

2. For computer operators:
   a. Forward e-mail to distribution lists to pass information from a single worker to a specified group of workers.
   b. Replace paper and cartridges in printers.

3. For auto equipment mechanics:
   a. Inspect equipment to determine whether repair or replacement is necessary for efficiency of operation or safety.
   b. Modify equipment to improve its efficiency of operation or safety.

4. For water and fuels analysts in an electric power plant:
   a. Inspect acid and caustic tank levels.
   b. Maintain fuel oil additive system to meet environmental standards.

5. For clerks:
   a. Fold, assemble, and staple papers.
   b. Check documents for accuracy.

When the level of detail to include in a task statement is in doubt, the statement should be more rather than less detailed during the first draft of the statements. Generally, 30 to 100 tasks are expected in the final task list for any particular job. If the first list numbers substantially more than 100 tasks, similar tasks should be combined wherever possible to reduce the number back to 100 or less.

THE TASK GENERATION MEETING

The first list of task statements is generated at a meeting of job experts. Five to seven workers and about two of their immediate supervisors are assembled at a convenient meeting place away from their work stations. With the aid of computers, the meeting could take place in cyberspace. Whatever the medium of the meeting, it is necessary to minimize distractions. The experts should be well experienced in the job under analysis and should also be able to communicate reasonably well orally and in writing. If possible, include experts of different ethnic backgrounds and both men and women. Their inclusion will ensure a well-rounded picture of the job and will enhance the legal soundness of the job analysis in the eyes of equal employment opportunity compliance officers. The purpose of the meeting is explained, namely, to generate tasks for the job under analysis. The experts are told to think about the job in general, not just about their own jobs. As a warm-up, they might be asked to comment about working conditions, such as amount of lifting that must be done or the proportion of time work is performed under dangerous conditions or in especially hot, noisy, or cold climates. Shift work, special hours, or other demands might also be explored. The information exchanged about these (and all other) items discussed in this meeting is carefully noted by a designated recorder or secretary.

Next, the definition of a task is provided and a couple of examples are given. Then the group members are instructed to prepare a list on their own, working as individuals rather than as a group. Each individual is given up to an hour to generate a list; each should be asked to put his or her name on the list. Each expert is asked to shoot for at least 50 tasks. When everyone has finished, a break should be provided. During the break, all lists are copied so that every group member and the group leader have copies of everyone's lists.

At this point, the group leader instructs everyone to review all the lists, delete tasks that are duplicates, and add any tasks that might have been missed. The group members should work on this individually but may raise questions for group discussion if a task statement is unclear. About 2 hours should be allowed for this phase of the meeting. Finally, all lists are collected by the group leader. The group members are thanked, and the meeting is adjourned.

The next phase of the analysis is the responsibility of the leader. He or she must screen the lists carefully, edit the tasks, and come up with a list of approximately 30 to 100 tasks in draft form. To simplify the process, the tasks might be listed on $3'' \times 5''$ index cards and sorted into 5 to 12 major duty or function categories, or the sorting could be done by computer. Such organizing schemes will usually make it easier to spot duplicate tasks or tasks that might be combined. If the analyst is not well versed in the job, he or she might enlist the aid of a supervisor or jobholder to prepare the draft.

Suppose this group approach does not work or a group meeting cannot be arranged. In that case, the task list may be generated by conducting a series of individual interviews with a representative sample of workers and their supervisors. *Representativeness* refers to inclusion of workers and supervisors at the various locations where the work is performed, and the inclusion of workers whose assignments are substantially different or unique within the job category under study. Representativeness also refers to the inclusion of people from diverse backgrounds.

How many workers should be interviewed? Unfortunately, there is no single number that is correct. The number varies with how many people there are performing the job, at how many locations, and so on. As a rule of thumb, at least six workers and two supervisors should be interviewed if there are that many available. A guideline for the maximum number to interview is to stop when few new tasks are unearthed. The correct number to interview should not be a major concern because there are at least two additional checkpoints built into this procedure to ensure that the task list is complete.

The interviews begin with a brief statement about their purpose. Then, if the interviewee is a jobholder, the jobholder is asked to think about his or her most recent complete work day (for example, yesterday) and to describe what he or she did from the start of the day to the end of the day. During the description, the interviewer should ask for more information if a task is unclear, or even for a sample of work products. After the description is complete, the worker might be asked about other tasks that were not done during the most recent work day but might be done during a particular week or month or at particular times of the year. By contrast, supervisors might be asked to describe a typical day for an employee under their direct supervision, and then to describe tasks that might come up at particular times during a week or month or particular times of the year.

After all interviews are completed, the interviewer will review all notes and prepare a draft list of 30 to 100 task statements, organized into 5 to 12 major duty or function categories. Again, the use of 3" × 5" cards may simplify the process; computer databases are increasingly popular as a substitute for cards. The outcome of either process, the group meeting or the interviews, is a list of tasks numbered consecutively and organized into functional categories.

THE TASK RATING MEETING

The next step is to assemble a group to rate the tasks. Five to seven job experts (perhaps the same ones who participated at the first meeting) are assembled at a convenient meeting site away from their regular place of work. Again, technology may be used to create a virtual meeting. The group leader announces the purpose of the meeting. Each of these job experts is then given the draft task list. The group leader asks that the members read over the list. Then he or she announces that each numbered statement will be reviewed individually by the group to see if it is okay as is, if it can be combined with another task, or if it must be separated into two or more tasks. The tasks are announced consecutively by number, and the discussion ensues. After all tasks are reviewed, the group is asked whether any tasks need to be added to the list. Finally, the group looks over the functional category labels to see whether they are satisfactory. A break might be taken at this point.

Now the group is instructed to rate all of the tasks on the list. The ratings may be made via comphuter, on a form designed for the purpose, or on a piece of paper that contains the number of each of the tasks on the task list. The original version of C-JAM used three rating scales. However, research indicated that eliminating one of the scales produced equivalent information for less work (Sanchez & Fraser, 1992; Sanchez & Levine, 1989). The current version of C-JAM uses two scales that should be carefully described to the group members. Copies of the scales should also be provided to each group member.

The scales cover (1) task difficulty and (2) criticality. Scale points and definitions are as follows:

1. *Task difficulty:* Difficulty in doing a task correctly relative to all other tasks within a single job
   1 = One of the easiest of all tasks
   2 = Considerably easier than most tasks
   3 = Easier than most tasks performed
   4 = Approximately half of tasks are more difficult, half less
   5 = Harder than most tasks performed
   6 = Considerably harder than most tasks performed
   7 = One of the most difficult of all tasks

2. *Criticality/consequences of error:* The degree to which an incorrect performance would result in negative consequences
   1 = Consequences of error are not at all important
   2 = Consequences of error are of little importance
   3 = Consequences are of some importance
   4 = Consequences are moderately important
   5 = Consequences are important
   6 = Consequences are very important
   7 = Consequences are extremely important

Ratings should be based on the job in general, not on the workers' own jobs or the positions directly supervised by the supervisory group members. The group members then proceed to rate each task on the two scales and may leave when they are finished. The original version of C-JAM also included a Relative Time Spent scale. This may be useful to include for such purposes as job design.

ANALYSIS OF TASK IMPORTANCE

The group leader then computes a task importance value for each task. The task importance value is the simple sum of task difficulty and criticality, thus

Task importance value = Difficulty + Criticality

A task importance value is computed for each rater, and the mean task importance value is computed over raters to give the overall task importance value for the task. This same process is repeated for all of the tasks rated. (Obviously, this type of data analysis could also be done by computer.) The values may range from a minimum of 2 to a maximum of 14. The production of a list of tasks organized within functional categories, in order of most important to least important tasks, with their overall task importance values typed in, is the final product of this phase of the analysis. In Table 4.1, there is a brief illustration of what the final product might look like for a clerical job. For completeness, the report should also include a little information about the qualifications of those persons who played a role in the analysis. Their race and sex, job-related education, and years and kind of work experience are the kinds of information that would be of interest to equal employment opportunity compliance agencies.

Table 4.1   A Brief Task List for Clerical Jobs

Typing	Task Importance Value
Prepare one or two page business letters from handwritten copy using a computer and software	10.5
Type entries onto forms according to standard instructions	7.5
Filing	
File incoming correspondence by date of receipt	7.2
File completed purchasing forms by date into vendor jackets	6.8

SOURCE: Adapted from Levine, E. L. (1983). *Everything you always wanted to know about job analysis.* Tampa, FL: Mariner. Reprinted by permission of the author.

EMPLOYEE KNOWLEDGE, SKILLS, ABILITIES, AND OTHER CHARACTERISTICS

Employee attributes needed to perform the tasks generated and rated in the previous phase may be grouped into types of knowledge, skills, abilities, and other characteristics. A *knowledge* is the degree to which employees have mastered a technical body of material directly involved in the performance of a job. A *skill* is the capacity to perform tasks requiring the use of tools, equipment, and machinery. An *ability* is the capacity to carry out physical and mental acts required by a job's tasks where the involvement of tools, equipment, and machinery is not a dominant factor. *Other characteristics* are interests, values, temperaments, and personality attributes suggesting what an employee is likely to do rather than how well an employee can do at peak performance.

Next we provide a smattering of these KSAOs. The examples have been matched against the examples of tasks provided earlier in this chapter.

1. For personal testing specialists:
   a. Knowledge of test item construction principles
   b. Ability to communicate orally with confused or angry applicants

2. For computer operators:
   a. Knowledge of computer hardware
   b. Skill in answering a computer-related question such that the asker is left more confused than ever; ability in obfuscation or pettifoggery (just kidding)

3. For auto equipment mechanics:
   a. Knowledge of automotive and heavy equipment systems
   b. Skill in using diagnostic equipment such as an engine analyzer

4. For water and fuels analysts in an electric power plant:
   a. Ability to work in standing, walking positions for long periods of time
   b. Willingness to work unusual work schedules

5. For clerks:
   a. Ability to read names and numbers
   b. Skill in operating office equipment such as a microcomputer, electric staple gun, or handheld calculator

THE KSAO GROUP MEETING

All KSAOs are generated and rated by a group of five to seven experts. The experts may be the same ones who generated and rated the tasks or another group of equally qualified employees. Trainers and supervisors may be used in greater numbers as compared to jobholders for this meeting because they are more often familiar with thinking about the kinds of people who are successful in the job than are jobholders. The meeting will usually take the better part of a full day. It consists of a morning session to generate KSAOs and an afternoon session to rate the KSAOs on a variety of scales.

The Morning Session

The meeting begins with a statement of its purpose. Then copies of the final product of the task phase (the list of tasks and their importance values within functional categories) are circulated to all group members, who are requested to review the list in detail. Several minutes are allowed for this. When all have completed their review, the group is asked if the list is complete and accurate. Group members are also asked if the functional categories are meaningful. Then they are asked whether the importance values are much different from what they expected.

Following any revisions in the task list (which should be very minor if any revisions are offered at all), the group is given the definition of each category of worker attributes—the KSAOs with examples. The members should be encouraged to ask questions to clarify the meaning of each category but are warned not to get too picky about whether an attribute is an ability or skill or other characteristic. For example, *flexibility* might be an other characteristic or it might be "the ability to alter one's behavior to meet unforeseen problems."

Once the definitions of KSAOs are clarified, the group is directed to think about the total job and generate any basic sensory and physical requirements. For example, the group should consider how vision, hearing, smell, touch, and, where applicable, taste are needed. Group members should also discuss requirements of strength for lifting, carrying, and so on and whether climbing, walking, or manual dexterity is needed. Especially with sensory and motor requirements, care must be taken to avoid excluding people unnecessarily (we describe this at greater length under the Americans with Disabilities Act in Chapter 6). For example, during a job analysis for a color photo finishing operation, we initially thought that color vision would be required. It turned out, however, that color-blind people were employed successfully in the job. The actual requirement was that the employee be able to calibrate the machine before and during operation. If the machine was properly calibrated, the colors were correct. Calibrating the machine did not require color vision.

When sensory and motor requirements are completed, the group is instructed to consider each functional category one at a time and generate all the KSAOs needed to perform the tasks in that category. On the other hand, if the number of tasks is small, KSAOs can be generated for each task. The objective is to generate up to 100 KSAOs but not fewer than 30. The group recorder or secretary lists all the KSAOs listed under each task or functional category. A means for sharing progress with the group is necessary. For example, the group leader could write each KSAO with a marker on a whiteboard so that the group could refer back to each KSAO as necessary. Or a computer network program could be used. The point is that all the group members should be able to see and review all the KSAOs. At the point where all task or functional categories have been covered, and no new KSAOs are generated, the group may break for lunch. Breaks should also be provided during the morning session whenever the group members' energy and attention are waning. An example of the form that might be used by the group recorder will be provided after the scales for rating KSAOs are discussed.

During the lunch break, copies of the recorder's KSAO list are created for group members and the group leader.

The Afternoon Session

The lists of KSAOs are shared with all group members, who review the wording and discuss any revisions with the group. Then group members are informed about the nature of the ratings they are to make. Copies of all the scales are given to each member, and the definition of each scale and the nature of the responses are discussed by the group leader.

The scales are as follows:

a. Is the K, S, A, or O necessary for newly hired employees? (yes or no)

b. Is the K, S, A, or O practical to expect in the labor market? (yes or no)

c. To what extent is trouble likely if this K, S, A, or O is ignored in selection (compared with the other KSAOs)?
   1 = Very little or none
   2 = To some extent
   3 = To a great extent
   4 = To a very great extent
   5 = To an extremely great extent

d. To what extent do different levels of the KSAO distinguish the superior from the average worker (compared with the other KSAOs)?
   1 = Very little or none
   2 = To some extent
   3 = To a great extent
   4 = To a very great extent
   5 = To an extremely great extent

(This also might look a bit familiar. If the job element method comes to mind, award yourself some chocolate. Otherwise, you might want a cup of coffee and a peek at Chapter 3.) The group leader first picks out a couple of KSAOs from the list to demonstrate the process. The group discusses the ratings of these KSAOs on all the scales and comes to agreement on each. Then the group members are told to go ahead and rate each KSAO on all the scales by themselves. If feasible, they should rate each KSAO one scale at a time. They are encouraged to raise questions for the group to consider where problems arise. The rating process continues until each member has rated every KSAO. The forms are then collected. If any of the group members in the KSAO session are different from those who served in the task meeting, they should supply in writing the same information about their previous education and experience as you gathered for the other experts.

You are probably asking, "Where is the form for rating KSAOs that you promised?" Okay, see Table 4.2 for a sample. The leader writes or types each KSAO. Each expert circles his or her choice using the scales we just described (for example, Necessary: Is the KSAO necessary in newly hired workers?).

The group recorder fills in all the KSAOs at the left of this form in the morning. The filled-in forms, when copied, serve very well for the experts to enter their ratings in the afternoon.

Table 4.2   Form for Rating KSAOs

KSAO	Necessary	Practical	Likely Trouble	Superior From Average
1. (Fill in)	YES or NO	YES or NO	1 2 3 4 5	1 2 3 4 5
2.	YES or NO	YES or NO	1 2 3 4 5	1 2 3 4 5
3.	YES or NO	YES or NO	1 2 3 4 5	1 2 3 4 5
4.	YES or NO	YES or NO	1 2 3 4 5	1 2 3 4 5

SOURCE: Adapted from Levine, E. L. (1983). *Everything you always wanted to know about job analysis.* Tampa, FL: Mariner. Reprinted by permission of the author.

ANALYSIS OF KSAOS

Now that the KSAOs have been generated and rated, they can be analyzed. The analysis is quite simple. For each "yes/no" question ("Necessary for new worker?" and "Practical to expect?"), tally the number of experts who said yes or no for each KSAO. For each of the two rating scales (Trouble Likely and Distinguish Superior From Average Workers), compute the average rating across all the job experts for each KSAO. The final product of the KSAO phase is a complete listing of all KSAOs with their accompanying ratings. After the KSAOs have been analyzed, job experts may be consulted once more to verify that the list is complete and that the ratings generally make sense.

USING THE RESULTS

Although the job analysis is done, still more analysis may be necessary to put the results to work. The C-JAM method has been targeted primarily for personnel selection and training. We briefly outline how the C-JAM results can be used for each. Where personnel selection and training are concerned, the KSAO portion of the analysis provides the most crucial information. The pattern of ratings on the KSAOs will indicate whether a KSAO is to be used for selection or training, and how it is to be used for those applications.

Starting with selection, each KSAO that is chosen to play a role in any examining or testing process must meet three criteria. First, a clear majority of the experts must have voted that a KSAO is necessary for newly hired workers. Second, a clear majority of the experts must have voted that a KSAO is practical to expect in the labor market. Third, the average rating on Trouble Likely must be 1.5 or greater. If any of these conditions do not apply, then the KSAO is not considered for selection.

"Wait a minute!" you say. "What if there is a 3–3 split on one or both yes/no questions, because in my meeting I had six experts?" This tied vote is not a clear majority, so the criterion is not met with a tie. Such KSAOs would not be used for selection. Suppose the decision has been reached to include a KSAO in selection. Now we look at the average rating on the Distinguish Superior From Average Workers scale. If it is above 1.5, then the KSAO should be used to develop a selection or screening measure that will rank applicants from most qualified to least qualified. If a KSAO is rated below 1.5 on this scale, it should be used to develop a selection or screening measure that will be used on a pass/fail basis. A concrete example may help build a bridge from the job analysis results to the development of an examination battery or test.

Let's assume we have arrived at three KSAOs to use in designing an examination battery for the job of personnel testing specialist: (1) ability to read and write, (2) knowledge of test item construction, and (3) ability to communicate with confused or angry applicants. Suppose also that ability to read and write was rated as being essential for new workers, practical to expect in the labor market, an average of 2.0 on Trouble Likely, but an average of 1.4 on Distinguish Superior From Average Workers. Knowledge of test item construction was rated essential for new workers, practical to expect in the labor market, 5.0 on Trouble Likely, and 5.0 on Distinguish Superior From Average Workers. Ability to communicate with angry applicants was rated essential for new workers, practical to expect in the labor market, 3.0 on Trouble Likely, and 5.0 on Distinguish Superior From Average Workers. These ratings mean that KSAO (1) should be used on a pass/fail basis, whereas KSAO (2) and KSAO (3) should be used to construct a scored examination or test battery used to rank the applicants.

Here is one exam plan that might come out of the analysis: Completion of a job application form by the applicant is evidence that applicants for this job can read and write. Then they are admitted into a combination test and interview exam battery. The test is used to measure knowledge of item construction; the interview is used to measure ability to communicate with angry applicants. The test and interview may be weighted by means of the KSAO ratings to come up with a final overall score on the battery. For example, we could multiply the Trouble Likely rating by the Distinguish Superior From Average Workers rating to arrive at an overall value of KSAO importance for selection. For our job of personnel testing specialist, KSAO (2) has a value of 25 (5×5), while KSAO (3) has a value of 15. The total importance of both KSAOs together is 40 (25 + 15), so we can weight the written test 25/40 or 62 percent of the final score and the interview 15/40 or 38 percent of the final score. A simpler way to arrive at weights for tests might be to stick with the rating on the Distinguish Superior From Average Workers scale only. The same reasoning would apply to weighing the importance of different parts of a single test according to the importance of the KSAO they are designed to measure. Obviously, it helps to know how to design tests, interviews, and other screening devices, but that's a topic for another book, or for consultation with a suitably trained expert.

How about the decision to use certain KSAOs for training? That decision is based on two scales only: the Essential for New Workers scale and the Distinguish Superior From Average Workers scale. If a KSAO is not rated as essential by a clear majority of the experts and is rated higher than an average of 1.5 on the Distinguish Superior From Average Workers scale, the KSAO should be used for training. The importance of the KSAOs for training may be determined by ranking them according to their rating on the Distinguish Superior From Average Workers scale. Another point is worth mentioning: If a KSAO designed for use in training is practical to expect in the labor market, then training need be provided only to those employees who are below a satisfactory level on it. However, when it is not practical to expect in the labor market, all employees should be trained on it.

To some of you sharp-eyed readers, it may seem that we are completely ignoring a major part of the job analysis for training and selection applications—the tasks. Because worker attributes are most important in these two applications, tasks do play a lesser role compared with KSAOs. But we may still use the tasks profitably. In selection, tasks may play a role in the construction of work sample tests. According to the "Uniform Guidelines on Employee Selection Procedures" (Equal Employment Opportunity Commission, 1978), when we validate tests by a content validity strategy we must use items that are representative of important aspects of job performance. The tasks and their importance ratings directly fill this requirement. So work sample tests may be designed directly from all, or a sample, of those tasks that are rated important in a job.

With regard to training, tasks associated with KSAOs that are designed for use in training may be used as the basis for a training program's content. Or the tasks may be used directly based on their importance ratings.

RESEARCH AND APPLICATIONS OF C-JAM

The method has been applied successfully in numerous contexts, such as power plants and government agencies. A full description of the successful use of C-JAM to build a selection process for emergency telephone operators is reported by Schneider and Schmitt (1986, pp. 419–426). A modification of C-JAM was employed to develop minimum qualifications requirements of 14 diverse jobs. Minimum qualifications are statements of education and experience needed to qualify for a job. An article by Levine, Maye, Ulm, and Gordon (1997) provides details.

Manson, Levine, and Brannick (2000) investigated the construct validity of scales used for rating task importance. Their evidence provided strong support for the scales assessing criticality, difficulty to learn, and relative time spent.

These parallel three of the scales employed in C-JAM. Another feature of C-JAM that has been studied is the use of teams of subject matter experts (SMEs) to collect data. Levine and Sanchez (1998) found that for 14 diverse jobs, team characteristics such as median level of education or functional diversity did not impair the quality of the job analysis data.

You have seen that raters can provide reliable ratings on scales used to evaluate tasks. Another important question for this method is the extent to which raters can provide reliable scale ratings of KSAOs. This would apply also to the job elements method. Recently a study by Van Iddekinge, Putka, Raymark, and Eidson (2005) provided positive evidence. They looked in depth at the sources of error when raters assessed two aspects of 118 KSAOs grouped into 10 dimensions—KSAO importance and whether KSAOs were needed at entry. Almost 400 raters across five organizations were used. The job was Customer Service Manager, and raters were managers themselves, store managers and district managers. In aggregate, ratings of KSAOs on these scales equaled or exceeded .87, a high level of reliability. Ratings were not influenced much by position level, organization, or demographic features of the raters. However, the reliability of individual raters was very low, and appeared due to individual differences in the rating styles of each rater. These results suggest relying on sizeable groups of raters. If small teams are used as is the case with C-JAM or JEM, standardizing the rating process and facilitating group discussions are critical in avoiding biases of individual raters. As a general rule, it is relatively easy to achieve reliable evaluations of perceptions or concrete objects, and relatively difficult to achieve reliable evaluations of concepts and abstract objects. Therefore it is not surprising that it is harder to get reliable evaluations of KSAOs than of tasks.

SUMMARY OF C-JAM

Two major sets of descriptors are used in C-JAM: tasks and KSAOs. Information gathering is usually done by teams of SMEs, especially incumbents and direct supervisors. These SMEs focus on the job as a whole, not on individual positions. They provide ratings of both the tasks and the KSAOs. The method is similar to the task inventory for the task part and similar to the job element method for the KSAO part. The ratings on the scales and the pattern of these ratings are then used to develop selection methods or training programs.

Multimethod Job Design Questionnaire

Many job analysis methods essentially consider jobs to be givens to which people are tailored by selection or training. Job design, on the other hand, attempts to alter jobs to better suit people. Such alterations may be common to the job or unique to the individual. For example, regardless of the individuals holding the job, some work areas are lit more brightly than are others. Hotel lobbies tend to be rather dim, but hospital operating rooms tend to be rather bright (there have been extensive studies of fitting light to work; there is even a Society of Illumination Engineers). On the other hand, some jobs allow workers to adjust the brightness of the light with which they work (for example, photographers, jewelers).

One purpose of the *Multimethod Job Design Questionnaire* is to gather information that can be used for job design. Not surprisingly, most of the information gathered by the MJDQ concerns work rather than worker attributes, although worker attributes must often be assumed in order to gather the needed task information. At another level, however, the MJDQ is also about looking at various theories of how jobs should be designed to better suit people. It turns out that the theories do not always agree, and so the designer is left with choices or trade-offs about the best job design. It is this integration of several different views of job design that caused us to place the MJDQ in this chapter on hybrid methods.

MJDQ DEVELOPMENT AND STRUCTURE

Campion and Thayer (1985) described the development and structure of the MJDQ. They began with a review of the research on job design (see, Morgeson & Campion, 2003, for a more up-to-date review). They developed a set of job design principles that they sorted into four categories: motivational, mechanistic, biological, and perceptual/motor. They then wrote items for the MJDQ based on design principles for each of the four groups. Each group and its contents are described next.

Motivational

The basic idea behind the motivational approach is that people want meaningful jobs. People find jobs to be meaningful when they feel that the work is significant and when the work allows for the development and exercise of skills. Thus, according to this approach, jobs should be designed to require multiple skills and to give jobholders responsibility for work outcomes. A concert musician, for example, needs to develop and maintain skill in playing an instrument. When it comes time to perform, the musician can play well or poorly, and is thus in large part responsible for the work outcome. The items that make up the Motivational scale are listed in Table 4.3. If you want to learn more about where the motivational design principles came from, start by reading work on job enlargement and job enrichment

Table 4.3   Contents of the Motivational Scale of the MJDQ

1. Autonomy, responsibility, vertical loading	9. Task significance
2. Intrinsic job feedback	10. Growth, learning, advancing responsibility
3. Extrinsic job feedback	11. Promotion
4. Social interaction	12. Achievement
5. Task/goal clarity	13. Participation
6. Task variety, horizontal loading	14. Communication
7. Ability/skill requirements and variety	15. Pay adequacy
8. Task identity	16. Job security

SOURCE: Adapted from Campion, M. A., & Thayer, P. W. (1985). Development and field evaluation of an interdisciplinary measure of job design. *Journal of Applied Psychology, 70*, 29–43. Copyright 1985 by American Psychological Association. Adapted by permission.

(for example, Herzberg, 1966), job characteristics theory (for example, Hackman & Oldham, 1975, 1980), and sociotechnical systems theory (for example, Pasmore, 1988; Rousseau, 1977).

Mechanistic

The main idea here is efficiency. The work is analyzed to find the most efficient way to do the job, and everyone is taught to do it that way. For example, in putting mushrooms on a pizza, the employee might be instructed to grab equal amounts of sliced mushrooms in each hand and to distribute them over the pizza using identical motions of both hands. The contents of the Mechanistic scale are shown in Table 4.4. If you want to learn more about this approach, start with early time-and-motion studies of industrial engineering such as practiced by Taylor (1911) and Gilbreth (1911) or more modern texts (for example, Mundel & Danner, 1994). You might even want to review our description in Chapter 2.

Biological

The design principles in this category come from studies of the human body. The idea is to design tools and the work context around the way people are constructed physically. For example, people can accomplish more in a day's work if they have rest breaks than if they do not have rest breaks. For another

Table 4.4   Contents of the Mechanistic Scale of the MJDQ

1. Task fractionalization/ specialization	8. Motion economy— pre-positioning of materials, tools
2. Specialization of materials, tools, procedure	9. Motion economy—eye and head movements
3. Task simplification	10. Motion economy—muscle movement
4. Skill simplification	11. Motion economy—muscle rhythm
5. Repetition/pacing	12. Motion economy—muscle movement style
6. Idle time/capacity	
7. Motion economy—materials handling	13. Mechanization

SOURCE: Adapted from Campion, M. A., & Thayer, P. W. (1985). Development and field evaluation of an interdisciplinary measure of job design. *Journal of Applied Psychology, 70,* 29–43. Copyright 1985 by American Psychological Association. Adapted by permission.

example, it is difficult for people to stand in one place for long periods; they do better if they can sit or rest on a stool. The contents of the Biological scale are shown in Table 4.5. To learn more about this approach, start with human physiology (how people function physically; see Astrand & Rodahl, 1977),

Table 4.5   Contents of the Biological Scale of the MJDQ

1. Seating	10. Wrists
2. Tool design	11. Stress concentration
3. Anthropometry	12. Vibration
4. Static effort	13. Noise
5. Endurance	14. Climate
6. Strength	15. Atmosphere
7. Lifting	16. Worker protection—safety
8. Posture, lower back	17. Work breaks
9. Muscular adequacy	18. Shift work

SOURCE: Adapted from Campion, M. A., & Thayer, P. W. (1985). Development and field evaluation of an interdisciplinary measure of job design. *Journal of Applied Psychology, 70,* 29–43. Copyright 1985 by American Psychological Association. Adapted by permission.

anthropometry (the study of body measurements, such as arm length; see Pheasant, 1996), and biomechanics (human movement and force production; see Kumar, 1999).

Perceptual/Motor

The idea is to design work and work aids that account for the way in which people perceive and process information. For example, automobiles have a standard layout for the accelerator and the brake. Imagine the fun if you got into a friend's car and the brake and accelerator were in positions opposite to yours. For another example, people perceive color well in the center of the visual field, but not on the periphery, where differences in black and white are more dominant. So if a workstation uses color to display information, the color displays should be placed in the center of the worker's visual field. The contents of the Perceptual/Motor scale are listed in Table 4.6. To learn more about this approach, start with human factors engineering and ergonomics (for example, MacLeod, 2000). Both the mechanistic and perceptual/motor approaches blend psychology and engineering for their recommendations, and so some of the descriptors overlap.

Table 4.6   Contents of the Perceptual/Motor Scale of the MJDQ

1. Workplace lighting—general	12. Warning devices
2. Workplace lighting—glare/contrast	13. Printed job materials
3. Control and display identification	14. Panel layout
4. Display visibility/legibility	15. Input requirements
5. Displays—information content	16. Output requirements
6. Control/display movement relationships	17. Information processing requirements
7. Control/display ratios	18. Memory requirements
8. Control resistance/feedback	19. Boredom
9. Controls—accidental activation	20. Arousal
10. Controls—anthropometry/biomechanics	21. Stress
11. Controls—motion economy	22. Workplace layout—safety
	23. Workplace layout—visual and auditory links

SOURCE: Adapted from Campion, M. A., & Thayer, P. W. (1985). Development and field evaluation of an interdisciplinary measure of job design. *Journal of Applied Psychology, 70,* 29–43. Copyright 1985 by American Psychological Association. Adapted by permission.

MJDQ RESEARCH

Formats

The MJDQ was developed for use by trained analysts, who observe the work and interview incumbents before completing the questions in the MJDQ (Campion & Thayer, 1985). The MJDQ was subsequently revised to allow it to be completed by incumbents (Campion, 1988). There are benefits to the self-report format, including ease of data collection for jobs such as management that are difficult to observe, as well as reduced expense. There may be drawbacks to incumbent reports as well. Incumbents do not necessarily have the same broad frame of reference as do observers when rating the target job. In other words, the observer and the incumbent may be comparing the target job to different jobs when making ratings. Incumbents may also bias the reports (for example, Caldwell & O'Reilly, 1982).

Reliability

There are several different types of reliability data reported on the MJDQ. For the observer format, internal consistency estimates for the four scales are all above .80, which is good. Observer (job analyst) agreement on the four scales was also reported good, ranging from .89 to .93 on a sample of 30 diverse jobs. For the incumbent format, internal consistency was reported good for three of the four scales. The reliability for the Mechanistic scale was .65, but the other scales had estimates above .80 (Campion, 1988). Campion (1988) also reported intraclass correlations that indicated the reliability (agreement) of the average incumbent ratings within jobs. The results suggested that an average of 10 incumbents was sufficient to get reliable results except for the Motivation scale, which was believed to be relatively more abstract than the other scales, and thus invites disagreement about the proper description of the job. In a sample of 11 clerical jobs, Campion and McClelland (1991) found good internal consistency estimates for MJDQ scales for incumbents, their managers, and a set of job analysts rating the same jobs. They also reported high correlations across jobs for the different sources (for example, incumbents with managers) on the scales with the exception of the Biological scale. In general, the MJDQ appears to reliably distinguish among jobs and can do so for both the incumbent and observer forms.

Correlations Among Scales and Correlations With Other Variables

Not surprisingly, the scales tend to show intercorrelations. In particular, the Motivational scale tends to be negatively correlated with the Mechanistic and Perceptual/Motor scales. In other words, a job high on the Motivational scale (where high-level skills are developed and used and there are high levels of autonomy) is likely to have a low score on the Mechanistic and Perceptual/Motor scales (which typically include simplified jobs). For example, a heart surgeon will have a great deal of discretion in how to decide to perform bypass surgery, and such an operation will involve a number of high-level skills. Such a job will score highly on the Motivational scale and score low on the Mechanistic scale. The Biological scale is relatively independent of the other three. The negative correlation appears to be due to the difference in theoretical approaches to job design. A job that is designed to be interesting and challenging and result in personal growth will tend to be more cognitively complex, thus resulting in a less mechanistic (routine, simplified) job. This represents a fundamental trade-off among the different work design approaches (Campion, Mumford, Morgeson, & Nahrgang, 2005; Morgeson & Campion, 2002).

The initial thrust of Campion's work was to show that there were trade-offs inherent in job design. For example, simplifying a job reduces training time but increases boredom. Consider the difference between preparing a meal from start to finish and just washing dishes. By and large, Campion and Thayer (1985) and Campion (1988) provided results across large numbers of jobs that support the notion of design trade-offs. There were some differences depending on whether analyst or incumbent data were used; the interested reader should consult the original articles for further detail. In general, they found that jobs high on the Motivational scale tended to be more satisfying to incumbents but less efficient and reliable in job performance. Jobs high on the Mechanistic and on the Perceptual/Motor scale tended to be efficient and reliable. Jobs high on the Biological scale tended to be comfortable. Campion (1989) found the scales of the MJDQ to be related to jobs' ability requirements much as one might expect and showed how job design and selection are connected. Campion and Berger (1990) showed that the MJDQ scales were related to compensation for different jobs as well.

Most of the studies concerning the MJDQ were correlational in nature, meaning that the ratings were made of different jobs as they existed, rather than looking at changes in the design of a particular job. However, a study in which jobs were examined after they had been changed (Campion & McClelland, 1991) did find that enlarged clerical jobs had higher scores on the Motivational scale and lower scores on the Mechanistic scale than a comparison group of jobs. The enlarged jobs were associated with higher job satisfaction, mental challenge, and customer service. On the other hand, the enlarged jobs required greater training and compensation. The information from this study provides support for the MJDQ as a source of information about what is likely to happen as a result of changing the design of a job. Yet a follow-up study by Campion and McClelland (1993) found that the long-term trade-offs depended on the nature of the initial changes made to the jobs. Task enlargement had primarily long-term costs, whereas knowledge enlargement had primarily long-term benefits. This suggested that there might be a way to avoid the trade-offs typically observed. Along this same line, Morgeson and Campion (2002) asked if specific changes to jobs could produce specific benefits (in terms of satisfaction and efficiency) and whether it was possible to avoid (or at least minimize) work design trade-offs. They found that it was possible to enhance satisfaction, efficiency, or both, suggesting that by explicitly identifying the trade-offs, one could minimize them. More work is needed before a definitive answer to the question of whether trade-offs are a necessary part of work design can be found. However, the studies to date are encouraging in that it may be possible to increase both satisfaction and work efficiency at once by improving job design.

The MJDQ as a General Measure of Work

The MJDQ occupies a middle ground between specific task measures and abstract attribute measures. As such, it may be useful as a general measure of work. Edwards, Scully, and Brtek (1999, 2000) subjected the MJDQ to a series of factor analyses in an attempt to understand its underlying factor structure and to examine its usefulness as a general measure of work. Factor analysis (see Chapter 9) is a method that can be used to group different variables into clusters or groups of variables that go together. In this case, the variables to be grouped are the items from the MJDQ. Interestingly, they found little support for the four major groupings described by Campion and Thayer (1985). Instead, Edwards et al. (1999) suggested that the four major groups be split into 10 more specific groups, which can be thought of as nested within the larger groupings. The nested groups are described next. The Motivational group included *feedback, skill,* and *rewards* scales; the Mechanistic group included *specialization* and *task simplicity* scales; the Biological group included *physical ease, work conditions,* and *work scheduling* scales; and the Perceptual/Motor group included *ergonomic design* and *cognitive simplicity* scales. Thus, each of the major approaches to job design appeared to be composed of more molecular design elements, each of which might potentially have an impact on work satisfaction and efficiency, though such research has yet to be completed. You might want to be one of those hardy research pioneers who braves the frontier to bring us new wisdom regarding this very issue! You may need coffee.

In fact, there is an additional issue at the same research frontier. Although the Edwards et al. (1999) scales represent a more comprehensive description of work, they are still limited because the resulting 10 scales do not fully represent a comprehensive description of work. Because some of the items from the MJDQ are the sole indicators of a given work dimension (for example, a single item is used to represent autonomy), they cannot be used to form scales. Additional items would need to be developed so these dimensions of work could be measured. (This is due to technical difficulties in factor analysis, which need not concern you further at this point as a job analyst.) Recognizing this limitation, Morgeson and Humphrey (2006) sought to develop a work design measure that addressed weaknesses in the MJDQ and other measures of work design. The resulting 21-factor Work Design Questionnaire (WDQ) included 21 factors (not 31; that would be a certain brand of ice cream), which are grouped into task and knowledge characteristics (comprising the commonly studied motivational characteristics), as well as the less frequently studied social (for example, social support, interdependence, feedback from others) and contextual (for example, physical demands, working conditions) aspects of work (Table 4.7). Therefore, the WDQ included all the elements contained in the MJDQ as well as adding additional work characteristics in order to offer a more complete description of work design. Initial evidence provided by Morgeson and Humphrey (2006) suggests that a more complex conceptualization of work can help avoid the trade-offs identified by the MJDQ. For example, one of the typical findings in research on the MJDQ is that jobs that are Mechanistically designed tend to be relatively boring and unsatisfying to perform. Yet an organization may wish to somehow enhance these kinds of jobs, in part because boring jobs tend to have higher levels of turnover. For business reasons it may be impossible to increase the motivational work characteristics (for example, enhancing may have negative implications for quality of efficiency), so what is an organization to do? (This is where you get to think like a manager . . . it is so exciting!) One possibility would be to redesign a job to have greater opportunities for social interaction and thereby enhance the

Table 4.7   Factors Contained in the Work Design Questionnaire (WDQ)

Task Characteristics	Social Characteristics
1. Work scheduling autonomy	13. Social support
2. Decision-making autonomy	14. Initiated interdependence
3. Work methods autonomy	15. Received interdependence
4. Task variety	16. Interaction outside organization
5. Task significance	
6. Task identity	17. Feedback from others
7. Feedback from job	**Work Context**
Knowledge Characteristics	18. Ergonomics
8. Job complexity	19. Physical demands
9. Information processing	20. Work conditions
10. Problem solving	21. Equipment use
11. Skill variety	
12. Specialization	

possibility for receiving social support. Morgeson and Humphrey (2006) found that jobs high in social support were also more satisfying to perform. Thus, the trade-off typically observed between Motivational and Mechanistic work design may be eliminated by considering other aspects of work design.

SUMMARY OF THE MJDQ

The MJDQ was developed to provide an integrated picture of job design and the trade-offs that are likely in any given job. The MJDQ appears to provide reliable data given trained job analysts or a reasonable (about 10, minimum) number of incumbents. The MJDQ also appears to provide data that predict various work outcomes (satisfaction, efficiency, comfort). Furthermore, the MJDQ provides data that are associated with jobs' ability requirements and compensation. On the other hand, there have been some recent criticisms of the factor structure of the MJDQ. The recently developed WDQ appears to address some of the criticisms of the MJDQ. Additional research is necessary to determine if WDQ can be useful for redesign efforts.

Occupational Information Network

IMPETUS FOR O*NET

The *Dictionary of Occupational Titles* (*DOT*) was produced by the U.S. Department of Labor. It is an encyclopedic source of job descriptions for more than 9,000 occupations. The *DOT* has been used by both government and private sector establishments for matching people to jobs and as a source of information for job analyses. In large part, the *DOT* was developed by field agents of the Department of Labor using the functional job analysis method we described in Chapter 2. Trained job analysts would observe and interview incumbents, and then summarize the job in terms of tasks and a few ratings. The latest version of the *DOT* (published in 1991) is a thick volume stuffed with information on so many occupations that you need to sit down with it and skim its contents to appreciate its size and scope.

The *Occupational Information Network* (O*NET) was intended to replace the *DOT*, and may yet do so. There are major differences between O*NET and the *DOT*. The changes were made in response to problems known or believed to be true of the *DOT*. What needed fixing? (For a more detailed answer than we provide, see Dunnette, 1999; Dye & Silver, 1999.)

1. The main content of the *DOT* is analysts' descriptions of tasks. Although everyone agrees that we need to know and describe tasks as part of a comprehensive job analysis, using the task as the heart of the system makes it difficult

to compare occupations or to organize them in systematic ways based on quantitative indices of their similarity.

2. Information on a substantial portion of occupations in the *DOT* is always out of date. It is time consuming and expensive to update the *DOT*.

3. The *DOT* contains little information beyond the task. True, there are sections for temperaments and for vocational preparation, but a much richer set of descriptors could be employed. For example, interests and abilities might be used.

The U.S. government formed a committee to examine the *DOT* and make recommendations for its future. The committee recommended that the successor to the *DOT* should be a database that is easily accessible. The information in the database should offer a wide range of descriptors so that different users might find value in the information. The database should also support multiple levels of detail or abstraction. Broader descriptors were needed to allow an occupation to be described in ways that allow cross-occupational comparisons. Narrow descriptors are needed to communicate the specific content of the job.

As previously mentioned, the *DOT* is expensive to revise. The committee noted the need for rapid, cost-effective data collection. On the other hand, the committee also noted that no single source would be able to provide all the information about a job that is needed for O*NET. Rather, the committee envisioned a partnership among government entities (the Department of Labor) and business establishments that would supply incumbents as well as vendors for developing and maintaining O*NET.

THE O*NET CONTENT MODEL

One of the main reasons for including O*NET here (besides the cool use of the Internet, our attempt to appear up to date, and our admiration for the architects of the system) is its comprehensive set of descriptors. The architects of O*NET wanted to cast a broad net, covering virtually everything that an industrial and organizational psychologist would want to know about a job. The O*NET content model is organized around six sets of descriptors, namely:

1. Worker requirements
2. Experience requirements
3. Worker characteristics
4. Occupational requirements
5. Occupation-specific requirements, and
6. Occupation characteristics

"But what *are* these?" you ask. Because you asked, we shall describe each in general terms. We also provide partial lists of descriptors for the first four factors. (Occupation-specific factors have yet to be developed extensively, and occupation characteristics are not contained in O*NET but rather in other databases that contain labor market information. Therefore, neither of these facets is described here in detail.) The lists of descriptors will help you to understand the meaning of the content model. If you want greater detail than we can provide here, you might start with the book by Peterson, Mumford, Borman, Jeanneret, and Fleishman (1999) or the summary of O*NET by Peterson et al. (2001).

Worker Requirements

The basic idea of worker requirements is to describe personal attributes that are developed through experience and that should prove helpful in performing a large number of tasks. For example, reading is a very useful skill in many tasks. Skill in reading is developed through many different experiences. This set of descriptors is divided into three categories labeled *basic and cross-functional skills, knowledge,* and *education, training, and experience.* Each of the categories is illustrated in Table 4.8.

Basic and Cross-Functional Skills. Basic and cross-functional skills help a person acquire specific job knowledge. For example, reading comprehension could be used in completing a training manual or a set of assembly instructions. Basic and cross-functional skills also refer to capacities that span multiple work activities. Persuasion, for example, could be useful in such tasks as sales and management.

Knowledge. As you can see in Table 4.8, knowledge refers to information about a domain or discipline such as art or music. Expertise in a knowledge domain is important for many jobs. A physician, for example, must know a great deal about human anatomy, physiology, and various diseases and their treatment.

Education. This category is for general education rather than specific vocational preparation. Some jobs are associated with minimal educational requirements, such as a cashier at a fast-food restaurant. Other jobs are associated with college degrees (for example, engineering), whereas others are associated with advanced degrees (for example, college and university instructors). In some sense, education stands for a collection of basic skills and cross-functional knowledges. College graduates are expected to perform better than high school graduates on tasks that require greater sophistication in critical thinking and communication. In Table 4.8, education is covered by the item General Education Level.

Experience Requirements

Experience requirements include specific vocational training, work experience, and licensure. It is useful to contrast experience requirements with

Table 4.8   Sample O*NET Descriptors for Worker Requirements and
Experience Requirements

Basic and Cross-Functional Skills	Knowledge	Education, Training, and Experience
1. Reading Comprehension	Art	General Education Level
2. Mathematics	Biology and Physiology	Instructional Program
3. Service Orientation	Building and Construction	Subject Area Education
4. Speaking	Chemistry	Licenses Required
5. Persuasion	Materials	Requirement to Obtain License
6. Idea Evaluation	Money	Who Requires License
7. Installation	Music	Related Work Experience
8. Time Management	Psychology	
9. Technology Design	Sales and Marketing	
10. Monitoring	Transportation	

NOTE: O*NET contains 46 descriptors for Basic Skills and Cross-Functional Skills, and 49 descriptors for Knowledge.

education. Education refers to general developmental activities that produce capacities applicable to a wide variety of tasks. Training and experience usually apply more narrowly to specific occupations and tasks. Training can be a matter of vocational training, such as in an auto shop, or apprenticeships or on-the-job programs. Work experience is figured in terms of time that a position was held, such as the number of years as an auto mechanic. Licenses are given to workers to certify that they are competent to complete certain tasks. Nurses and forklift drivers need licenses to do their work legally. In Table 4.8, experience requirement descriptors are shown in the third column, below General Education Level.

Worker Characteristics

This set of descriptors deals with enduring personal characteristics needed by individuals for successful job performance. In Chapter 3, we described several methods that are relevant to worker characteristics. The set of worker characteristics in O*NET is further divided into three categories: *abilities, occupational values and interests,* and *work styles.* Examples of each are shown in Table 4.9.

Abilities. These descriptors deal with enduring human capacities that are less subject to development by experience than are basic skills and knowledge. Examples of the full set of abilities in O*NET that are shown in Table 4.9 include mathematical reasoning and manual dexterity. The Ability Requirements Scales (ARS; Fleishman & Mumford, 1988) and the Threshold Traits Analysis System (TTAS; Lopez, 1988) that we described in Chapter 3 both use standard sets of abilities. Fleishman's work is similar to the abilities used in O*NET.

Table 4.9   Sample O*NET Descriptors for Worker Characteristics

Abilities	Occupational Values and Interests	Work Styles
1. Oral expression	Ability utlization	Achievement/effort
2. Originality	Achievement	Persistence
3. Mathematical reasoning	Company policies	Energy
4. Memorization	Creativity	Cooperation
5. Manual dexterity	Moral values	Concern for others
6. Reaction time	Responsibility	Self-control
7. Stamina	Security	Dependability
8. Near vision	Social status	Integrity
9. Night vision	Variety	Independence
10. Hearing sensitivity	Working conditions	Analytical thinking

NOTE: O*NET contains 52 descriptors for Abilities, 21 descriptors for Occupational Values, and 17 descriptors for Work Styles.

Occupational Values and Interests. This set of descriptors is less focused on whether a person *can* do the job and more focused on whether the person *will* do the job. What does a person find interesting? What does a person find reinforcing or gratifying at work? The answers to such questions are useful in matching people and jobs. Examples drawn from the full set of O*NET descriptors and shown in Table 4.9 include security and variety. People value job security particularly when the economy is bad. Security also becomes more important as people age, begin a family, or think about retirement. People find working at a variety of activities stimulating and helpful for a sense of skill development.

Work Styles. Work styles also refer to enduring capabilities of workers much like abilities. However, abilities refer to tests of maximum performance (for example, a vocabulary test); work styles refer to tests of typical performance and personality. Again, here we are talking *will do* rather than *can do.* The most capable person may not always work the hardest. (The race goes not always to the swift.) Examples drawn from the full set of O*NET work styles that are shown in Table 4.9 include persistence and integrity. There is a bit of overlap between work styles and occupational values and interests. Perhaps the simplest way to distinguish between the two is to consider occupational values and interests to be work-related sources of gratification and work styles to be types of behaviors ordinarily exhibited at work.

Occupational Requirements

The three main sets of descriptors for the O*NET content model that we have discussed thus far (worker requirements, experience requirements, and worker characteristics) are all on the worker side of the job analysis (recall Chapter 3). The occupational requirements descriptors, however, fall on the work side of job analysis (recall Chapter 2). As you know, the work side of job analysis typically reports on what the worker does, and this usually means a description of tasks. In the O*NET model, occupational requirements are built from three categories of descriptors: *generalized work activities, work context,* and *organizational context.* Examples drawn from the full set of O*NET descriptors for each type of descriptor are shown in Table 4.10.

Generalized Work Activities. The generalized work activity (GWA) is a task that is written at a broad level so that it can apply to multiple occupations. Example tasks in Table 4.10 include getting information needed to do the job and interacting with computers. Both these tasks are general enough that they could apply to many occupations. For example, getting information needed to do the job would apply to a lawyer researching case law and to a geologist analyzing water samples. For another example, both a computer programmer and a secretary interact with a computer. O*NET is designed so that occupations

Table 4.10   Sample O*NET Descriptors for Occupational Requirements

Generalized Work Activities	Work Context	Organizational Context
1. Getting information needed to do the job	Social interaction	Empowerment
2. Judging the qualities of objects, services, or persons	Unpleasant individuals	Autonomy
3. Making decisions and solving problems	Privacy of work area	Task identity
4. Thinking creatively	Radiation exposure	Skill variety
5. Handling and moving objects	High places exposure	Role conflict
6. Interacting with computers	Body positioning	Goal specificity
7. Documenting and recording information	Work attire	Risk-taking values
8. Coordinating the work and activities of others	Decision latitude	Leader: Visionary
9. Teaching others	Level of automation	Number of teams
10. Staffing organizational units	Constant awareness	Number of reorganizations

NOTE: O*NET contains 42 descriptors for Generalized Work Activities, 39 descriptors for Work Context and 33 descriptors for Organizational Context.

can have specific tasks that are nested within the GWAs. For example, the computer programmer can interact with the computer by writing code in C++ and the secretary can interact with the computer by typing a letter using a word processor. The occupation-specific tasks belong to the occupation-specific requirements category rather than the occupational requirements category, however.

Work Context. This set of descriptors concerns the conditions under which the work must be completed. An obvious concern is weather for people who work outdoors. Example descriptors in Table 4.10 include unpleasant individuals and constant awareness. We would expect to encounter unpleasant individuals in the job of prison guard, for example. Prison guards are sometimes assaulted by inmates, so this should qualify as dealing with unpleasant individuals. Constant awareness would apply to an air traffic controller, who must be aware of his or her aircraft at all times. Failure to do so could result in aircraft collisions and the resulting destruction and death.

Organizational Context. This set of descriptors is the most experimental of all the descriptors in O*NET. Such descriptors are absent from the *DOT.* Many of these descriptors have come from the study of "high-performance" organizations. The idea is that many attributes of organizations can affect the way in which jobs are completed. For example, if an organization is relatively flat, meaning that there are few layers of supervision, then most jobholders will have more decision-making authority and more choices about the tools used and sequence of steps used to complete the work (that is, flat organizations result in jobs with more autonomy). Examples of such descriptors in Table 4.10 include autonomy and risk-taking values. Risk-taking values will influence whether relatively risky job-related behaviors will be tolerated. Differences in such values might be reflected in messages such as "Just do it" versus "Safety first." If you noticed the similarity between these and the MJDQ Motivation scale, give yourself a pat on the back.

Occupation-Specific Requirements and Occupation Characteristics

Occupation-specific requirements refer to the work of the occupation. Here we expect to see occupation-specific tasks that fall under the GWAs. Recall that O*NET is supposed to have multiple levels of abstraction. The GWAs join occupations into similar larger entities; the occupation-specific tasks distinguish the occupations from one another. Although O*NET includes data on occupation-specific tasks, there are generally very few tasks listed for each occupation (typically about 10). As such, for many purposes (for example, designing a training program), additional task-level detail will need to be collected. The O*NET's tasks are a good starting point for conducting one's own task-level job analysis. Also covered are specific occupational knowledges and skills and machines, tools, and equipment. The occupation-specific requirements are similar to the descriptions that are currently in the *DOT* and described in "Functional Job Analysis" in Chapter 2.

Occupation characteristics are not incorporated directly into O*NET. Rather, O*NET is designed to link to other databases that contain the relevant information. The descriptors under this category include labor market information, occupational outlook, and wages. Such information is important for vocational planning and preparation as well as the national interest for employment.

O*NET RESEARCH AND DEVELOPMENT

O*NET has been subjected to a pilot study that is described in Peterson et al. (1999). First, the content model was developed. Complete trial versions of the four general sets of descriptors illustrated in Tables 4.8 to 4.10 were developed (that is, worker requirements, experience/occupational preparation requirements, worker characteristics, and occupational requirements). Next, occupations were selected, and business establishments were contacted to provide incumbents who would complete questionnaires about sets of descriptors. At the same time, trained analysts were asked to provide ratings on some of the same descriptors as the job incumbents so that the reliability of the judgments could be estimated. Task inventories were adapted to provide content for a sample of occupations for the fifth category, occupation-specific requirements.

The original sampling plan called for 80 occupations and 30 incumbents per occupation so that the data would be available for a representative sample of occupations and there would be a large enough sample of incumbents to provide stable estimates of means for each descriptor. However, due to problems in data collection, fewer than half of the occupations at the end of the study had four or more incumbents responding to all the descriptors. Therefore, both the representativeness of the occupations and the stability of the results might be called into question.

In general, the pilot study showed that it is possible to collect data for O*NET. However, the source of information may be problematic. For example, for the GWAs, incumbent ratings were compared with analyst ratings (Jeanneret, Borman, Kubisiak, & Hanson, 1999). There were 35 occupations and 42 items. For each item, researchers computed the correlation between the incumbents and analysts (this is the correct method to use for this comparison). The mean correlation (reliability) was .71 (the median was .69; the range was .47 to .88). They also computed tests to see whether the mean ratings were higher for incumbents or analysts (the test is a statistical test of significance used to decide if two means are really different from one another). They found that there were significant differences in means for 22 of the 42 GWA items, thus indicating that incumbents and analysts provided different means for over half of the items. In our opinion, the results do not support the equivalence of incumbent and analyst ratings for the GWAs.

Analogous results were reported for incumbent and analyst ratings of basic and cross-functional skills (Mumford, Peterson, & Childs, 1999). There were again 35 occupations but 46 items. Again reliability was calculated for each item across the two types of raters, as was a test for the difference in means. The mean correlation (reliability) was .74 (the median was .75; the range was .53 to .88). They found significant differences between mean ratings for 37 of 46 items. Again, in our opinion, the results do not support the equivalence of incumbent and analyst ratings. Without further research, we cannot say whether one source of information (incumbent or analyst) is superior to another, either overall or for specific types of descriptors.

Data collection to populate the O*NET database with complete incumbent-provided data continues. The data used for the initial version of O*NET consisted of job analyst ratings of O*NET descriptors based on information contained in the DOT. In 2001, data collection designed to replace the job analyst ratings began. This involves having job incumbents in various occupations complete O*NET surveys. The goal of O*NET is to collect such survey data on 200 occupations each year, with the database being updated every 5 years. In addition, a Spanish-language version of O*NET is available.

The design of O*NET is innovative and the data can be accessed through a computer database via the Internet. Much more detailed information about the status of the data collection and other tools can be found online at http://www.onetcenter.org/. For example, the surveys used to collect the job incumbent data are available at the O*NET Web site and can be downloaded and used by anyone. Thus, if a job analyst needs to collect data on jobs not in the O*NET database, the O*NET surveys can be administered to the appropriate incumbents (or used by a trained analyst).

The content model, that is, the set of descriptors, is excellent in our view. However, there are at least two potential limitations in O*NET. First, there is significant expense and difficulty in collecting and updating the data to be contained in O*NET. There currently appears to be sufficient federal government support for the data collection effort designed to replace the job analyst ratings. Yet, for O*NET to remain viable over time, periodic updates are essential. Second, beyond the evaluation provided by the pilot study, there has been relatively little published evaluation of the O*NET. Although there has been some initial evaluation (Eggerth, Bowles, Tunick, & Andrew, 2005; Hadden, Kravets, & Muntaner, 2004) and uses of O*NET for specific purposes (for example, Converse, Oswald, Gillespie, Field, & Bizot, 2004; Jeanneret & Strong, 2003), much more research is needed. It is essential that the O*NET be scrutinized so that its limitations are understood and addressed. Despite its limitations, the *DOT* benefited from the many years of research conducted on it. Unless there is a body of empirical, peer-reviewed research, O*NET may never replace the *DOT* as an accepted source of information about jobs in the United States. Given its potential for enhancing the management of jobs and people across the whole economy, we believe further development and evaluation of O*NET would be a wise investment.

Chapter Summary

In this chapter, we described three hybrid methods of job analysis, the combination job analysis method, the Multimethod Job Design Questionnaire, and the Occupational Information Network. All three methods require that multiple attributes of jobs be studied. In terms of process, C-JAM uses a fixed or standard set of procedures, but the items are different for each job that is analyzed. The MJDQ uses a given or standard set of items for completion. O*NET uses some standard items, but also some items that change from occupation to occupation. In terms of purpose, C-JAM was intended primarily for selection and training, which are two of the most common uses of job analysis information by industrial and organizational psychologists. The MJDQ was developed to describe a job in terms of design features that result in different work outcomes, such as job satisfaction, efficiency, and comfort. O*NET was designed to replace the *DOT*, so its main applications are matching people to jobs and describing the content of jobs. In addition, O*NET may be much more useful for comparing jobs on multiple attributes than is the *DOT*. In all, the methods presented in this chapter are something of a mixed bag. However, they help to cover many of the purposes for which job analysis information is collected.

5

Management and Teams

The previous three chapters have been devoted to work-oriented methods, worker-oriented methods, and hybrid methods, respectively. All of the methods of job analysis in those chapters are suited for a broad variety of jobs. In this chapter, we describe more specialized methods of analysis that are targeted toward specific types of jobs. In the first half of the chapter, we describe the *Management Position Description Questionnaire* (MPDQ), which (surprise!) is used to analyze managerial jobs. We also discuss the practice of competency modeling, which is a newer form of work analysis typically targeted at managerial and leadership positions. The second half of the chapter is devoted to analyzing the work of teams.

Although there are other methods for analyzing managerial jobs, we chose the Management Position Description Questionnaire for inclusion in this chapter because it appears to be the most comprehensive in scope. We also chose it because it was one of the first job analysis methods developed with software that allows the results of the job analysis to be displayed and used directly for purposes such as job evaluation and performance appraisal. We discuss competency modeling because it has become extremely popular in the business community, but there exists considerable confusion about exactly what it is and how it differs from more traditional job analysis methods. We hope to clarify what competency modeling is and how it fits in (or doesn't!) with the larger work analysis literature.

For the section on job analysis for teams, we present three different sets of descriptors for teams. The first set of descriptors concerns job design. We describe both input and process features that are believed to influence the success of teams. Next we describe the knowledge, skills, and abilities (KSAs) that team members should have to be effective as part of any team. The third set of descriptors concerns team functions. Team functions are things that all teams need to do to reach their goals. For example, teams have to maintain member motivation.

The last part of the chapter is devoted to the *MAP system* (multiphase analysis of performance system). The MAP system is a method of analyzing the work of teams that shows how the team attains its goal and how the work of individuals within the team relates to the work of other individuals within the team. We provide a simple illustration of how the MAP system can be used to develop team training.

Management and Leadership

In this section, we discuss analyzing managerial jobs. Such jobs usually involve the supervision of other people. For example, in the comics section of many newspapers, we see Dagwood Bumstead's boss kicking Bumstead's chair to wake him up and get him back to work. Other examples of discord between supervisor and subordinate can be found in such comic strips as Beetle Bailey and Dilbert. Managerial jobs also involve functions such as deciding what the business should do. For example, a company near us makes aircraft instruments such as altimeters (What's our altitude?) and vertical speed indicators (How fast are we falling?). Management has decided recently to expand beyond conventional mechanical devices to use electronics for displays, thus illustrating a major decision about the strategy of the business.

Managerial jobs present challenges for job analysis. For one thing, many important managerial tasks are difficult to observe. A case in point is the decision to expand from mechanical to electronic instrument manufacture. One can observe a manager collecting data and informing others of a decision, but the actual decision is primarily mental and therefore difficult or impossible to observe. Some activities that are observable are not very informative. For example, we may observe a manager reading a report or examining a spreadsheet, but that doesn't tell us what information the manager is extracting, what the manager is doing with it, or why it's interesting. Therefore, it is difficult for observers to describe many managerial tasks.

There are other challenges as well. On the interpersonal side, it is difficult to specify what the manager does in behavioral terms. It is usually easier to describe the objectives or goals of the interpersonal interactions than to describe what the manager actually does. For example, it is easier to say that the goal of performance appraisal is to provide performance feedback than it is to describe what the manager is actually doing during a performance review (listening, speaking, pointing, shouting, jumping up and down, warding off blows . . .).

We do not mean to imply that the analysis of managerial jobs is impossible. Even if mental work is more difficult to observe than is physical work, the content of the work can still be described in terms of tasks. It may have occurred to you that cognitive task analysis (which you relished in Chapter 3) might be applied profitably to the headwork involved in managerial jobs.

If one were to attempt to analyze many different managerial jobs in terms of functions, however, one would soon realize that managerial jobs differ in the actual behavioral content and task expertise depending on the nature of the work supervised. For example, although the functions are similar, the content of the actual work of the manager of a grocery store is different from that of the branch manager of a bank.

There are several functional or role-oriented analyses of managerial work. The simplest of these comes from the Ohio State University leadership work and concerns the broad-level functions of consideration (person centered) and initiating structure (task centered) (for example, Halpin & Winer, 1957; Hemphill & Coons, 1957). A more elaborate analysis based on roles was developed by Mintzberg (1973). Fleishman, Mumford, Zaccaro, Levin, Korotkin, and Hein (1991) summarized the history of taxonomic efforts in the description of leader behavior and offer their own 13-dimension model, which includes the four superordinate dimensions of information search and structuring, information use in problem solving, managing personnel resources, and managing material resources. Borman and Brush (1993) offered a four-factor model based on data from prior studies. Their model covers interpersonal skills, leading others, administrative skills, and instrumental personal behavior. Other trait-based systems are used in managerial assessment centers (business simulations used for selection and training; see Heneman & Judge, 2003). Although these kinds of systems are widely applicable, they are not associated with any specific job content or a structured, standardized job analysis procedure. It is a challenge to describe managerial jobs in ways that are both behavioral and general enough to apply to a large number of jobs. The method that we describe attempts to analyze a broad range of managerial and executive jobs in common behavioral terms.

DEVELOPMENT AND STRUCTURE OF THE MANAGEMENT POSITION DESCRIPTION QUESTIONNAIRE

Page (1988) cited the work of Hemphill (1960) and Tornow and Pinto (1976) as being influential in the development of the Management Position Description Questionnaire (MPDQ). Hemphill had about 90 executives respond to about 575 items in order to describe their jobs. There were problems in the analysis of his data due to having more items than people. Tornow and Pinto expanded on Hemphill's work by including statements relevant to supervisory as well as executive positions; that is, they moved from the top of the organization down the management hierarchy to include more jobs. Page described the thorough development of the MPDQ at Control Data Corporation subsequent to Tornow and Pinto's work. The development was reported to take about 10 years; during that time various versions of the questionnaire were given to more than 7,500 managers (Page, 1988).

Like many of the job analysis instruments we have described, the MPDQ uses quantitative responses to standard items for the analysis of the job. The MPDQ was designed to use managers' self-reports of their jobs. Such self-reports have obvious advantages and disadvantages. Advantages include speed, lower cost of administration, and that the source of information is the person who knows the job best. An obvious disadvantage is that if the results are used for job evaluation (see Chapter 7), it will be in the incumbent's financial interest to present a puffed-up picture of the job.

Items in the final version of the MPDQ were chosen from a large pool of items based on analyses of managers' answers to the items. Items that remained in the MPDQ proved useful in identifying the managerial level of the job. The items also provided information useful for developing job evaluation dimensions; performance appraisal dimensions; job descriptions; and knowledge, skills, abilities, and other characteristics (KSAOs). Last, the chosen items were clear and easily understood. A description of the MPDQ's sections is shown in Table 5.1.

As you can see from Table 5.1, the major contents of managerial and executive work are summarized by the MPDQ. The main things that managers and executives do might be described as headwork, paperwork, and people-work. Under headwork, or cognitive tasks, we have such areas as decision making, planning and organizing, controlling, and consulting and innovating. Such tasks have a very strong intellectual requirement. People who hate thinking long and hard will be unhappy with this kind of work. Under paperwork, we have administering, and to a smaller extent, controlling. Such tasks require keeping accurate and timely records. For peoplework, the MPDQ lists supervising, contacts, coordinating, and representing. Each of these categories of behavior requires interpersonal skills to be effective.

There is also a section that lists more than 30 KSAs, that is, what is required by the job rather than describing what managers do. Selected KSAs from the MPDQ include leadership, planning, human relations/sensitivity, oral expression, information management, and professional/technical knowledge (Page, 1988, p. 875). The KSAs in the MPDQ parallel the task dimensions of the MPDQ. One can imagine other attributes that might be useful in managerial work that are not tapped by the MPDQ. For example, managerial work often requires that incumbents accept responsibility for decisions that do not work out. For another, managerial work often requires resistance to stress of various kinds, such as time pressure or tolerance of financial risk.

Response Scales

For most of the items in the MPDQ, the incumbent responds to a scale such as the following (Page, 1998, p. 864):

0 = Definitely not part of the position
1 = Minor significance to the position
2 = Moderate significance to the position
3 = Substantial significance to the position
4 = Crucial significance to the position

Table 5.1   Structure and Content of the MPDQ

MPDQ Section	Illustrative Content	Number of Items
1. General Information	Name and title. Description of HR and financial responsibilities.	16
2. Decision Making	Complexity of decisions. Make final and mostly irreversible decisions.	22
3. Planning and Organizing	Long-range planning. Choice of business activities.	27
4. Administering	Record keeping. Documentation. Send requisitions.	21
5. Controlling	Analyze projects. Analyze budgets.	17
6. Supervising	Schedule subordinate activities. Coach subordinates on technical aspects.	24
7. Consulting and Innovating	Contribute special expertise to specific problems. (Usually done by technical experts such as lawyers or industrial psychologists.)	20
8. Contacts	Type of individual contacted and purpose of contacts. (See the matrix example in Table 5.2.)	16
9. Coordinating	Cross existing organizational boundaries to coordinate efforts of others that are not under the incumbent's control.	18
10. Representing	Sell or market products. Negotiate contracts.	21
11. Monitoring Business Indicators	Review information on local market or U.S. economy (usually executive function).	19
12. Overall Ratings	Estimate importance and time spent in categories described by the MPDQ.	10
13. Knowledge, Skills, and Abilities	Estimate proficiency required by the job in each KSA or competency.	31
14. Organization Chart	Attach copy of organizational chart showing location of focal job in relation to other supervisory jobs.	1
15. Comments and Reactions	Provide feedback on the questionnaire.	7

SOURCE: Adapted from Page, R. C. (1988). Management Position Description Questionnaire. In S. Gael (Ed.), *The job analysis handbook for business, industry, and government* (Vol. II, pp. 861–879). New York: Wiley. Reprinted by permission of John Wiley & Sons, Inc.

These are the instructions to the incumbent to rate significance:

> Indicate how significant each activity is to your position by entering a number between 0 and 4 in the column next to it. Remember to consider both its importance in light of all other position activities and frequency of occurrence. (Page, 1988, p. 864)

Note that the significance scale is not defined precisely. Presumably, a task would be significant if it were either important to the job or frequent in occurrence. However, it would be reasonable to expect different people to judge differently the significance of a single task. A few other response scales are used as well, including a scale for the nature of the decision-making role and a scale for the importance of functions in the overall ratings section. The contacts section provides a matrix in which the manager places a number indicating significance into each box (see Table 5.2). In Table 5.2, the matrix for internal contacts is shown. There is another similar matrix for external contacts.

RESEARCH AND APPLICATIONS OF THE MPDQ

The MPDQ has been used for several different applications, including job evaluation, job design, training and development, performance appraisal, staffing, and job description. We briefly describe a few of these applications. There has also been some research on the reliability of the MPDQ and its value for job evaluation, which we also describe.

The MPDQ contains more than 250 items and takes about 2.5 hours to complete for the average incumbent (Page, 1988). Not surprisingly, the first order of the day is to reduce the quantity of information into fewer, more manageable numbers of scales. The data from the items have been combined into scales using both data-based and judgmental methods. The specific dimensions differ depending on the intended use of the MPDQ.

Management Work Factors

One set of dimensions was labeled *management work factors* (see Table 5.3). This set of dimensions was derived mainly from a kind of data analysis called *factor analysis* that places similar items into groups or clusters called factors (this is discussed a bit more in Chapter 9, on doing job analysis). The management work factors are used mainly to help distinguish jobs based on clusters of relatively independent contents. An illustration of the use of the dimensions can be seen in Figure 5.1, in which a specific job is compared with the average of a group of similar managers.

Because the MPDQ is proprietary, we have created simplified graphs that do not present all the information shown by the MPDQ. They do, however, illustrate the kind of presentation possible. As can be seen in Figure 5.1, several of the work dimensions are listed. Each bar graph shows the levels of significance

Table 5.2   Internal Contacts Section of the MPDQ

	Purpose of Contact		
Internal Contacts	Share information regarding past, present, or anticipated activities or decisions	Influence others to act or decide in a manner consistent with your objectives	Direct the plans, activities or decisions of others
1. Executives	4	4	2
2. Group managers (managers report to position)			
3. Managers (supervisors report to position)			
4. Supervisors (no supervisors report to position)			
5. Professional/ Administrative (exempt)			
6. Clerical or support staff (nonexempt)			
7. Other nonexempt employees			

SOURCE: Adapted from Page, R. C. (1988). Management Position Description Questionnaire. In S. Gael (Ed.), *The job analysis handbook for business, industry, and government* (Vol. II, pp. 861–879). New York: Wiley. Reprinted by permission of John Wiley & Sons, Inc.

for each work dimension. The target position (our manager, Jane Doe) is represented by a solid bar; a reference group of managers (for example, other human resources managers) is represented by a light bar. Figure 5.1 shows that the target manager finds planning and organizing less significant than the average manager, decision making and administering to be about the same as the average manager, and consulting and innovating more significant than does the average manager. Such a graph allows you to see at a glance both where the target manager has the most significant involvement and how the target manager relates to a comparison group of managers.

Table 5.3   Work Factors of the MPDQ

1. *Decision Making*. Evaluating information and options; taking appropriate considerations into account in making decisions; making decisions that might have a substantial impact on the organization.

2. *Planning and Organizing*. Formulating long-term and short-term plans, including planning long-range objectives, business activities, and strategic business plans as well as short-range planning and scheduling, such as planning the design, development, production, and/or delivery of products/services.

3. *Administering*. Preparing and maintaining records or documents; monitoring and implementing action to ensure compliance with policies and regulations; obtaining and distributing information; providing staff services to management.

4. *Controlling*. Controlling and adjusting the allocation of human, financial, and material resources; requisitioning materials, equipment, or services; establishing expense controls.

5. *Consulting and Innovating*. Applying advanced techniques to address unique problems, issues, or questions; providing decision makers with crucial inputs; identifying and developing new products or markets; keeping up to date with the latest technical developments.

6. *Coordinating*. Coordinating with other units to achieve organizational goals; directing and integrating the efforts of others over whom you exercise no direct control; negotiating for organizational resources; handling conflict or disagreements when necessary.

7. *Representing*. Interacting with groups/individuals, such as customers, suppliers, government and community representatives, stockholders, and applicants; promoting or selling the organization's products or services; negotiating contracts or terms.

8. *Monitoring Business Indicators*. Monitoring key business indicators, such as total net income, sales volume, international business and economic trends, and competitors' product lines and services.

SOURCE: Adapted from Page, R. C. (1988). Management Position Description Questionnaire. In S. Gael (Ed.), *The job analysis handbook for business, industry, and government* (Vol. II, pp. 861–879). New York: Wiley. Reprinted by permission of John Wiley & Sons, Inc.

Job Evaluation Factors

The MPDQ has also been used extensively for job evaluation. The dimensions used for job evaluation are described in Table 5.4; they also appear in Figure 5.2. Job evaluation points shown in Figure 5.2 provide an estimate of

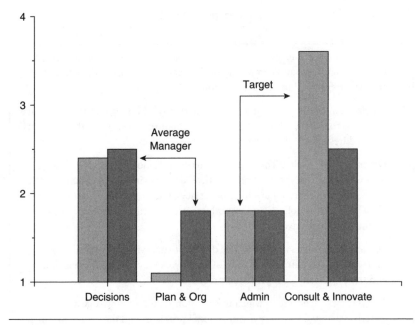

Figure 5.1   Individual Position Profile Adapted From the MPDQ

the value of the job to the company. These can be converted into salary levels as will be described in Chapter 7. The dimensions were initially developed through expert judgment. Later work changed some items to make them more applicable to a wide variety of jobs and organizations. We mentioned earlier that using the MPDQ for job evaluation might cause problems because self-reports are used. The evidence to date for its use, however, is actually quite positive. Page (1988) reported several different studies in which MPDQ responses were used to predict salary grade levels for various jobs. Correlations between actual and MPDQ-predicted salary grade levels were all high, ranging from .79 to .96. People at Control Data who were the users of the MPDQ job evaluation system found it preferable to other systems that the company used.

Computer Use

The MPDQ was one of the first computerized job analysis systems. The system produced professional quality customized reports and graphics. Simplified examples of the kind of reports available can be seen in Figures 5.1 and 5.2. As you can imagine, there is a great saving in time and energy realized when respondents input data directly to the computer, which will then compute, display, and print any desired report. The MPDQ can also create tailored

Table 5.4   Job Evaluation Dimensions of the MPDQ

---

1. *Decision Making.* The level of authority in making decisions, considering the nature, magnitude, and complexity of the decisions as well as the amount of autonomy exercised in making decisions.

2. *Problem Solving.* The level of analytical or creative thinking required to resolve problems that arise, taking into account the nature and scope of the problems to be addressed and the inventiveness of the solutions.

3. *Organizational Impact.* The magnitude of organizational impact, including the extent to which the position is critical for achieving organizational goals, developing or delivering products or services, creating strategic or business plans, developing policies and procedures, and meeting revenue, profit, and performance objectives.

4. *Human Resource Responsibility.* The degree of supervisory responsibility as measured by the number and level of employees reporting to the position, and the complexity of supervision provided.

5. *Know-How.* The degree to which the position requires knowledge and expertise that will solve key organizational problems and the degree to which this knowledge and expertise must be applied to special problems, issues, questions, or policies facing the organization.

6. *Contacts.* The scope and level of internal and external contacts defined by the level of the contact, the purpose of the contact, and the frequency with which contacts are made.

SOURCE: Adapted from Page, R. C. (1988). Management Position Description Questionnaire. In S. Gael (Ed.), *The job analysis handbook for business, industry, and government* (Vol. II, pp. 861–879). New York: Wiley. Reprinted by permission of John Wiley & Sons, Inc.

performance appraisal forms so that those items that were endorsed as most significant by the manager under given dimensions will appear on the appraisal form along with the dimension descriptions.

Reliability

There have been several different kinds of estimates of the reliability of the responses to the MPDQ. Because it takes so long to complete, fatigue might be an issue. To explore this, one study examined the consistency of responses to items that were deliberately repeated in the questionnaire and found the median item reliability to be .83. This indicates good response consistency at

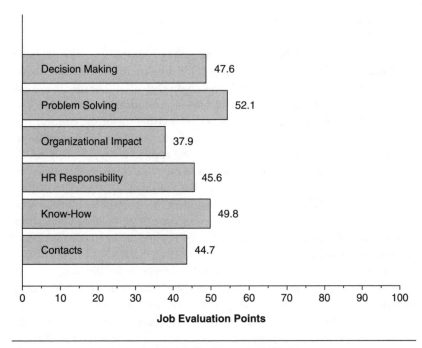

Figure 5.2   Job Evaluation Graph Similar to the MPDQ

least for most items. Agreement between different people reporting on the same job has been much lower. For example, when incumbents and their managers were asked to complete MPDQs for the incumbents' jobs, the median item reliability was about .40. Furthermore, managers who completed a short form of the MPDQ and repeated the short form about 3 months later showed a median item reliability of .55. On the other hand, when managers and incumbents were asked to complete MPDQs for job evaluation purposes and the reliability of the job evaluation scales (not items) was examined, the reliability was again above .80 (Page, 1988), which is quite good.

SUMMARY OF THE MPDQ

As we stated at the beginning of the chapter, the MPDQ appears comprehensive, with about 250 questions and typically requiring more than 2 hours to complete. Because it is standardized, results can be compared across incumbents and managerial jobs. The MPDQ appears to have several applications, including job descriptions, performance appraisal, and job evaluation. It also has software that allows users to generate professional, custom reports based on the job analysis.

Competency Modeling

A more recent approach to understanding managerial jobs has occurred under the broad label of "competency modeling." At the core of competency modeling is the notion of managerial or leadership competencies. The idea that competencies are important for success (as opposed to more cognitive attributes) was articulated by McClelland (1973). Despite criticisms of the concept (for example, Barrett & Depinet, 1991), a focus on managerial or leadership competencies has become quite prominent in the applied and consulting realm. The process of identifying competencies and then linking them to a variety of human resource management systems has been termed competency modeling.

Shippmann et al. (2000) found that between 75 and 80 percent of surveyed companies are currently using some form of competency-related application. Given its popularity, it is important to describe some of the major features of competency modeling. Unlike work on the MPDQ, there is no accepted taxonomy of competencies nor is there consensus on methods to use in competency modeling. In addition, there is less published research on competency modeling methods than other forms of work analysis. In fact, competency modeling is primarily practiced by business consultants using proprietary systems. Nonetheless, because of its popularity, we thought it was important to summarize some of the major features of competency modeling. It is important to recognize that what we discuss here is something of a composite of different approaches. Actual results may vary!

As a practice, competency modeling appears to have been given a boost by the influential work of Prahalad and Hamel (1990), who described core competencies of businesses. Their idea was to focus on the essential skills that form the competitive advantage of the business (not the individual). This general idea was taken up by the consulting community and then taken down to the individual level (where job analysis typically is practiced). Competency modeling concerns identifying organizationally valued personal characteristics required of individual employees by jobs or roles. The key idea in competency modeling is to somehow link the specific business strategy to the competencies needed in people to pursue the strategy. Suppose an organization decided it valued innovation (think 3M and Post-it notes or Pfizer and finding the next blockbuster drug like Viagra). Such an organization would want to hire, develop, and reward individuals who possessed competencies—for example, creativity—that enabled them to be innovative. You might find it helpful to think of competency modeling as a search for characteristics that separate the best workers from the rest. Recall that this was also the main question asked by the Job Element Method. Competency modeling practice typically gathers information about such traits across jobs, often across all managerial jobs within an organization; it tends to ignore tasks.

The human attributes identified in competency models tend to be broad, and not linked directly to specific tasks (Jackson & Schuler, 1990; Snow & Snell, 1992). Proponents of competency modeling have suggested that once articulated, competency models can form the foundation for all human resource systems (for example, selection, training, performance management, and so on) across all manner of different jobs in an organization.

Literally hundreds of competencies have been identified in a range of academic and practitioner publications (for a sample, see Bartram, 2005; Borman & Brush, 1993; Boyatzis, 1982; Lucia & Lepsinger, 1999; Spencer & Spencer, 1993; Tett, Guterman, Bleier, & Murphy, 2000). Even the federal government has gotten in on the act, with the U.S. Department of Labor identifying a set of critical competencies in the Secretary's Commission on Achieving Necessary Skills (SCANS) report (http://wdr.doleta.gov/SCANS/), the Office of Personnel Management's set of competencies across occupational groups (http://www.opm.gov/workforceplanning/tools/), and last but not least, the various descriptor domains of O*NET (which some might suggest detail the range of competencies needed for successful job performance).

This proliferation of lists of competencies is a little bewildering. As one example, Bartram (2005) recently described the competency approach utilized by the consulting firm SHL (see Table 5.5). This system includes eight competency factors (dubbed "the Great Eight," no doubt in homage to the Big Five personality factors. Never underestimate the power of a "grabby" label), 20 competencies, and 112 components. Similarly lengthy lists of competencies can be found in any of the above referenced sources. Although achieved through different means, all attempt to describe the breadth of managerial work (similar to the work of Mintzberg, 1973, and Fleishman et al., 1991, noted earlier). Despite the variety of labels across systems, there is considerable overlap among the desirable characteristics. If you are curious about the degree of overlap, we recommend that you compare the work factors of the MPDQ in Table 5.3 to the Great Eight competencies in Table 5.5.

In the interests of scientific parsimony it would be desirable if there could be some way to reconcile these different sets, but given their proprietary nature, such an outcome is unlikely (and unfortunate, in our minds). Consulting organizations have developed their own proprietary dictionaries of fixed sets of competencies that can be applied to a range of jobs or roles. They also provide a means to translate customized sets or others' dictionaries into their own lexicon. Alternately, they offer a means to customize their dictionaries or modify them in the face of newly discovered or company specific competencies.

One of the fundamental problems facing competency modeling is that there is no agreed-on definition of a competency (Shippmann et al., 2000). For example, competencies have been defined as demonstrated knowledge, skills,

Table 5.5   Description of the "Great Eight" Competencies

Competency Label	Description
1. Leading and Deciding	Tells other people what to do. Decides what action to take.
2. Supporting and Cooperating	Works well with other people; team player.
3. Interacting and Presenting	Persuades others; has social confidence and presentation skills.
4. Analyzing and Interpreting	Analyzes problems effectively; comfortable with data.
5. Creating and Conceptualizing	Deals effectively with change. Moves things forward according to the big picture.
6. Organizing and Executing	Plans work to meet objectives; ensures customer satisfaction.
7. Adapting and Coping	Handles pressure and bounces back after setbacks.
8. Enterprising and Performing	Focuses on results. Understands finances.

or abilities (Ulrich, Brockbank, Yeung, & Lake, 1995); a mixture of knowledge, skills, abilities, motivations, beliefs, values, and interests (Fleishman, Wetrogan, Uhlman, & Marshall-Mies, 1995); a motive, trait, skill, aspect of one's self-image or social role, or a body of knowledge (Boyatzis, 1982); a knowledge, skill, ability, or characteristic associated with high performance on a job (Mirabile, 1997); a written description of measurable work habits and personal skills used to achieve work objectives (Green, 1999); and "sets of behaviors that are instrumental in the delivery of desired results or outcomes" (Bartram, Robertson, & Callinan, 2002, p. 7). You may have noticed that academics such as ourselves dwell on definitions, just as statisticians dwell on assumptions of their models. Is this really worth all the time and paper spent, or are authors receiving kickbacks on the sales of aspirin and coffee?

There has been a debate about whether competency modeling is superior to job analysis or whether competency modeling is simply another name for job analysis (for example, Pearlman, 1997). Shippmann et al. (2000) addressed this question by polling experts from a number of different areas to address systematically the similarities and differences between job analysis and competency modeling. Experts were asked to evaluate both job analysis and competency modeling as they are typically used on the following attributes: method of investigation, type of descriptor, procedures for developing descriptor content, level of detail of descriptors, link to business goals and strategies, content review, ranking of descriptor importance, assessment of reliability, process of content revision, and documentation of the procedure. (What a load of work! Maybe you can send them a box of chocolates for their effort.) The gist of their findings was that job analysis was judged superior to competency modeling with one exception: the link to business goals and strategies. Although job analysis tends to do a better job of obtaining the right information, it comes up short on communicating the value of what it does. Both the procedures used and the descriptors used in competency modeling speak to business management in a way that makes clear the value of the information gathered. Competency modeling usually involves a concerted effort to understand the organization's context, strategy, and goals (Shippmann et al., 2000). Furthermore, it usually proceeds to link explicitly the results of the modeling effort with the organization's outcomes of interest.

The use of broader rather than narrower traits may help cope with broader jobs with ill-defined boundaries. On the other hand, job analysis typically is focused on the task performance for a job as the outcome of interest (although the training cycle is an exception; see Chapter 8).

Yet there are well-known problems with more global or holistic judgments about work (Butler & Harvey, 1988). If a competency modeling process involves the identification of numerous abstract competencies, the potential for a misspecified competency model may result. For example, Morgeson, Delaney-Klinger, Mayfield, Ferrara, and Campion (2004) found that global competency ratings were inflated compared to more decomposed task and ability ratings. This could have the effect of producing long lists of "important" competencies even though some might not be so important. Interestingly, research has found that the quality of competency modeling is improved by using more rigorous job analysis techniques (Lievens, Sanchez, & De Corte, 2004). Clearly it would be worth attempting to link traditional job analysis efforts more closely to business goals and strategies. Such a strategy would eliminate the one identified weakness of job analysis while retaining the rigor that is needed when using job analysis to develop human resource systems.

On the other hand, in support of competency modeling we have received information that in-house, proprietary research and development efforts resulted in numerous successful applications of competency modeling, and in more refined specifications of competencies themselves. We look forward to seeing more of this research in rigorous, peer-reviewed outlets.

After all this debate we expect that you may want a description of an actual competency modeling process. Here is an example drawn from a research study conducted by Lievens et al. (2004; study 2 to be exact). These authors relied on subject matter expert (SME) panels to formulate competency models for three jobs—design and manufacturing engineer, technical production operator, and management accountant. A different SME panel was assembled for each job and consisted of a job incumbent, supervisor, human resources (HR) specialist, and internal customer (ideally we would like to have larger SME panels). Familiarity with the focal job and knowledge about the organization's business and human resource strategies were required to be included on an SME panel. To begin, the SMEs completed a half-day training session that familiarized them with the particular competency modeling approach to be used. Each trained participant then received a set of 67 commercially available cards on which were listed a standard set of behaviorally linked competencies, one per card. Their task was to sort the 67 cards into five categories ranging from "essential for success" to "not important." Their sorts had to follow guidelines such that the number of cards falling into each category was fixed and resembled a normal curve with most falling into the middle category and few at the extremes. Although such a "forced distribution" will aid in prioritizing the competencies, this approach has undesirable measurement properties. (The technical term is that this type of rating process produces an ipsative set of scores. This produces dependency in the competency ratings that can pose problems when conducting statistical analyses. There, now you know the rest of the story.) An alternative to this rating process would be to have SMEs simply rate each competency in terms of its importance. Because their analyses were designed to answer research questions and not be used for job analysis purposes, Lievens et al. (2004) do not describe what to do with the SME results. Let us fill in the gap. From this point a number of analytic strategies could be used. One might be to do scale ratings for each card (for example, 1 = essential for success, 5 = not important) and average these to prioritize the competencies. Or the subject matter experts could meet and decide which competencies belonged in what categories.

SUMMARY OF COMPETENCY MODELING

Although you might think of competency modeling as a quick and dirty worker-oriented method of job analysis, its practice is likely here to stay in one form or another. It explicitly addresses the link between business strategy and goals and the attributes needed in the workforce to compete effectively. As such, it addresses a common weakness in job analysis. In addition, it has helped highlight a broader set of attributes that are likely to be helpful when thinking about managerial work, particularly at higher organizational levels. Yet, there are many weaknesses in competency modeling that are not yet addressed in the scientific literature. Research has begun to investigate and improve competency modeling, but much more needs to be done. Or, where in-house proprietary research has been done, it needs to appear in rigorously reviewed scientific publications. These recommendations are particularly crucial in light of potential legal challenges to human resource management systems built upon a competency modeling approach.

Job Analysis for Teams

People are limited in what they can do individually. However, when people organize and work together in harmony, there is virtually no limit to what can be accomplished. Also, many tasks simply cannot be carried out by a single person. Such tasks include performing a symphony, operating a submarine, and refueling a jet in flight, among many others.

The definition of a team and the difference between a team and a group are slippery concepts that are not universally agreed on. It is useful to think about teams in terms of at least three attributes: (1) multiple people, (2) interdependent work, and (3) a shared goal. To have a team, clearly there must be at least two people (some people say three, but we don't see a compelling reason for this, so never mind). By interdependent work, we mean that the team members' tasks are connected in some important way, and each member has a defined role to play. For example, the surgeon cannot proceed (better not!) until the anesthesiologist has the patient sedated. Or for another example, two programmers may divide the task of writing code for a program, but when the two pieces of code are compiled, they must share data or pass the data properly from one part of the program to the other. In essence, the two pieces of the program have to fit together like two legs on a pair of pants. The shared goal defines the team by establishing its purpose. The shared goal also provides some idea of how to tell the effectiveness of the team. Examples of goals include winning a competition, providing service to a customer, building a machine, and maintaining equipment.

"Why," you wonder, "should we worry about analyzing the work of teams?" Analyzing work for teams serves many of the same functions as it does for jobs. That is, we want to know about selecting people for teams, training teams, compensating teams and team members, and designing jobs for teams. We also analyze the work of teams to reduce a very complex whole into more manageable parts. You might also ask why we cannot simply analyze the jobs of each of the team members instead of analyzing the work of the team as a whole. Well, of course we can and we will, but if that is all we do, then we will lose sight of the forest for the trees. Another analogy is the group of folks describing an elephant: One who examines only a leg says an elephant is like a tree trunk, another who looks only at the trunk says it's like a rope, another who sees only the ear says it's like a giant leaf. Sometimes you need the big picture.

Teams are an increasingly popular type of work organization. There is at present a great deal of interest in business and the military in creating, managing, and evaluating teams of every description (for example, Brannick, Salas, & Prince, 1997; Jones & Schilling, 2000; Wheelan, 1999). Job analysis for teams should be helpful for all these purposes.

Job analysis for teams is similar to job analysis for jobs in that we can think about the same building blocks for teams as for jobs, namely (you guessed it), the descriptors, the methods of data collection, the sources of information, and the units of analysis. We introduce a fifth building block, information storage, retrieval, and dissemination. As you will see, analyzing the work of teams forces us to consider a number of issues that typically do not arise when analyzing single jobs.

JOB DESIGN FOR TEAMS

Most theories of team effectiveness follow an input-process-output model (for example, Dickinson & McIntyre, 1997; Gladstein, 1984; Guzzo & Shea, 1992; for exceptions, see Sundstrom, De Meuse, & Futrell, 1990, and Ilgen, Hollenbeck, Johnson, & Jundt, 2005). The input factors include such items as organizational resources and other contextual factors. The process factors concern what the team actually does, such as communicate. The output factors typically include effectiveness measures (Did they win?) as well as satisfaction with the team (Can the team members stand to work together again?). Campion and his colleagues (Campion, Medsker, & Higgs, 1993; Campion, Papper, & Medsker, 1996) reviewed the literature and compiled a list of factors that they believed could be used to design effective teams. They developed a survey that can be used to measure teams on the characteristics of interest. The factors and a sample item for each factor are shown in Table 5.6.

Four of five factors considered under job design are factors considered in the job characteristics theory (Hackman & Oldham, 1980). The factors from job characteristics theory are autonomy, variety, task identity, and task significance. Self-management in teams is analogous to autonomy in individual jobs. Teams may have formal leaders who are given responsibility and authority to make decisions such as the assignment of tasks and hiring and firing members of the team. As self-management increases, the leader becomes more of a coach than a boss, and in extreme cases, there may be no formal leader; the functions of management are taken over by the team. Participation refers to the degree that all members contribute to team decision making, and it is highly related to self-management. Self-management and participation are thought to help promote feelings of responsibility in team members.

Task variety, task identity, and task significance are all attributes of jobs that are thought to motivate people. A job with variety causes people to develop and use multiple skills. Task identity refers to the work being a whole entity rather

Table 5.6   Team Design Elements

Characteristic	Sample Item
Job Design	
1. Self-management	My team rather than my manager decides who does what tasks within the team.
2. Participation	My team is designed to let everyone participate in decision making.
3. Task variety	Most everyone on my team gets a chance to do the more interesting tasks.
4. Task significance	My team helps me feel that my work is important to the company.
5. Task identity	My team is responsible for all aspects of a product for its area.
Interdependence	
6. Task interdependence	Within my team, jobs performed by team members are related to one another.
7. Goal interdependence	My work goals come directly from the goals of my team.
8. Interdependent feedback and rewards	My performance evaluation is strongly influenced by how well my team performs.
Composition	
9. Heterogeneity	The members of my team vary widely in their areas of expertise.
10. Flexibility	Most members of my team know each other's jobs.
11. Relative size	The number of people in my team is sufficient for the work to be accomplished.
12. Preference for group work	I generally prefer to work as part of a team.
Context	
13. Training	The company provides adequate technical training for my team.
14. Managerial support	Higher management in the company supports the concept of teams.
15. Communication/ cooperation between groups	Teams in the company cooperate to get the work done.

(Continued)

Table 5.6 (Continued)

Process	
16. Potency	My team can take on nearly any task and complete it.
17. Social support	Members of my team help each other out at work when needed.
18. Workload sharing	Everyone on my team does their fair share of the work.
19. Communication/ cooperation within the work group	Members of my team cooperate to get the work done.

SOURCE: Adapted from Campion, M. A. Medsker, G. J. Higgs, A. C. (1993). Relations between work group characteristics and effectiveness: Implications for designing effective work groups. *Personnel Psychology, 46,* 823–850. Adapted by permission of Personnel Psychology.

than a fraction (for example, building a whole car versus just seat covers). Task significance refers to the impact of the work on other people (for example, a surgeon has a significant job). Identity and significance are thought to influence team members' sense that their work is meaningful and important.

The interdependence factors include task and goal interdependence, which are two of our defining properties of teams. The interdependent feedback and rewards concerns the degree to which individual members' feedback and rewards depend on team outcomes. The interdependence of the work will influence the degree to which members feel that they are part of a team. The greater the interdependence, the greater the feeling of being part of a team.

The composition factors refer to the mix of people that belong to the team. *Heterogeneity* refers to the variability of backgrounds in team members in such characteristics as race, sex, and cognitive ability. *Flexibility* refers to the degree to which team members can change their assignments. To be flexible, the team must have the authority to change assignments and the skill by some members to cover the jobs of other members. *Relative size* refers to the number of people relative to the amount of work that needs to be done. As the size of a team increases, coordination demands also increase. According to the theory, there is an optimal size for each team.

The context factors are so labeled because they come from outside the team. *Training* of team members is a support activity provided by management that is intended to increase the effectiveness of the team either through improved task functioning, improved process such as better decision making, or both. *Managerial support* concerns other types of support such as provision of materials and information. *Communication and cooperation* between groups concerns the quality of relations across teams within an organization. The organization may be characterized as relatively cooperative or relatively competitive.

According to input-process-output models of team effectiveness, all of the factors we have described so far fall into the input part of the model. The process factors fall into the process part of the model (surprise!). *Potency* is the team's belief in its own competence. For example, a football team may feel confident that it will win an upcoming game or it may feel that a win would be miraculous. *Social support* refers to team members getting along well interpersonally. *Workload sharing* is the adjustment of work across individuals to avoid slacking by some team members. *Communication and cooperation* within the team refers to passing information among members. The process variables are thought to influence team effectiveness either by motivating team members to work hard and to persist (potency and social support) or by directly increasing the effectiveness of work (workload sharing and communication).

Campion and colleagues developed a survey to measure the properties of teams in organizations. They also measured the effectiveness of teams in several ways. They examined both the productivity of the teams and the satisfaction of the team members with their work. They found that most of the team characteristics were related to most of the outcome measures. This evidence supported their model of team design characteristics.

According to the theory, the factors are supposed to be related to effectiveness and subject to control by management (that is, they can be changed). The research to date, however, deals only with differences in existing teams rather than the results of experiments in which team characteristics were manipulated. Therefore, whether manipulating these factors will result in improved effectiveness remains to be seen. However, this line of research has provided a rich source of descriptors to consider when analyzing the work of teams.

TEAM KNOWLEDGE, SKILLS, AND ABILITIES

As we describe in Chapter 10 on the future of job analysis, many people predict that work in the future will be accomplished by small teams of people who have flexible, dynamic jobs. In that case, it is difficult to analyze specific tasks to infer the required KSAs. One solution to the problem is to select people for *generic* traits that are valuable for a range of jobs. In the case of teams, researchers have developed a list of KSAs thought to be helpful, and even a paper-and-pencil test that attempts to sort people into better and worse prospects for team membership (Stevens & Campion, 1994, 1999).

The list of 14 KSAs for teams is presented in Table 5.7. As you can see, there are two main types of KSAs: interpersonal skills and self-management skills. Both of these main types are further subdivided. Included under interpersonal skills are skill in conflict resolution, problem solving, and communication.

Table 5.7   Generic Teamwork Skills

I. Interpersonal KSAs

  A. Conflict Resolution KSAs

    1. The KSA to recognize and encourage desirable, but discourage undesirable team conflict.

    2. The KSA to recognize the type and source of conflict confronting the team and implement an appropriate resolution strategy.

    3. The KSA to employ an integrative (win-win) negotiation strategy, rather than the traditional distributive (win-lose) strategy.

  B. Collaborative Problem Solving KSAs

    4. The KSA to identify situations requiring participative group problem solving and to utilize the proper degree and type of participation.

    5. The KSA to recognize the obstacles to collaborative group problem solving and implement appropriate corrective actions.

  C. Communication KSAs

    6. The KSA to understand communication networks, and to utilize decentralized networks to enhance communication where possible.

    7. The KSA to communicate openly and supportively, that is, to send messages which are (a) behavior- or event-oriented, (b) congruent, (c) validating, (d) conjunctive and (e) owned.

    8. The KSA to listen nonevaluatively and to appropriately use active listening techniques.

    9. The KSA to maximize the consonance between nonverbal and verbal messages and to recognize and interpret the nonverbal messages of others.

    10. The KSA to engage in small talk and ritual greetings and a recognition of their importance.

II. Self-Management KSAs

  D. Goal Setting and Performance Management KSAs

    11. The KSA to help establish specific, challenging, and accepted team goals.

    12. The KSA to monitor, evaluate, and provide feedback on both overall team performance and individual team member performance.

  E. Planning and Task Coordination KSAs

    13. The KSA to coordinate and synchronize activities, information and tasks between team members.

    14. The KSA to help establish task and role assignments for individual team members and ensure proper balancing of workload.

SOURCE: Reprinted from Stevens, M. J., & Campion, M. A. (1994). The knowledge, skill and ability requirements for teamwork: Implications for human resource management. *Journal of Management, 20,* 503–530, with permission from Elsevier Science.

The self-management skills involve performance management, including goal setting and feedback and planning and task coordination. Take a few minutes to read through the list in the table. Try to imagine a situation that requires each of the KSAs. For example, conflict may be desirable when it concerns the best way to accomplish an agreed-on goal in an atmosphere of trust (for example, "How can we keep our competition from selling to our clients?"). For more on the benefits of conflict, see Amason (1996), Amason, Thompson, Hochwarter, and Harrison (1995), or Nemeth (1992). Conflict is usually not desirable when it is personal or reflects deep differences in values (for example, "I'm going to get you, you stupid #$%*!").

A sample item from the teamwork test is as follows:

> Suppose that you find yourself in an argument with several co-workers about who should do a very disagreeable, but routine task. Which of the following would likely be the most effective way to resolve this situation?
> 1. Have your supervisor decide, because this would avoid any personal bias.
> 2. Arrange for a rotating schedule so everyone shares the chore.
> 3. Let the workers who show up earliest choose on a first-come, first-served basis.
> 4. Randomly assign a person to do the task and don't change it. (Stevens & Campion, 1999, pp. 225–226; the keyed answer for this question is 2)

Researchers have tried using the test to select members for teams. Although there is some support for the idea that the test helps identify better team members, a surprising finding is that scores on the team KSA test were very highly correlated with scores on cognitive ability tests. In other words, the teamwork test pretty much amounts to testing how smart somebody is. Also note that the team KSA test does not assess agreeableness or other personality traits that might be desirable in team members. Research indicates that teamwork KSAs, several personality traits, and social skills contribute uniquely to performance in team environment (Morgeson, Reider, & Campion, 2005), suggesting that teamwork KSAs are only one important part of success in team environments.

We have included the team KSA test here because it is also a rich source of descriptors that may be useful in describing the work of teams, especially some of the interpersonal aspects. The descriptors appear especially useful for self-managed work teams. Many of the descriptors are things that might fall under leadership or management in traditional hierarchical organizations. For example, conflict resolution is something likely to be required of any work group manager.

TEAM FUNCTIONS

As you just saw, teams are likely to require certain kinds of knowledge and skill of their members, regardless of the specific work of the team. Another approach to analyzing the work of teams that is not tied to the specific task content is to analyze team functions that are thought to be generic or universally required. A set of such functions was identified by Nieva, Fleishman, and Reick (1978; see also Fleishman & Zaccaro, 1992). There are five general functions, each of which is divided into two or more specific functions.

1. *Orientation* functions allow team members to know what they are doing, that is, what the team's goal is and what resources they have to achieve the goal. During orientation, the team must also exchange information about environmental features and assess what tasks need to be completed in what order.

2. *Resource distribution* functions allow the team to place people into tasks so that people have work and there is some matching of individual talent to the task requirements.

3. *Timing* functions deal with the patterning of activity within the team. Timing is concerned with the general pace of activities, both for the team and for the individuals.

4. *Coordination* concerns the requirements for patterning of team members' actions.

5. *Motivational* functions deal with team members' level of effort as well as managing conflict among the members. Norms for performance must be developed and adopted. Team rewards need to be established.

Researchers have developed a set of scales so that judges can rate different teams and their functions (Shiflett, Eisner, Price, & Schemmer, 1982). The scales have been used to show differences in requirement profiles for different military teams. The team functions taxonomy has not been widely applied to teams in companies, however. Again, we have provided the list as a rich source of descriptors for analyzing the work of teams. In our view, the team function approach leads to a fairly complete picture of what a team needs to do. It is left for other approaches to describe how the team accomplishes the required functions.

THE MULTIPHASE ANALYSIS OF PERFORMANCE SYSTEM

The multiphase analysis of performance (MAP) system was developed to analyze team tasks primarily for team training (Levine & Baker, 1990; Levine, Brannick, Coovert, & Llobet, 1988). The idea is to start with the team's mission or goal, and then move to the functions that people must fulfill to achieve the goal, and then to the tasks that individuals must fulfill to carry out the functions. Once the tasks are identified, several different types of analyses can be carried out to determine the content of training. The term *MAP* was also chosen in part because of a geographical analogy. One starts with a big picture to locate the general position of the team, and then fills in finer detail as needed to get to where one wants to be in terms of training. The exercise is something like planning a trip from Tampa to a specific street in Detroit. You would start with a country map, move to state maps, and conclude the trip with a city map.

Building Blocks for Team Job Analysis

The MAP system is based on four of the building blocks that you have come to know and love over the course of this book, namely, the descriptors, sources of information, the methods of collecting data, and the units of analysis (we now recognize planning for using the information after the job analysis is important, but that is not part of the original MAP system beyond a final report). Comprehensive lists of each of the building blocks were given in Chapter 1 (see Table 1.3; add "team" to "job" and "worker" as appropriate). Levine and Baker (1990) organized the building blocks for the MAP system in a series of feasible sets that depend on the kind of training to be done. For example, if we are training a team on an entirely new piece of equipment, team members are not feasible sources of information for job analysis data because there are no team members working on the job until after the training. On the other hand, equipment designers or other experts could be used.

The organizing principle used by Levine and Baker to generate the feasible sets was composed of three factors. The first factor was whether the training was intended to be applied to individuals or the team as a whole. For example, even though pilots may fly together as a crew, the pilot training may or may not involve other crew members; some tasks require other members but some do not. The second factor was whether the training was intended primarily for interpersonal relations or primarily for production of products or services, that is, the technical aspects of the job. The third factor was whether the team was mature or immature. By immature teams we do not mean adolescent or giggly; rather, we mean teams that do not have prior experience with the task. Together the three factors create a grid of eight cells for training. For each cell, a subset of building blocks is recommended.

Using Levine and Baker's (1990) example of simulated training for jet fighter pilots, Table 5.8 presents a grid of recommended building blocks for each cell. (The numbers in the cells are taken from Table 1.3 in Chapter 1. Each number refers to a particular building block.) Cell 1, for example, is for providing individual training on interpersonal aspects of teamwork for mature (experienced) team members. Cell 1 lists the feasible descriptors, sources of information, methods of data collection, and units of analysis. Some useful descriptors (D) include physical and psychological demands on team members. Useful sources of information (S) include team members and team trainers. Useful methods of data collection (C) include interviews and questionnaires, and units of data analysis (A) include job dimensions such as leadership behaviors and team member attribute requirements such as assertiveness.

Table 5.8   MAP Building Blocks

	Individual Training	
	From Mature Team	*From Immature Team*
Interpersonal	Cell 1 D: 5,9, 12, 13, 14 S: 4, 6 C: 2, 4 A: 4, 5, 6, 7	Cell 2 D: 5, 9, 12, 13 S: 2, 5, 6 C: 2, 3 A: 4, 5, 6, 7
Production	Cell 3 D: 5, 7, 8, 12, 13 S: 4 C: 2, 4 A: 1, 2, 6, 7	Cell 4 D: 1, 5, 7, 8, 12, 13 S: 2, 5, 6 C: 2, 3, 7 A: 1, 2, 6, 7
	Team Training	
	From Mature Team	*From Immature Team*
Interpersonal	Cell 5 D: 3, 5, 9, 12, 13, 14 S: 2, 4, 5, 6 C: 2, 3 A: 4, 5, 6, 7	Cell 6 D: 3, 5, 9, 12, 13 S: 2, 3, 5, 6, 9 C: 2, 3 A: 4, 5, 6, 7
Production	Cell 7 D: 3, 5, 7, 8, 12, 13, 14 S: 2, 3, 4, 6, 9 C: 2, 4 A: 4, 5, 6, 7	Cell 8 D: 1, 3, 5, 7, 8, 12, 13 S: 2, 3, 5, 6, 9 C: 2, 3 A: 4, 5, 6, 7

SOURCE: Adapted from Levine, E. L., & Baker, C. V. (1990). *Team task analysis: A test of the multiphase analysis of performance (MAP) system.* Contract No DAAL03–86-D-001. Orlando, FL: Naval Training Systems Center. Adapted by permission of the author.

NOTE: D refers to descriptors; S refers to sources of information, C refers to methods of data collection; A refers to units of analysis. Numbers are keyed to Table 1.3.

As we mentioned earlier, the analysis begins with the team's mission and proceeds through increasingly fine-grained phases until the information needed for training is complete. Levine and Baker (1990) illustrated the use of the MAP system by analyzing a laboratory team task in which two people work together to "fly" a microcomputer simulation of a jet fighter. The task was set up so that one of the two people works the joystick and the other works the keyboard. The joystick controls the direction of the jet. The keyboard controls the speed of the jet and the weapons used to fire on an enemy fighter. The task is structured so that neither crew member can complete the task alone; they must work together to achieve their goal, which is to shoot down an enemy fighter.

Levine and Baker (1990) began by considering the type of training that would be most desirable. Because they were dealing with a laboratory task, teams had no prior experience with it, and so the immature teams were chosen (cells 2, 4, 6, and 8) as the most relevant. Then production training was chosen as the most relevant (cells 4 and 8) for the demonstration.

Descriptors

The descriptors that they chose correspond to the numbers 1, 3, 5, 7, and 12 (see Table 1.3 for an explanation of these numbers). To conserve space, we will mention only those items most directly connected to teams. The second item in the list (item 3) was responsibilities and mission of the team and team members. The first goal of the analysis was to determine the main goal or mission of the team. In this case, the mission was to shoot down an enemy jet. After the mission is established, the functions of the team members should be discovered and described in a general fashion as they contribute to reaching the team mission. In our example, one member steers the jet in position to lock on target and holds it there. Then the other member fires the weapons, and so forth.

The fourth item (item 7) was machines, tools, work aids, and equipment. This will be a major item in equipment-intensive tasks such as the current one. The analysis should focus on the computer, joystick, keyboard, maps, head-phones, and other machines and tools that are part of the job. In a typical job analysis (not for teams), all the mechanical devices refer to the target job. In job analysis for teams, however, there needs to be some indication of the relations between the mechanical items and each of the team members. In our case, only one member uses the joystick, but both use headphones.

The fifth and final descriptor they chose was team and team member tasks and activities (item 12). Levine and Baker (1990) developed a list of tasks and activities for each team member by gathering a panel of subject matter experts (SMEs), who were directed to develop a task inventory (see Chapter 2). In the development of the inventory, the SMEs were reminded of the overall mission and the functions that are relevant to the accomplishment of the mission. Then each function was broken into a series of tasks by individual position. For example, for the joystick position, the aiming function was broken into search, approach, and maintain (lock) steps. The first two steps involve interpreting information displayed by radar, but the third involves interpreting information displayed through and on the cockpit window.

Flowcharts and Time Charts

Team members are connected to one another by the work. Teamwork always involves coordination of task performance through sequence (for example, imagine a bucket brigade in which each person passes a bucket of water to the next until the last person douses a fire), simultaneity (for example, in an orchestra, different musicians must play different notes at the same time), or both. Sequence may involve physical things as in auto assembly, or it may involve the passage of information as in air traffic control, where one controller "hands off" an aircraft to another controller. Simultaneity can involve physical effort such as when multiple people have to pull together to remove a tank tread. It can also involve sending information through multiple channels such as two different types of radio, one for signaling an emergency and one for transmitting speech. A flowchart can diagram the teamwork necessary to accomplish a task.

An example of a flowchart is shown in Figure 5.3 (Levine & Baker, 1990). In this flowchart, actions (task performance) are shown in rectangles and decisions are shown in diamonds. The sequence of activities is shown by arrows. Thus, one of the main descriptors associated with flowcharts is the relations among actions. That is, the flowchart tells us whether one action precedes another. Flowcharts also allow us to illustrate loops or repetitive sequences of actions. For example, if we fire at the enemy and miss, then we try again.

Time charts can also be useful for understanding a work process. An example of such a chart is shown in Figure 5.4. Typically, three people are needed to operate a tank. One person drives the tank to put it in proper position for action (see the top line in Figure 5.4). A second person decides on a target and what type of ammunition to use (the line second from the top). A third person aims and fires the main gun (the third line in Figure 5.4). A couple of points are worth noting in this example. First, each arrow represents one activity. Time is represented as a line passing from left to right. Therefore, sequences of activities are shown as sets of arrows pointing from left to right. The three different arrow heights indicate how the task is typically done by the three crew members. Such a representation is much like a musical score used by the conductor of an orchestra. It shows all that is done, and how the parts relate to one another through time. Such charts are helpful in understanding how the work is done and in thinking about how to change the work to make it more effective or efficient.

In a musical score, there is little discretion in terms of timing—all the notes are shown in temporal relations to one another. However, in representations such as Figure 5.4, some of the relations are fixed, but others can be changed. For example, one has to decide on the type of ammunition and load it before firing, so the relations among these tasks are rigid. On the other hand, one can aim the tank before, during, or after maneuvering it, so the relations among maneuvering and aiming are flexible. It is possible to mark graphs such as Figure 5.4 in such a way to show which relations are rigid and which are flexible.

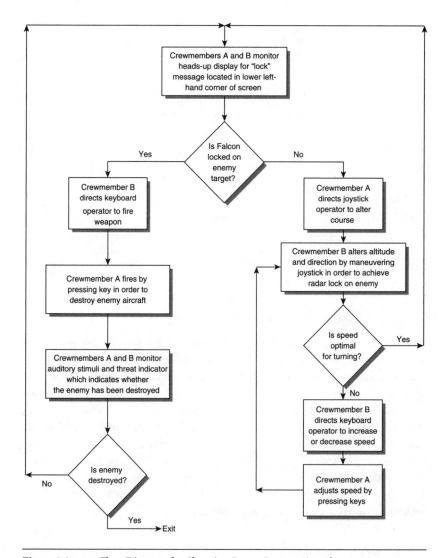

Figure 5.3   Flow Diagram for Shooting Down Enemy Aircraft

SOURCE: Adapted from Levine, E. L., & Baker, C. V. (1990). *Team task analysis: A test of the multiphase analysis of performance (MAP) system.* Contract No DAAL03–86-D-001. Orlando, FL: Naval Training Systems Center. Adapted by permission of the author.

Flowcharts and time charts are valuable not only for team training. They can be used for the design of team tasks (Dieterly, 1988) and for inferring ability requirements (Mallamad, Levine, & Fleishman, 1980) that might be used for selection as well.

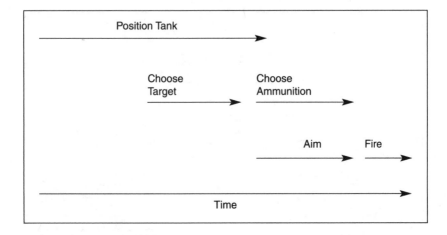

Figure 5.4   Time Flow Diagram for the Process of Firing a Tank's Main Gun

Sources and Methods of Data Collection

Before we began describing the beauty and wonder of flowcharts and diagrams, we were describing the Levine and Baker (1990) study that analyzed a simulated air combat mission. Let us resume thinking about that study, and specifically, about the sources of information and methods of data collection they used. The feasible sources of information included officers/supervisors, high-ranking officials, experts, trainers, and written documents. The people actually used in the study to provide information were experts and trainers. The feasible methods of data collection included observation, interviews, technical conferences, review of relevant documents, and doing the work (if feasible). They watched experts perform the job, interviewed experts, and called a technical conference to develop a task inventory.

Ratings (Units of Analysis)

Levine and Baker (1990) recommended that the task generation meeting should have a goal of 12 to 15 team functions and at least 50 individual position tasks. The position tasks should be listed hierarchically under the functions. After the tasks have been generated and organized, another meeting of SMEs is called to generate the KSAOs needed to complete each task successfully (note that these steps are very similar to C-JAM, described in Chapter 4). After the list of tasks and KSAOs are completed and revised as necessary, they can be rated by SMEs to provide information used in specifying the training content.

Each task should be rated for both difficulty to learn and criticality. The ratings can be analyzed later to provide a composite index of importance for training. The KSAOs should be rated on two factors. The first factor is whether the attribute is essential in new team members. The second factor is whether the given KSAO distinguishes the superior from the average team member.

Data Analysis

Once the ratings are completed for each task and KSAO (difficulty to learn, criticality, KSAOs essential to new workers, and distinguishes average from superior), summary statistics can be computed for each task and KSAO. The summary statistics can then be presented to those responsible for developing the actual training. We would expect tasks that are rated higher on criticality and difficulty to learn, and KSAOs rated higher on distinguishing average from superior performance to be good candidates for training. Typically, there is a fair amount of judgment in the final decisions about what to train. These decisions also depend on other factors such as the amount of time and money available for the training program.

Storing and Retrieving Information

At the end of the job analysis, a report will be written that documents the process and outcomes (for example, task inventory and ratings) of the analysis. Job experts will be invited to review the report for accuracy and completeness. Any necessary revisions will be made at this time. Although Levine and Baker (1990) did not consider this issue beyond filing a final report, we know now that it is an important concern. Much of the work on job analysis is very applied, and so, even though it is very useful, it is not easy to publish and so it is hard to retrieve. Putting such a report on the World Wide Web would make it much more accessible (for example, see O*NET; the address is listed in Chapter 4). Also, data can be organized into a database that might allow retrieval of information about the individual positions or the team as a whole.

Chapter Summary

THE MPDQ

The Management Position Description Questionnaire was designed to analyze managerial and executive jobs for multiple purposes, including job evaluation, job description, performance appraisal, and job design. The MPDQ was developed and refined over several years to be useful in a wide variety of jobs. The items of the MPDQ are largely behavioral in nature, although there is a section on managerial KSAOs as well. The instrument is completed by the job incumbent. The rating scales for the MPDQ are not precise and require the responses of several incumbents to describe a job reliably at the item level.

The MPDQ features a useful array of software that allows the results to be tailored to the user's purposes.

COMPETENCY MODELS

Competency modeling focuses on describing a set of (most frequently) managerial attributes that are specifically linked to an organization's business strategy and goals. It has been well received in the business community, but there are a number of potential shortcomings associated with its use. Combining elements of a competency modeling approach with more rigorous job analysis procedures is likely to result in a more useful and valid competency model.

TEAMS

We provided snapshots of four different approaches to understanding the work of teams. The first approach was job design for teams. Researchers reviewed the literature to identify aspects of teams that might be controlled and that contribute to team effectiveness. The factors were organized into five main clusters. The first of the clusters was labeled job design, and included factors comparable to those in the job characteristics for motivation literature such as task variety and task significance. The second set of factors (labeled interdependence) are those that distinguish teams from groups, namely, task interdependence, goal interdependence, and feedback and reward interdependence. The third set of factors was labeled composition, and included such characteristics as heterogeneity or diversity and relative size. The fourth set of factors was labeled context, and included such factors as training and managerial support. The fifth and final set of factors was labeled process, and included such factors as potency, the belief of a team about its own capacity to accomplish its mission, and social support.

We next described the team KSA approach. In this approach, the work of teams is thought to depend on two classes of generic skills. One class of skills concerns interpersonal relations. Team members need to know how to resolve conflicts, collaborate on work-related problems, and communicate effectively. The other class of skills concerns . . . both planning and organizing one's own work and managing the connected or cooperative part of the work.

The third approach involved examining functions that teams fulfill to achieve their goals. For the orientation functions, team members need to exchange information about the team's goal and about the members' resources and constraints. The resource distribution functions take care of assigning tasks to the members so that there is some balance of the work across members and members are assigned work that is appropriate for their skills. Timing functions help the team set a good pace for the work. Response coordination functions are used to achieve proper patterning of task performance. Motivational functions help to establish norms of behavior in the team and to reinforce individual contributions toward the team's goal.

The fourth and final approach that we described was the MAP system. The idea in the MAP system is to start with the team's mission and proceed through increasingly detailed phases to develop team training of various sorts. The system provides an organizing principle based on the type of team and the type of training desired that resulted in a feasible set of building blocks for each analysis. We then reviewed a trial of the MAP system using a two-person microcomputer flight simulator. The illustration showed specific descriptors, methods of collecting data, sources of data, and units of analysis. Of particular interest were flowcharts and time charts, which may be particularly useful for understanding the work of teams.

The last issue we considered was storing and retrieving information about job and team analysis. Use of the World Wide Web or other computer networks offers a solution to the problem of accessibility.

6

Job Analysis and the Law

A s you now know, job analysis forms the basis for most human resources approaches to employment practice. Employment practices sometimes result in lawsuits and court cases, so it is not too surprising that job analysis is often linked to legal battles. In this chapter, we take a peek at the battlefield and the combatants. Although laws regulating employment practices exist in many other countries, our chapter covers only the legal system in the United States. And even more specifically, only the U.S. Constitution, federal laws, and executive orders are covered. The chapter is divided into two parts, the first of which is about legislation and regulations. We begin by mentioning constitutional law, and then key pieces of U.S. federal employment legislation, including the Equal Pay Act, the Civil Rights Acts, the Age Discrimination in Employment Act, the Rehabilitation Act, and the Americans with Disabilities Act. Together, these laws regulate much of what employers can and cannot do in terms of hiring, promoting, paying, and otherwise treating employees. We must note that U.S. states, counties, and cities also have their own applicable constitutions and laws. Often these mirror those at the federal level. However, we could not do justice (no pun intended) to all of the state and local laws, so we are sticking to the most widely applicable ones—the federal laws. Human resource managers know quite well that they must also be aware of state and local regulations.

We then turn to the enforcement of the laws and provide an overview of the court system and the Equal Employment Opportunity Commission (EEOC). Professional standards also act like laws in regulating what professionals do when they practice. Therefore, we conclude the first section of the chapter with a description of professional standards from the American Psychological Association and the Society for Industrial and Organizational Psychology that bear on job analysis.

In the second section, we describe how the laws and standards are linked to job analysis. We have included sections on personnel selection, pay, and job design. Although the laws, guidelines, and professional standards themselves make for some pretty dry reading, there is good reason for interest in the legal aspects of employment practice. Companies, government agencies, labor unions, and employment agencies that fail to comply with employment law may treat individuals unfairly and at the same time expose themselves to severe legal penalties. Let us apologize in advance for the legalese that might creep into the text. Hard as we tried, we could not avoid it completely. To get through some of this you might have to reach for coffee, aspirin, chocolate, or perhaps all of them.

Federal Legislation

As much as possible, we present the following federal legislation in chronological order, so you can see the development of federal law. The common theme through the various laws is fairness in access to work. The general principle is that people should be chosen to work by their merits for the job rather than by their mere membership in social groups identified by such features as sex, religion, race, age, or disability.

THE CONSTITUTION

Occasionally, individuals bring suit against organizations under the Fifth and Fourteenth Amendments to the U.S. Constitution. Both amendments state that no person shall be denied life, liberty, or property without due process of law. The Fourteenth Amendment applies to state governments, and the Fifth Amendment applies to the federal government. The use of constitutional laws is rare for two reasons: (1) The language is general and does not mention specific employment practices, and (2) the burden of proof on the person bringing suit is greater under the constitutional amendments than under the subsequent federal legislation (Arvey & Faley, 1988; the most likely alternative to constitutional law for bringing suit is the Civil Rights Acts, which we will share with you soon). Interestingly, however, the Fourteenth Amendment has become a major vehicle for "reverse discrimination" claims (Gutman, 2000). Reverse discrimination refers to claims of unlawful discrimination brought by members of a *majority* group, such as the white male group, which is also protected under the law.

EQUAL PAY ACT

The Equal Pay Act (1963) requires employers to pay men and women the same salary for the same job, that is, equal pay for equal work. Companies cannot get around the law by taking the same job or essentially the same job and giving it two different titles, one for men and another for women. The Equal Pay Act does not require equal pay for jobs that are different. Comparable worth (equal pay for different but comparable work) is not covered by the Equal Pay Act.

CIVIL RIGHTS ACTS

In the early 1960s, it was common employment practice in the United States to reserve some jobs for whites and other jobs for blacks. An example of such a practice could be found at Duke Power, an electric power generating plant. At Duke Power, laborer jobs were given to blacks, whereas management, skilled, and semiskilled jobs went to whites. The Civil Rights Act of 1964 made such a practice illegal. Duke Power's response was to allow blacks to apply for the rest of the jobs in the factory. Initially, Duke Power required laborers to have a high school diploma to apply for other jobs. It dropped the diploma requirement for those who could pass two tests (the Wonderlic Personnel Test and the Bennett Mechanical Comprehension Test). The passing score was set at the median for high school graduates. Although the company may not have intended this, the effect of this procedure was to eliminate most blacks from moving to the more desirable jobs. One of the black workers sued Duke Power, claiming that the procedure was illegal. The case ultimately went to the U.S. Supreme Court. In *Griggs v. Duke Power Company* (1971), the Supreme Court ruled that Duke Power's procedure was unlawful because Duke never established the job relatedness of the selection procedure; that is, the company never proved that the high school diploma and test scores were related to job performance. The ruling stated that testing could be used by companies, but the tests were not to be used to measure people generally (for example, we want smart, happy people) but rather used for measuring how well individuals fit a specific job. Nor did it matter what the company's intent was; results were the key. In a power plant, for example, a worker might need to know some facts about the way electricity behaves in order to be safe. It might also be the case that the electric plant needs smart or happy people, but employers have to prove this to be the case rather than to just say it. The court also noted, by the way, that setting the passing score at the median of high school graduates would eliminate half of those with diplomas from applying for the jobs.

Title VII of the Civil Rights Act (1964) and its amendments (1972 and 1991) prohibit employers from discriminating on the basis of race, color, sex, religion, or national origin. The Civil Rights Act (1964) created the Equal Employment Opportunity Commission in order to enforce it. The law applies to all "conditions, or privileges of employment" and is therefore broader in coverage than just hiring and promotion practices. The law states that employment practices that do not affect members of one of the protected groups (that is, race, color, sex, religion, or national origin) are legal unless covered by another law. Therefore, some employment practices that seem unfair or even downright dumb are legal. For example, it would be legal to refuse to hire people because they confessed to eating cherry tomatoes, wore purple clothing, or owned a collection of comic books. On the other hand, practices that tend to reject a higher percentage of one protected group than of another protected group may be illegal unless they are job related and consistent with business necessity. Such procedures are said to produce *adverse impact* or *disparate impact*. Several practices that might seem neutral at first glance are likely to have adverse impact if actually used. For example, if all job applicants with brown eyes are rejected, disproportionate numbers of Asians, blacks, Hispanics, and Native Americans would be rejected. If minimum weight or arm strength requirements are used, a disproportionate number of women would be rejected, and so forth. In addition, it is illegal to deliberately treat someone differently just because of factors such as race or sex. For example, it would be illegal to toss aside all applications from women for the job of truck driver because the employer thought women were not strong enough to be truck drivers.

AGE DISCRIMINATION IN EMPLOYMENT ACT

The Age Discrimination in Employment Act (1967) and later extensions or amendments prohibit discrimination against people 40 years of age and older. This law does not force employers to be blind to age in general but creates a special protected class of those 40 and older. Therefore, it would be legal, though possibly an unsound business decision, to prefer a 20-year-old applicant to a 39-year-old applicant because of age, but it would not be legal to prefer a 20-year-old applicant to a 40-year-old applicant because of age (go figure). Nor would it be legal to prefer a 40-year-old worker to a 60-year-old worker. The law does not force employers to hire less qualified older workers over more qualified younger workers.

REHABILITATION ACT

The Rehabilitation Act (1973) prohibits discrimination based on handicap. It says that "no otherwise qualified individual with handicaps . . . shall, solely by reason of his handicaps, be excluded from participation in, or denied the benefits of, or be subjected to discrimination under any program or activity receiving federal assistance." The term *handicap* means essentially the same thing as *disability* to be described in the next section. The Rehabilitation Act applies only to federal contractors; the Americans with Disabilities Act applies to all companies that employ 15 or more people.

AMERICANS WITH DISABILITIES ACT

The Americans with Disabilities Act (1990) prohibits employers from discriminating against people with disabilities. *Disability* is broadly defined as referring to both physical and mental impairments that limit a major life activity of the person (for example, breathing, walking, or working). Disability also includes those individuals who have a history of impairment and those who are regarded as disabled, regardless of their actual level of impairment (for example, those with facial scars). The laws we have discussed prior to the ADA can be interpreted as prohibiting an employer from denying employment to groups of people. The ADA goes further, however, in that it requires employers to make adjustments for, or *accommodate,* people with disabilities.

The ADA protects a *qualified individual with a disability.* A qualified individual with a disability is a person who, with or without *reasonable accommodation,* can successfully complete the *essential functions* of the job. (For once, we're not to blame for all this jargon. Blame the U.S. Congress.) Suppose our job is that of data entry, where a person is given slips of paper that he or she reads and then enters into a computer using a keyboard. Further suppose that the job does not involve answering the phone and that all the major duties of the job do not involve hearing. Now suppose that a person who is skilled at data entry but is unable to hear applied for the job. Such a person would be a qualified person with a disability. The person could do the job without accommodation because the person need not hear to do the job. Further suppose that a person applied for the job who was skilled at data entry but had some trouble with his or her vision so that the person had trouble seeing numbers close up. If it turns out that a simple accommodation, such as providing a magnifying glass, allows the person to do the job, then this applicant would be a qualified applicant with a disability because the accommodation took care of the problem.

Whether an accommodation is reasonable is something of a matter of opinion. The law is deliberately vague on this point. In general, accommodations are thought to be reasonable unless they would cause the employer "undue hardship." The law states that specific dollar amounts and fractions of salary of the applicant's job are not to be considered in the determination of what is reasonable. The EEOC provides numerous examples of reasonable accommodations, including physical changes to the work environment, such as installing wheelchair ramps, providing aids such as readers and interpreters, changing work schedules, and adapting testing and training materials to give the person access to the job.

Enforcement of Equal Employment Opportunity Laws

Two major organizations are devoted to the enforcement of equal employment opportunity (EEO) laws: the EEOC, which we have already mentioned, and the

U.S. Office of Federal Contract Compliance Programs (OFCCP). The OFCCP regulates companies that have contracts with the federal government. The EEOC regulates most other businesses. During the 1970s, there were several sets of guidelines issued by federal agencies that were intended to regulate personnel selection. The earliest guidelines were issued by the EEOC in 1970 and were used by the courts in determining whether illegal discrimination had taken place. Industrial psychologists and businesspeople eventually became concerned about the use of the guidelines because the courts tended to use them as a checklist, and it wasn't clear whether any business could meet all of the terms of the guidelines without spending a fortune. Also, other agencies, including the U.S. Department of Labor (DOL), which includes the OFCCP, had their own guidelines. Eventually, the "Uniform Guidelines on Employee Selection Procedures" (Equal Employment Opportunity Commission [EEOC], 1978; from now on, simply the Guidelines) were developed through a process of open discussion and negotiation among the interested parties. The Guidelines were adopted by five federal agencies: the EEOC, the Office of Personnel Management (OPM), the Department of Labor, the Department of Justice (DOJ), and the Department of the Treasury. The Guidelines are still in effect today and are used by the EEOC and the courts in determining unlawful discrimination.

Executive Orders

Executive orders come from the president's authority to make rules and regulations for the federal government and also for those doing business with the federal government. As you know, lots of people work for the federal government, and even more work with the federal government, so an order from the president can have a wide impact. If a company is found in violation of an order, it can be barred from doing business with the government.

Executive Order 11246 covers both nondiscrimination and affirmative action based on race, color, religion, sex, and national origin (Gutman, 2000, p. 236). The OFCCP has issued guidelines that require affirmative action by the employer to hire minorities and women. For example, companies must set up goals and timetables to make their employment workforce match the labor market's demographic characteristics. Such actions go beyond that required by the Civil Rights Acts, which state that employers should ignore demographic features of applicants when hiring.

Professional Standards

The American Educational Research Association, in partnership with the American Psychological Association and the National Council on Measurement in Education, published its most recent *Standards for Educational and*

Psychological Testing in 1999. The document describes what is good practice in the development and use of tests that are used to make decisions about people. The *Standards* make a distinction between test fairness and selection bias. Selection bias is a technical term that relates test scores to job performance. The use of a test results in selection bias when minority and majority members who have the same (arithmetic mean) test scores have different (arithmetic mean) standings on job performance. Test fairness, on the other hand, is a nontechnical moral or ethical issue that depends on social and political views. The *Standards* describe how to avoid test bias, but cannot address test fairness per se.

In 2003, the Society for Industrial and Organizational Psychology published its most recent version of the *Principles for the Validation and Use of Personnel Selection Procedures*. The *Principles* describe good practice in the development and evaluation of tests used in personnel selection. Like the *Standards,* the *Principles* are also concerned with the development and use of tests that are used to make decisions about people. However, the *Principles* are directly focused on personnel selection, whereas the *Standards* cover broader territory.

Prescriptions for Job Analysis

In this part of the chapter, we describe how the laws and standards are linked to the practice of job analysis. Most of the links are found in personnel selection, although pay can be an issue, as can job design. And of course determining what is an "essential function" under the ADA is clearly related to job analysis (Brannick, Brannick, & Levine, 1992).

SELECTION

Personnel selection is the employer's process of deciding whether or not to hire or promote job applicants. In making such a decision, employers typically want to know whether applicants will be successful if they are hired. Employers usually gather information designed to inform the hiring decision. The information is gathered through several techniques, including application blanks, interviews, paper-and-pencil tests, reference checks, job simulations, and other types of tests.

Test Validation According to the Principles and the Standards

Test validation is the process of gathering data to determine the usefulness of a test in making hiring decisions. The *Principles* are directly relevant to test validation for personnel selection. The *Principles* discuss three primary sources of validity evidence:

1. Relationships between our chosen tests and other measures, especially measures like job performance ratings

2. The degree of match between test contents and requirements and the job's contents and requirements, and

3. Whether the items or scales of our test fit together as suggested by the way we define the construct the test is supposed to measure (for example, whether there are strong relations among all the items intended to assess critical thinking)

However, these sources all bear on the quality of our decisions when we use a test; they are not separate types of validity. Although it is common to talk of "valid tests," strictly speaking validity is not a property of a test; it is better to think of validity as an argument (for example, the test is useful in this employment context) supported by evidence and theory. The more supportive the evidence, the stronger is the argument.

In exploring the first source of validity evidence, one first defines a measure of job performance that is of interest to the organization. In police work, for example, such measures might include the number of arrests made, the number of complaints about an officer received from members of the community, or a rating of overall job performance from a supervising officer. In industrial psychology, such measures are called *criteria* (*criterion* is singular). After identifying the criterion, the tests are chosen or developed and either job applicants or current employees take the tests. Then the test scores are related to the criterion measures. If the test is valid, we expect to see that test scores are associated with a measure of job performance. Suppose we had a personality test that measured persistence. Further suppose that we tested police cadets in a police academy and locked away the tests without scoring them. We then waited a year and looked at the number of arrests by each officer. Finally, we dug up our tests of persistence and scored them. We could then compare the test scores to the number of arrests (see our chapter on doing job analysis and analyzing data for more detail on this). Figure 6.1 shows this kind of comparison. In the graph each point represents an officer whose score on the test and the criterion is indicated. It shows in general terms that the higher one's score on persistence, the more arrests one makes. There are statistical approaches to evaluating significance and magnitude of the association between the test scores and the criterion (described later in the book). However, the main point to note here is that a criterion-oriented test validation strategy compares test scores with criterion scores. Evidence in support of the validity of a test is a statistically significant relation between test scores and one or more criteria. Nowadays it is common to supplement this kind of evidence by lumping together these kinds of validation studies and computing an estimate of what the "true" relationship across jobs and people is between our test and some criterion of interest (see for example Hunter & Schmidt, 2004). This type of evidence is labeled a *validity generalization study*.

A *content-oriented* test validation strategy is based on sampling the content of the job and using that sample to construct a test. For example, suppose

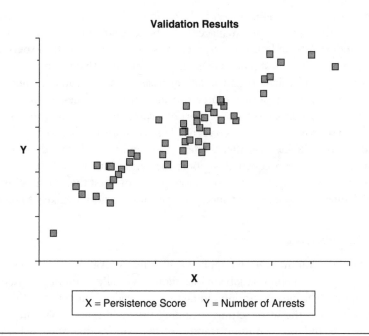

Figure 6.1   Results for a Hypothetical Validation Study

a job consisted of typing letters into a computer. Then a test could be designed in which the job applicant had to type a letter into a computer. We could even sample actual letters from a current employee to be sure that the sample was representative of the letters to be typed. Under this strategy, much of the work is in showing that the test is a representative sample of the important task or tasks of the job. Evidence supporting the validity of the test is documentation and judgments about the relation between the content of the job and the content of the test.

An *internal structure* validation strategy is complementary to the criterion-related and content-oriented strategies, in that it focuses on the development of selection procedures. It was a new addition to the 2003 *Principles*. Internal structure concerns the interrelationship among test items, components of selection procedures, or relationships between scales and constructs. For example, if a test of computer knowledge is used in a selection process, evidence concerning the internal structure of the test would be obtained if there were positive relationships among the separate test items. It is important to recognize, however, that internal structure is not sufficient in and of itself to establish the usefulness of a selection procedure in predicting future job performance.

There are two other sources of validity evidence that are less frequently employed. One has to do with the processes people engage in when taking some action on their job. For example, we might build a test that is aimed at capturing the way an expert manager goes about deciding whether to market a new product. We could use a variety of ways to establish how the expert does it and then see if the test reflects these. If you remember that this type of information is provided by a cognitive task analysis, we salute you and count you among our faves. The other source considers the consequences of test use. What happens after a test becomes part of a company's selection program can serve as a source. If the test was designed to select more productive people, and production levels increase after the test has been used in hiring decisions for some time, then consequences support the validity of the test. When a job analysis has pointed the way to the development of a test that predicts important elements of high performance, positive consequences are likely to result.

Job Analysis Under the Principles

Some recommendations apply to all kinds of validation studies. The *Principles* recommend that job analysis should typically result in a written job description. The job description should help the reader to understand the work performed and the work setting, including the main tasks, tools and equipment used, and any important features of the work setting, such as hazards. A second purpose of the job analysis is to identify worker characteristics, such as the general level of knowledge or skill required by the job (Society for Industrial and Organizational Psychology, 2003, pp. 10–11).

The *Principles* also provide recommendations that are tailored to the kind of validation study. In the criterion-oriented strategy, development of the criterion depends on the job analysis. The *Principles* do not advocate any one method of job analysis for this purpose. The *Principles* simply note that "criteria should represent important organizational, team, and individual outcomes . . . as indicated by a review of information about the work" (p. 16). For the content-oriented strategy, the *Principles* indicate that job analysis is needed to provide an accurate and thorough understanding of the content of the job. The *Principles* state that the content domain of a job should be based on "analysis of work behaviors and activities, responsibilities of the job incumbents, and/or the KSAOs prerequisite to effective performance on the job" (p. 22). For the internal structure approach, the *Principles* suggest that a job analysis can be helpful in establishing the dimensionality of the KSAO requirements.

Federal Law

There are no federal laws that require a job analysis by name. However, several laws require job information at a level that cannot be obtained without some systematic study of the job. For example, the ADA requires employers to determine what parts of a job are essential, and in determining whether to offer a job to an applicant, to focus solely on the essential functions of the job if the applicant is disabled. Clearly, to comply with this law, the employer has to know the essential functions of the job. Similarly, for the Equal Pay Act, one has to understand the nature of the jobs held by men and women before one can render a judgment about whether the jobs are the same.

EEOC and OFCCP

"Uniform Guidelines on Employee Selection Procedures." The EEOC uses the Guidelines to help it determine whether an employer is illegally discriminating. Employers and industrial psychologists have an interest in the Guidelines because they are a clear statement of what the EEOC thinks is important. The Guidelines, including the earlier versions issued by the EEOC, have also been used by the Supreme Court. In *Griggs v. Duke Power Company* (1971), the Supreme Court examined the Guidelines when determining the job related-ness of the test in question. In a later case (*Albemarle Paper Co. v. Moody*, 1975), the Court said that the earlier EEOC guidelines were "entitled to great defer-ence," meaning that, in effect, whatever it said in those guidelines was nearly as good as law. This was seen as applying to the "Uniform Guidelines" as well. Since 1975, the Court has softened its position on the Guidelines somewhat in recognition that best practices change with time and technical advances. You will note that the discussion of validation that follows differs from the current conception we just described based on the more recent *Principles* and *Standards*. The EEOC, however, has continued to follow the Guidelines.

The Guidelines state that the choice of a selection procedure should be based on an understanding of the job. Some form of job analysis should be used to gain an understanding of the job. Any method of job analysis can be used if it provides the information appropriate to the validation study about the job for which the selection procedure is to be used (Sec. 14A, p. 38300). However, as Sparks (1988, p. 42) pointed out, the Guidelines also provide definitions of several terms; we have summarized them in Table 6.1.

The Guidelines refer to job analysis as a product rather than a process. What they call a job analysis, we would call a *job description*. However, it is clear that what they have in mind concerns work behaviors, that is, what the worker does. Sparks (1988) has argued that the Guidelines also suggest that job analy-sis involves direct observation of the work. Let's review what the Guidelines have to say about validation strategies and the role of job analysis.

Criterion-Based Validity. The Guidelines state that there should be a review of job information to determine measures of work behavior(s) or performance that are relevant to the job or group of jobs in question. These measures or criteria are relevant to the extent that they represent critical or important job duties, work behaviors, or work outcomes as developed from the review of job information

Table 6.1   Definitions from the "Uniform Guidelines"

Term	Definition
Job analysis	A detailed statement of work behaviors and other information relevant to the job.
Work behavior	An activity performed to achieve the objectives of the job. Work behaviors involve observable (physical) components and unobservable (mental) components. A work behavior consists of the performance of one or more tasks. Knowledges, skills, and abilities are not behaviors, although they may be applied in work behaviors.
Observable	Able to be seen, heard, or otherwise perceived by a person other than the person performing the action.
Knowledge	A body of information applied directly to the performance of a function.
Skill	A present, observable competence to perform a learned psychomotor act.
Ability	A present competence to perform an observable behavior that results in an observable product.

(Sec. 14B(2), p. 38300). As a special case, the Guidelines note that success in a training program can be used as a criterion if the content of the training program can be linked to important work behaviors on the job or if success in training can be shown to be related to success on the job (Sec. 14B(3), p. 38301).

> Where a job analysis is required a complete description of the work behavior(s) or work outcome(s), and measures of their criticality or importance, should be provided (Essential). The report should describe the basis on which the behavior(s) or outcome(s) were determined to be critical or important, such as the proportion of time spent on the respective behaviors, their level of difficulty, their frequency of performance, the consequences of error, or other appropriate factors (Essential). Where two or more jobs are grouped for a validity study, the information called for in this subsection should be provided for each of the jobs, and the justification for the grouping (see Section 14B(1)) should be provided (Essential). (EEOC, Sec. 15B(3), p. 38304)

The thrust of the Guidelines remarks on criterion-related validity suggests that job analysis should be focused on (1) tasks and observable behaviors and (2) the important and central tasks rather than the peripheral tasks.

Content Validity. Evidence of the validity of a test or other selection procedure by a content validity study should consist of data showing that the content of the selection procedure is representative of important aspects of performance of the job for which the candidates are to be evaluated (Sec. 5B, p. 38298). The Guidelines call for a job analysis that focuses on observable work behaviors. The Guidelines also call for a selection of content that covers most of the job rather than just a part of it (Sec. 14C(2), p. 38302).

In terms of the job analysis that is required, the Guidelines have this to say:

> A description of the method used to analyze the job should be provided (Essential). The work behavior(s), the associated tasks, and if the behavior results in a work product, the work products should be completely described (Essential). Measures of criticality and/or importance of the work behavior(s) and the method of determining these measures should be provided (Essential). Where the job analysis also identified the knowledges, skills, and abilities used in work behavior(s), an operational definition for each . . . [of the KSAs] as well as the method used to determine [the relationship between the KSAs and the work behavior(s)] should be provided (Essential). The work situation should be described, including the setting in which work behavior(s) are performed, and where appropriate, the manner in which knowledges, skills, or abilities are used, and the complexity and difficulty of the knowledge, skill, or ability as used in the work behavior(s). (EEOC, Sec. 15C(3), p. 38305)

The Guidelines also call for explicit links between the contents of the test that is developed and the contents of the job. For example, the Guidelines require the employer to show that the behaviors on the test are representative of behaviors on the job. This includes identifying what behaviors are intended to be sampled by each part of the test and showing where in the job each behavior fits. If the test is intended to be a work sample (for example, a welding test or a word processing sample), then the test setting and complexity should match the job. For example, if the job requires the person to input mathematical equations, then this should be reflected in the test. On the other hand, if the job does not require the input of equations, then the test also should not (Sec. 15C(5)).

Here again, we see that the Guidelines focus on the important tasks or core of a job. In addition, however, two other factors are mentioned. The first factor is the work products. For example, if a person assembles ballpoint pens, the pens are products and are part of the analysis. Second is the notion of sampling tasks from a job. The Guidelines essentially require an employer to sample most or all of the important tasks for testing.

Construct Validity. Note that the *Principles* and *Standards* do not refer to this approach. It is embedded in the sources of evidence they describe. *Constructs* refer to the underlying psychological factors that a test or measure is supposed to assess. The first thing the Guidelines say is that the bottom line in construct validity is evidence that the trait or construct being measured is important to success on the job (Sec. 5B, p. 38298). The Guidelines go on to call for a job analysis that will show the important work behaviors. For construct validation, the job analysis should include the identification and definition of each construct that will be tested (Sec. 14D(2), p. 38303).

Specific details include the following:

> A description of the method used to analyze the job should be provided (Essential). A complete description of the work behavior(s) and, to the extent appropriate, work outcomes and measures of their criticality and/or importance should be provided (Essential). The report should also describe the basis on which the behavior(s) or outcomes were determined to be important, such as their level of difficulty, their frequency of performance, the consequences of error or other appropriate factors (Essential). Where jobs are grouped or compared for the purposes of generalization of validity evidence, the work behavior(s) and work product(s) for each of the jobs should be described, and conclusions concerning the similarity of the jobs in terms of observable work behaviors or work products should be made (Essential). (EEOC, Sec. 15D(4))

Once again, the Guidelines focus on important tasks as being central to job analysis. In construct validity, however, the additional focus is primarily on linking the job behaviors with constructs to be tested, that is, knowledge, skills, abilities, and other characteristics (KSAOs).

Case Law

From time to time, employers are taken to court by applicants, employees, or organizations representing employees, such as the EEOC. At the end of the trial, the judge or jury renders a decision, which becomes a case or record. Other lawyers and judges pay close attention to prior judgments and allow these to influence their views. Precedents are set and rulings have the effect of law. Case law is important because it shows how the courts have interpreted legislation, and unless there is new legislation, case law becomes what controls whether employment practices are legal.

Thompson and Thompson (1982) reviewed case law regarding job analysis for personnel selection. They provided a set of guidelines that is intended to help job analysis for personnel selection withstand legal scrutiny:

1. A job analysis must be performed for the job for which the selection instrument is to be used.

2. Results of the job analysis should be reported in writing.

3. Job analysts should describe in detail the procedure used.

4. Knowledgeable job analysts should collect job data from a variety of current sources.

5. If job incumbents are used as the source of information, lots of workers should be used, and the workers should hold the job of interest.

6. Tasks, duties, and activities should be included in the analysis.

7. The most important tasks should be represented in the selection device.

8. Standards of job performance for entry-level jobs should be specified.

9. Knowledge, skills, and abilities should be specified, particularly if a content validation model is followed. (pp. 872–873)

Arvey and Faley (1988) provided a summary of court cases related to content validity. In addition to the advice provided by Thompson and Thompson, they noted that

1. The content of the test needs to be weighted to correspond to its importance on the job.

2. The records of how a content valid test is developed are important in defending the test.

3. The courts appear more interested in the quality of information provided by the job analysis than by the methods or techniques used to analyze the job.

Brumback (cited in Levine, Thomas, & Sistrunk, 1988) suggested that job analysis for content validation should include

1. Task frequency data

2. Standardization of job analysis procedures to allow someone else to repeat the analysis

3. A way to determine the importance of job requirements

4. A measure of the trainability and/or difficulty of job requirements

SUMMARY FOR SELECTION

Hiring people in the United States is subject to a fair amount of legal control. Much of the legal prescription is fairly simple: If you want to reject job applicants, be sure that you are rejecting them on the basis of predicted job performance. The only way you can do this, of course, is if you know what the job requires and you have some means of measuring the fit of the person to the job. The laws do not require the employer to conduct a job analysis or to measure fit for the job. It is perfectly legal to choose from the job applicants by lottery. As our adviser used to say, "You can be fairly stupid as long as you are stupid fairly."

Much of the legal control over job analysis for selection deals with how the analyst collects data to understand the job and the worker requirements to complete the job successfully. There is also a substantial amount of material dealing with test validation. Such control is aimed at ensuring that the information produced is job related.

PAY

The Equal Pay Act (1963) states:

> No employer . . . shall discriminate . . . on the basis of sex by paying wages to employees in such establishment at a rate less than the rate at which he pays wages to employees of the opposite sex in such establishment for equal work on jobs, the performance of which requires equal skill, effort and responsibility and which are performed under similar working conditions except where such payment is made pursuant to (1) a seniority system, (2) a merit system, (3) a system which measures earnings by quantity or quality of production or (4) a differential based on any other factor other than sex.

The important thing to note is that the law refers to equal work that requires equal skill, effort, responsibility, and working conditions. It seems clear that to resolve a dispute under the Equal Pay Act, one will have to know what jobs are being done by both sexes. Levine, Thomas, and Sistrunk (1988) suggested that a job analysis should include "job information relating to job context, worker traits required, and worker and work activities" (p. 343).

DISABILITY AND JOB DESIGN

The ADA prohibits employment discrimination against disabled job applicants based solely on their disabilities. If some part of the job is not essential and the person is otherwise qualified, the employer may have to change or redesign the job so that the disabled person does not have to do it. Employers also must provide reasonable accommodations to allow qualified people with disabilities to perform the essential functions of the job. The essential functions of a job are the main parts or most important parts of the job. Precisely what is essential is something of a judgment call. However, the EEOC suggests that the following factors be examined to determine whether a function is essential:

1. The position exists to perform the function.

2. There are a limited number of other employees available to perform the function, or to whom the function may be distributed.

3. The function is highly specialized and the person in the position is hired for special expertise or ability to perform it.

Evidence that can be considered in determining essential functions includes

1. The employer's judgment

2. A written job description prepared before advertising the position

3. The amount of time a worker spends doing the function

4. The effects of not having the person to perform the function

5. The terms of a collective bargaining agreement

6. The work experience of people who have performed the job in the past

7. Other relevant factors (for example, organizational structure)

The EEOC does not require a formal job analysis in complying with the ADA. It does note, however, that a job analysis would be valuable, and it is difficult to see how an employer could comply with the ADA without some systematic study of the job. The EEOC notes that there are many different kinds of job analysis and that some kinds of job analysis are more likely to be of value than others. It favors an analysis that focuses on the objectives of the job, that is, on the tasks and duties of the job. The EEOC recommends *avoiding* descriptions of processes used to complete the tasks and duties, however. For example, if a job requires knowledge of material contained in manuals, the requirement should be to *learn* the materials in the manuals rather than to *read* the materials in the manuals. For another example, a task might be to lift materials onto a conveyer belt rather than to *manually* lift materials onto a conveyer belt. Task statements that specify a process can be used to disqualify an otherwise qualified applicant with a disability.

Brannick, Brannick, and Levine (1992) discussed how to analyze jobs for selection under the ADA. They recommended that job analysis be conducted on a case-by-case basis for determining the essential functions of the job in question and what accommodations are available and reasonable. The job analysis need not be comprehensive; it should focus on that part of the job that causes a problem for the qualified applicant with a disability.

Chapter Summary

In the first section of this chapter, we described laws and regulations. We began by describing the most important U.S. federal employment legislation, such as the Civil Rights Acts, the Americans with Disabilities Act, and constitutional amendments. Together, these help define legal employment practices. Next we described the enforcement of the laws by the EEOC and OFCCP. We then described an executive order issued by the president. We concluded the first part with a description of professional standards adopted by the American Education Research Association in partnership with the American Psychological Association, and the National Council on Measurement in Education and principles by the Society for Industrial and Organizational Psychology.

In the second section, we described good practices of job analysis under the laws and standards. Most of the second part of the chapter was devoted to issues in personnel selection. We began by describing sources of evidence that may support the judgment that a test is a valid basis for making decisions about people. These sources included correlations between our test and measures of job performance, comparisons between test and job content, studies of the internal structure of our test, and less commonly, consideration of the mental and psychomotor responses people make when taking the test, and the consequences of test use. Cumulations of studies that looked at the relationship between tests and criteria were defined and labeled validity generalization studies. We then described proper job analysis according to the *Principles* and according to the Guidelines, noting specific practices for the different test validation strategies. We also noted the impact that case law has had on the practice of job analysis. Finally, we described job analysis procedures related to issues of pay and disability.

7

Job Description, Performance Appraisal, Job Evaluation, and Job Design

You are now armed and potentially dangerous. You have learned enough about the methods of job analysis and the related legal requirements to consider putting them to use. Here and in the next two chapters we talk about the key purposes served by job analysis and how to do a study, so that you can see how to use the tools. The more you know about the interface between methods and applications, the better able you will be to avoid potential pitfalls.

In this chapter, we describe some of the common human resources applications of job analysis. The spotlight is on the following for this chapter:

- Job description
- Performance appraisal
- Job evaluation for compensation
- Job design/redesign

In Chapter 8, we discuss staffing and training.

Our objective here is to tell you a bit about each application and to show how information from the job analysis provides the foundation for the application. One of the themes of the chapter is that different applications require different sorts of information. The implication is that you should know your application or purpose before you start.

Job Description

The job description is the most common application of job analysis. A *job description* is a brief summary or snapshot of the job. There is a fair amount of confusion in terminology about job descriptions in the business world. Because the most common use of job descriptions is for job evaluation, people in compensation often make no distinction between job evaluation and job description. Job *evaluation* is the process of assigning value to a job for compensation purposes within an organization, and it is described later in this chapter as part of compensation. People also confuse job analysis and job descriptions. "Where is the job analysis?" they say, as if a job analysis were kept in a file drawer. Job analysis is the process of discovery and understanding of a job that results in a written report or summary; a job description is an abbreviated written summary of what was learned during the job analysis. (Yes, we covered this in Chapter 1; sorry.)

There is also confusion about the difference between a job description and a position description. Some references (for example, some U.S. Department of Labor [DOL] publications) mean what we mean when we say "job description" when they say "position description." In our view, a *position* is what one person in the organization does. Therefore, a position description is a detailed description of what that one person does. It is often written for unique managerial positions as a tool for communicating what is expected of the person who holds the position. It is also used for classifying positions into categories for compensation and staffing purposes. A position description is essentially a contract between the organization and an individual about what is to be done at work. A job is a collection of positions that are enough alike to be treated as equivalent from a management standpoint. Thus, a job description refers to an abstraction that is intended to apply to multiple people who hold the job.

The most important function of the job description is to communicate the essential nature of the job. The job description is not written primarily for the job expert but rather for the job novice. True, a job expert should recognize the job when reading the job description, but its main purpose is to communicate with someone who is not that familiar with the job. Because the point of the job description is to communicate the essence of the job to someone who is not familiar with it, it is very easy to write a bad job description but surprisingly hard to write a good one.

STRUCTURE OF THE JOB DESCRIPTION

Job descriptions should be short. Gael (1988) recommended one to three pages in length. Ghorpade (1988) also recommended that job descriptions be short, but avoided specific page limits. There is no universally accepted content or format for the job description. Based on our experience, most job descriptions contain the following pieces or sections:

1. Identifiers (job title plus other classifying information)

2. Summary (mission or objective statement)

3. Duties and tasks (what, why, how)

4. Other information, such as responsibility, including nature of supervision given and received; knowledge, including education experience or other minimum qualifications; and context, such as hazardous working conditions or rotating shift work

Tables 7.1, 7.2, and 7.3 show examples of job descriptions for the jobs of supervisor of data processing, dough mixer, and receiver, respectively.

Table 7.1   Information Services Supervisor Job Description

Supervisor of Information Systems Operations	Exempt	012.168
Job Title	Status	Job Code
July 3, 2005		Olympia, Inc. Main Office
Date		Plant/Division
Arther Allen		Info Technology
Written by		Department/Section
Juanita Montgomery		12 740
Approved by		Grade/level Points
Manager of Information Systems		[classified]
Title of Immediate Supervisor		Pay Range

Summary

Directs the operation of all database, data control, and data acquisition requirements. Performs other assignments as required.

Job Duties

1. Follows broadly based directives.
    a. Operates independently.
    b. Informs Manager of Information Systems of activities through weekly, monthly, and/or quarterly schedules.

(Continued)

Table 7.1   (Continued)

2. Selects, trains, and develops subordinate personnel.

   a. Develops spirit of cooperation and understanding among work-group members.
   b. Ensures that work-group members receive specialized training as necessary in the proper functioning or execution of machines, equipment, systems, procedures, and methods.
   c. Directs training involving teaching, demonstrating, and advising users on productive work methods and effective communications in information technology.

3. Reads and analyzes a wide variety of instructional and training information.

   a. Applies latest concepts and ideas to changing organizational requirements.
   b. Assists in developing and/or updating manuals, procedures, specifications, and other matters relating to organizational requirements and needs.
   c. Assists in the preparation of specifications and related evaluations of supporting software and hardware.

4. Plans, directs, and controls a wide variety of operational assignments performed by five to seven subordinates, works closely with other managers, specialists, and technicians within Information Systems as well as with managers in other departments and with vendors.

   a. Receives, interprets, develops, and distributes directives ranging from the very simple to the highly complex and technological in nature.
   b. Establishes and implements annual budget for department.

5. Interacts and communicates with people representing a wide variety of units and organizations.

   a. Communicates both personally and impersonally, through oral and written directives and memoranda, with all involved parties.
   b. Attends local meetings of professional organization in the field of information technology.

Accountabilities

Successful completing of scheduled activities. Increased use of facility services through expansion of user understanding and satisfaction with delivered product.

Table 7.2   Dough Mixer Job Description

JOB ANALYSIS SCHEDULE

1. Estab. Job Title <u>DOUGH MIXER</u>

2. Ind. Assign <u>(Bake. Prod.)</u>

3. SIC Code(s) and Title(s) <u>2051 Bread and other bakery products</u>

4. JOB SUMMARY:

   Operates mixing machine to mix ingredients for straight and sponge (yeast) doughs according to established formulas, directs other workers in fermentation of dough, and cuts dough into pieces with hand cutter.

5. Description of Tasks:

   1. Dumps ingredients into mixing machine: Examines production schedule to determine type of bread to be produced, such as rye, whole wheat, or white. Refers to formula card for quantities and types of ingredients required, such as flour, water, milk, vitamin solutions, and shortening. Weighs out, measures, and dumps ingredients into mixing machine. (20%)

   2. Operates mixing machine: Turns valves and other hand controls to set mixing time according to type of dough being mixed. Presses button to start agitator blades in machine. Observes gauges and dials on equipment continuously to verify temperature of dough and mixing time. Feels dough for desired consistency. Adds water or flour to mix measuring vessels and adjusts mixing time and controls to obtain desired elasticity in mix. (55%)

   3. Directs other workers in fermentation of dough: Prepares fermentation schedule according to type of dough being raised. Sprays portable dough trough with lubricant to prevent adherence of mixed dough to trough. Directs DOUGH-MIXER HELPER in positioning trough beneath door of mixer to catch dough when mixing cycle is complete. Pushes or directs other workers to push troughs of dough into fermentation room. (10%)

   4. Cuts dough: Dumps fermented dough onto worktable. Manually kneads dough to eliminate gases formed by yeast. Cuts dough into pieces with hand cutter. Places cut dough on proofing rack and covers with cloth. (10%)

   5. Performs miscellaneous duties: Records on work sheet number of batches mixed during work shift. Informs BAKE SHOP FOREMAN when repairs or major adjustments are required for machines and equipment. (5%)

SOURCE: U.S. Department of Labor (1972). *Handbook for analyzing jobs.* Washington, DC: U.S. Government Printing Office.

Table 7.3   Receiver Job Description

Job Title:	Receiver	*FLSA:* Non-Exempt
Immediate Supervisor:	Receiving Supervisor	
Department:	Distribution	

General Summary:

Verifies and keeps records of incoming shipments of computer parts and software using computer system. Moves incoming shipments safely to storage area using forklifts and other machines.

Essential Duties and Responsibilities:

1. Compares identifying information from freight bills and packing lists by counting, adding, subtracting, and multiplying shipped items.
2. Unpacks and examines products for damage and shortages.
3. Contacts shipper to notify of damages and shortages.
4. Records product quantities and identifying information into computer.
5. Verifies computer records against physical counts and investigates and reports any discrepancies.
6. Identifies location for storage of received items.
7. Prints bar-code labels and put-away documents using computer and printers.
8. Operates forklifts and other machines to move and lift shipments from receiving area to storage area.
9. Records quantities and location of items stored manually or with scan gun and enters information into computer.
10. Works closely with packing department to ensure customer satisfaction through proper handling of product orders.

Supplementary Information:

Job incumbents can be expected to work in conditions that require the certified use of forklifts and other machines. Work may involve exposure to heights. It is also expected that the job will require walking, bending, and carrying to move product from receiving area to storage area. Environmental conditions may include dust; however, areas are well ventilated.

Identifiers

Jobs are always identified by their titles. Jobs in industry usually include the physical and/or functional location of the job. Our receiver, described in Table 7.3, works in a warehouse (a distribution center). Our supervisor of data processing works in the main office in the information technology department. Job descriptions usually provide information about reporting relationships (who supervises the job and who reports to the job). Reporting relationships are often recorded in the identification section of the job description. Notice that reporting relationships are among job titles and not among named people. The supervisor of information services reports to the manager of information services, for example, and not to Ms. Jones. Jobs may also be identified by various codes. The dough mixer has a code of 2051, which within the DOL *Handbook* means bread and other bakery products. As you can see from the job descriptions, the identification section includes a job title and other qualifying information. Some of the details depend on local practices and needs.

Job Summary

The job summary is a concise statement of the essence of the job. Upon reading the summary, the reader should know why the job exists, that is, what mission the job is to fulfill. The dough mixer job, for example, exists to mix ingredients, ferment dough, and cut the dough into pieces for baking. The receiver gets (receives) computers and parts from shippers, verifies that the goods received match the paper receipts, and puts the goods away. Summaries are very hard to write. Judgment is required about what to include and what to omit. The dough mixer summary is excellent as long as the reader knows that dough is used to make bread (which we think is a reasonable assumption).

There is a tendency for writers to include other items that are not very informative. For example, in the supervisor summary, we find "Performs other assignments as required." This statement is uninformative and is probably included for reasons that have little to do with the job. Most likely, the authors of the summary wanted to avoid having supervisors of data processing refuse to complete assignments because such assignments were not clearly listed in the job description.

Duties and Tasks (What, Why, How)

In this section, the content of the job is described more fully. Typically, the content is described in terms equivalent to what we have called *duties* rather than tasks. A typical job may be described by about 100 tasks, but only about 5 to 10 duties. The central, main, or essential functions of the job are listed in this section. The dough mixer summary statement is expanded in the description of tasks to describe more fully what the job entails. This is true as well for the other two job descriptions.

The duties and tasks typically answer three questions:

1. What does the jobholder do?

2. How does the jobholder do it?

3. Why is it done?

What is done is explained by the action verb and direct object. *Why* the task is done is explained by reference to a goal, objective, or outcome of the task. *How* the task is done is explained by reference to tools, equipment, materials, and so forth. Task statements should always describe what is done. Task statements may describe why and how if the information is important or not certain to be inferred by the reader. For example, in the dough mixer job, we have "Observes gauges and dials on equipment continuously [what] to verify temperature of dough and mixing time [why]." For the receiver, we have "Unpacks and examines products [what] for damages and shortages [why]," and "Prints bar code labels and put-away documents [what] using computer and printers [how]."

The grammar for writing task statements that we described in Chapter 2 applies to the writing of duty and task statements in this chapter. In general, the statement should start with an action verb that is followed by a direct object. Qualifying statements are provided as needed. The inclusion of qualifying statements is up to the author and is a difficult judgment call. Some tend to write longer task statements and others tend to write shorter statements. As a general rule, one should consider who will be reading the job descriptions and especially for what purpose. Readers who are more familiar with the job will need less detail. Some applications require more detail, others less.

Other Information

The first three items (identifiers, job summary, and duties/tasks) are essential for the job description. Other information is often used for specific applications that can be separated from the job description on logical grounds but is included for administrative reasons. The most common application is job evaluation. Many job evaluation systems reward autonomy and responsibility, so statements about worker discretion are often found in job descriptions. For example, the statement in the supervisor description that reads "Operates independently" is probably a stock phrase from the company's job evaluation system that denotes a specific level of autonomy.

Any other information of special note may be included in a job description. Note the item labeled "Accountabilities" found at the end of the supervisor of data processing job description. The Job Analysis Schedule in the *Handbook for Analyzing Jobs* (U.S. DOL, 1972) contains sections not shown in our Table 7.2. Examples include involvement with data, people, and things and several worker trait ratings, including general and specific educational preparation, aptitudes, temperaments, interests, physical demands, and environmental conditions.

An item often found in the "Other" category is working conditions. For example, the receiver job mentions exposure to heights and dust. Job descriptions often list unpleasant or hazardous working conditions such as extreme temperatures, noise, vibration, or chemicals that might pose a risk to workers. Another factor listed under context is shift work, particularly if the shift rotates so that the job requires people to go to work at different times of the day and night.

A final bit of information often contained in a job description is the classification of the job under the Fair Labor Standards Act of 1938 (FLSA) as being either "exempt" or "nonexempt" (see Table 7.1, where the status box contains the word *Exempt;* also see Table 7.3, where the Receiver classification is noted). Note that *nonexempt* means "covered" by the FLSA. (Don't ask us why they didn't just say "covered." This is the federal government we are talking about.) The FLSA applies to a company's employees, who are either hourly (nonexempt), or salaried (exempt). Exempt employees are excluded from the FLSA minimum wage and overtime pay requirements. If you are exempt, you get the same salary no matter how many hours you work. If you are nonexempt, you must receive overtime pay for working more than 40 hours per week. The exemption applies to four kinds of workers: executives (for example, company CEO), administrators (for example, school principal), outside sales people (for example, traveling salesperson for a manufacturing company), and professionals (for example, lawyers, accountants, and high-level computer-related workers such as systems engineers). There are specific tests related to classifying jobs as exempt or not. The PAQ (see Chapter 3) now has items that cover this. The specific tests need not concern us here; the point to know is that the tests depend upon the nature of the job, and the process of the discovery of the nature of the job is, of course, job analysis.

ISSUES IN JOB DESCRIPTION

Descriptive Versus Prescriptive

Job descriptions are typically written based on data collected from current employees (observations, interviews, surveys, and so on). Because jobs tend to be modified over time to fit individual differences in incumbent interest and skill, management may want to describe jobs as they should be (were intended) rather than as they currently are. We recommend, however, that job descriptions typically describe how the jobs are actually done. The problem of job content drift for individual differences should be solved by examining multiple jobholders. The job description should be broad enough to cover most or all of the current incumbents. Expect problems if the job is described as how it ought to be rather than how it is. For example, if one of the task statements is "Walk on water," then there will be problems with hiring and job evaluation and the training staff won't like it either.

Present Versus Future

The job description typically presents a snapshot of the job as it is now (or if not now, at least when the job analysis was done). Because of the fast pace of change, particularly with regard to technology, many may be reluctant to spend the time and energy to produce a job description that is quickly out of date. Some have even gone so far as to suggest that job analysis is pointless because the job as a static entity is a thing of the past. We certainly agree that the more quickly things change, the more often a job description must be updated to be accurate. However, management of work requires an understanding of the current system, whatever it is. That is, managers have to know what their workers are doing in order to monitor, evaluate, guide, plan, and generally carry out the functions of management. Therefore, job analysis, whether formal or informal, becomes increasingly important as change increases because management has to understand what is happening in order to be effective. How often job descriptions should be updated is something of an open question.

Means for doing so efficiently (quickly, easily, cheaply, but still accurately) is an important topic that we hope will see increasing attention in the future. One approach that enjoyed success at a large financial services company relied on a computerized database. Whenever a manager needed to fill a position, the job description in the database was sent to that manager for review and revision as needed. Of course, before revisions are made to a part of the job description, other managers can be consulted to see if the change is applicable to most other positions with that job title.

KEY CONSIDERATIONS

Job analysis begins with the identification of a job by its title and perhaps other code information. At a minimum, the job analysis must produce the essential duties and tasks. In other words, the job analysis must uncover *what* the worker does so that the work content can be communicated to individuals who are not job experts. What the worker does should be shown in the job description as sentences containing action verbs and direct objects. Any method that provides work-oriented descriptors such as *functional job analysis,* the *critical incident technique,* or the *combination job analysis method* (C-JAM) is appropriate for producing information needed for job descriptions. The purpose or goals of the job must also be discovered by the job analysis to provide a meaningful summary. To the extent that there are applications of the job description beyond explaining the gist of the job in terms of what gets done and why, the job analysis must also provide this information. The applications drive what additional information must be collected.

Performance Appraisal

Performance appraisal is a formal process used to evaluate what individual workers do at work. One might ask, for example, how effective a college professor is in presenting lectures and in designing exams. Performance management systems, of which performance appraisal is an important part, have two primary goals:

1. To support administrative rewards and punishments for past performance (for example, raise in salary versus counseling that may lead to termination for poor performance)

2. To improve performance through feedback (coaching)

Although it is beyond the scope of this discussion, researchers (for example, Meyer, Kay, & French, 1965) have often found that it is unlikely that one appraisal system can achieve both administrative and performance improvement goals well.

There is a third goal, but it is mainly of interest to industrial and organizational psychologists. So, unless you really, really want to know, we won't tell. Oh, all right, since you insist. Performance appraisal may be used as a standard or criterion to allow us to validate tests or evaluate interventions such as new training programs. We describe test validation in the following chapter.

Performance appraisal systems are typically set up so that at a certain period (for example, once a year on the employee's hire date anniversary) the supervisor completes an evaluation using a performance appraisal form and then discusses the evaluation with the employee. The discussion will often focus on the supervisor's impressions of the employee's work, ideas for improvement, and the raise or salary increase that the employee will receive.

Industrial and organizational psychologists have had some input into the kind of job analysis that will best support a performance appraisal system, the types of forms or formats that might be used for administrative purposes, and ways in which the performance appraisal meeting might be carried out. For an extended discussion of issues related to performance appraisal, useful sources include Motowidlo (2003), Murphy and Cleveland (1995), and Smither (1998). A recent look at issues concerning the use of pay as a motivator for good performance is provided in a thorough summary by Rynes, Gerhart, and Parks (2005). In this section of the chapter, we focus on the methods of job analysis and consider how the products of job analysis might support the purposes of performance appraisal. To do so, we start with a brief description of some commonly used formats for performance appraisal.

RATING FORMATS

Performance appraisal usually requires the manager to make quantitative ratings of various aspects of the worker's job performance. We briefly describe the following formats:

- Graphic rating scales
- Behaviorally anchored rating scales
- Behavioral observation scales
- Forced-choice scales

Graphic Rating Scales

Graphic rating scales are a popular rating format in industry. An example is shown in Table 7.4. Such scales are popular because they describe workers in familiar, comfortable ways that we ordinarily use to describe people. Sometimes the scales are based on personal traits. When we think of managers, for example, a trait that comes to mind—we hope—is leadership; when we think of bankers, we think of (hope for?) integrity; and so forth. Other commonly used scales include both traits and generic work aspects. Examples include quality of work, quantity of work, absence, lateness, cooperation, and loyalty to the company. Although graphic rating scales are easy to develop and use for a large variety of positions, they have drawbacks of two major kinds.

Table 7.4 Graphic Rating Scales Based on Traits

1 = Strongly Disagree 2 = Disagree 3 = Neutral 4 = Agree 5 = Strongly Agree	Trait	SD	A	N	A	SA
	Friendly	1	2	3	4	5
	Courteous	1	2	3	4	5
	Kind	1	2	3	4	5
	Cheerful	1	2	3	4	5
	Thrifty	1	2	3	4	5
	Brave	1	2	3	4	5
	Clean	1	2	3	4	5
	Reverent	1	2	3	4	5

Probably the most serious drawback is related to legal soundness. Scales based on personal traits have done very poorly in lawsuits arising from the use of performance appraisals for administrative decisions such as firing an employee. The courts have found trait ratings to be too subjective and not clearly related to job performance. For example, we might agree that someone is a good leader but for very different reasons. Or more likely, we might disagree about the quality of leadership even though we agree about what behaviors we saw. Not that there is anything wrong about evaluating leadership for managerial jobs. The problem is that leadership by itself is not defined in terms of job behaviors. What we need to do is to specify what we mean by leadership, so that anybody who sees it will know it. For example, it might be considered good leadership for a department manager to delegate the task of keeping a financial balance sheet current, but bad leadership to delegate the entire process of developing a department budget. Kluger and DeNisi (1996) offered yet another critical point about trait-based ratings. The further feedback departs from the job's tasks and the more it focuses on traits, the less will feedback result in improved performance.

The courts have also ruled that a job analysis is necessary to understand what the requirements of the job are. It will not do simply to choose rating scales on the basis of a job title. It might be, for example, that even though the job has "manager" in the title, the job requires no supervision of others. For both the administrative and coaching aspects of performance appraisal, it is helpful to have formats that are full of job-related, behavioral descriptions. An alternative that is more likely to pass muster with the courts is the use of these types of rating scales where the rating factors are the major functions of a person's job. For example, it is common for college faculty to receive ratings on each of three domains: scholarly or artistic productivity, teaching, and service. We will mention this again later. More sophisticated variations of rating scales are discussed in the next two sections.

Behaviorally Anchored Rating Scales

The main idea with behaviorally anchored rating scales (BARS) is to provide behavioral descriptions ("anchors") to help people understand what the points on a rating scale mean. An example is shown in Figure 7.1, which students (or a faculty evaluation committee, or the department chair, for that matter) might use to evaluate the examination practices of a faculty member. The behaviors and associated numbers are intended to provide guidance to the rater, who can compare the employee's behavior to the examples given and see where it fits on the rating scale. BARS incorporate observable behavior into the rating process, and so are an improvement on traits or other simple labels. However, people sometimes have difficulty using the format. They complain

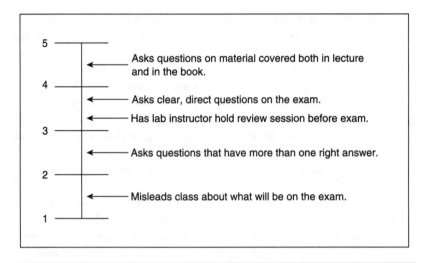

Figure 7.1   Behaviorally Anchored Rating Scale

that the employee's behavior is both better than some of the behavioral examples and worse than some of the worst; they would like to put multiple ratings
on the same scale for a single employee. Rarely do employees' behaviors match
the examples exactly.

Behavioral Observation Scales

Behavioral observation scales (BOS) are similar to BARS in that they also
use behavioral statements to illustrate the meaning of a category. However,
they do so by having the rater respond to each item rather than to the category
as a whole. An illustration is provided in Table 7.5 for the job of professor.
Notice that some of the behaviors in the BOS are the same as those used in the
BARS. Just as in BARS, several behaviors are listed under each category.
However, in BOS, each behavior is rated, and the ratings are more straight-
forward. The rater simply reports the frequency with which a behavior occurs.
This requires more work of the rater (because there are more total ratings), but
people feel more comfortable making each rating. Another advantage of
having multiple ratings per category is that it is possible to estimate internal
consistency reliability, which cannot be estimated with single-item scales.

Forced-Choice Scales

One way to use this format is to require the rater to choose two statements
from four that are given. For example, suppose that a college's department

Table 7.5   Hypothetical Behavioral Observation Scales

Lecture Practices

1. Shows up late for class.

      Almost Never   1 2 3 4 5   Almost Always

2. Fails to use the blackboard or to use other means to present notes or outlines.

      Almost Never   1 2 3 4 5   Almost Always

. . .

Examination Practices

1. Asks clear, direct questions on an examination.

      Almost Never   1 2 3 4 5   Almost Always

2. Asks exam questions regarding material covered both in lecture and in the text.

      Almost Never   1 2 3 4 5   Almost Always

---

chair were to evaluate a faculty member. The chair might be given the following statements (taken from Table 7.5):

1. Shows up late for class
2. Fails to use the blackboard or to use other means to present notes or outlines
3. Asks clear, direct questions on an examination
4. Asks exam questions regarding material covered both in lecture and in the text

The chair would be asked to choose the statement that *most* describes the faculty member (either 3 or 4, we hope) and the statement that *least* describes the faculty member (either 1 or 2, we hope). Thus, the chair is forced to choose the statements that are most and least descriptive of the faculty member. The development and scoring of forced-choice scales is a bit tricky. But if it is done correctly, one of the two nice-sounding statements indicates superior work performance, but the other one does not. Similarly, if it is done correctly, one of the two nasty-sounding statements is associated with poor performance, but the other is not. There is quite a bit of research showing that forced-choice scales work well because (1) the scales are reliable so that different raters tend to agree with one another in their choices regarding particular individuals, and (2) the scales provide good quality information about the relative standing of employees in terms of job performance. Unlike BARS and BOS, the raters (that is, managers) find it hard to "see through" the forced-choice rating task to tell who is getting a good rating and who is getting a poor rating. This is at once a good and a bad feature.

COMPARISON OF FORMATS

All three of the formats (BARS, BOS, and forced-choice scales) require a good deal of work to develop. Subject matter experts such as incumbents and their supervisors must generate statements that are indicative of excellent to poor performance for several categories. Effort is required to ensure that the statements belong to a single category and that the value or "goodness" of the behavior is clear. In other words, the statements that survive the process from generation to a performance appraisal form must be clear both in how good or bad the behavior is and to which category the behavior belongs. This means (you guessed it) additional judgments are needed from the experts. The forced-choice format requires even more work to match items that truly differentiate good from poor performers with items that do not do so, but are similar in terms of social desirability. For example, it might turn out that "Checks own work before passing it on" accurately sorts people by job performance, but "Volunteers to help others" does not (or vice versa).

User (manager) acceptance is typically best for the BOS format. As we mentioned earlier, by having the rater respond to each item, the rater finds the rating task less demanding. The forced-choice scale typically provides the most informative evaluations, at least initially. Managers hate the forced-choice format because they cannot see through it. After it is implemented, they tend to figure out ways to defeat the system (for example, rate everyone the same, pretend that they are rating X when they are rating Y).

Psychologists think about performance appraisal something like this: "Let's carefully collect performance data on an employee and organize the data into meaningful categories. Let's use a helpful format to pull it all together (performance appraisal form). Now that we have the behavior descriptions, we can evaluate the employee's performance and give feedback. We can then decide what kind of a raise the person's performance indicates." The idea is to first describe the behavior, then to evaluate it, and finally to reach an administrative decision. Managers think about performance appraisal for their subordinates something like this: "What raise do I want to give this person? How do I have to fill out this stupid form to justify the raise I want to give? Why do I have to sit in a room and talk to this person about her performance when we both know how she's doing?" This may be why managers hate the forced-choice format.

So far we have focused on the administrative purpose (reward or punishment) associated with performance appraisal. There is also a coaching or performance improvement purpose. Coaching and evaluation have rather different objectives. For evaluation, numbers or other grades are useful in distinguishing the levels of performance between individuals. They are also useful in communicating relative strengths and areas for improvement within individuals. For example, our data processing supervisor might be super at training subordinates (10) but poor in making work assignments (3).

However, numerical evaluations and global behavioral statements are rarely useful as feedback in a coaching session. Being told that you are a "3" in making work assignments tells you little or nothing about what to do to improve. Improvement hinges upon knowing specific contexts and specific appropriate behaviors. For example, it might be that our data processing supervisor's problem in work assignments is matching the programming skills of individuals to the appropriate projects. Or it could be that the same individuals were assigned to too many different projects or that the priorities for various projects were not made clear or that deadlines were never communicated, and so on. Here we merely note that none of the formats that we have described are particularly useful for coaching. We also note that coaching needs to be done on an ongoing basis rather than, say, once a year. Imagine a figure skating coach who waits until the season is over before giving feedback to any of the skaters.

KEY CONSIDERATIONS

Recall that performance appraisal is a management tool that has two primary goals:

1. To support administrative decisions based on past performance (for example, raise in salary versus counseling that may lead to termination for poor performance)

2. To improve performance through feedback (coaching)

(We are biting our respective tongues lest we launch into jargon regarding the third goal.) Job analysis, therefore, needs to produce information that will help management focus on employees' *job-related behavior*. Furthermore, the kind of behavior that receives attention should be (1) largely under the control of the incumbent and (2) capable of distinguishing good from poor performance.

Although managers can and very much should be concerned with job outputs or so-called bottom-line considerations, they must also be concerned with coaching the process of job performance, the moment-to-moment behaviors that influence the job outcomes. For our receiver job, for example, performance can be defined in terms of the number of items received per hour minus some function of losses (damaged items stocked, items signed for as received but never stocked). Knowing that a receiver is slow or loses items is obviously important, but it doesn't tell us what to do to fix the problem. Job analysis, therefore, should present the kind of information that allows for coaching work behavior rather than simply providing a description of the desired outcome.

The second point was that the information should be useful in distinguishing good from poor performance. This point is mainly about efficiency. If everyone is doing something well, there is little point in coaching anyone on it. If everyone is doing something poorly, there is probably some other issue that needs attention, such as job design. For merit pay or similar administrative decisions, the only important information concerns how employees differ from one another in the performance of their duties. Therefore, the job analysis should provide information that highlights differences in behavior under control of the employee that results in good or poor job performance.

The job analysis method most favored for performance appraisal is the critical incident technique (Chapter 2). Recall that critical incidents include (1) the context of a situation, (2) what the person did in the situation, and (3) what happened as a result. For performance appraisal, the context should be that of the focal job. The critical incident technique helps to restrict the job analysis information by ignoring typical or ordinary job behavior. Job experts (incumbents, supervisors, or observers) provide incidents in which the worker's behavior in the situation and not some outside factor was the cause of the outcome. Therefore, the critical incident method appears to satisfy both requirements of the job analysis, namely, that the information should be under the control of the incumbent, and that the job behavior should result in good or poor performance. Critical incidents are clearly helpful in developing the behaviorally anchored rating scales, behavioral observation scales and forced choice scales used in a performance appraisal.

Other methods that provide information about the work requirements of the job may also be used profitably for performance appraisal. Functional job analysis and *task inventories* can provide information about the specific tasks that are required to complete the job successfully. When tasks are combined into duties, the duties provide a good structure for the appraisal of job performance (where important duties are viewed as major dimensions of job performance). Our data processing supervisor (Table 7.1), for example, might be evaluated on such duties as training and developing subordinate personnel, planning work, making work assignments, establishing and administering a budget, and so forth.

One of the aspects of the Management Position Description Questionnaire (MPDQ; Chapter 5) that we liked was its ability to create customized performance appraisal forms based on the task content of the job and even tailored to the level of the position, so that the emphasis or time spent on various tasks or duties might be considered. Ideally, the performance appraisal system will help the manager focus on the employee's job performance. Such a focus provides the best defense against attacks on the performance appraisal system, because the content of the job matches the content of the performance appraisal (which is positive evidence supporting the validity of the appraisal). The task focus also helps to support the coaching function because of its emphasis on the content of the work itself.

Job analysis methods that focus on worker attributes are not as useful for performance appraisal. For example, the Position Analysis Questionnaire (PAQ) and threshold traits analysis (TTA) tend not to provide the kind of information needed for performance appraisal. Performance appraisal is about rewarding or punishing people for their past performance and coaching them in how to do better in the future. Worker attributes are more concerned with capacity for behavior (for example, Can the person train others? Can the person operate a mixing machine?). Performance appraisal focuses not so much on the person's capacity, but rather on the actual on-the-job behavior (for example, Did the supervisor assign subordinate computer programmers to appropriate training? How many batches of dough had to be thrown out because of mixing errors?).

Behavioral Job Description

Although the primary function of performance appraisal is a management tool for rewarding and coaching, performance appraisal systems can be developed essentially to substitute for management. The so-called behavioral or results-oriented job description (Gael, 1988) incorporates standards into the task descriptions so as to indicate what constitutes successful job performance in objective terms. A conventional task statement could read, "Communicates effectively with subordinates." A behavioral version of the same statement might read, "Approves or denies subordinate requests for equipment in writing no later than 5:00 p.m. the day following the request." For another example, compare "Balances cash drawer" with "At the end of the shift, the cash drawer will not be out of balance by more than $10.00; at the end of the month the total out of balance will not exceed $50.00." Including performance standards in the task description accomplishes two related objectives. First, it sets objective performance standards, thus relieving the supervisor from separating performance observation and evaluation. The system sets the evaluation standards for the manager. Second, it communicates clearly to the incumbent what is expected in the way of job performance.

Despite the obvious advantages of a behavioral or results-oriented job analysis for performance appraisal, there are drawbacks to the approach as well. Because job performance is so multifaceted, there is bound to be some judgment needed in appraising job performance. For example, one might have a bank teller who is extremely accurate in handling money (cash drawer always balances exactly, entries are never posted to the wrong account, and so on) but who is rude to customers, antagonizes other tellers, and ignores instructions from the branch manager. Such a teller will be regarded as a performance problem, even though the teller meets or exceeds written task requirements.

Job Evaluation

Job evaluation is the formal process of assessing the value or worth of jobs in an organization. Generally, job evaluation is done in large companies and government agencies as opposed to small family businesses where salaries and compensation are set by less formal means. Job evaluation either directly or indirectly sets the base pay (wages or salary) for jobs. Job evaluation is part of compensation, which includes the administration of pay and benefits that employees receive in exchange for their work. Typically, the largest component of compensation is base pay, which is the hourly amount or salary that the employee receives for time spent on the job. In addition to base pay, there may be commissions, incentives, merit pay, bonus pay, and pay for time not worked (sick leave, vacation). The employer may also pay for health and life insurance, contribute to a pension, and generally buy things of value for the employee. Finally, the employer may provide perquisites (perks) such as a company car, membership in a club, or other desirable benefits. Compensation, and particularly base pay, is important for a business firm because it is typically among the largest items in the company's budget and so has a serious impact on the company's profits.

Because of the importance of compensation to both the employer and the employee, job evaluation is a topic of serious interest to managers. In this section, we first describe what job evaluation is supposed to accomplish. Then we discuss the most common methods of carrying out job evaluation. Finally, we describe research on job evaluation that bears on how well job evaluation is carried out.

EQUITY

Many of us base our self-worth, at least in part, on what we are paid at work. Being social creatures, people tend to look around to see what kind of rewards other people receive. Even if salaries are not posted, people tend to infer what others make and some rewards (for example, vacation time and that coveted parking space) are clearly visible. Equity theory (Adams, 1965) says that people compare their inputs (credentials, experience, effort) and outcomes (compensation, rewards) to other people's inputs and outcomes. People perceive equity (fairness) if their ratios of outcome to input are similar to other people's. For example, suppose that I am fresh out of high school, I refuse to work hard, and I have a low-paying bank teller job. According to equity theory, I will look around at other people. If I see other people who have similar qualifications that don't work hard and receive a poor salary, that will appear equitable (fair) to me, and I should be satisfied with what I've got. If I look around and I see someone else with good qualifications who works hard and is well paid (say, the head teller or the branch manager), that should also appear equitable because the ratio of outcomes to inputs is balanced; that is, they get more than I do, but they put in more than I do. On the other hand, if I see someone else with minimal qualifications and who doesn't work hard, but who also gets well paid (the bank president's son has been made branch manager even though he has no more qualifications than I do), then I will have an equity issue and be dissatisfied as a result.

There are three kinds of equity for an organization to worry about: (1) same job, same company; (2) different jobs, same company; and (3) same job, different companies. In the same job, same company scenario, the equity issue has to do with maximally similar comparisons. For example, tellers in the same bank branch compare their work and rewards with one another. This kind of equity is considered under performance management by the organization and is considered in performance appraisal rather than in job evaluation. The reason is that the equity comparison is between individuals or positions rather than between jobs. On the other hand, if the bank has branches all over the country, it is important to ensure equity across the branches. This may allow easier transfers of employees across locations.

The equity concerning different jobs in the same company has to do with creating an internally coherent ordering of jobs according to the jobs' worth. According to equity theory, some jobs require greater inputs (credentials, experience, effort, and so on). Such jobs ought to be better compensated. How would we know what jobs require in the way of input? Job analysis provides the answer to such a question, as we explain shortly.

The equity concerning the same job but different companies is the problem of market value. If our bank pays tellers less than other banks nearby, then it will be difficult for our bank to attract and retain good tellers. If people can get a raise by walking down the street, they will. On the other hand, if our bank pays tellers more than other banks nearby, we will attract good people, but our bank's profits are likely to suffer because we are paying more for the same work. Companies use salary surveys to find out what other companies pay for similar jobs and adjust their salaries based on the information taken from the surveys. Companies usually participate in such surveys in exchange for a copy of the results of the survey. Everyone wants to be in the same ballpark (that is, paying similar wages) to balance profits against a solid labor pool.

JOB EVALUATION METHODS

The goal of job evaluation is to order a series of jobs (not positions) according to their worth or value to an organization. Many methods have been devised to do this. In terms of job analysis, there are two major classes of job evaluation methods: (1) those that are based on a job description and (2) those that are based on direct assessment of components of the job (work and/or worker attributes). The methods based on job descriptions can further be classified by whether (among other things) they (1) consider the whole job versus compensable factors and (2) compare jobs to jobs or compare jobs to attributes.

Whole Job Versus Compensable Factors

The simplest method of job evaluation is the *ranking method*. With this method, the job evaluation committee (the group of people entrusted with the job evaluation function) receives a job description for each job. The committee proceeds to rank order the jobs in terms of their overall worth. This can be done individually and then collectively among the members or done as a consensus meeting.

Although the entire job can serve as a basis for judging worth, it is more common to consider attributes of jobs instead. Such attributes are believed to be the reasons that some jobs pay more than others do. Therefore, such attributes are called *compensable factors*. Four general attributes are *skill, effort, responsibility,* and *working conditions*. These four attributes are particularly important as they are codified in the Equal Pay Act of 1963. Think of the four general attributes as an umbrella covering a host of more specific attributes. For example, factors that might fall under *skill* include analytical ability, social skill, judgment, physical skill, accuracy, and dexterity. Factors indicative of *effort* could include attention demand, concentration, mental effort, physical effort, monotony of work, and volume of work. Factors falling under *responsibility* might include accuracy in details, commitments, property, money or records, contact with the public, accuracy in weighing, and product quality. *Working conditions* might include such factors as hazards, out-of-town travel, danger from lifting, and environmental conditions.

The most commonly used job evaluation systems use a panel or committee that examines each job for its standing on several compensable factors. Early job evaluation systems had the committee make comparison of jobs using job titles directly. In the *factor comparison method,* the panel ranks jobs separately by each factor. The panel then assigns a dollar value to each job in each factor. The dollar values across the factors must sum to the dollar value (wage or salary) for the job as a whole. Table 7.6 shows an example of the factor comparison method. The Total Job Rate column shows the hourly pay for the entire job. There are five compensable factors in this particular model. As you can see from Table 7.6, the most important factor in terms of pay appears

Table 7.6   Factor Comparison Results for Hypothetical Internet Company

Key Job	Job Rate	Job Factor									
		Skill		Mental Demand		Physical Demand		Responsibility		Working Conditions	
		$	R	$	R	$	R	$	R	$	R
Network designer	$ 41.50	$ 26.00	1	$ 6.50	1	$ 2.00	10	$ 6.00	2	$ 1.00	8
Systems administrator	39.20	25.00	2	6.20	3	2.00	8	5.00	4	1.00	7
Network installer	40.30	21.00	3	6.30	2	4.00	2	5.00	3	4.00	2
Hardware support	34.75	16.00	4	6.00	4	3.75	3	6.00	1	3.00	3
Web designer	27.50	15.00	5	5.00	5	2.00	9	4.50	5	1.00	9
Systems analyst II	23.80	12.00	6	4.80	6	2.00	7	4.00	6	1.00	10
Systems analyst I	19.75	10.00	7	3.75	7	2.00	6	3.00	8	1.00	5
Receptionist	14.20	4.00	8	3.40	8	2.80	4	3.00	7	1.00	6
Clerical	13.60	3.50	9	3.30	9	2.80	5	3.00	10	1.00	4
Janitor	16.80	2.50	10	2.80	10	4.50	1	3.0	9	4.00	1
M	27.14	13.50		4.81		2.79		4.25		1.80	
SD	11.09	8.69		1.41		0.97		1.23		1.32	

NOTE: Ranks for tied entries are assigned randomly for this example.

to be skill. Notice the large mean and large variance for this column. In the *point method,* the panel again compares jobs within compensable factors. In the point method, however, jobs are assigned points rather than dollars for each factor. The points are totaled across factors, and the total is used to classify the job into a pay grade.

Comparing Jobs Versus Attributes

The most commonly used current methods of job evaluation are called *point-factor methods.* Like the factor comparison method and point method, the point-factor method evaluates each job on each compensable factor. However, instead of using job titles to create the evaluation scale, narrative descriptions of each *level* or *degree* of the factor are used to give the committee guidance in its evaluations. Examples of guidance for a single compensable factor are shown in Table 7.7 and Table 7.8. Both tables are attempts to provide guidance to raters in their evaluations of the attribute *job complexity*. Once the level or degree is chosen, then the point value is automatically assigned. The difference between Tables 7.7 and 7.8 is that Table 7.8 has been modified to apply specifically to secretarial jobs according to the people who wrote the tables; the secretarial jobs never get more complex than level 3. The more relevant information that is provided to the committee as guidance, the easier their job of judgment becomes.

For the point-factor method to work well, two conditions must be met. First, the evaluation committee must have accurate and detailed job descriptions. Furthermore, the kind of information the committee needs concerns the standing of the job on the compensable factors. Take a minute to review the job description in Table 7.1. (Diligence, we note, is its own reward.) In Table 7.1 (the data processing supervisor), you can see that the job received 740 points from the company's point-factor method of job evaluation.

The second requirement for quality job evaluations is an understanding of the evaluation system. The evaluation panel must have explicit guidance in how to evaluate the jobs. Because jobs are evaluated on general attributes such as skill and responsibility, there is a big inferential leap between the content of a job and its standing on the attribute of interest. Henderson (1988) recommended that the panel be given both the narrative descriptions common to the point-factor method and job titles that are representative of each level or degree for each compensable factor.

Direct Assessment Methods

Point-factor methods require judgments based on job descriptions. However, other job evaluation methods have been devised that work directly on job analysis data about work and worker attributes. We describe two main approaches, one based primarily on work attributes, and one based primarily on worker attributes. Both methods use statistical means rather than human judgment to relate the job information to pay. In point-factor methods, the importance of the compensable factors is determined by the number of points allocated to the levels of each factor. With statistical methods, however, weights are derived for measures of job attributes that take the place of compensable factors.

Statistical approaches begin with a set of *key jobs*. Key jobs are those jobs believed to be equitably paid or fair according to the market. For each key job, we have a salary or wage that serves as a criterion measure. We then use job analysis to measure a generic set of work and/or worker attributes for each job.

Table 7.7   Complexity Described in Universal Terms

Factor 4: Complexity
This factor covers the nature, number, variety, and intricacy of tasks, steps, processes, or methods in the work performed; the difficulty in identifying what needs to be done; and the difficulty and originality involved in performing the work.
Level 4–1   25 points
The work consists of tasks that are clear-cut and directly related. There is little or no choice to be made in deciding what needs to be done. Actions to be taken or responses to be made are readily discernible. The work is quickly measured.
Level 4–2   75 points
The work consists of duties that involve related steps, processes, or methods. The decision regarding what needs to be done involves various choices requiring the employee to recognize the existence of and differences among a few easily recognizable situations. Actions to be taken or responses to be made differ in such things as the source of information, the kind of transactions for entries, or other differences of a factual nature.
Level 4–3   150 points
The work includes various duties involving different and unrelated processes and methods. The decision regarding what needs to be done depends upon the analysis of the subject, phase, or issues involved in each assignment, and the chosen course of action may have to be selected from many alternatives. The work involves conditions and elements that must be identified and analyzed to discern interrelationships.
* * *
Level 4–6   450 points
The work consists of broad functions and processes of an administrative or professional field. Assignments are characterized by breadth and intensity of effort and involve several phases being pursued concurrently or sequentially with the support of others within or outside of the organization. Decisions regarding what needs to be done include largely undefined issues and elements, requiring extensive probing and analysis to determine the nature and scope of the problems. The work requires continuing efforts to establish concepts, theories, or programs, or to resolve unyielding problems.

SOURCE: U.S. Civil Service Commission, *Instructions for the Factor Evaluation System*. Washington, DC: Government Printing Office, May 1977.

Table 7.8   Complexity Described for Secretarial Jobs

Level 4–1   25 points

The work consists of a few clear-cut tasks. The secretary typically provides typing or stenographic services, maintains simple office files, sorts mail into a few categories, and refers phone calls and visitors to staff members. There is little choice in deciding what needs to be done or when it should be done. Work is performed either as it arrives or in an order set by someone else. Actions to be taken are readily discernible (e.g., phone calls are simply referred to the requested staff member); otherwise, the secretary requests assistance.

Level 4–2   75 points

The work consists of duties that involve various related steps, processes, or methods. In addition to duties as varied as those described at level 4–1, secretaries at this level perform a full range of procedural duties in support of the office, including such duties as requisitioning supplies, printing, or maintenance service; filling out various travel forms for staff members; arranging for meeting rooms; and preparing scheduled reports from information readily available in the files. Decisions regarding what needs to be done involve various choices requiring the secretary to recognize the existence of and differences among clearly recognizable situations. Actions to be taken or responses to be made differ in such things as the sources of information, the kind of transactions or entries, or other readily verifiable differences. Decisions at this level are based on a knowledge of the procedural requirements of the work coupled with an awareness of the specific functions and staff assignments of the office.

Level 4–3   150 points

The work includes various duties involving different and unrelated processes and methods. For example, in addition to duties described at levels 4–1 and 4–2, the secretary performs a number of duties comparable to the following:

- Prepare one-of-a-kind reports from information in various documents when this requires reading correspondence and reports to identify relevant items, and when decisions are based on a familiarity with the issues involved and the relationships between the various types of information; and
- Set up conferences requiring the planning and arranging of travel and hotel accommodations for conference participants when this is based on a knowledge of the schedules and commitments of the participants.

Decisions regarding what needs to be done, and how to accomplish them, are based on the secretary's knowledge of the duties, commitments, policies, and program goals of the supervisor and staff, and involve analysis of the subject, phase, or issues involved in each assignment. The chosen courses are selected from many alternatives.

SOURCE: U.S. Civil Service Commission, *Instructions for the Factor Evaluation System.* Washington, DC: Government Printing Office, May 1977.

Statistical approaches require that a quantitative measure of each attribute be available for each job. After job analysis, we have a set of measures for each job. The measures serve as predictors. The statistical technique called *multiple regression* is then used to derive a set of weights to be used in a formula (multiple regression is described in more detail in Chapter 9). Each of the weights is multiplied by the value of the relevant attribute. Then all the products are added together. The sum represents estimated salary. The formula derived by the mathematical pairing of the features of jobs with known fair salaries can then be applied to new jobs to assign a wage or salary that is in line with the key jobs.

The PAQ (described in Chapter 3) has been used widely for job evaluation, and its inventors have made big bucks for this, so pay attention. The PAQ contains a large number of worker-oriented attributes that can be used to describe most any job. McCormick, Jeanneret, and Mecham (1972) described a study that illustrates the use of the PAQ for job evaluation. PAQ data were available for 340 jobs in 45 different organizations. Wage and salary data in one form or another were available for each job and were converted into a uniform scale of measurement. The jobs were randomly divided into two samples (Sample A with 165 jobs and Sample B with 175 jobs). For each sample, information from the PAQ was used to predict salary. Weights for the PAQ were derived and applied to the remaining sample. In other words, multiple regression was used in Sample A to derive weights and predict salary for Sample A. The weights from Sample A were then used on Sample B data to predict Sample B salaries without deriving new weights. (Such a process is called *cross-validation;* it is used because the derived weights tend to overstate the quality of results on the initial sample but not for the cross-validation sample.) Sample B was used to derive weights that were then applied to Sample A data, for a second cross-validation. The cross-validation multiple correlation coefficients averaged about .85 (where the maximum is 1.0), which indicates that the information taken from the PAQ was able to predict differences in salary across jobs very well. Since then, the PAQ has been used many times for job evaluation with positive results. Such success indicates that worker-oriented characteristics of the job taken directly from the job analysis can serve as a basis for job evaluation.

Work-oriented (task) information has also been used in job evaluation. Job evaluation work by Ray Christal and associates of the U.S. Air Force illustrates the task inventory approach (for example, Christal & Weissmuller, 1988). The task inventory is a questionnaire that lists the task content of jobs in detail (see Chapter 2). Task inventories are typically narrower in scope than the PAQ. That is, task inventories are generally designed to describe a smaller range of jobs than is the PAQ. If a task inventory is designed to cover a large range of jobs, then it becomes very long (more than 1,000 tasks) and an incumbent will be able to check only a few of the tasks as applicable. However, the process of job evaluation with a task inventory is very similar to that with the PAQ. Each job is represented by a set of scores that relate to specific tasks or to task composites (responses summed over related items). Multiple regression is used to derive weights to use with the task inventory responses as estimates where salary is the criterion. Results of such studies also show that salary is predictable. So both work and worker attributes have been used successfully to form the basis of job evaluation. However, Christal and Weissmuller (1988) noted that task inventories may not by themselves provide all the information needed for job evaluation if a point system is to be used. They recommended that incumbents and supervisors be allowed to provide amplifying information that could help a panel to correctly evaluate a job.

KEY CONSIDERATIONS

Job evaluation results in an ordering of jobs on the basis of relative worth. To do this well, job analysis has to provide information that is comparable across jobs. That is, job analysis has to provide information on the same attributes across jobs to be useful. Because the task content is qualitatively different across jobs, task content can be used only to compare similar jobs. Otherwise, an inference is needed that bridges the task content to worker attributes or to more abstract job requirements such as skill, effort, and responsibility. Such an inference can take place in a panel entrusted with job evaluation based on job descriptions, or it can take place at the time of the job analysis by a trained analyst with an instrument such as the PAQ. It is worth mentioning that the O*NET provides a standardized set of both abilities and generalized work activities. Therefore, it appears to offer a foundation that might be used for job evaluation.

RESEARCH ON JOB EVALUATION

Is there a best method of job evaluation? Although there has not been a great deal of research that directly compares job evaluation methods, it appears that most methods tend to agree with one another in the global ordering of jobs by worth. In other words, the value of jobs rendered by one job evaluation system tends to be highly correlated with the value of jobs rendered by another system. Thus, at a gross level at least, the accuracy of the job evaluation method is not the deciding factor in the choice of systems. Practical concerns such as cost and perceived fairness may be as important.

Can job evaluation systems be improved? As we noted earlier, to be useful, job evaluation has two main requirements: (1) to provide accurate information about the jobs and (2) to evaluate the obtained job information in a consistent manner. Although we are unaware of comparisons of direct (component) and job description (evaluation committee) job evaluation results, logical analysis leads us to suppose that the direct methods have an edge in consistency across jobs and settings, whereas panel methods have an edge in terms of taking more specific and varied information into account.

Several studies have examined the reliability of judges' assessments of points for compensable factors. Results consistently indicate that panels of judges are reliable (Spector, Brannick, & Coovert, 1989). Snelgar (1982) found that different companies' evaluations of the same set of jobs resulted in very similar orderings of worth for the jobs. Thus, despite the heavy dose of judgment involved in job evaluations, the evidence to date suggests that job evaluation systems can produce reliable and valid assessments of the relative worth of sets of jobs.

With the emergence of team-based approaches to accomplishing work, new problems have emerged for the traditional, job-based evaluation systems. Companies are trying a variety of new things including compensation based on team contributions rather than individual contributions. In skill-based compensation, for example, team members increase pay as they learn more of the tasks across a series of jobs that comprise the team. To illustrate, in a warehouse, a worker might start by learning to pack and ship outgoing orders, then to search for items stored in the warehouse, then to receive and stock items from outside the warehouse, and finally to troubleshoot problems. Because skill-based compensation typically results in higher wages over time than does setting wages according to fixed jobs, management must be concerned about whether increases in efficiency justify the switch to skill-based compensation.

Job Design/Redesign

Much of the work on job design belongs more to industrial engineering than to industrial psychology (see, for example, Salvendy, 1982). If you are going to design or redesign jobs, you might want to involve an industrial engineer in the process. In this section, we describe some aspects of job design/redesign that are most closely related to industrial and organizational psychology and describe some approaches that may help satisfy the psychological requirements.

GOALS OF JOB DESIGN/REDESIGN

Job design is intended to meet three kinds of organizational needs: production system needs, social-organizational needs, and individual worker needs. The designer needs to attend to each of these while considering possible physical and functional work layouts.

Production System Needs

The logic of the production system is easiest to see if you think about an assembly line, but it applies to all kinds of organizations. The idea is that jobs should be designed to be efficient, so that maximum output will result from the lowest possible input. Jobs should also be designed to deal with technological uncertainty, so as to deal with unreliable equipment, degree of automation, and so forth. In recent years, improving product and service quality has been increasing in importance. In essence, jobs need to be designed to contribute to the accomplishment of an organization's mission.

Social-Organizational Needs

There is a social structure to any organization. Such a structure includes roles, tradition, reporting relationships, career paths, interactions among workers, and so forth. Organizations need hiring and training to maintain the structure as individual people enter and leave the organization. Job design/redesign needs to consider how the structure of jobs will affect the social structure generally. More specifically, the process of job design/redesign needs to consider the impact on turnover, training, and selection.

Individual Worker Needs

People join organizations not only to pay their bills but also to fulfill such needs as growth, status, belonging, and preference for different types of work. At a minimum, job design should consider the following (Davis & Wacker, 1988, p. 160):

Physical environment factors, including

- Safety
- Comfort

Job content factors, including

- Autonomy
- Feedback
- Skill variety
- Task variety
- Task significance

Internal social relations factors, such as

- Achievement recognition
- Social contact/interdependence among workers
- Leadership and mentoring
- Social support

Career path factors, such as

- Career paths
- Personal development

To recap, the job design/redesign needs to consider three main sets of needs: production system needs, social-organizational needs, and individual worker needs. Next, we turn to the process of design or redesign.

DESIGN DECISIONS

Three types of decisions must be made in allocating tasks for job design: deciding what tasks will be accomplished by people, allocating tasks to jobs, and deciding how jobs will relate to each other. Such decisions represent the process of job design.

Accomplished by People

When the work is simple and can be accomplished by following clear rules, machines have a distinct advantage over people because machines tend to be more reliable and less subject to fatigue. When the work requires devising solutions to problems that are exceptions to rules, or when the work is complex, people have a distinct advantage because people invent original solutions to problems. Design always involves choices about what to give to people and what to give to machines. Doing what is cheapest or most technologically advanced may or may not be the best choice. An operator with nothing to do but watch a machine is likely to fall asleep. In commercial aviation, for example, it is possible to program the flight management computer to fly the jet and land it without further human input. However, to do so is to leave the human so far out of the loop that if the computer fails, the human in the cockpit will likely be unable to take over the operation of the aircraft safely. Joint custody of the flight by pilots and the computer helps the pilots to keep abreast of developments during the flight so that they are ready to take complete control of the aircraft if need be.

Task Allocation

Tasks are grouped together to form jobs. In some cases, the jobs are largely determined by the equipment. Large pieces of equipment such as cranes, bull-dozers, and trucks are all designed to be operated by a single person. Larger pieces of equipment such as tanks, some aircraft, and submarines are operated by multiple people, but still the equipment mostly dictates what each jobholder does. Jets typically have as few as one and as many as three people assigned to the cockpit. Psychologists may work with engineers to help decide how many people will be used to fly a jet, or given that two will be used, whether the two will sit next to one another or one behind the other, or what instrument displays will be common to the two and unique to each and where the displays will be located.

Technology can be devised to increase the flexibility of assigning tasks to jobs. For example, in a Volvo assembly plant, an assembly line was replaced by a large motorized base that the assembly crew could move from station to station. The crew was designed to be cross-trained so that eventually, each crew member could nearly build an entire car. Organizational system factors also affect such designs. If there is no incentive for crew members to train each other, cross-training may not be achieved. Where such groups are used, it is common to pay crew members according to their skills, so that as they learn more they get paid more.

Ford (1969) suggested the following questions be asked when considering adding responsibility to a job:

1. What does the supervisor now do for the incumbent that the incumbent could do?

2. What steps that now precede the incumbent's work could be included in the job to make it more meaningful and responsible?

3. What steps that are now done after the incumbent's work could be included in the job to make it more meaningful and responsible?

4. What tasks should be pushed down to a job at a lower level of classification?

5. What could be automated completely?

6. Was there once a way of handling this work that was more meaningful or satisfying in some respect?

7. What do we let an employee do in an emergency or in the absence of his or her supervisor that he or she might be allowed to do all the time?

8. Can accounts or customers be divided into meaningful classes (all TV or radio accounts, all department stores, all hotels, and so on) so that an employee might be given responsibility for a certain type of customer?

9. Are there any verifiers or checkers who might be dropped?

10. What training could employees give each other? What specialized knowledge might they be encouraged to build up? What new things could they learn to do that someone else does now? (cited in McCormick, 1979, p. 289)

Notice that many of the questions are related to task content. The first question refers to autonomy. The next two questions concern task identity, and so forth.

Job Relations

Much of the relations that develop between jobholders is due to physical proximity—people get to know other people nearby. The functions of work may also tie workers together. For example, a race car driver has to rely on his or her pit crew to change tires, refuel, and so on, and this leads to discussions of how well they are doing as a team. Modern communication technology can also influence the amount and type of interaction that coworkers have. Job design influences how jobholders relate to one another by how tasks are allocated, by the physical design of machines and equipment (for example, using glass instead of steel allows people to see one another), and by the functional design of equipment (for example, electronic mail versus closed-circuit television).

Job Design for People With Disabilities

Jobs are sometimes adjusted for people with disabilities. This may be an aspect of reasonable accommodation called for by the Americans with Disabilities Act. The process of job analysis in such cases is more focused than typical methods we have described (Brannick, Brannick, & Levine, 1992; Kochhar & Armstrong, 1988). The job analysis will consider (1) the specific disabled person and the nature of his or her disability, (2) whether the disability in fact causes trouble for the completion of the job as it is done now, and if there is a problem, (3) whether the problem can be remedied within reason.

Kochhar and Armstrong (1988) described an example in which a paraplegic man applied for a hospital messenger job. The job involved picking up blood and plasma samples from one refrigerator and delivering them to another refrigerator within the hospital. This required moving along corridors, opening and closing refrigerator doors, lifting and holding samples, and using the elevator. The job applicant was confined to a wheelchair. For part 1, the analysis involved testing the applicant's reach and strength of arm, hand, and grip. These were compared against the job. For part 2, they discovered that the applicant was strong enough to move the wheelchair through the corridors around the hospital quickly enough to meet the job requirements. They found that the applicant could successfully open the refrigerator doors and reach far enough into the refrigerators to pull the samples. The applicant's hand strength was weaker than normal, but still strong enough to do the job (lift the blood samples). There was only one thing the applicant could not do: reach the emergency alarm in the elevator. Thus, for part 3 the analysts solved the problem by giving the man a stick that he could use to push the elevator alarm.

KEY CONSIDERATIONS

Kinds of Information

For most applications of job analysis, there is a single, most important type of information that job analysis must provide. For example, for job descriptions, job analysis needs to provide the duties and mission to communicate the gist of the job. Job design is often so broad in scope that it is difficult to specify what the required information must be. However, it is very likely that job analysis for job design/redesign will need to provide information about the relations of tasks to one another and to the desired goal. A flow diagram, for example, is very likely to prove helpful, because the tasks are those that we have to choose from for allocation to jobs. A matrix that shows how performance on one task influences performance on another task may also prove helpful (for example, Englestad, 1979). In software development, for example, it may be that certain modules only affect certain other modules. It often makes sense to assign interacting tasks to the same job so that a single jobholder has responsibility for the related tasks.

Beyond sequences and dependencies, job analysis methods such as the *Multimethod Job Design Questionnaire* (MJDQ) described in Chapter 4 (on hybrid methods) are helpful because they provide much of the information related to individual outcomes mentioned at the beginning of this section. The MJDQ covers efficiency, safety, comfort, and job content such as task significance. As Campion (1988; Campion & Thayer, 1985) suggested, job design is likely to create trade-offs in outcomes. If the job becomes more efficient, it may also be poorer in task significance. The critical incident technique (Chapter 2) may also prove useful by pointing out problems in job performance. Such performance problems may point to opportunities for improved design.

A Redesign Process

Morgeson and Campion (2002) described a four-step process that can be used to redesign jobs.

Step 1. Define task clusters. The task cluster is the smallest collection of logically related tasks that are normally performed by a single person such that they form a whole or natural work process. Morgeson and Campion (2002) described the work of data entry analysts, which consisted of 13 task clusters (following redesign). These included 10 relatively routine data entry task clusters (for example, defining data collection requirements, building and testing the system, completing documentation) as well as three participation-oriented task clusters (that is, participate in creation/modification of design, participate in mapping data, and participate in design, construction, and implementation of infrastructure changes). One advantage of using task clusters as the unit of analysis is that once they are defined, they can be combined or grouped in many different ways so that alternative job configurations can be evaluated.

Step 2. Rate clusters. The clusters are the things that can be recombined into new jobs. The obvious question concerns how to assign the clusters to jobs. This step requires subject matter experts (SMEs) rating the clusters in a way that helps the redesign effort. In the Morgeson and Campion approach, the ratings concern motivational and mechanistic properties of the clusters, the interdependencies among the clusters, the extent to which clusters from other jobs should be integrated into the focal job, and the extent to which the clusters should be kept as part of the job or assigned to another job (or not performed at all). Table 7.9 provides an example of the rating form used to make ratings on one particular task cluster for the data entry analyst. Because there were 12 clusters in the original data entry analyst job, SMEs were asked to rate each task cluster individually, then indicate its connection to the other 11 task clusters. This obviously requires some stamina on the part of SMEs.

Step 3. Combine clusters. The third step involved combining the task clusters back into jobs by simultaneously considering the ratings, the goals of the redesign project, recommendations of subject matter experts, and logical analysis. That is, alternative job configurations were considered in light of:

a. Their ability to enhance the job characteristics desired (for example, either motivational design, mechanistic design, or both)
b. Their composition, that is, that the resulting jobs must be composed of task clusters that are at least moderately interdependent, and
c. Their ability to absorb other task clusters from other jobs. For example, the data entry analyst job in a pharmaceutical company was originally designed to collect and enter data for clinical drug trials. The job was thought to be too routine, mostly dealing with data entry. The job was found to contain 12 task clusters, 10 of which were retained. Three new clusters were added that concerned the development or implementation of data entry systems. The new clusters were believed to be more involving and autonomous, thus increasing the motivational properties of the job.

Step 4. Evaluate the result. The fourth step involved evaluating the reconfigured job (at the job level). The incumbents holding the data entry jobs were surveyed both before and after the changes in task clusters regarding the motivational and mechanistic properties of their jobs. The surveys showed that the employees described the redesigned jobs as higher in motivational properties than were the original jobs. Employees were also more satisfied with the redesigned jobs.

Table 7.9   Example Form Used to Rate Task Clusters

Task Cluster #1: _____

5—Strongly agree, 4—Agree, 3—Neither or neutral, 2—Disagree, 1—Strongly disagree

Please rate the **satisfying** aspects of the cluster.

1. This cluster allows autonomy or freedom in terms of methods, sequencing, or decision making.
2. The cluster has a variety of activities.
3. The cluster is important to the mission of the organization.
4. The cluster allows opportunities for learning and growth in terms of skills and competence.
5. The cluster is interesting and motivating to perform.

Please rate the **efficiency** aspects of the cluster.

6. The cluster is quite simple and uncomplicated to perform.
7. The cluster allows efficiency gains through repetition.
8. The cluster requires fairly little skill and training.
9. The cluster requires minimal waiting for others to do their work.
10. The cluster is efficient to perform.

Please rate the **interdependence** between this task cluster and each of the other task clusters on the job. In other words, are these two task clusters related in that the performance of one cluster influences the performance of the other in some manner, such as work flow, information needs, quality implications, etc.?

(3—Highly related, 2—Moderately related, 1—Unrelated)

Cluster 2.
Cluster 3.
Cluster 4.
Cluster 5.
Cluster 6.
Cluster 7.
Cluster 8.
Cluster 9.
Cluster 10.
Cluster 11.
Cluster 12.

Should this Cluster be **retained** as part of the job?
Yes   Uncertain   No

If the Cluster should **not** be retained or uncertain, in which job should it be performed?

NOTE: This form has been modified to remove identifying information. When used for job redesign purposes, the actual task clusters and other potential jobs would be listed for the rater.

Implementation

Job redesign has implications for other organizational systems described in this chapter and the next. Changing the nature of the job will affect the job description, performance appraisal, compensation, staffing, and training. When redesigning jobs, it is a good idea to involve multiple parties in addition to an industrial engineer. Those incumbents likely to be affected, their managers, and human resources professionals also should be included in planning and carrying out the changes.

Chapter Summary

In this chapter, we have described some of the most common applications of job analysis for human resources purposes, including job description, performance appraisal, compensation, and job design/redesign.

JOB DESCRIPTION

A job description is a brief description or snapshot of the job as it exists. The most important function of the job description is to communicate the essential nature of the job. The content of the job description typically consists of identifiers such as the job title, a summary statement that tells why the job exists, and a list of duties or global tasks that tells what gets done on the job, how it gets done, and often, why it gets done. There may be other information on the job description that varies across organizations; the most common other information is used in job evaluation. The job description should describe the job as it is rather than the job as it should be. There is some controversy about the usefulness of job descriptions in today's dynamic business environment.

PERFORMANCE APPRAISAL

Performance appraisal systems are intended to help management in rewarding or punishing past job performance and in coaching future improvements in job performance. To further the performance appraisal process, job analysis needs to provide information about the job that will help identify job behavior that is largely under the control of the incumbent and that tends to result in good or poor work outcomes. Job analysis methods that focus on work activities or tasks are suited to this purpose. The critical incident technique is particularly appropriate. The critical incident technique focuses on behavior that is under the control of the incumbent and that has been associated with good or poor outcomes in the past. We also discussed several performance appraisal formats, including graphic rating scales, behaviorally anchored rating scales, behavioral observation scales, and forced-choice scales. Although the graphic rating format is easy to develop and understand, it tends to be unacceptable for legal reasons, and may result in less effective feedback. The other methods all require serious work to develop. Although the forced-choice format can provide the highest-quality information, it is usually not acceptable to those who must use it. Therefore, either the BARS or BOS formats are usually better than forced-choice formats. On the other hand, standard rating scales derived from job analysis can also be useful. Political considerations may make a greater difference in usefulness than scale format, but job analysis is at the heart of any good system and a key element in its legal defensibility.

JOB EVALUATION

Job evaluation is the formal process of assessing the value or worth of jobs in an organization and is used mainly by large organizations. Job evaluation is important in part because it establishes equity by balancing what the job requires in the way of skill, effort, responsibility, and working conditions against what the job pays. There are numerous methods of job evaluation; some methods evaluate the whole job at once, and others consider the job as a set of attributes called compensable factors. The most commonly used methods today are called point-factor methods. Such methods typically evaluate jobs by examining job descriptions and relating the description to a set of compensable factors to determine the level or degree of the factor for the job. The level or degree sets a point value for the factor. The point values across factors are added to give a point value for the job. The job's point value establishes a pay grade for the job. There are also job evaluation methods in which job attributes are measured directly through job analysis and related to pay through statistical means. A widely used method for this purpose is the Position Analysis Questionnaire. To work effectively, job evaluation requires information about jobs that is comparable across jobs, such as skill and effort. Job evaluation also requires a policy that relates such information to value or worth. Available research indicates that both the point-factor method and the direct evaluation method appear to produce reliable and reasonably valid estimates of job worth.

JOB DESIGN/REDESIGN

The other applications in this chapter generally consider the job to be a fixed or at least slowly changing entity. Job design/redesign, however, deliberately considers jobs that are changed or are new. Three main kinds of decisions must be made in job design/redesign: (1) what tasks will be done by people (versus by machines), (2) what tasks will be grouped into what jobs, and (3) how the jobs will relate to one another. The decisions must be made in light of three organizational criteria: (1) system production needs, (2) social-organizational needs, and (3) individual worker needs. Because job design/ redesign creates or changes the job itself, it affects all the other human resources applications. Job design/redesign generally has implications for many jobs in the organization, and so the information needed from job analysis tends to be varied and complex. Job design/redesign is likely to involve trade-offs in outcomes such as quality of output, efficiency, skill requirements, and motivational properties of the job. Most applications of job design/redesign in the psychological literature show how jobs have been changed either (a) to make them more meaningful by having workers complete a whole rather than a part (for example, a whole car rather than partial assembly) or (b) to give workers more autonomy to increase feelings of responsibility. On the other hand, jobs may sometimes be adjusted for people with disabilities, especially if reasonable accommodation is required under the Americans with Disabilities Act.

Expertise in activities such as developing performance appraisal systems or redesigning jobs requires mastery of both job analysis and the specifics of the particular activity. Mastery is a journey rather than a destination, however, because we have not yet achieved scientifically grounded answers to all the issues that must be considered.

8

Staffing and Training

In this chapter, we describe two of the purposes that are dearest to the hearts of industrial and organizational psychologists, namely, staffing and training. Staffing concerns attracting people to the organization and placing them in jobs where they will be of benefit to the organization. In large companies, staffing also concerns plans for the future. It is important to have a pool of people that we are developing for jobs that have increasing responsibility. In staffing, the job is considered essentially fixed or given and people are chosen so as to match the job.

In training, people are given experiences that enhance their knowledge and skills. Thus, rather than being picked for their match with the job, people are changed to better match the job. More than any other purpose in human resources, training has a well-developed systems approach that covers the entire process from design to evaluation.

Staffing

A company without people is an empty shell. People make the place (Schneider, 1987), and finding the right people to fill the company is the point of staffing. There are three main staffing functions:

1. Recruitment

2. Selection

3. Placement

Recruitment usually involves getting people from outside the organization to apply for a job inside the organization. However, in large companies, there is often a system in which jobs are first advertised inside the company and then outside the company if no suitable internal candidates are found, so recruiting can be both from inside and outside the company. Recruiting is done to attract job applicants. Selection involves choosing people to hire from among the pool of job applicants. The organization tries to discover information about the applicants that will tell who will be best suited for the job. The applicants try to discover what it will mean to work at the organization. If all goes well, the organization and the applicant choose each other, and the applicant becomes an incumbent. Selection is about choosing the right person for the job. Placement, on the other hand, is about choosing the right job for the person. If an organization hires someone believed to be useful to the organization, but considers that person for more than one job at a time, then placement is an issue. Outside the military, placement is not usually a concern because people are hired for specific jobs rather than for a range of jobs. Therefore, we will have little to say about placement in this chapter. We describe recruitment and selection in a bit more detail. We describe the functions that recruitment fulfills and show how job analysis provides the necessary information to write job specifications that communicate job requirements to job applicants.

Selection has an extensive history in industrial and organizational psychology. Books by Gatewood and Feild (1998), Guion (1998), Heneman and Judge (2003), Ployhart, Schneider, and Schmitt (2006), and Schmitt and Borman (1993) offer more detail than we can provide here. Selection is closely associated with testing, so we outline procedures used for choosing and constructing tests and ways of knowing whether the tests are working for their intended purpose. We distinguish between tests that are intended to measure specific constructs (for example, color vision) and those that are intended to provide work samples (for example, a typing test). Finally, we show how several different methods of job analysis can be used profitably to support personnel selection activities.

Staffing is about matching people to jobs. From a staffing standpoint, jobs are typically considered givens. People are to be found that fit the jobs rather than the jobs being tailored to fit people. The trick in staffing is to know what is required by the job in the way of human knowledge, skills, abilities, and other characteristics (KSAOs). Once we know what is required, we can find the people with those characteristics. Finding people that fit a job is not the only way to enhance performance; training changes people, leaders motivate people, and job redesign alters jobs (Chapter 7).

Because quite a few industrial psychologists (and many more people in businesses) have been looking at the fit between people and jobs for quite a few years, you might expect that the means for creating a solid match has been worked out. You might expect that there is a reference like a dictionary where one can go to look up the job and see the associated human requirements (job requirements). Although several such systems have been devised (for example, Ability Requirements Scales, job element method), none are yet considered the final word. Part of the problem is that although many human capacities are well understood (for example, perception of length and color), their specific applications are too varied to catalog. For example, both the cabinet installer and the graphic artist make use of perception of length and color, but the installer uses the information to fit pieces together while the artist uses it to produce eye-catching compositions.

Some important human attributes are not well understood or measured. Take resistance to monotony or boredom, for example. Such a trait is very important in inspection work where the vast majority of products pass inspection, but exceptions have nasty consequences (consider poultry and tires, to name only two). In theory, all jobs can be described in terms of elements that require some human capacity. In practice, jobs are dynamic abstractions. Think of the jobs of Web master and Web designer, which did not exist a few years ago. If there were a dictionary linking jobs and job requirements, it would either be incomplete or constantly under revision.

Whenever we move away from the performance of the task itself and consider what the task requires in terms of human capacity, we have to make an inferential leap from the task to human capacity. The more abstract the capacity and the less the capacity resembles the task itself, the greater the leap and thus the greater the possibility of landing off base. It requires a fairly small leap to infer that accountants must have knowledge of addition and subtraction of numbers. On the other hand, it is a considerably larger leap to infer that an accounting job requires a certain number of years of experience, a high level of verbal ability, or resistance to stress. What we need is a classification system that simultaneously treats the essential attributes of both jobs and people. Despite some notable attempts, the required taxonomy is not yet available, and so we have to proceed as best we can on a case-by-case basis. Harvey (1991) presented an extended discussion of the problem. He described two main inferences that are typically made in selection: (1) from the job to the KSAOs and (2) from the KSAOs to the tests or other methods used to assess differences in applicants on the KSAOs.

RECRUITMENT

When employers have jobs to fill, they encourage people to apply for them, that is, they recruit applicants. Recruiting methods are as varied as companies; some rely on word of mouth, and some are required by law to place written advertisements in specific publications. Accepted methods include classified ads in newspapers or trade journals, walk-ins, job fairs, college campus recruiting, and whatever clever activities recruiters can devise. For example, a recruiter for a software company puts her business cards in C++ (a programming language) books in bookstores (Harris & Brannick, 1999). Another puts her recruiting ads on drink coasters at a restaurant frequented by people who are likely to be good applicants (Harris & Brannick, 1999). Recruitment serves at least the following functions:

1. To let people know that there is a job opening, including people of diverse backgrounds as part of equal employment opportunity (EEO) efforts

2. To entice people (especially those suited to the job) to apply (that is, to market the company as a good place to work)

3. To inform potential applicants about the requirements of the job and the nature of the company or agency

The first function is easy to fulfill with most any approach, as long as the message is clear. Take a look at the want ads in your local paper. One in our paper today reads:

> JOIN US. *Cabinet Installers Wanted* for the Tampa Bay area. Must have tools, Workman's comp & liability. Excellent pay. [telephone number]

The first line clearly lets us know that they are looking to hire someone to install cabinets. The bit about excellent pay is intended to entice the applicant. The job requirements are tools and insurance. The job title clearly suggests carpentry skills and experience are expected, although that is not explicitly stated. Formal communications such as advertisements or job listings should ideally both entice applications and screen applicants. Recruiting has a marketing function (selling the organization to the potential applicant) that has received little attention from industrial psychologists, but really deserves more. Part of the lack of attention may be because the enticement function has more to do with the company (its culture, compensation package, locations, and so on) than with the job itself. Instead, job analysis tends to be most closely related to the discovery and communication of job requirements in recruitment. On the other hand, especially when unemployment is low, recruiting is very important. Psychological research ought to be able to help employers find ways to reach or create pools of qualified applicants.

Job Specification (Job Spec)

A job specification is a written description of job requirements. Job specifications offer a way of communicating "This is who we are looking for" to recruiters and applicants. The job specification is typically written from the job description (Wernimont, 1988). It may include exactly the same types of KSAOs that are used for testing (discussed under selection), such as verbal ability or resistance to stress. It may also include degrees and work experience required or other essentials, such as the tools and insurance required for our cabinet installer.

Statements contained in such specifications should tell applicants and those hiring about the requirements that the job imposes in terms of KSAOs. Thus, the obvious descriptors include licensing, job context, personal job demands, worker activities, and especially human attribute requirements. However, personnel selection is heavily regulated by law and the kind of job analysis required to support personnel requirements is influenced by legal considerations (for example, Gatewood & Feild, 1998; Gutman, 2000; Thompson & Thompson, 1982).

Key Considerations for Recruitment

Job analysis for recruitment has to communicate the essential nature of the job and the most important job requirements (worker attributes). Want ads nearly always give the job title, but usually give little more in the way of a job description. Want ads typically seek people with experience in the job for which they are recruiting; qualified applicants may be presumed to have a good idea about the nature of the job. On the other hand, college recruiters are often given more information about the jobs they are trying to fill. Both the recruiters and the potential job applicants will want more information to assess the fit between the person and the job.

A decent job description will provide a descriptive title and a description of the purpose and major duties of the job. However, the job description is not likely to provide a good list of worker requirements unless the job analysis was designed to do so from the start. In practice, job specifications may be written solely by looking at task descriptions without taking a look at the job itself (Wernimont, 1988). Such a practice is risky. Expect trouble if the requirements in the specification cannot be linked directly to the job analysis. For example, it is very difficult to defend requirements of degrees and length of experience (for example, requires high school or GED and 2 years' experience of X). Levine, Maye, Ulm, and Gordon (1997) discussed such requirements at length. If you remember that an example of how to set these specifications (also called *minimum qualifications*) was presented way back in Chapter 1, reward yourself with a trip to the local spa. The results of a worker-oriented job analysis (see Chapter 3) can be used to create job specifications by summarizing the most important worker requirements. Such a "direct estimation" method for determining the needed KSAOs has become increasingly popular (Morgeson & Campion, 2000). In any event, good job specifications allow applicants to self-screen. If the potential applicant sees a match, the applicant will throw his or her hat into the ring. If not, the applicant searches elsewhere.

SELECTION

Selection is about choosing the best applicants. Stated more formally, *selection* is the process of choosing from among the applicants those whom the company wishes to hire. The logic of selection is to examine the job to find the tasks and KSAOs, examine the applicants to find their standings on either the tasks or the KSAOs, and then to offer the job to those with the best (or at least some minimally qualified) predicted job performance. (It gets easier if the applicant is close kin to the company president, but that's another story.) Although the process is very simple in theory, it gets rather complicated in practice. Part of the practical difficulty comes from laws about hiring practices, and part comes from what we know about psychological tests and their use.

TEST VALIDATION

"So, what are psychological tests?" you wonder. They come in a wide variety. The most common are the paper-and-pencil variety (although most of these are presented these days via computer, so perhaps point-and-click would be a better description). Of the point-and-click, we can distinguish two major types: those intended to assess maximum performance and those intended to tap typical performance. In the maximum performance category, we have all sorts of tests of abilities, such as the infamous SAT and/or professionally developed tests of analogies, vocabulary, arithmetic reasoning, and so forth. Tests of specific bodies of knowledge (for example, real estate law for realtors, local geography for cab drivers) would also fall here. The item types typically present a problem and ask you, the test taker, to choose the best answer from those available. An item stem might be something like "Keats is to Shelley as Byron is to [Blank]," and the correct response would be "Some other dearly departed British poet." For the typical performance tests, we have measures of personality, interest, and so forth. The typical item presents a statement and the test taker indicates its applicability in some way. An item might be "I am the life of the party," and you would be asked to say how accurately that statement describes you. Another popular type of test is the work sample. A welder might asked to weld something that can then be tested (perhaps by X-ray) to see if the weld is done properly. All sorts of simulations would apply here as well (the assessment center includes a series of business simulations often used to select upper-level managers). Although the interview is not really a professionally developed psychological test, it is a test according to the law because it is a means of gathering and evaluating information to make a selection decision. Therefore, the rules that apply to psychological tests also apply to employment interviews, both structured and unstructured.

The law allows employers to use psychological tests to help make employment decisions unless the tests are intended to discriminate against people in protected classes such as race and sex. (We presented the legal basis for job analysis in some detail in Chapter 6. Bet you're just itching to go back there and have another look!) The way testing actually works, though, is a bit more complicated. Initially, employers can use any test they want. But if the test shows "adverse impact," meaning that it tends to disproportionately exclude members of a protected group from employment opportunity, then employers are in trouble (they can lose a costly lawsuit) unless they can show that the test is job related and consistent with business necessity. Many tests are likely to show adverse impact against one group or another. For example, vocabulary tests tend to favor whites over blacks. Physical tests such as grip strength tend to favor males over females. Employers may choose not to use such tests, or they may attempt to justify their use in terms of job relatedness and business necessity.

Psychologists tend to talk about validity rather than job relatedness; validity is actually a broader concept, but it will be the key to demonstrating job relatedness. *Test validation* is what psychologists call the process of discovering the meaning of test scores. In the case of employment testing, test validation is about investigating the job relatedness of the test for the job(s) of interest. For example, we might investigate whether a vocabulary test is associated with individual differences in the job performance of clerks in a bank or whether a grip strength test predicts the job performance of auto mechanics. Psychologists have devised several different methods of test validation, but they are all aimed at understanding the meaning of test scores. Next we describe the most commonly used validation methods for employment testing. Try to think of test validation as an argument supported by theory and data. Some arguments are stronger than others, and some arguments fit certain situations better than others.

Content-Oriented Strategies. Content-oriented test validation (wow, what a compound noun) aims to link the content of the test to the content of the job. This is easiest to do when there is an obvious link between the job and the test.

The argument in support of the test provided by content-oriented methods is strongest when selection is to be based on work samples, simulations, or tests of task knowledge required by the job. In such a case, KSAOs can be defined in terms of the tasks of interest and do not require much of an inferential leap from the task to the test. If the job requires welding, for example, one can devise a welding test that samples the important tasks on the job. When evidence for validity flows from judgments about test content, the job analysis should generally focus on tasks. The major interest will be work activities. Other descriptors may also be of interest, including products and services; machines, tools, equipment, and job aids; and work performance indicators and standards. Job analysts should be used, and, from a legal standpoint, a large sample of incumbents and supervisors is ideal. A variety of methods of data collection are possible, including observation, interviews, technical conferences, questionnaires, and doing the work. The units of analysis should include the task and scales applied to units of work. According to the "Uniform Guidelines on Employee Selection Procedures" (EEOC, 1978; see Chapter 6), the tasks should be rated for importance or criticality, and most or all the critical tasks should be sampled. The basic idea is to show that the personnel requirements match or represent the important tasks on the job.

Recall, if you will, our distribution center receiver job (Table 7.3). The list of 10 essential functions for the job resulted from a process in which the job analysts first observed and interviewed incumbents; they also did part of the work (all but driving the forklift). Analysts wrote a list of tasks and shared them with distribution center managers and human resource professionals at the company, who revised and approved the list.

To recapitulate the gist of the job, the receiver's function is to receive merchandise from the manufacturer and store the merchandise in the distribution center. There are five main steps to the job (if you skip ahead to Table 8.7, you will see each of these steps broken into finer detail).

1. Unpack the truck. The receiver has to unload the parts from the truck using a forklift.

2. Unpack the skid. The receiver needs to verify the parts against the packing slip to ensure that the parts sitting on the loading dock are exactly what was intended and what will be paid for.

3. Receive the parts into the computer. The receiver then enters code numbers into the computer so that the warehouse inventory is updated and the computer can place each part into a bin, also for inventory.

4. Label the parts. The receiver prints labels using the computer and printer, and affixes the labels to the parts.

5. Put away parts. Finally, the receiver will move the parts from the loading dock to bins specified by the computer in the distribution center. (The parts will be subsequently pulled from the bins and shipped to a retail outlet, but that is another job.)

Suppose that we have decided to select receivers using two work sample tests. The first test will involve verifying parts against a packing list. The applicant will be given a packing slip that has the names, identification numbers, and quantities of a series of parts that are laid out on a receiving dock. The applicant has to count the number of parts of each kind and compare it to the packing list, noting any discrepancies. Some of the parts will be bundled with shrink wrap, requiring the receiver-to-be to multiply to find the correct quantity. Some parts will be bundled so that the applicant must subtract parts from the total in order to get the correct count. There will also be some parts that are on the dock but not on the packing list, and some on the list, but not on the dock. We will score the test by examining the number and nature of mistakes, if any, made by the applicant.

The second test will be a forklift operation test. This test will require an applicant to pick up a full pallet using a forklift and move the pallet to a labeled bin. Once at the bin, the applicant must use the forklift to store the pallet on the top shelf. It just so happens that high storage with a forklift is hard to do, and anyone who does much of this kind of work will be able to judge the skill of a forklift operator by watching this operation. We score this by a judgment of the applicant's competence to operate a forklift.

In Table 8.1, we have reproduced the receiver's essential functions from the job description in Table 7.3. We have indicated with an *X* the job content that appears on the two tests. You can see that the tests represent some, but not all, of the job's content. Because of their obvious relevance to the job, work

Table 8.1   Matrix Linking Essential Duties to Tests for Content Validity

Task	Packing List	Forklift
Compares identifying information from freight bills and packing lists by counting, adding, subtracting, and multiplying shipped items	X	
Unpacks and examines products for damage and shortages		
Contacts shipper to notify of damages and shortages		
Records product quantities and identifying information into computer		
Verifies computer records against physical counts and investigates and reports any discrepancies		
Identifies location for storage of received items		X
Prints bar code labels and put-away documents using computer and printers		
Operates forklifts and other machines to move and lift shipments from receiving area to storage area		X
Records quantities and location of items stored manually or with scan gun and enters information into computer		
Works closely with packing department to ensure customer satisfaction through proper handling of product orders		

sample tests are well received by managers and applicants. Such tests are relatively unlikely to be challenged. From the standpoint of the Guidelines, however, for a test to be justified on the basis of test content, it must sample all or nearly all of the content of the job. This makes little sense to us, because the tests possess obvious relevance to the job. Part of the job (knowledge specific to the operation of the computer program) would be trained rather than selected for, so there would be little point in representing that in a valid test. However, scientific practice and legal practice do not always coincide. Note also in this case that no quantitative ratings of criticality or importance were collected. Rather, the set of essential functions used by the company for the job description were considered to be the important tasks.

Let us consider a second example of an attempt at developing a valid test based on its content. An insurance company was interested in developing a test of the decision making of claims supervisors to be used for development (that is, feedback to employees about their skills). In consultation with the client, the consultant decided to develop a situational judgment test (SJT). An SJT presents scenarios in which problems arise and then lists several possible courses of action. The test taker must decide which of the actions are best and worst. Some items looked something like this:

> You receive a call from a grumpy customer. Her claim was not resolved, and the claims representative who handled her claim is no longer with the company. What should you do?
>
> a. Find the old claims representative to find out what happened, then process the claim yourself.
>
> b. Apologize to the customer. Give the claim to your best claims representative.
>
> c. Give the claim to your newest claims representative as a learning opportunity.
>
> d. Review the file to see what additional information is needed. Get a claims representative to collect any needed information, then resolve the claim yourself.

If you were taking this test, you would pick the best and worst choices. (This is a paraphrased version of an item, and sorry, we do not know the keyed responses. We guess that response (c) is the worst choice.)

Experts provide the keys (that is, the actual best and worst choices for the situation) that are used to score the test taker's responses. The experts are chosen because they are recognized as the best or most knowledgeable about the subject matter. In this case, top company executives with experience in the claims supervisor job were used to provide the keys.

For the job analysis, two analysts began by reviewing job descriptions. Then they interviewed incumbents (12 of them) and supervisors (four of those) of the job. The interviewers asked the incumbents and supervisors about the job in question, focusing on the kinds of decisions made on a daily, monthly, quarterly, and annual basis. They recorded lots of examples. The examples were analyzed for themes. The result was essentially a taxonomy of decision making for claims supervisors. The types of decisions were labeled (1) identifying talent, (2) developing talent, (3) achieving business results, (4) creating a positive work environment, and (5) handling claims. The analysts wrote at least 10 scenarios to represent each of the five categories. The analysts sorted each other's scenarios into the five categories to ensure that the scenarios matched the decision type. The surviving scenarios were edited and revised by supervisors of the job and representatives from the human resources department. The resulting SJT had five items per decision making area. The SJT could then be linked back to the content of the job through the job analysis. The idea is that the scenarios in the test represent (sample) scenarios encountered on the job.

In both these cases, the tests represent a part of the content of the jobs in question. In neither case does the test represent all of the job's content. The two types of tests also vary in the fidelity with which they represent the focal job. The receiver work sample tests can be made to be quite faithful to the job by sampling actual parts and packing lists, using the actual distribution center, forklift make and model (they do come in various shapes and sizes), and so forth. The claims supervisor scenarios abstract problem situations rather than present problems as they actually occur in the workplace. In any such case, it is clear to the job applicant that the test is not the job.

In some validation efforts where test content is at issue, experts are used to judge the degree to which the test content represents the job. Such techniques are not often used when work samples form the basis of the test in question, but are more likely when a domain of knowledge is being tested. For example, someone who teaches history in high school must know a great deal about U.S. history. One might argue to test potential history teachers using a test of history (actually teachers are certified in other ways, but this example helps make clear the intent of the validation effort). Experts might be used to judge the degree to which the content of a test of U.S. history represents the domain of interest, the body of knowledge in U.S. history that might be taught. A test that was judged to be representative of the domain of U.S. history might be supported with content-oriented evidence.

In our view, the argument for validity based on test content is strongest when the test content is sampled directly from the job. For example, the receiver job clearly requires some skill in arithmetic. To verify the packing list, the receiver needs to count, multiply, and subtract. If we test such skills by having the applicant verify a packing list, the content validity argument carries maximum force. However, if we develop a very good test of arithmetic and give that to the applicant, then content validity is less persuasive because the analyst has made an inference about qualities that are necessary to do the job, and the test is justified based on that inference rather than on the performance of the task itself. It sometimes happens that KSAOs that are "obviously" important are not required by the job. For example, we once analyzed the job of photo processor and discovered that, contrary to what we believed going into the analysis, color-blind people could do the job successfully.

Although the argument in favor of a test based on its content is strongest when it is applied to tasks that are sampled from the job, the argument is never as compelling as it might be because the inferences we make about people are based on test scores. We decide whom to hire based on test scores. The content argument, however, only applies to test stimuli, that is, the contents or items of the test, and not to the scores based on the responses to those items. Our inference is that the scores will be meaningful or valid because the test content reflects important components of the job. Therefore, for most tests, and particularly for those tests chosen on the basis of KSAOs inferred from the job rather than tasks sampled from the job, the argument for validity is stronger when correlations of test scores with, say, measures of job performance supplements our inferences based on test content alone. This criterion-oriented test validation strategy is described next.

Criterion-Oriented Strategies. In many cases, the personnel requirements are not simply a sample of the job tasks. For example, we might be interested in the conscientiousness of a mechanic. There is nothing about the steps involved in adjusting brakes that indicates conscientiousness per se, but careless work in adjusting brakes can have terrible consequences. In such cases, there is an inferential leap from the work information to worker information, that is, from the tasks to the KSAOs. In such cases, it is still necessary to collect information about the tasks. However, task information alone is no longer sufficient to support the personnel requirements. In such cases, criterion-related validity evidence obtained from local validation or test transportability might be used.

Criterion means measure of job performance (or lack of performance, as when someone quits) to the industrial psychologist (*criterion* singular; the plural is *criteria*). In the criterion-oriented test validation strategy, the researcher shows how test scores are related to scores on a criterion measure. For our dough mixer job from Chapter 7, for example, we might measure ingredients used and dough produced over some period of time to determine the amount of waste (spilled flour, forgot to add yeast, and so on). We might test each dough mixer with a measure of conscientiousness (attention to detail, punctuality, personal discipline), which will provide our test scores. Then we can compute a correlation (typically the correlation coefficient; see Chapter 9) to show the association between the test and criterion scores. We would expect to see that more conscientious dough mixers would have less wasted dough.

Construct-Oriented Strategies. We have not yet covered the psychologist's favorite method of validation—construct validation. It's our favorite because we can say in good conscience that novices should not try this at home. Here we are trying to make several complex judgments. One is whether a construct, a variable that exists in the psychologist's imagination, fits nicely into a good theory. For example, the variable anxiety may in our theory be linked with anger or depression, on the one hand, and some kinds of job performance and job satisfaction, on the other. We can then collect data to test hypotheses drawn from the theory. For example, does a measure of anxiety predict angry outbursts at work?

Construct validity deals with the meaning of test scores by examining a pattern of relations of our focal measure with other measures that are theoretically relevant. For example, let's say we have developed a measure of anxiety for surgeons (for example, "I get nervous when I see blood," and "I get distracted when other people are watching me work"). We could give our new measure of anxiety to a group of surgeons and also give them another older, established test of anxiety. We would expect there to be a substantial correlation between the two measures. We could also give the surgeons a job satisfaction survey that may index things like social support the surgeons get. We would expect a substantial but negative correlation between anxiety and job satisfaction because high anxiety is associated with low job satisfaction. Because construct-oriented evidence of validity is concerned with a pattern of relations among variables, it subsumes criterion-related evidence. That is, you can think of criterion-related evidence as a special case of a construct-oriented strategy. We expect our measure of anxiety to be related to a measure of job performance. For example, surgeons who have high anxiety may have unsteady hands. We could examine the relations between anxiety and a measure of surgical performance (straight cuts, clean sutures, time to completion, and so on) taken from a simulation at a medical school. (Surgery being what it is, we prefer to avoid research on live people.) You sharp-eyed readers will make the connection that the types of evidence we are describing here fall under the rubric of evidence based on relationships between tests and other variables—one of the accepted sources of evidence for validity listed in the *Principles* and the *Standards*. We emphasize once again that there are not different kinds of validity but rather different types of evidence that bring meaning to scores on tests and other methods to assess the attributes of people.

Research yielding evidence bearing on psychological constructs is the most interesting type of research from a scientific standpoint. It offers the most information helpful in developing psychological theories. It is, therefore, the psychologist's favorite approach. Construct-oriented studies are rarely conducted as such in organizations because of practical constraints. The organization wants to improve its workforce and to improve its bottom line. Organizations are typically not interested in learning more about the meaning of test scores other than whether they successfully predict job performance.

Applicant Job Experience and Validation. Applicants differ in their job experience. Our cabinet installer want ad is intended for experienced cabinet installers. In other cases, most or all of the applicants may lack experience in the job. Beginning managerial and professional jobs (manager trainee, medical residents, and such) do not have experience in the job when they are hired. Vocational training programs for jobs such as the cabinet installer are also aimed at less experienced applicants. When the applicant pool contains lots of experienced people, it makes sense to evaluate them on the specific knowledge and skills required by the job. Under such circumstances, content-oriented validation strategies are reasonable. When the applicant pool is inexperienced, applicants will not have the specific knowledge and skill needed for the job. In such cases, it makes sense to evaluate the applicants on more general abilities and other characteristics needed for the job. For the cabinet installers, we might be interested in spatial reasoning and interest in realistic occupations that require working with one's hands. General knowledge of the use of tools might also be a good bet, not so much because of the specific job skills, but because it indicates interest in the use of tools (using tools to work on real objects).

Predictive and Concurrent Designs. Criterion-oriented strategies come in two kinds of design for data collection: predictive and concurrent. In the predictive design, job applicants are given the test. The applicants that survive the selection process are hired, and at some later point, those hired are evaluated on their job performance. Levine and Weitz (1971) offered advice based on their research that suggests how long to wait before measuring job performance. For simple jobs, they said to wait only a short time. For more complex jobs, they said to wait a good bit longer. At any rate, after the wait we measure job performance. Then the correlation between test scores and job performance is computed. In the preferred form of the predictive design, the test under study is not used as part of the selection process. Instead the test response sheets are locked up somewhere and later scored after the criterion measure is obtained. If this design is used, then we can see what the impact of testing is likely to be. Note that some people who would presumably have failed the test will be hired, and if the test is job related, those people should not do well on the job. Note also that if the tests are locked away, they cannot have an influence on the incumbents' supervisor or the incumbents themselves. The less preferred (but more commonly used) predictive method is to use the test for selection purposes, so that some applicants are rejected for poor scores on the test. Job performance measures are gathered at a later time and compared to test scores. Such a design provides poorer information about the value of the test for selection because people who are predicted to do poorly are rejected and therefore not available for the job performance measure. You might be thinking, "But that's the whole point of the test! You want to avoid hiring people who will perform poorly!" There is a certain force to that argument, which is why the preferred design is not used routinely. We merely note that there is a difference between a test working and showing that a test is working. It will be easier to show that the test is working if you use the preferred method. Also, in the predictive design in which the test is used, supervisors may know the test scores and therefore treat the incumbents differently. A common source of job performance measures is supervisory ratings, and such ratings could be contaminated by knowledge of test scores.

In the concurrent design, the researcher tests incumbents and gets job performance measures from the same people at the same time (hence the term *concurrent*). The concurrent design is nice because it allows the researcher to collect and analyze the test validation data in relatively short order. However, because current employees rather than applicants are tested, the results of the study may not apply as well to future applicants as do the results of a predictive study. Concurrent designs are more commonly used than predictive designs for practical reasons. On the other hand, unless forced by legal challenges, actual or potential, employers are not likely to carry out validation studies. This does not go over well with psychologists, who love to do such research.

Synthetic Validity. All criterion-oriented strategies involve collecting data on a number of people for both tests and a criterion. The data are usually summarized with a correlation coefficient. It turns out that the correlation coefficient is not very stable or accurate in a statistical sense when it is based on small numbers of people. Although statistics books are reluctant to give minimum numbers, in our experience, validation studies based on fewer than 100 people are suspect. It is good to have 250 or more people for a criterion-related validation study. The typical validation study includes people from one job. As you might guess, it is unusual for a company to have more than 100 people doing the same job. Of course, such jobs do exist, including bank tellers, clerical assistants, cashiers, and so forth. However, for many jobs and many companies, the criterion-oriented strategy for a single job is not feasible. The idea in synthetic validity is that the performance of different jobs or tasks requires some of the same human attributes. For example, counting buttons and counting cash both require counting. Training tellers and serving customers both require some interpersonal skills. Graphic design and watch repair require good vision; watch repair and surgery require precise controlled movements of the hands and fingers, and so forth. So the idea in synthetic validity is to use different jobs or tasks to indicate individual differences in the same human attributes. Adding people across jobs can create large enough numbers of incumbents to make a criterion-oriented study feasible.

A very different version of synthetic validity comes about when a test is validated in a setting other than that of the target job. If the job on which the test is validated can be shown to be very similar to our target job, the "Uniform

Guidelines on Employee Selection Procedures" (EEOC, 1978) allow this. A more abstract approach not anticipated by the Guidelines is called *validity generalization*. Here many studies of the validity of a test type, say, a cognitive ability test, are pooled across different jobs and settings. If the test type works in predicting performance across the board, we then make a judgment that it should work for our job also. Obviously, this is a controversial approach. More conservative scientists will not buy the results unless the jobs and settings on which the test has been validated are very close to the one in which we are interested.

Still another approach that might be classified as synthetic validity is the J-coefficient described as part of the *job element method* in Chapter 3. If you remembered this and are of age, have a glass of fine champagne on us, or rather on our publisher.

Signs and Samples. Consider our receiver job once again. Suppose we are considering two tests: a paper-and-pencil personality test of the construct of conscientiousness, and a work sample test of driving a forklift. Consider the personality test first. Clearly, we want distribution center employees who handle expensive computers to be attentive rather than sloppy in their work. Mistakes are invariably irritating and may be costly as well. Although the test is labeled "conscientiousness," the activities in taking the test do not appear anything like receiving and putting away computers. The test is a *sign* or index of a psychological construct called *conscientiousness* that we use to summarize a lot of different behaviors such as showing up to work on time and counting parts accurately. Taking the test, however, requires reading some material and marking an answer sheet with a pencil. On the other hand, our forklift driving test looks just like what receivers do on the job. The test corresponds well to a specific task that is part of the job. In a sense, the test is a *sample* of the work required for the receiver job.

Many people feel that there is a qualitative difference between the two types of tests (signs versus samples). In particular, people are often more comfortable with samples as tests for selection than they are with signs. Although not a formal strategy for validation, we sometimes use the term *face validity* to refer to the degree of surface similarity between the test and the job. In practice, it is more common to justify samples with content-oriented strategies and to justify signs with criterion-oriented strategies. For example, for the receiver job, we might use a content-oriented strategy to demonstrate the job relatedness of the forklift driving test, but a criterion-oriented strategy to demonstrate the job relatedness of the conscientiousness test.

Despite the obvious difference in the two types of tests, the interpretation of both is essentially the same: Differences in test scores are interpreted as predictions of job performance. Thus, scores that indicate highly conscientious behavior and scores that indicate skill in driving a forklift would be interpreted as indicating (predicting) good job performance for receivers. Whether different test validation procedures are really necessary for the two types of tests is somewhat controversial. For example, compare the views of Harvey (1991) and Wernimont (1988).

Comparison of Designs. As we mentioned earlier, there are two main inferences in selection, (1) from the job to the KSAOs and (2) from the KSAOs to the tests methods used in selection (Harvey, 1991). The criterion-oriented validation design offers a means to confirm the accuracy of the inferences using data. By comparing test scores with job performance measures, we can essentially see whether our inferences were correct. If there is an association between test scores and job performance, this bolsters our argument that we figured out the job requirements and presented people with methods of measuring them.

The content-oriented method is both better and worse than the criterion-oriented method, depending on your point of view. The content method attempts to match the test directly to the job. Thus, especially with work samples, it can actually bypass the determination of KSAOs. For example, if we devise a forklift-driving work sample, the KSAOs required to do the task do not have to be named. They are whatever is required to do the task on the job and on the test. This is helpful because it essentially eliminates one of the inferences in the selection process. On the other hand, validation is about understanding the meaning of test scores. Content validation strategies don't deal directly with test scores. They deal with test stimulus materials. Thus, we could devise two different tests for determining a receiver's knowledge of driving a forklift. In one test, we could use a multiple-choice format rather like the driver's license exam and ask about safety (What is the maximum load? maximum speed?). Or we could create a simulation in which receivers would be asked to move some pallets quickly and would then be graded on how well they did or the number of mistakes they made. A content-oriented strategy would proceed in essentially the same way for either test; it doesn't include the scores as such. Thus, the content-oriented approach *can* avoid the job to KSAO inference, but it necessitates an inference (or assumption) about the relation between the test scores and job performance that is not checked against data. Even with a good simulation, it is impossible to duplicate the job in all its detail as a test, so we still have to assume that whatever KSAOs are needed for the job are manifested in the test.

Research on Judging KSAOs for Validation

The central problem in selection is the matching of people to jobs, and the key to doing so is to infer the KSAOs that are necessary for successful job performance. How good are people at inferring KSAOs? The answer to this question is complex, and it is based on rather skimpy data. Overall, we can say that people who are well informed about the job and who use a systematic procedure can infer KSAOs with some degree of accuracy.

Reliability. The reliability (particularly interjudge agreement) of KSAO judgments is important because the reliability of such judgments sets a limit on the validity or accuracy of the judgments. Put another way, if two people make independent judgments of the KSAOs required by a job and they agree, fine. If the two people make judgments of the KSAOs required and they disagree, we have a problem. Although data on the issue are scarce, existing data suggest that individual judges are not very reliable in their judgments of required KSAOs. For example, Hughes and Prien (1989) had job experts examine 343 task statements regarding the job and then make ratings of KSAOs. They found that the average agreement of importance for the KSAOs was rather low at .31, and they concluded that interjudge reliability was a serious problem. Cain and Green (1983) studied trait ratings used by the U.S. Department of Labor, Unemployment Insurance and Employment Service, for ratings provided in the *Dictionary of Occupational Titles* (U.S. Department of Labor, 1977). They also found rather low reliability of ratings. The reliability of ratings due to differences in judges can be largely controlled by using panels of judges rather than individual judges (Van Iddekinge, Putka, Raymark, & Eidson, 2005). If a panel of about 10 expert judges can be assembled, their mean judgment of the importance will tend to be much more reliable than that of the individual judges (for example, if the correlation between two judges is .30, then we would need 10 judges to achieve a reliability of .80 for the mean importance rating; see Nunnally & Bernstein, 1994, for the appropriate computations). Of related interest, Langdale and Weitz (1973) found that personnel interviewers agreed with each other more about the suitability of applicants when the interviewers were armed with a job description than when they were given only a job title.

Validity of KSAO Judgments. A study by Trattner, Fine, and Kubis (1955) examined how well job analysts could predict the test scores of job incumbents in 10 different jobs. There were two panels of eight job analysts. Each panel reviewed information about each of the 10 jobs and estimated aptitude test scores. One panel examined job descriptions; the other also got to observe the jobs in question. The job analysts' ratings were averaged within panels, and then correlated with the mean test scores of incumbents in each of the 10 jobs. The results are summarized in Table 8.2. As you can see from the table, the panels were able to predict mean test scores fairly well for mental and perceptual tests. They were less able to predict physical test scores. Observation of people doing the job appeared to help the analysts make more accurate judgments than simply reading a job description. One must regard these results with caution because the number of jobs was quite small.

Table 8.2   Validity of Job Analysis Judgments

Aptitudes	Analysts Using Job Descriptions	Analysts Using Observation
Mental and perceptual	.60	.71
Physical	.01	.27

SOURCE: Reprinted from *Job Analysis: Methods and Application*, by Ernest J. McCormick. Copyright 1979 AMACOM. Published by AMACOM, a division of American Management Association International, New York, NY. Used with the permission of the publisher, via Copyright Clearance Center. All rights reserved.

Parry (1968) asked job analysts to estimate validity coefficients rather than mean test scores. He found only moderate validity for the judgments. More recent work by Schmidt, Hunter, Croll, and McKenzie (1983) indicated that panels of people can estimate the validity of tests to a reasonable degree. They noted that the prediction of actual test-criterion correlations is difficult because such correlations vary quite a bit due to the small samples typically found in industrial settings.

The U.S. Air Force has conducted several studies (cited in McCormick, 1979) that are relevant to job analysis for selection. U.S. Air Force researchers found that psychologists and instructors could estimate the relevance of various tests for predicting success in technical training. They also found that psychologists could judge aptitude requirements for tasks and that these judgments could be pooled to estimate the ability requirements for jobs. Note that this is the same idea behind the job element approach.

So far as we know, there are no studies that examine the ability of people to judge a person's competencies. Note that the judgment required for competencies is qualitatively different from that for the typical job. Competencies are usually considered in light of business goals. A company thought to be innovative might value creativity, for example. Therefore, competencies are not typically thought of as job requirements, but more as attributes on which to judge the fit of the individual to the organization.

To examine the validity of such judgments, we need research that spans multiple organizations that would show that, for example, creative people were more successful, productive, or satisfied in Company A than they were in Company B. On the other hand, as we have seen, competencies are often shorthand for managerial functions such as planning, financial management, and representation to people outside the organization. Such competencies would appear to be required for success in most managerial jobs.

Position Analysis Questionnaire Studies. McCormick (1979) reports a study of the PAQ used for predicting test scores of the General Aptitude Test Battery (a test battery, mostly cognitive, used by the federal government) and validity coefficients (test-criterion correlations) for a sample of 163 different jobs. The database used dimension scores for each job as predictors and either mean test scores or validity coefficients as the criterion. Results indicated that the job incumbents' mean test scores across jobs were quite predictable for the cognitive tests (intelligence, verbal, numerical, spatial, form perception, and clerical perception). The correlations between the PAQ and the mean scores ranged from .61 to .83. The correlation between the PAQ and the mean motor coordination test was also impressive (.73). Correlations between the PAQ and test scores for finger and manual dexterity, however, were lower (.41 and .30, respectively). The correlations between the PAQ and *validity coefficients* were much smaller, however, ranging from .04 to .39. Validity coefficients for the cognitive tests and the motor coordination test were much less predictable from the PAQ than were the mean test scores. Correlations between the PAQ and validity coefficients for the manual and finger dexterity test were .15 and .39, respectively.

A similar study was reported by Gutenberg, Arvey, Osburn, and Jeanneret (1983), who looked at a database of test validation studies. They used dimension scores from the PAQ to predict the size of test-criterion correlations. The logic of the study was that if the PAQ results indicate that the job requires a good deal of cognitive ability, then the correlation between a criterion and a cognitive ability test for that job should be large. If the PAQ indicates that the job does not require much cognitive ability, then the correlation between a criterion and a cognitive ability test should be small. Results of the study indicated that the PAQ did predict the size of the correlations for cognitive tests, but less so for perceptual and physical tests. As we mentioned earlier, validity coefficients are hard to predict because most studies are based on small samples of data, so the PAQ findings are impressive.

Summary of Judging KSAOs. Panels of analysts armed with good job information can provide reliable and valid estimates of job requirements. Analysts are better at judging mean test scores of incumbents than they are at judging the validity of tests (but there may be several technical reasons for this apart from the judgment task itself). Although there is little in the way of empirical data on the issue, we suspect that reliability and validity of judgments about KSAOs will increase to the extent that the KSAOs are relatively concrete and closely tied to specific tasks. For example, consider the job of surgeon and the KSAOs "hand and finger dexterity" and "verbal reasoning." Although verbal reasoning tests may predict performance in surgery quite well, this is not obvious from considering what happens in a typical surgery as seen on your favorite medical television drama.

Key Considerations for Selection

Attributes Closely Linked to Tasks. For selection, you need information about worker attributes, that is, the KSAOs needed to successfully complete the job. These days, a variation on this theme is "competencies," which are sometimes seen as more business-oriented and broader versions of KSAOs. Whatever term is chosen, worker information is used to pick tests, create interview questions, and generally communicate what the job requires for success. To complete a validation study, however, also requires work attributes, mainly task information. Information about tasks is needed for at least one of three purposes. First, if we are going to conduct a content-oriented validation study, we have to know the task content of the job so that we can relate the tasks on the job to the tasks on the test. Second, if we are going to conduct a criterion-oriented validation study, we have to know the task content of the job to select one or more criteria. Finally, we need to collect task information to satisfy federal legal requirements for conducting validation studies (the "Uniform Guidelines"). There are exceptions. If the criterion is an objective measure such as scrap or turnover, task information may not be needed.

One approach to job analysis that meets the requirements for selection is the *combination job analysis method* (C-JAM; see Chapter 4 on hybrid methods). C-JAM begins with a comprehensive list of tasks and follows up with a list of KSAOs that are needed to complete the tasks successfully. C-JAM uses panels of expert judges to develop both the tasks and KSAOs. The tasks can be used for criterion development or to form the basis of judgments of content validity. The KSAOs can form the basis for the choice of tests to be used in selection.

Another method that has been used for selection is the *critical incident technique* (see Chapter 2 on work-oriented methods). The critical incident technique requires that job experts recall specific incidents of either very good or very poor performance on the job. Each incident begins with a statement of context (what led up to the incident), what the worker did, and what the result of the worker's action was. When a large number of incidents have been compiled, they may be sorted into dimensions that represent tasks, KSAOs, or both. The task dimensions can be used to create rating forms that are used to collect judgments such as managers' or peers' judgments of job performance; these could be used as criteria in test validation studies. The KSAO dimensions can be used to select or develop tests.

The *job element method* (see Chapter 3 on worker-oriented methods) is similar to the critical incident technique in that it takes specific bits of the work and combines them to form dimensions. Because the terminology used in job elements is that of the worker or job expert, resulting dimensions could be used both to pick or devise tests and to create rating forms. A hypothetical example linking job dimensions to inferred abilities and tests is shown for a manager's job in Table 8.3. The main difference between critical incidents and job elements is that the critical incident technique begins with examples of good and poor performance, and the job element method begins directly with judgments of what is required to be successful on the job.

Table 8.3   Job Dimensions, Inferred Abilities, and Sample Tests
             Based on Critical Incidents

Job Dimension	Importance Rating*	Abilities Inferred	Relevant Tests
Planning (coordination of information and projection to future)	1.2	Intelligence	WAIS Watson-Glaser Wesman
		Verbal Comprehension	Terman Concept Mastery Quick Work Test
Supervision of subordinates	1.6	Leadership	Fleishman Leadership Opinion Questionnaire
		Dominance	California Personality Inventory
Communication with higher level personnel and other agencies	2.5	Verbal fluency	SRA Verbal Fluency Guilford Fluency Test
		Self-Confidence	California Personality Inventory

*These ratings are based on a 5-point scale of importance, where 1 = extremely important and 5 = hardly important at all.

Generic Traits

Structured methods such as the Position Analysis Questionnaire (PAQ), the Threshold Traits Analysis System (TTAS), and Ability Requirements Scales (ARS) (see Chapter 3 on worker-oriented methods) have also been used for selection, particularly to justify the choice of tests. (Although newer, the O*NET could also be used.) Such methods require the job analyst to review the job and then to complete a standardized questionnaire that describes the job mostly in terms of worker requirements. Because the PAQ, TTAS, ARS, and O*NET provide a great deal of information on the worker side and because the information provided is directly comparable across jobs, such methods have promise for furthering the scientific basis of selection. Unlike C-JAM, critical incidents, or job elements, the PAQ, TTAS, ARS, and segments of O*NET such as basic skills and cross-functional knowledges are not tailored, and therefore they apply the same attributes to each job. Because they are structured to be standard across jobs, the information that they provide is more comparable across jobs and thus easier to cumulate.

On the other hand, they do not provide much in the way of descriptions of the work itself. A list of KSAOs derived from a study of generic traits required for the receiver job is shown in Table 8.4. Note that there are a large number of KSAOs listed in the table. Not all of the KSAOs identified during job analysis will be used for selection. A subset of the KSAOs and associated tests is shown in Table 8.5. An interesting feature of the table is that several different kinds of tests may be used to measure a single KSAO; this feature highlights Harvey's (1991) second inference that links KSAOs to tests.

Table 8.4   KSAO List for the Receiver Job

Knowledge
Product identification
    Arithmetic (count, add, subtract, multiply) to find quantity
    Vendor and part identification

    Knowledge of paperwork
        Meaning of items on packing list (for example, part numbers, payment numbers)
        Meaning of items on freight bill
        Meaning of items on put-away document

    Knowledge of machines
        Knowledge of operation of computer system
            Names and commands for different screens
            Screen places (for example, part numbers)
            Error messages
        Knowledge of operation of printers
        Knowledge of operation (rules) of forklifts
        Knowledge of operation of scanner

    Knowledge of D. C. Layout
    Knowledge of safety regulations and procedures

(Continued)

Table 8.4   (Continued)

Skills
> Operation of forklift
> Reading and writing words and numbers

Ability
> Perceptual speed and accuracy (visual)
> Physical
>> Strength
>>> Lifting
>>> Dragging
>>> Pulling
>> Agility
>>> Stooping and bending
>>> Climbing
>>> Reaching
>>> Twisting
>
> Depth perception (vehicle operation)
> Spatial orientation and visualization (packing and storage)
> Multi-limb coordination (vehicle operation)
> Hearing (warning signals)

Other-Personality
> Conscientiousness
>> Attendance
>> Punctuality
> Attention to detail
> Work motivation (pace and endurance)
> Assertiveness (signing freight bill)
> Integrity
>> Theft avoidance
>> Drug and alcohol avoidance
>> Interpersonal hostility and violence avoidance
>
> Vigilance (resistance to monotony)
> Team orientation (agreeableness and customer orientation)

Levine, Bennett, and Ash (1979) surveyed experts to compare the PAQ, the critical incident technique, task analysis, and the job element method for personnel selection. They found that the experts most often used task analysis and the job element method. However, the experts were not highly favorable in their evaluations of any of the methods. Further research on the four methods by Levine, Ash, and Bennett (1980) showed that the critical incident technique

Table 8.5   KSAOs and Tests for the Receiver

	App/ Interview	Paper & Pencil	Simulation	Other
KNOWLEDGE OF:				
Arithmetic (add, count, subtract, multiply)	Interview	1. Customize 2. Saville & Holdsworth (Published test)	Number of items in a carton Number of items missing from a carton	
SKILL IN:				
Reading words and numbers	Application Interview		Read packing slip Read PC screen	
ABILITY IN:				
Eyesight (acuity; see well enough to read letters and numbers)		Number checking		Eye exam
Perceptual speed and accuracy		1. Number checking 2. Guilford-Zimmerman Aptitude Survey (Published test)	Find and select parts from bins matching part numbers to written orders	

resulted in slightly better test plans than the other methods, but the PAQ was the least expensive to use. The PAQ was not as popular for the development of test plans, probably because it does not provide task information. Levine et al. (1980) further noted that none of the methods provides information about minimum qualifications.

Training

Like staffing, training typically considers the job to be a fixed entity to which people are fit. In staffing, good fit between jobs and people is achieved by selecting the person who best matches the requirements of the job. In training, people are tailored to fit the job; that is, people are trained so that they come to possess the knowledge, skill, attitudes, values, or other requirements of the job, such as certificates. Abilities and personality characteristics are rarely trained.

Consider our receiver job. Receivers must quickly and accurately compare names and numbers on packing slips with names and numbers on delivered merchandise. Therefore, we might select them for perceptual speed and accuracy (an ability). Receivers have to compare the quantity of items on a packing slip to the quantity received, so they need to be able to count, add, subtract, and multiply quickly and accurately (often parts come in boxes that are only partially full, so it is much more efficient to multiply and subtract than to count). People can be either selected or trained for arithmetic (a knowledge). Most likely they will be selected, because it is reasonable to assume that most applicants will have the needed background in arithmetic. On the other hand, many receivers will be trained and certified in operating a forklift (knowledge of its operation, and skill in actually driving it). Most applicants know how to drive a car, but not a forklift.

The kind of training we are talking about in this book is training designed for jobs at work. Rather than being aimed at workers in general, such training is intended to facilitate job performance on tasks that constitute a job held or aspired to by incumbents. For example, a general class in human relations skills offered to all employees in a bank is not likely to be the sort of training we are describing. On the other hand, human relations skills in the context of instruction about how to conduct performance appraisal meetings for managers in the same bank would be considered training. The distinction is one of tailoring training to specific tasks that belong to a job currently held or shortly to be held by trainees. We applaud corporate efforts to further employee development through general education and skill development such as human relations skills classes, reimbursement for college credit, and so forth. Such instruction, however, is not typically based on a careful analysis of the job, nor are the instructional objectives defined in behaviors of interest to the job. Although general education is likely to benefit employees and ultimately prove beneficial to employers, it is not designed with the goal of immediate transfer.

Some form of training is necessary for virtually every job. If nothing else, people have to know where their workstations and tools are. Like recruiting, training comes in endless varieties from formal to informal. Formal training may take place away from the workplace over a long period of time. For example, mechanical flight trainers are used to train pilots in how to respond to emergencies such as engine fires. Or training may be rather informal and take place on the job. For example, a supervisor may ask a subordinate to instruct a new employee in how to use the telephone.

Training is expensive. People trained away from the job still get paid. The people doing the training need to be paid, and any space and equipment used in the training has to be supported. The cost of using a mechanical flight simulator for training may be more than $1,000.00 per hour. If the training is done on the job, then someone else usually has to take time away from his or her usual job to provide the training. Such time away creates a loss in efficiency—either some work fails to get done, or it gets done more slowly.

On the other hand, the cost of *failing* to provide training generally outweighs the cost of training. Many jobs will be done poorly or simply will not be done without some training. A computer programmer who is denied access to an account will not be effective. An untrained sales representative can lose business in many ways. People who handle hazardous materials can injure themselves or their coworkers. People who operate powerful machinery can create a real menace. Therefore, training is necessary to promote successful job performance and to avert disaster. From the employee's perspective, training can reduce stress by promoting feelings of confidence and competence.

We begin this section with an outline of what we call the "training cycle." The training cycle is a big-picture approach to solving an organizational problem through training. Training is unusual in its comprehensive problem-solving approach. Such an approach is a very good way to think about all applications of job analysis (for example, staffing, compensation, and job design) and not just training. After we present the training cycle, we describe the kinds of information that job analysis needs to provide in order to answer questions about training. As you will see, training is similar to selection in the kind of job information required, but training usually requires more specific information about the tasks (work attributes) than does selection.

THE TRAINING CYCLE

Training cycles of various kinds have been developed by different authors (for example, Gagne & Briggs, 1979; Goldstein & Ford, 2002). They are all alike in that they provide a means-ends analysis to meeting organizational goals. The cycle that we describe is developed in Goldstein and Ford (2002) and is shown in Table 8.6. The table contains four columns labeled Needs Assessment, Training and Development, Evaluation, and Training Goal. Each is briefly described.

Needs Assessment

Needs assessment is called different things by people responsible for training. Needs assessment is sometimes called "front-end analysis," because it must be done *before* the training is developed. Needs assessment is crucial to developing a good training program. Of the four phases of the training cycle, needs

Table 8.6   Training Cycle

Needs Assessment	Training and Development	Evaluation	Training Goal
1. Needs Assessment 　a. Organizational Support 　b. Organizational Analysis 　c. Task and KSA Analysis 　d. Person Analysis 2. Instructional Objectives	1. Selection and Design of Instructional Programs 2. Training	1. Development of Criteria 2. Use of Evaluation Models 　a. Individual Difference 　b. Experimental 　c. Content	1. Training Validity 2. Transfer Validity 3. Intra-Organizational Validity 4. Inter-Organizational Validity

SOURCE: From I. L. Goldstein (1993), *Training in Organizations*, 3rd ed. Copyright (c) 1993. Reprinted with permission of Wadsworth, a division of Thomson Learning.

analysis is the phase that is most closely tied to job analysis. The basic idea is that before we begin training, we need to have a good idea of what the training is supposed to accomplish. If the ultimate goals of training are not specified prior to training, there is a good chance that they will not be met. For example, Goldstein & Ford (2002) pointed out that firefighters may face dramatically different conditions and must do different things when fighting fires in high-rise buildings than when fighting fires on the docks of a river. Failure to specify goals regarding both types of fire combat will produce inadequate training programs.

Needs assessment involves three main entities: the organization, the tasks and KSAOs, and the people to be trained. *Organizational analysis* considers the job to be part of a larger organization. The job exists to fulfill some function. For example, our dough mixer job prepares dough to be baked into bagels and crullers and buns. If our customers are complaining about bad bagels, it could be because the dough mixer doesn't know how to mix the dough properly. We could have bad bagels for lots of other reasons, too, but the point is that the dough mixer job provides an output that is used by another job. The output provides some objectives that can be used to inform training.

Another way of saying this is to consider what management wants the training to achieve. The organizational analysis should tell us how to know whether our training is effective. For example, organizational analysis of the grocery clerks might point to customer satisfaction with the speed of service. Organizational analysis informs the training objectives; in other words, organizational analysis answers the question of *why* training takes place.

Task and KSAO analysis provides training content. All job-oriented training must consider the job itself, that is, the tasks contained in the job or common to several jobs. For example, there are aspects to driving a forklift that are determined by the machine and its use. The forklift driver needs to be able to steer the forklift to place the tines of the fork into a pallet, to operate controls that lift the pallet, and so forth. For simple jobs, the tasks that are found in the job description may be sufficient for understanding what needs to be trained. For most tasks, however, additional knowledge, skill, or other characteristics must be trained. For example, the forklift operator needs to know rules for safe operation of the forklift, such as speed limits, maximum weight for lifted loads, maximum heights and angles for lifting, and so on. Many years ago we experienced what could happen if these rules are not followed. At a soda bottling plant forklifts stacked pallets, each five soda cases high, up to three pallets high. An inexperienced driver failed to use the right angle in placing the top pallet at the end of a row. As a result an entire row of soft drinks came tumbling down like dominoes. It took two full shifts of three workers to clean up the mess. Task and KSAO analysis provides the substance of the training. That is, task and KSAO analysis (in part) answers the question of *what* is to be trained.

Person analysis concerns the KSAOs that trainees bring with them. A native French speaker will have little use for a course in conversational French. A student enrolled in calculus without first mastering algebra will be unprepared to handle the new material. It is a waste of time to train people on things they already know. The receiver job does not contain an arithmetic training module. Incumbents are expected to know how to add, subtract, multiply, and divide before they are hired. On the other hand, training will not be useful if the training incorrectly assumes that trainees possess skills that they do not. If most of the incumbents are native Spanish speakers with little exposure to English, the elaborate English instruction manuals may be largely wasted. Person analysis requires that information be gathered about the potential trainees before the training is developed. Person analysis helps to make sure that training is efficient by providing no more or less than what trainees need to achieve the training goals. Person analysis helps to answer (in part) the question of *what* is to be trained. It may also help us learn who is deficient on what skills, so the question of *who* should take our course is addressed.

Together, organizational analysis, task and KSAO analysis, and person analysis help to determine the *instructional objectives* for the training. Instructional objectives are statements that describe the behavior of properly trained people. Well-written instructional objectives contain enough context so that both the stimulus situation and the appropriate response are clear. Furthermore, good instructional objectives also contain statements about standards; that is, such statements specify a minimum acceptable level of performance. For example, in a course on the operation of a forklift, the immediate goal of the training is for the trainee to pass a certification exam and receive a certificate (license) to operate a forklift. The instructional objectives of the course are the things that a person has to do to pass the test. The operator might have to use a forklift to pick up a pallet and move it from one end of a warehouse to the other within 2 minutes without collisions or loss of objects from the pallet.

You are wondering about the term *organizational support* that appears in the table but has not been described. You *are* sharp this late in the chapter. Goldstein and Ford (2002) noted that gaining acceptance and support of top management and other organizational members, and their willingness to commit time and resources is critical to the whole needs assessment enterprise. However, it is less central to our mission here of focusing on the role played by job analysis.

Training and Development

Training and development activities are the heart of the training itself. The needs assessment provides instructional objectives. Instructional objectives say what properly trained people are supposed to do. Training and development provides the setting and activities that get the trainees to learn what it is that they are supposed to do, and if the training program works well, the learning will be maintained on the job. This phase involves both the selection and design of the instructional environment and the training itself. Lots of questions have to be answered in the design of the instruction.

- Where will the instruction take place?
- What media will be used?
- Who will provide the training?
- What instruction is already available? How suitable is it? How expensive is it?
- How much time and money are available for training?

Decisions about the training get made and the training gets developed one way or another. As we mentioned earlier, training programs vary enormously. Instruction on a single topic can be done as a lecture or a film, in small group discussions, through interaction with a machine such as a computer or simulator, by reading a book or other printed material, through other media (for example, closed-circuit TV), observation of a worker completing the task or practice on the job, preferably accompanied by well-timed feedback, or some combination of these.

Evaluation

It is easy to say that we favor effective and efficient training. It is harder to know that we have it. How can we show the effectiveness of training? This is the question of evaluation. Part of the answer to such a question is provided by the instructional objectives. The objectives should provide statements about

- The context or stimulus situation
- The behavioral requirement (what the person does), and
- The minimally acceptable response

Training should involve testing, so that the trainee can demonstrate what has been learned. If assertiveness is being trained, the trainee should demonstrate assertive behaviors in a social situation. If the training is about how to operate a forklift, the trainee should use a forklift to complete a task.

Evaluation Models. The evaluation models listed in this phase include *individual difference, experimental,* and *content.* Each of these models provides a data collection strategy that generates information about the quality of training. The individual difference model involves collecting data about the relative standing in training and relative standing on job performance and relating the training data to the job performance data. For example, we might compare police academy grades with subsequent patrol officer performance measures. If the two measures are correlated, training evaluations can be used for selection. Unfortunately, such correlations do not necessarily mean that much was learned in training.

The experimental model involves using trained and control groups and/or pretest-posttest designs to show the effects of training. We would expect that knowledge tests given at the beginning and end of training would show gains. For example, we might give tellers a test of the required bits of information needed to cash a check both before and after training. If the training is effective, we expect to see better performance on the test after training than before training. Performance on a test for a group that has just received a new kind of training may be compared with the performance of a group that received the old (status quo) form of training (or no training). By so doing, we can see how the new training compares with the prior method. Note that in both the individual difference and experimental evaluation models, the comparison is between people (correlations show standings relative to the mean; ANOVA (analysis of variance) shows mean differences between groups). This is different from a comparison to a standard of performance on the task itself as we required for the instructional objectives.

For example, suppose we are instructing people to serve in tennis. Our method involves giving people practice and feedback in serving the ball. Our test of proficiency is the number of serves out of 20 tries that are hit from behind the baseline into the service box at a speed of at least 50 miles per hour. Each trainee at the end of training gets 20 tries that are timed by a speed gun and judged by a lines person as either in or out. We just count the number that land "in" at more than 50 miles per hour. The individual difference method would involve comparing our service scores with later indices of tennis proficiency, such as tournament standings, points won, "aces," and so forth. The experimental method might use the same test both before and after training to see whether the serve improves over the course of instruction. A good instructional objective might state that upon completion of the training, the trainee must achieve a score of 10 or more on the test. Note that for the other two methods, no minimum score is needed to complete training. The content model merely requires that the training be connected to the KSAOs discovered by the job analysis.

Training Goals. Because training is developed to achieve organizational goals, it is a good idea to check whether the training results in the desired outcomes. The trainee may have learned to be assertive during training and be able to show appropriate assertive behaviors at the end of training, but the behavior may not be seen on the job because work group norms discourage it. Different authors organize training goals differently. Kirkpatrick (1959, 1960) has suggested assessing

> *Reactions:* Trainee reactions to instruction
>
> *Learning:* Measures of proficiency taken at the end of training
>
> *Behavior:* Measures of performance on the job subsequent to training, and
>
> *Results:* Organizational effectiveness measures that are believed to show the results of increased effectiveness on the job

If we were training data processing supervisors in skill in dealing with subordinates, for example, we would first ask the trainees at the end of training what they thought of the training. Was it useful? enjoyable? Next we would test them on the content of the course, to see whether they had learned the principles taught in the course (for example, balance positive and negative feedback). Third, we would examine performance on the job to determine how well they dealt with their subordinates. Finally, we would look at indices such as data processing service records and complaints about data processing from other departments, which would provide evidence of the functioning of the entire department.

Goldstein and Ford (2002) described four training goals:

1. Training validity

2. Transfer validity

3. Intraorganizational validity, and

4. Interorganizational validity

The first two of these are similar to two of Kirkpatrick's effectiveness categories. Training validity concerns whether anything was learned during training. Training validity is similar to Kirkpatrick's "learning," that is, measures of proficiency taken at the end of training. Training validity can be assessed using the experimental approach or the instructional objectives approach. The most useful information to establish training validity is the quality of trainee performance on tasks that were supposed to be trained. Transfer validity concerns how well the material learned in training applies to the job setting. Transfer validity is analogous to Kirkpatrick's "behavior," or measures of job performance. Here we are concerned with job performance that should be influenced by the training.

Two of the Goldstein and Ford's (2002) goals are different from Kirkpatrick's. Intraorganizational validity concerns how well the training evaluation results taken on one group of trainees applies to another group of trainees in the same organization. When training programs are new or when they are being formally evaluated, there may be pressure on the trainers and trainees to behave in ways that they otherwise would not. When classroom instructors are graded by the test scores that their students receive, for example, the instructors become motivated to "teach to the test." The question asked by *intra*organizational validity is whether the results of a training evaluation effort apply to ongoing training programs. In *inter*organizational validity, the question is whether training evaluated in one organization is likely to have similar effects when used in another organization. Going back to our data processing supervisor example, suppose we have a new subordinate relations training program and that both the instructors and supervisors know that the program will be evaluated by looking at the supervisors' scores on tests at the end of training and also by looking at supervisors' later job performance. Intraorganizational validity concerns whether the evaluation results for the training will apply when the training no longer involves evaluating trainees' scores at the end of training. Interorganizational validity would apply if we were borrowing the supervisor training from another company and looking to apply the results of that company's training evaluation study to our company.

We have described training evaluation in terms of a cycle because the results of the evaluation can be incorporated into a new needs analysis in order to improve training. Proceeding through the cycle will result in data that (a) show that training is effective, (b) show where training needs improvement, or (c) show that training is not the best way to solve the problem.

There is obviously more to the training story than we can get into here. As but one example, our approach to evaluation focuses on final outcomes or comparisons of training and job content. But what if the training decays over time because the trainer begins to leave out big chunks of the program? Lots of sources cover this complex and fascinating topic. The Web site of the American Society for Training and Development (www.astd.org) is an excellent source.

Key Considerations of Training

The content of the work itself, that is, the tasks, are central to training. KSAOs may also be important for training because they support task performance. For example, mixing the dough (a task) is the heart of the dough mixer's job. To carry out the task, the dough mixer has to know how to operate a mixing machine (specific knowledge of how to turn the machine on, operate safely, and so on). The level of detail required for the tasks will depend on the intended application. One application of task statements is to determine whether the task should be trained, and if so, where. Task statements in such a case can be written fairly broadly, as they are for job description and selection. Such task statements will often be rated by experts, and the ratings will be used to decide, for example, whether the task is to be trained.

When tasks are to be trained, that is, when job analysis is to provide the basis of the content of training, then the level of task description must be much more detailed. Otherwise, the training must be developed by one or more job experts (which is a good idea anyway, but not always practical). Task statements written for the receiver job as input to training are shown in Table 8.7. If you compare the tasks in Table 8.7 to the tasks in the job description in Table 7.3 you will see that Table 8.7 contains a larger number of tasks and that the tasks tend to be more detailed. Notice that the intent of the job description in Table 7.3 is to communicate the gist of the job. In Table 8.7, however, the job is described in terms of a series of steps as they typically occur on the job. Such a list of tasks could be used to inform training for employees who are new to the receiver job to be sure that the entire job is covered in training.

Table 8.7   Detailed Task List for the Receiver Job

Step 1: Unpack truck

1. Receive freight bill from trucker.
2. Operate forklift to move pallets from truck to storage.
3. Count pallets and cartons.
4. Sign freight bill if skid count agrees with freight bill.
5. Notify driver if skid count disagrees with freight bill and he will also recount.
6. Call for exception if driver and receiver agree with new count.
7. Contact supervisor if driver and receiver disagree with the count.
8. Fax notice of overage or underage to shipper.
9. Call shipper to notify them of overage or underage.
10. Call shipper to notify them to search for the missing part if exception is under-received.
11. Search all parts for labels and then call shipper to ask whether they want to sign over (receive) the part or send it back if exception is over-received.

Step 2: Unpack skid

1. Sign freight bill for piece count.
2. Find shipper's packing list.
3. Fill out alternate packing list if packing list is lost.
4. Look up PO in computer and print screen to create a packing list if the packing list is lost.
5. Cut shrink wrap with pallet knife.
6. Pull shrink wrap off boxes and discard.
7. Layout pallets to place unpacked order.
8. Check boxes and products for damage.
9. Put damaged box and product in designated "Bad Box" section to be sent for repacking if only box is damaged.
10. Set product aside for inspection if product is damaged or believed to be damaged.
11. Examine boxes for identification.
12. Move boxes containing the same part numbers to a common location if more than one part is stacked on the pallet.
13. Open boxes with more than one kind of part inside.
14. Multiply and add to determine the total number of each part in the order after parts are separated and collected by number.
15. Underline the vendor part number and circle or write in the quantity received if the packing slip is found.
16. Write the vendor part number and quantity of each part received on the alternate packing slip if the packing slip is not found.
17. Stack boxes so that vendor part number is visible to bar coders.
18. Stack boxes that look alike but have different part numbers in different locations.

Step 3: Receive parts into computer system

1. Enter password to log onto system.
2. Punch choice for receiving screen at main menu.
3. Punch PO number to find order of interest at receiving screen.
4. Identify local part numbers from vendor part numbers and other identifying information when order appears.
5. Enter quantities received for each part number received.
6. Compare quantities ordered (Qty Open) to quantity received.
7. Investigate discrepancies between quantity open and quantity received.
8. Fill out alternate packing slip for the discrepancy if parts are found.
9. Compare computer screen to paper to verify that all received entries are correct (verified).
10. Identify current places where product is stored using the computer.
11. Troubleshoot any computer error messages (red displays).

(Continued)

Table 8.7   (Continued)

12. Enter shipping information into computer (that is, use freight bill screen to enter number of packages, shipper, weight, shipping fee, zip code, and so on).
13. Locate part numbers using computer searches.
14. Locate part numbers by calling manufacturers.
15. Assign part numbers different POs.
16. Recount items to avoid receiving errors.
17. Troubleshoot parts to be received that do not match part numbers.
18. Call supervisor if troubleshooting is unsuccessful.

Step 4: Do paperwork and labeling

1. Print bar code labels and put-away document.
2. Reprint mangled bar codes.
3. Color special bar code labels with markers to help bar coders apply labels properly.
4. Collect bar code stickers from printer.
5. Affix order number sticker to packing list.
6. Initial and date sticker.
7. Collect put-away document from printer.
8. Place bar code stickers and associated put-away documents together on the floor in a separate location.
9. Take bar code stickers and put-away docs to parts received on the loading dock (storage area).
10. Replace stickers in bar code printer.
11. Replace paper in put-away document printer.
12. Compare bar code and boxes to verify that bar code stickers are placed on the correct boxes (spot check).

Step 5: Put away

1. Operate forklift to pick up pallets.
2. Operate other machines (for moving pallets) to pick up pallets.
3. Identify place that parts are to be stored from put-away document.
4. Operate forklift to store pallets.
5. Place boxes onto pallet.
6. Remove boxes from pallet and place onto storage rack.
7. Place boxes so that bar code faces pickers.
8. Scan the product number bar code and the storage location bar code to note location.
9. Enter the quantity of the product stored in a particular location in the scan gun.
10. Note new storage locations using the computer.
11. Place scan gun in computer cradle in order to transfer put-away orders from the scan gun to the computer.
12. Print out the transferred put-away orders.
13. Check the original packing slips to the transferred put-away orders for accuracy.
14. Send the put-away orders to corporate in order to validate them.

The training itself typically requires a level of detail that is much greater than is supplied by the task statements. This is because learning task performance requires a linking of specific stimulus conditions to specific desired responses. The specific hazards of the dough-mixing machine are not apparent from the task statements, but are readily apparent when you are standing next to the machine (it can rip off your arm). The computer screens that a receiver has to work through to enter inventory and to troubleshoot are not described in the kind of detail in task statements that one needs to use the screens on the job. In the receiver job, one can learn on the job by watching another person go through the computer screens. One could learn off the job through a workbook or a computer simulation. If training is done off the job, a great deal of care needs to be taken that the correct stimulus situations are presented to avoid training the wrong behaviors. We delight in retelling the story of a new cashier in a department store who was having difficulty with a credit card purchase. She told her supervisor that she was doing it exactly like she was taught in training. Her supervisor responded, "Forget everything you learned in training and watch me."

Rating Scales. It is often the case that training does not encompass the entire job; rather, only some of the tasks are trained. Training is expensive, and many tasks can be learned quickly on the job with minimal risk. Rating scales are often used to help decide how to treat different tasks. Examples of commonly used rating scales include the following:

- Importance or criticality
- Consequence of error
- Difficulty to learn
- Frequency of occurrence
- Location of training

Tasks are good candidates for training if they are important or critical, occur frequently, or are difficult to learn. Police officers do not often shoot guns at work. However, the task is critical and it has serious consequences if there are errors, so shooting must be trained. Firefighters rarely fight fires, but that is the essence of their job. A sales job may involve the use of a computer system to book and track orders that are shipped to customers. If the computer system requires some sophistication to use, it will probably be trained prior to actually doing the job. The location of the training may be asked directly (for example, "Where should the task be learned?").

SELECTION VERSUS TRAINING

Both selection and training tend to focus on tasks that are critical, occur frequently, or are difficult to learn or perform. In short, both are concerned with the job's most important tasks. One major distinction between selection and training has to do with the characteristics of the applicant pool. If most applicants have the knowledge or skill, it makes sense to require the skill upon entry rather than train the skill. On the other hand, if most of the applicants do not have the knowledge or skill, or if a company is specifically looking for beginners to learn "the company way," then it makes sense to train the knowledge or skill. This is the reason job analysts try to establish whether it is practical to expect a skill in the applicant pool and whether new workers need the skill right away.

Chapter Summary

STAFFING

We described links between job analysis and two of the three main staffing functions, recruitment and selection. Job analysis for recruitment must provide information to communicate the gist of the job and its essential requirements to recruiters and applicants. Job analysis for selection must provide the information needed to infer the knowledge, skills, abilities, and other characteristics (KSAOs) required for successful job performance. A variety of methods are useful in providing the worker attributes or KSAOs (for example, C-JAM, PAQ, ARS, job elements, critical incident technique). Once the KSAOs are determined, they can be used to devise or choose tests or other methods to evaluate the applicants on them. Validation studies can (should) be conducted when feasible to establish the job relatedness of the chosen tests. Job analysis must provide work-oriented (task) information for this purpose. For content-oriented validation, task information generally provides the strongest basis for inferring validity when it is used to judge the appropriateness or relevance of the test's content. KSAO information, although relevant, requires somewhat more risky judgments that scores will be valid based on test contents alone. For criterion-oriented validation, tasks provide the basis for establishing criteria used in evaluating the empirical relations between test scores and job performance. For construct-oriented strategies, job analysis provides the basis for judgments about relations among measures that are theoretically relevant to the focal test and job performance.

TRAINING

Training, like selection, considers jobs to be fixed entities. Both training and selection are most concerned with central or critical tasks of the job. Unlike selection, in which people are chosen to match the job, training uses instruction to change people to fit the job. The training cycle is a process used to make sure that training is effective in achieving organizational goals. The training cycle tailors the training to fit its objectives. In the needs assessment phase, the requirements of the organization and job are compared to the skills available in the potential trainees to make training effective and efficient. Later phases of the training cycle help evaluate the effectiveness of the training. Job analysis provides input to training by specifying the task content of jobs. It also provides information that is useful in deciding which tasks should and should not be trained and if the task is to be trained, where. In addition to task knowledge, training may also enhance KSAOs to support task performance.

9

Doing a Job Analysis Study

A s much fun as job analysis is to study, it is even more fun to do. Even the incumbents usually like it. Once people get over their disbelief that you actually want to know the details of their work, they become more than willing to share. In this chapter, we discuss how to carry out a job analysis. Before you actually analyze one or more jobs, you have to make some decisions. First, you have to decide what kind of job analysis to do. What descriptors will you use? What sources of information? What methods of data collection? How will you analyze the data? Who gets the information? In large part, the purposes or functions of the job analysis should provide the answers to such questions. If your aim is job evaluation, you will want different information than you would if your aim is training for a specific task.

In addition to the purposive questions, you need to answer some practical questions before you start. Who will be in charge of the job analysis? Who will carry it out? What are the costs and constraints of the techniques that you might use and how do these compare to your budget and resources? If you want to observe the job and your job incumbents are all within easy reach, great. But what if they are located all over the world? Yes, it would be nice to go visit each one (particularly those in places you've always wanted to see like Bali, Hong Kong, Paris, and Singapore), but your boss isn't going to let you have the time or money for that.

Deciding what to do for a job analysis requires that you answer both sets of questions (functional and practical). Then there is the collection of data through observation, interview, surveys, or whatever means. We offer tips on each of these. After the data are collected, there are issues about the quality of the data that should be addressed (inquiring minds will want to know about the reliability of the data). The data must then be analyzed to provide information that can be used for the original purposes of the job analysis. At the end of the study, some report or other action should be taken in relation to the original purpose of the job analysis. Issues of how the information will be disseminated, stored, and retrieved for future uses conclude the whole process. We describe each step in turn.

Matching Purpose and Job Analysis Attributes

PURPOSES

The method of job analysis should be chosen to provide information required to fulfill one or more purposes or objectives. We covered the main purposes of job analysis in Chapter 1 and again in Chapters 7 and 8. For the sake of review, we list purposes identified by Levine, Thomas, and Sistrunk (1988, pp. 340–341). Brief descriptions are offered for those purposes that have not been covered earlier in the book.

1. *Job description* (see Chapter 7).

2. *Job classification.* Job classification is the assignment of a target job to a category of other jobs that are similar in some way. Job classification results in job families, which are groups of closely related jobs. Multiple ways of defining job similarity have been used. For example, outcomes and products of the job, knowledge and skill required by the job, and compensation paid for the job have all been used.

3. *Job evaluation* (see Chapter 7).

4. *Job design/redesign* (see Chapter 7).

5. *Personnel requirements/specifications* (see Chapter 8).

6. *Performance appraisal* (see Chapter 7).

7. *Worker training* (see Chapter 8).

8. *Worker mobility.* Worker mobility concerns the planned movement of people through a series of jobs (sometimes called succession planning). Such series are often called job ladders, career ladders, or job lattices. Worker mobility is closely related to vocational and career development. At times, this may refer to unplanned mobility, like turnover, which could be a result of one job feature or another.

9. *Efficiency/safety.* Various programs can be developed to improve safety at work, including redesigning jobs, selecting "safe" people, and implementing programs to motivate safe behavior.

10. *Workforce planning.* Workforce planning concerns explicit plans by an organization to recruit, select, and develop people through worker mobility so as to ensure that both organizational needs in terms of skilled workers and individual needs in terms of career development are met.

11. *Legal/quasi-legal requirements.* Employers are required to supply some reports to the federal government, such as the EEO-1 report. Job analysis also supports the legal foundation for many other purposes, such as selection (see Chapter 6).

The purposes that are listed here are not mutually exclusive. For example, job classification is closely linked to job evaluation. Rather, we have attempted to provide a fairly comprehensive list of uses to which job analysis information may be put.

ATTRIBUTES

We described the many attributes of job analysis in Chapter 1. Take a moment to review Table 1.3 to recall the numerous descriptors, sources of information, methods of data collection, and units of analysis (we'll wait for you right here). For further detail, you might want to consult Levine, Thomas, and Sistrunk (1988). These attributes are applicable to jobs performed by individuals. Analyzing the work of teams may require more options (see Chapter 5). When you consider that multiple attributes can be used, it should be clear that a very large number of combinations are possible for a single job analysis project.

Selecting Approaches

In this section, we remark on job analysis attributes that are particularly suited or unsuited for specific purposes. The remarks are based on some combination of (1) empirical research on the methods, (2) the stated purpose of the development of the method, and (3) our experience. Although empirical research is the most important source of information to consider, there is a shortage of studies that compare the outcomes of different job analysis methods for the same purpose. There has been research on expert opinions about the usefulness of various techniques, however, and we report on that. Levine, Ash, Hall, and Sistrunk (1983) surveyed job analysis experts regarding their opinions of seven commonly used job analysis methods for 11 purposes. A summary of mean ratings given by the experts is shown in Table 9.1. In that table the scale ranges from low = 1 to high = 5.

Table 9.1 shows mean responses of job analysis experts to questions about the usefulness of various approaches for various purposes. For example, it shows that the experts believe that the *task inventory* and *functional job analysis* are the most useful for informing job descriptions, and the *Ability Requirements Scales* are not very useful for job descriptions. For another example, the *critical incident technique* is seen as most useful for developing performance appraisal materials. Here we cover those purposes not covered in Chapter 7 (job description, job evaluation, performance appraisal, job design/redesign) and Chapter 8 (training, staffing). For those purposes, refer to the relevant chapter under "Key Considerations."

Table 9.1   Effectiveness of Job Analysis Methods for Different Purposes

Purpose	TTA	ARS	PAQ	CIT	TI	FJA	JE
Job description	2.95	2.15	2.86	2.59	4.20	4.07	2.66
Job classification	3.11	2.61	3.67	2.19	4.18	3.81	2.73
Job evaluation	2.80	2.44	3.70	2.37	3.46	3.52	2.72
Job design	2.73	2.28	2.99	2.52	3.72	3.64	2.59
Personnel requirements/ specification	3.68	3.51	3.36	2.86	3.19	3.58	3.64
Performance appraisal	2.80	2.75	2.72	3.91	3.24	3.58	3.07
Worker training	2.74	2.78	2.76	3.42	3.65	3.63	3.33
Worker mobility	2.67	2.47	2.78	2.20	3.34	3.07	2.62
Efficiency/safety	2.34	1.90	2.46	3.08	2.79	2.81	2.30
Workforce planning	2.61	2.32	2.83	2.24	3.41	3.11	2.60
Legal/quasi-legal requirements	2.65	2.44	3.03	2.66	3.67	3.38	2.79

SOURCE: Levine, E. L., Ash, R. A., Hall, H., & Sistrunk, F. (1983). Evaluation of job analysis methods by experienced job analysts. *Academy of Management Journal, 26,* 342. Copyright (c) 1983 by Academy of Management (N&). Reproduced with permission via Copyright Clearance Center.

NOTE: TTA is Threshold Traits Analysis, ARS is Ability Requirements Scales, PAQ is Position Analysis Questionnaire, CIT is Critical Incident Technique, TI is Task Inventory/CODAP, FJA is Functional Job Analysis, and JE is the Job Elements Method.
Ratings are on a 1 (low) to 5 (high) scale.

It would be nice if we could hear about your goals, and then prescribe the one and only correct job analysis approach. It would be nice, but it is not possible (at least, not if we are going to be honest about it). In some cases, we can eliminate some approaches. For example, we would probably avoid the Threshold Traits Analysis System or the PAQ as the primary means for developing a training program, because such methods focus on human attributes rather than task-based skill development. But there are several approaches that do focus on tasks, such as critical incidents, the task inventory, and observation/ interviews. Any of these might prove useful. Of those methods that are most relevant to your purpose, you will need to consider pragmatics. How much time and money do you have? If you have lots, your choices are many. The less time and money you have available, the fewer your choices. What kind of access to job holders (and/or supervisors) is possible? Is it feasible to do the work yourself, that is, can an analyst try it? Will you want quantitative ratings of criticality? Someday it may be possible to hold a conversation with an artificial intelligence program that will give you expert advice. Today, you need to keep an eye on your purpose and think carefully about how the job analysis method will get you where you want to go. It will often be the case that more than one method is feasible and effective and the choice may boil down to pragmatics, politics, or your comfort level with the method.

JOB CLASSIFICATION

Job classification requires the placement of each job into a category on the basis of similarity so that each job goes into the category that it most resembles. There have been several means of defining similarity in terms of job attributes. McCormick (1976) described four types of attributes (and we mention a fifth):

1. *Job-oriented systems.* The focus is on the outcome of the job, such as a product or service.

2. *Worker-oriented systems.* The focus is on the observable human requirements or demands made by the job, such as worker activities, and elemental motions plus physiological demands.

3. *Attribute requirements.* The focus is on the knowledge, skills, abilities, and other characteristics (KSAOs) required by the job (the unobservable, but inferred attributes), such as personal job demands and human attribute requirements.

4. *Overall job systems.* The focus is on the job title and type of work performed.

5. *Compensation.* Jobs are clustered into bands or levels based on salary.

Because the descriptors vary so widely, a large number of sources of data and methods of data collection apply. An important requirement is that the descriptors are common across jobs so that classification based on similarities among the same descriptors can be evaluated. Sometimes descriptors may be job specific; in such a case, judges must infer similarities. The classification operation can be carried out by judgment or by a numerical algorithm such as cluster analysis. Cluster analysis will place each job into a category defined to be most similar according to a specified rule. There are many possible rules, so it is possible that a job will belong to different categories depending on how the cluster analysis is done. Research indicates that the type of cluster analysis is not as important as the type of descriptor, however (Levine, Thomas, & Sistrunk, 1988).

WORKER MOBILITY

Mobility refers to the movement of people between jobs within an organization. Typically, a large number of jobs will be involved in a mobility study. Therefore, job incumbents and supervisors are likely sources of data. Job analysts are also useful, but often too expensive and slow to complete the entire study. Questionnaires are likely to be distributed to gather the needed information. A quantitative analysis such as cluster analysis is likely to be computed based on scales applied to work or to trait requirements. Placing career ladders and lattices along with job bidding procedures online with associated job descriptions can aid in career planning.

EFFICIENCY/SAFETY

The most appropriate descriptors for job analysis for efficiency/safety depends on the job in question (Levine, Thomas, & Sistrunk, 1988). The analysis of production and assembly jobs is typically completed by a very skilled analyst who observes incumbents working in what is called a *time-and-motion study* (see Chapter 2). The analyst often uses special recording equipment such as video or special transcription notation to record incumbent body movements.

Other frequently used methods focus on the machines, tools, equipment, and work aids required by the job (for example, functional job analysis, the Position Analysis Questionnaire). An analysis of the equipment can be done by an expert analyst or other technical experts, by reviewing technical documents, and by incumbent interviews. Task information can also be used to create more efficient or less stressful sequences of tasks or to develop job aids such as checklists that will minimize errors.

There are three main approaches to improving safety (Landy & Trumbo, 1980):

1. The engineering approach, which involves the design of equipment and processes of task accomplishment (that is, ergonomics for prevention of injury and increasing efficiency; see MacLeod, 2000; Mital, Kilbom, & Kumar, 2000)

2. The personnel psychology approach, which involves the selection of people with traits suited for the work

3. The industrial/social approach, which involves the development of programs to motivate employees to behave safely (for example, Geller, 2001)

The procedures we already described appear useful for the engineering approach. In addition, critical incidents may prove useful because the technique can highlight behaviors that are unsafe or behaviors that avert or mitigate accidents. The personnel psychology approach requires an analysis of the job in terms of the human attributes required for safe performance of the job in question, which could include such attributes as conscientiousness and physical strength. The industrial/social approach appears less job oriented, so job analysis may be needed primarily to customize or tailor the approach to specific job content.

WORKFORCE PLANNING

Workforce planning is the complement of workforce mobility. With planning, the organization is trying to make sure that it will have people with the needed skills both now and especially in the future. To create plans, the organization must take stock of where it is and where it expects to be in terms of jobs and their requirements, on the one hand, and people and their skills, on the other. Although tasks can be used as descriptors for this purpose, the most likely descriptor will be human attributes, particularly skills. The likely sources of data include supervisors, experts, and incumbents. The methods of data collection include group and individual interviews and the questionnaire. The most likely units of analysis are worker trait requirements and scales applied to such requirements.

LEGAL/QUASI-LEGAL REQUIREMENTS

Legal requirements vary by the purpose or human resource application. However, legal requirements should be analyzed to plan for legal challenges. Areas for consideration include collective bargaining agreements, equal opportunity requirements, licensing requirements, and Occupational Safety and Health Administration (OSHA) regulations (Levine, Thomas, & Sistrunk, 1988). As a general rule, tasks and work activities are useful descriptors for legal requirements because people usually think of jobs in terms of tasks (Ash, Levine, & Sistrunk, 1983).

PRACTICAL CONSIDERATIONS

As we have said many times, the choice of job analysis methods should suit the purpose of the job analysis. However, completing any project requires resources. In this section, we describe practical concerns and choices that must be made either before the job analysis project begins or during the project itself.

Issues to Consider

Levine, Thomas, and Sistrunk (1988, p. 348) presented a list of 11 practical issues to consider when choosing a job analysis method:

1. *Operational status.* Has the method been tested and refined enough to be considered ready for use in its current form?

2. *Off-the-shelf availability.* Is the method ready to use, or must it first be redesigned or custom tailored to the particular job being analyzed?

3. *Occupational versatility/suitability.* Is the method suitable for the analysis of a variety of jobs, or at least the various types of jobs that are to be analyzed in the current project?

4. *Standardization.* Is the method capable of yielding norms, thus allowing the comparison of data obtained from different sources at different times?

5. *Respondent/user acceptability.* Is the method, including its various information-gathering requirements and report format, acceptable to the job analysis respondents and users?

6. *Amount/availability of job analyst training.* How much training is required for job analysts to be able to use the method independently, and how readily available is the training?

7. *Sample size.* How many respondents or sources of information does the method require in order to ensure adequately dependable data?

8. *Reliability.* Will the method yield similar results upon repetition?

9. *Cost.* What is the estimated cost of the method? The cost includes the cost of materials, required training, consultative assistance, and person-hours by salary for job analysts, respondents, and clerical staff.

10. *Quality of outcome.* Will a particular method generally produce high-quality outcomes (that is, legally defensible, valid examinations, effective training programs) relative to other methods?

11 *Time to completion.* How many calendar days will it take to collect the data and produce a final written report?

Levine et al. (1983) also surveyed job analysis experts about their opinions regarding the practicality of several commonly used job analysis methods. The results are summarized in Table 9.2. Again the scale ranges from 1 = low practicality to 5 = high practicality. The experts indicated that the job analysis methods differed most on four of the practicality issues. One such issue was standardization. Relatively standardized methods included the PAQ and the task inventory (TI/CODAP), whereas the critical incident technique was found to be relatively unstandardized. A second issue was time to completion, where the relatively quick methods were the PAQ, Ability Requirements Scales, and Threshold Traits Analysis, and the relatively slow methods were the task inventory, functional job analysis, and the critical incident technique. A third issue was off-the-shelf availability. The PAQ was considered very practical in this regard; the critical incident technique was least practical. The fourth issue was reliability. The task inventory and the PAQ were given the highest ratings for

Table 9.2   Practicality Ratings of Job Analysis Methods

Practical Issue	TTA	ARS	PAQ	CIT	TI	FJA	JE
Occupational versatility/ suitability	3.74	3.61	3.82	3.86	4.13	4.06	3.58
Standardization	3.37	3.40	4.28	1.99	3.97	3.54	2.88
Respondent/ user acceptability	2.96	3.00	3.12	3.19	3.43	3.44	3.16
Amount of job analyst training required	2.73	3.00	2.78	3.04	2.39	2.57	2.68
Operational	2.96	3.09	4.20	3.42	4.04	3.85	3.52
Sample size	2.78	2.51	3.53	3.04	2.08	3.26	3.16
Off-the-shelf	3.20	3.27	4.51	2.43	2.98	3.28	3.03
Reliability	3.04	3.10	3.84	2.67	4.05	3.49	2.93
Cost	2.87	3.23	3.29	2.57	2.29	2.80	2.96
Quality of outcome	2.67	2.61	3.17	2.74	3.63	3.53	2.76
Time to completion	3.31	3.36	3.43	2.17	1.93	2.57	2.93

SOURCE: Levine, E. L., Ash, R. A., Hall, H., & Sistrunk, F. (1983). Evaluation of job analysis methods by experienced job analysts. *Academy of Management Journal, 26*, 344. Copyright (c) 1983 by Academy of Management (N&). Reproduced with permission via Copyright Clearance Center.

NOTE: TTA is Threshold Traits Analysis, ARS is Ability Requirements Scales, PAQ is Position Analysis Questionnaire, CIT is Critical Incident Technique, TI is Task Inventory/CODAP, FJA is Functional Job Analysis, and JE is the Job Elements Method.
Ratings are on a 1 (low) to 5 (high) scale.

reliability, followed by functional job analysis, which was more highly rated than the other methods.

Organizational Issues

The issues raised by Levine et al. (1983) are tied to the job analysis methods. For example, methods differ in their reliability and time to completion. Other practical issues in job analysis concern choices that are more closely linked to the organization than to the method per se. Such issues include the following:

- Time and budget
- Project staffing
- Acceptability of the process and outcome

Time and Budget. The amount of time available to complete the project and the budget available for its completion may be negotiated with management or may be set by management at a level higher than those who actually complete the project. That is, you may find yourself with a given budget and deadline and told to do what it takes to get the job done on time and under budget. Clearly, such constraints will influence the job analysis method chosen. Questionnaires take longer to develop and administer, so if time is short, the questionnaire is a poor choice unless a commercially available questionnaire suits your needs.

Project Staffing. Someone has to lead the job analysis project, and someone has to carry out the work. Sometimes the same person gets to do both; often the project leader is responsible for multiple projects of which this job analysis is only one. The formal project leader will almost certainly belong to the host organization. However, the people responsible for carrying out the project may be hired as consultants specifically because of their expertise. Consult Van de Voort and Stalder (1988) in deciding whether to hire a consultant or staff the project internally.

Acceptability. At least three of the Levine et al. (1983) practical issues are relevant to the organizational acceptability of the job analysis project: respondent/user acceptability, quality of outcome, and time to completion. Additional organizational concerns were discussed in Hakel, Stalder, and Van de Voort (1988). They noted that a job analysis project needs a sponsor (the person who wants the project done for whatever reason). The more visible and powerful the sponsor, the easier it will be to complete the project. In communicating with the higher levels of the organization, it is important to show how the job analysis will contribute to the organization's objectives, but to avoid overstating the benefits of the project.

Data collection will involve contact with members of the organization, perhaps a few, perhaps many. Acceptance of the method will be influenced by the time required. If a survey is used, then the cosmetics of the survey will influence acceptance. Either way, managers of those affected by the project must be notified of the project. Involvement of incumbents or experts will require that those contacted be told the purpose of the job analysis and the organization members' role in the process.

Once the data are collected, the main thrust is to make sure that the data are analyzed and reported in a manner that facilitates the intended purpose. The report must be clear and relevant, and if a product of the analysis is a database, it must be easy to access and ready for use. If possible, incumbents or experts should be involved in reviewing the report and verifying its contents so that they support it. The report should also be geared toward the needs of the project's sponsor.

Observations and Interviews

Sometimes the job analysis project involves a staff and laborious data collection. Other times, the job analyst does the whole project in short order. In the latter case, the job analyst will usually observe incumbents working, interview incumbents, or both. It is preferable to interview the incumbents while watching them because you can ask questions immediately about how and why something is done. Sometimes interviewing incumbents during the work is not a good idea. The interview could interfere with the performance of the job, resulting in unsafe practices or poor productivity for the worker (for example, surgeon, racing pit crew, piece rate workers). In such cases, observation can be followed by an interview. The observation may be video-taped as well and then the interview can incorporate the video.

PREPARING FOR THE OBSERVATION/INTERVIEW

Before you go, find out as much as you can about the job. Places to start include the following:

1. Prior job descriptions from the organization

2. Training manuals and other training materials

3. Job descriptions from the *Dictionary of Occupational Titles* (U.S. Department of Labor, 1991), O*NET, or studies reported in the professional literature

4. Operations managers or human resource professionals who can tell you the gist of the job

Try to learn any special jargon used on the job so that you will understand what the incumbent or experts are telling you. Write down things that you don't understand going into the meeting so that you are sure to clear them up during the interview. The observation/interview will then provide a chance to check what you think you know about the job going in.

Your dress should not be the object of comment at the site chosen for observation/interview; no matter where you are going, dress like the people who will be there. If you are going to a warehouse, people will be wearing T-shirts or sweatshirts, jeans or overalls, and work shoes. If you are going to a bank, people will be wearing jackets and ties (as of this writing, casual Fridays are the norm in business, but you can always take your tie off). Safety equip-ment such as hard hats and safety goggles are usually provided by people at the site, but check ahead of time to see what is needed and how to get it.

You will need to keep records of the observation/interview. Most people use a notebook or clipboard and a pen to take notes. We usually print a series of questions and write answers or take observation notes directly on the same paper (as an alternative you can use notebook computers or personal digital assistants). If you are going to write out questions ahead of time, leave space for your answers. You can also use video and/or audio recording devices for observations and interviews. If you do, make sure that your incumbents or experts know what you're up to and that they agree to allow you to do so. Video and audio recordings tend to make people nervous.

Schedule your meetings in advance, typically 1 to 2 weeks out. Both the incumbents or experts and their managers need to know that you will be conducting an observation/interview. If you will be conducting an interview away from the job site, try to schedule a room for the interview that is good for an interview. That is, it should be clean, well lit, and free from distractions. Simultaneous observation and interview is nice because you can ask questions about things you are observing. On the other hand, interviews away from the job are nice because the incumbents or experts are focused on the job analysis rather than trying to get the job done. Such interviews are more efficient.

MAKING CONTACT

When you go to the site to do the observation/interview, you will ordinarily make contact with the supervisor first (this won't be the case if, for example, you are interviewing a receptionist). The supervisor will usually introduce you or arrange for an introduction to the incumbent or expert. When you meet the supervisor and the incumbent/expert, you should (Hakel et al., 1988):

1. Introduce yourself. Tell them your role in the project.

2. Tell them why you are conducting a job analysis and what will be done with the information. This is especially important if you are collecting data for purposes other than job evaluation.

3. Explain what information you are trying to obtain from them. If you have written questions, show them what you have written and let them know that this is what you will be asking.

4. If the incumbent or expert can expect any changes as a result of the project, let them know when they might expect to see the change.

5. Ask them if they have questions; if so, answer them to the best of your ability.

What you are trying to do is establish open, honest, nonthreatening communications between you and whoever is to be observed or interviewed. People are often threatened by someone coming from outside and watching them work because they fear a negative evaluation. Once they believe that you are there to analyze the job rather than evaluate their performance, however, they usually cooperate.

CONDUCTING THE OBSERVATION/INTERVIEW

Several strategies can be used for observations and interviews including the typical day, task cycles, and tasks listed by importance. For the "typical day" strategy, ask the incumbent or expert to take you through a typical day, starting with arrival at work. This method helps to provide a complete list of tasks. On the other hand, the incumbent can become bogged down in details. "First, I put my key in the lock. Then I turn it. Then I open the door. Then I turn on the lights. . . ." Most jobs have a cycle of tasks that is repeated. In photo finishing, for example, the technician gets film from a customer, develops the film, creates prints from the developed film with a printer, packages the prints and negatives, and then rings up a sale when the customer returns for the prints. For such jobs, try to observe a complete cycle or two. In an interview, have the incumbent or expert tell you about the job in terms of a sequence of steps, explaining how one step leads to the next. After the main cycles are covered, ask to see or have explained parts of the job that are less frequent. In the photo technician job, less frequent tasks include maintaining the printer by replenishing fluids, calibrating the printer, and so forth. If the job does not have clear cycles, ask for a list of tasks with the most important tasks listed first. The photo technician might list printing first or perhaps customer interactions, and then proceed to the next. The task list by importance strategy is helpful to ensure that the most important tasks are covered.

In our experience, interviews with incumbents and technical experts are best suited to gathering task- or work-oriented information. Incumbents rarely think about worker requirements or traits that separate the more and less successful incumbents. Supervisors do think about worker-oriented information, especially if the supervisors are responsible for the selection or training of their people. If you need to gather human attribute requirements, go ahead and ask both supervisors and incumbents for their opinions. But do not be surprised if you get better information on attribute requirements from the supervisors. On the other hand, incumbents often have a better understanding of how the job is currently done (task requirements) than do supervisors.

After the interview or observation, you may want to check back with the supervisor to report on what you have learned and to let him or her know you are finished.

Remember to thank your contacts for their time and cooperation. Avoid taking more time from them than you scheduled.

Questionnaires

PLANNING AND PREPARING

Unless you use an off-the-shelf product such as the PAQ, task inventories and other surveys require time and effort to develop. All surveys require time to distribute, collect, and analyze. Once the survey goes out, your mistakes are pretty much permanent, so it makes sense to take time up front to get it right. Collect *only* the information you need, but *all* the information you need. When you collect data from members of an organization, you set up the expectation that something will be done with the information. If members learn that survey information is not used, they will not be motivated to complete the survey. Therefore, avoid collecting superfluous data; collect only the information you need. Questionnaires allow you to collect large amounts of precise, quantitative data. Such data can be used to represent even small differences in the criticality, time spent, or other attributes of various tasks. But surveys tell you nothing about things that you forgot to put in the survey. And you typically cannot go back and collect the missing data. Therefore, ask for all the information you need the first time.

Your task list should be complete. Tasks should be organized by duty, either alphabetically or in the sequence required by the job. Duties should stand out from tasks, either by font size, boldface type, or layout. At the end of each duty, there should be space for the incumbent to write in tasks that are not listed on the questionnaire. The reason for the organization is so that respondents (usually incumbents) can easily tell whether a given task is included in the task inventory without having to search the entire list. Incumbents usually do not fill in missing tasks, but occasionally someone will write in something important that indicates an omission on the questionnaire.

Writing Tips

Writing good task statements is difficult and time consuming; it is something of an art. Hints on writing them gleaned from various sources include the following:

1. Be clear. If the respondents fail to understand the tasks, the results will be worthless.

2. Be brief. Shorter statements can be read more quickly by respondents. When qualifying statements are used, they should serve some purpose. Consider the purposes of the job analysis while reviewing the task statements.

3. Follow standard job analysis grammar. The first word in the statement is an action verb, followed by a direct object plus optional qualifiers.

4. Be specific. The task should be stated so that there is no doubt whether the respondent does the task. This implies (a) the statement contains a single action and a single object, and (b) the task is narrow enough that the respondent does all or none of it, rather than part of it.

5. Use common words or jargon familiar to the employees. The respondent must understand the statement.

Distribution

The survey is a major effort to develop and may require several hours of each subject matter expert's (SME's) time in responding to the questionnaire. Because surveys are typically mailed or sent via the Internet, there is generally nobody to answer any questions the SME might have in responding to the questionnaire. It is a good idea to pilot test the questionnaire to be sure that the task statements are clear, the task list is complete, and the instructions on how to complete the questionnaire are clear.

Have a care with the appearance of the questionnaire. It should look professionally prepared. There should be no typographical errors or formatting problems. Directions should be clear. Today's word processors allow anyone to prepare excellent documents, so the preparation is not as expensive as it once was. If you have 100 or fewer respondents, a response form in which the incumbent circles a number directly on the questionnaire is a good choice. Dummy up responses to a few and see how long it takes to punch them into a computer database. This will let you estimate how long it will take to enter the data.

If you are administering a survey to a large number of people, you may wish to print a document that can be scanned by a computer. For very large applications, you may want to hire a firm that does surveys for a business. In many cases, it is now feasible to administer surveys over the Internet or a computer connected to a telephone. In either case, the incumbent contacts the computer for the survey by visiting a designated Web site or dialing an assigned phone number. The computer asks questions and the incumbent responds by typing numbers or letters, or pushing buttons on the telephone. For large-scale applications, the expense of setting up the survey for the computer is less than the clerical effort that would be needed to take the paper-and-pencil responses and enter them into a computer.

The choice of scales to include will depend on the purpose of the job analysis. If training is the purpose, then a question about whether the task should be trained on the job or off the job is reasonable. The same question would not be reasonable if the purpose were selection. Another question might ask about how difficult a task is to learn. Consider how the scales will be used, singly or in combination, before you collect the data. The number of response options should fit the question, so we would not choose four response options to a question about whether the incumbent does or does not do the task. For graded response options such as criticality or the amount of time spent, there are typically five, seven, or nine response options provided. Give people the largest number of response options that they can use reliably and meaningfully. If you give them fewer than they can use reliably, you throw away information. If you give them more than they can use reliably, instead of getting finer distinctions, you get more error.

COLLECTING DATA

Although most people like to talk about their work, they don't like to fill out surveys, especially long ones. If at all possible, gather your respondents in a single room, distribute the surveys, and have them fill them out and turn them in. If you do this, you will have a terrific response rate. If the incumbents cannot be herded into rooms to fill out the surveys, they usually receive them by mail or email at work or they can access the survey via a computer network. If so, they should be granted time at work to complete the survey. If incumbents are told to take the survey home and complete it on their own time, the response rate will be very low and those who complete the surveys may not be representative of the workforce as a whole. If surveys are completed individually, set a deadline (typically about 1 week from receipt of the survey) for the incumbent to complete the survey.

Questionnaires should be anonymous to promote open responses to the items. However, demographic data should be collected to document the characteristics of the respondents. For example, job analysis should include people with more and less tenure on the job, both men and women, and so on, and response data can be used to document this. The demographic characteristics can also be compared with information provided by the organization about the workforce. For example, if 80 percent of the job incumbents are female, then questionnaires can be counted to determine how close to 80 percent of the respondents are female.

Analyzing Data

In this section, we discuss the analysis of quantitative data gathered by survey or provided by job analysts. More specifically, we discuss the analysis of responses to scales applied to either tasks or human attributes. Two major considerations influence the interpretations of such scales. The considerations are those of reliability and validity. *Reliability* is about the amount of error or disagreement contained in the responses. For example, we often want to know how well two job analysts agree in their responses to the same jobs. The more they disagree about identical jobs, the lower the reliability. *Validity* is about the quality of the responses in relation to what we want to know or infer. For example, we may want to use dimension scores from the PAQ to predict the salaries for a set of jobs. The closer the relations between the PAQ dimensions and the salaries, the greater is the validity of the PAQ for predicting salary.

The analyses of reliability can all be handled by a spreadsheet or desk calculator. For an understanding of the statistical aspects of the presentation, it would be helpful to have an undergraduate-level introductory statistics course or to read an introductory book on statistics (for example, Sanocki, 2001). Many of the analyses for validity are more complex, and we merely describe what they do. A proper understanding of the more complex statistics can be obtained through graduate courses in social sciences or advanced undergraduate statistics courses. Computer packages are now available for virtually all of the applications we describe. For readers who wish further detail, we have provided references to methodological papers that report the development and use of the techniques we describe.

REPORTING STUDY RESULTS

Suppose we have developed a task inventory questionnaire. We have received responses from a total of 50 incumbents. We have "time spent" information for each task. That is, each incumbent responded to a scale for time spent in which 1 = very much below average, 2 = below average, 3 = about average, 4 = above average, and 5 = very much above average. At a minimum, we will want to report the mean, standard deviation, and N (number who do the task). Table 9.3 shows the kind of results that should be reported.

Table 9.3   Task Inventory Results

Task	M	SD	N	SEM
1.	3.5	1.4	49	0.2
2.	4.2	1.4	49	0.2
3.	2.5	1.2	36	0.2
4.	4.5	0.5	25	0.1
5.	2.5	2	25	0.4
6.	3.5	1	25	0.2

In the column labeled "Task," we would print the task to which the incumbents responded. For a photo finishing operation, the first task might read, "Develop black-and-white negatives." To find the mean, we would just add each respondent's ratings for the task and divide by the number of people who responded. In symbols, we have

$$\bar{M} = \frac{\sum X}{N},$$

where M is the mean, Σ means to add up whatever is on the right (which is X, the incumbent ratings), and N is the number of people. Not everyone's rating will be the same; some will be above the mean and some will be below the mean. We would like an index of how variable the ratings are. The standard deviation is used for this purpose. The standard deviation is essentially the average distance of the ratings from the mean. The larger the standard deviation, the more spread out are the ratings. The standard deviation is computed by

$$SD = \sqrt{\frac{\Sigma(X - M)^2}{N - 1}},$$

where the radical sign means take the square root, and the other symbols are defined as they were for the mean. There is also a fifth column labeled "SEM" for standard error of the mean. Statisticians have worked out how much study results in the form of a mean are likely to vary given the variability of the data (estimated by the standard deviation) and the size of the sample (indexed by N). The formula for the standard error of the mean is

$$SEM = \frac{SD}{\sqrt{N}},$$

which says that the standard error of the mean is the standard deviation of the variable divided by the square root of the sample size. The standard error of the mean gets large as the standard deviation is large and the sample size is small. Large, properly chosen samples of people tend to yield precise results. The practical benefit of the standard error of the mean is that it can be used to place a band around our study results that is proportional to the precision of the results. We recommend that data summaries such as that shown in Table 9.3 be prepared routinely and included in the technical portion of the job analysis report.

ASSESSING RELIABILITY

Why Estimate Reliability?

Reliability concerns the amount of error in our data. Whenever we collect data, we need to gather some evidence about reliability. If the data are full of error, then the decisions we make based on the data are likely to be wrong. It is generally better to spend the effort to go back and get better data than it is to act on data known to be full of error. If we do not estimate the reliability of the data, then we have no way to know what kind of confidence to place in them. Thus, it is important both scientifically and practically to estimate the reliability of job analysis data.

There are several sources of error in job analysis data, including human judgment, the specific item contents of scales (for example, decision-making items that form a decision-making scale in the PAQ), and changes in job content over time. The most commonly studied source of error is human judgment. Such judgments are frequently the heart of job analysis, for example, the amount of time spent on a task or the importance of spatial ability for accomplishing a job. Because we ask people to make judgments of time spent or spatial ability requirements, we need to know how much people differ in their judgments. By collecting data that show the amount of error and thus the reliability, we can judge the precision of our data and whether some corrective action is needed (for example, to collect more or better data). Several different methods are used to assess the reliability of job analysis data. We describe the most commonly used methods.

Interjudge Agreement

There are two commonly used methods that consider agreement: percentage agreement and $r(wg)$. Percentage agreement is simply the number of ratings for which the judges agree divided by the total number of judgments. Suppose we have two incumbents responding to the same task inventory. For the first task, suppose that the first incumbent records a 3 (average) for time spent on a scale that ranges from 1 to 7. If the second incumbent also records a 3, then we have an instance of agreement. If the second incumbent records anything but a 3, then we have a disagreement. To find the percentage agreement for the two incumbents, we would simply count the number of tasks for which the incumbents agree and divide by the total number of tasks in the inventory.

Although percentage agreement is easy to compute, understand, and communicate to others, it is not used much because it has been heavily criticized. You are probably thinking that of course it's been criticized; if it's easy and clear then statisticians will have nothing to do with it. But unfortunately, that's not the problem. One problem with percentage agreement is that it can be very high even when there is little or no variance in the judges' ratings. So if one of our judges rates everything a 2 and the other judges use the 2 category 80 percent of the time, then the percentage agreement will be 80 percent. This is a problem because, in a sense, there is nothing to predict if the judge always uses the same category.

Another reason for the criticism of percentage agreement is that there is no comparison between our observed results and what we would expect to get by chance. If the judges use only two categories each and they both respond at random, they will still agree about half of the time. On the other hand, if each judge uses a large number of categories, then the percentage agreement due to chance will be much lower. If you want to report percentage agreement, you should probably use a method that adjusts for chance agreement. One good method for doing this is called *kappa,* and it is described by Siegel and Castellan (1988).

Often, however, we would like to estimate reliability when we have only one job. Such an instance would occur, for example, if we asked 50 incumbents, all of whom held the same job, to estimate time spent, importance, criticality, or difficulty to learn for a series of tasks. In such a case, we can use $r(wg)$ (the so-called within-group correlation; James, Demaree, & Wolf, 1984) to estimate agreement of the 50 good souls compared with agreement we would expect if all 50 responded randomly. What $r(wg)$ does is to compare the observed standard deviation with the standard deviation that would be observed if incumbents responded randomly to the scale (that is, with a uniform or rectangular distribution). If the observed distribution has a small spread compared with the random distribution, then we conclude that there is relatively good agreement among our judges. Both $r(wg)$ and kappa compare observed agreements and disagreements to theoretical distributions based on chance. Kappa would be used with categorical data; $r(wg)$ would be used with continuous data (for example, on a scale for a task inventory) when there is only one job but multiple judges.

Interjudge Reliability

In the professional literature on psychological measurement (for example, Nunnally & Bernstein, 1994), there is a difference between reliability and agreement. *Agreement* simply refers to a function of those judgments that are identical and those that are different. *Reliability*, however, refers to two sources of variance: variance due to random errors and variance due to systematic differences among the items of interest. Reliability cannot be assessed meaningfully unless there is some true variance among the items of interest. For us, the items of interest are most often jobs. Suppose we wanted to assess the reliability of judgments of the importance of spatial ability in performing a job. To conduct a study of the reliability of such judgments, there must be (1) several jobs (three is a theoretical minimum, but good estimates will need many more jobs), (2) true differences in jobs in terms of the importance of spatial ability, and (3) at least two judges.

The simplest true index of reliability is the correlation coefficient, r (you can find a detailed description of this in any introductory statistics textbook). Suppose we have two job analysts, each of whom judges the importance of spatial ability for a set of jobs. If we line up the judgments side by side by job, we will have two columns, one for each judge. We can compute a correlation between the two columns, that is, the two analysts' judgments across jobs. Such a correlation will estimate the amount of error due to analysts. In general, large correlations indicate little error and thus good reliability.

An alternative to the ordinary correlation is the intraclass correlation. Intraclass correlations are associated with a broad and flexible theory of measurement called *generalizability theory* (for example, Crocker & Algina, 1986; Cronbach, Gleser, & Rajaratnam, 1963; Shavelson & Webb, 1991). The basic idea is to look at the correlation between measures taken under different conditions to see how one set generalizes to the other. For example, we might want to know how well job analyst ratings compare with incumbent ratings or with supervisor ratings of the same jobs. If the correlation between job analyst ratings and incumbent ratings is high, then we can have confidence that one set of ratings will predict the other and we will be happy to have either set of ratings (probably we will go with the quickest or cheapest way to collect the data in such a case). On the other hand, if the correlation between analyst and incumbent ratings is low, then we will be getting different information from the two sources and we will want to know which set is better for our given purpose.

Intraclass correlations have not been used much to assess the reliability of job analysis data (for an exception, see Webb, Shavelson, Shea, & Morello, 1981), although their use has been advocated (Cornelius, 1988, p. 357). We have two reasons beyond their appropriateness for job analysis data for introducing them here. First, intraclass correlations allow us to deal with differences in means across judges. Second, they offer a convenient way to estimate the number of judges that would be needed to achieve a level of reliability that we desire for our study.

We mentioned earlier that agreement has been criticized because it is possible to have good agreement without having any variance in the ratings. On the other hand, the correlation has been criticized as a measure of reliability because it fails to account for differences in means across raters. Proponents of agreement indices complain that the correlation indicates high "agreement" (really reliability) when there is no actual agreement at all. As long as the pattern of relations is the same for both sets of ratings, the correlation can be quite high even though the individual numbers are quite different. Consider the following ratings on a 5- (high) point scale for time spent on a job given by two judges:

	Judge A	Judge B
Task 1	5	3
Task 2	4	2
Task 3	3	1

For these ratings, the correlation coefficient is perfect (1.0) even though there is no agreement. This is where the intraclass correlation helps.

The ordinary correlation and intraclass correlation are used when the raters provide quantitative, relatively continuous ratings or judgments. Ratings of the amount of time spent or of the difficulty to learn a task are the kind of scales that are appropriate for such techniques. Intraclass correlations are particularly useful for situations in which either there are multiple raters or tasks to be summed and we want to know the reliability of the resulting sum.

Intraclass correlations are also helpful when we want to account for differences in mean ratings for our raters.

Internal Consistency and Temporal Stability

As we mentioned earlier, human judgment is an important source of error in job analysis data. Two other sources of error are often worth investigating as part of a job analysis: error due to specific item content and error due to changes over time. To investigate error due to specific item content, we estimate internal consistency. Internal consistency describes how a measure composed of several items "hangs together" or has a structure that is coherent. Large estimates of internal consistency indicate that there is a small amount of error due to specific item content. One method of assessing internal consistency is the split-half estimate. To compute a split-half estimate of internal consistency, you assign the items of a scale to two different pieces, add up each piece separately, and then find the correlation between the two pieces. For example, suppose we had ratings of four decision-making items from the PAQ on a set of 100 jobs. We could assign items 1 and 3 to scale A and items 2 and 4 to scale B. For each of the 100 jobs, we now have two scores, A and B. We can compute the correlation between A and B to estimate internal consistency.

Notice that we could also assign questions 1 and 2 to A and 3 and 4 to B. If we did, we would have a different estimate of internal consistency. With a large number of items, there can be a very large number of different estimates of internal consistency, which is a problem. The split-half method is not used much anymore, but it can be useful when a measure consists of a mix of different factors. Today, a method called *alpha* is used instead.

The correlation coefficient (r) is often used when we have two judges, items, or tests to compare. Often, however, we have multiple judges or items that are totaled to yield a score. For example, we may have three job analysts making ratings or we may create a score for a duty by summing responses to several different tasks for an incumbent. In such cases, we need an index of reliability that summarizes the reliability of the total score rather than summarizing the data in pairs. Alpha (Cronbach, 1951) provides such a summary (this is the same alpha used for multiple items in a scale).

Alpha is probably the most commonly used estimate of reliability. It is often used when there are multiple judges rating multiple jobs. However, alpha is not limited in use to judges. It applies to items or scales just as well as judges. Therefore, alpha is also used on items when rating scales are formed, for example, in performance appraisal ratings. Alpha is commonly used for tests as well, when the individual test items are summed to form a total score. In that case, the test items take the place of judges. Alpha is properly used when all test items or judges are expected to give similar results or ratings. If we expect differences, say, between incumbents and supervisors, then we need a method to account for such differences. One way of doing so is with intraclass correlations, which we mentioned earlier.

Temporal stability is estimated when we take a measure once and then take the same measure again later. We could ask a set of incumbents to tell us about time spent or importance of the tasks that comprise the incumbents' job in January and then ask them to do it again in June. For each task, we would have a mean rating of importance or time spent at two different times. We could compute the correlation between the two measures. The correlation would show how similar the mean ratings were across time, and hence the term *stability.* When temporal stability is high, there is little error due to changes over time.

VALIDITY

As we mentioned earlier, validity of measurement concerns the meaning of the numbers or scores. In job analysis, validity of measures is typically bound up with the use or purpose of data collection. For example, if we use the PAQ for job evaluation, we expect that scores from the PAQ correlate highly with salary data for a set of key jobs. In this section, we describe several data analysis techniques relevant to the validity of job analysis data. For the most part, these techniques require computers and cannot be accomplished by hand in any reasonable period of time.

Correlation and Regression

Correlation is used when we want to summarize the relations between two variables with a single number. We could use a correlation to express the relation between task ratings of the difficulty to learn and average training time to proficiency for a set of tasks, for example. Regression is closely related to correlation. The main difference is that regression is used when we want to make numerical predictions of the value of one variable when given values of another variable. Correlation can tell us that PAQ scores are closely related to salary for a set of jobs. However, regression can give us a predicted salary in dollars for a job when given some PAQ data. Regression is very useful for job evaluation. Although we have presented correlation only in the context of two variables, correlation and regression can be extended to any number of predictor variables. So, for example, several different scales from the PAQ can be used at once to predict salary. This is called *multiple regression.* For in-depth coverage of such techniques, see Pedhazur (1997).

Factor and Cluster Analysis

Both factor analysis and cluster analysis help us to group things. Several of the structured job analysis techniques (for example, Job Components Inventory

[JCI], PAQ) have a large number of items. Although a large number of items helps to ensure that our coverage of the job is relatively complete, the price to pay for all this detail is that there is just too much information about each job to keep in mind. It would be much simpler to combine a number of items into more global scales that have a sort of summary meaning. For example, several of the PAQ items might be combined into a problem-solving scale, or several of the JCI items might be combined into an arithmetic scale. Factor analysis is often used to create such scales. If we measure a large number of jobs on each item, we can compute a correlation matrix among our items. The correlation matrix will show the similarity of items to one another across jobs. Factor analysis will pull from such a matrix several variables called factors that show which of the items in the questionnaire go together. With a small number of items, one can simply inspect the matrix to see what goes with what. However, such a task quickly gets out of hand as the number of items increases, and a computer program is immensely helpful here. Factor analysis is often used in scale development, especially in the development of structured job analysis techniques. For more detail on factor analysis, see Kline (1994). A technique called *multidimensional scaling* is quite similar to factor analysis and could be used for the same purposes as factor analysis. For further information on multidimensional scaling, see Borg & Groenen (1996).

Cluster analysis also is used to group things. However, cluster analysis is usually used to group jobs rather than items. Like factor analysis, cluster analysis operates on data that tell about the similarity of the items in question. In the case of cluster analysis, the items are usually jobs. The similarity data can be a correlation matrix where jobs are correlated with one another, or the data can be profiles of jobs on various attributes, such as time spent on various tasks. In either case, cluster analysis builds groups of jobs by assigning jobs to clusters based on the jobs' similarity to one another. The most similar jobs get grouped first, then the next most similar jobs get grouped, and so forth. Cluster analysis starts with each job in its own group and finishes with all jobs in a single group. In the middle somewhere, there is usually a grouping that makes sense and has a reasonable number of clusters (maybe 3 to 10 or more, depending on how different the jobs are). The computer provides various cluster solutions, but it is up to the researcher to decide which one to choose to best represent the data. Cluster analysis is useful for job classification. It may also be useful for grouping jobs for purposes of selection and training. For more detail on cluster analysis, see Bailey (1994).

Other Multivariate Techniques

Other multivariate techniques are sometimes used to analyze job analysis data. Such techniques include multivariate analysis of variance (MANOVA), canonical correlation, and discriminant analysis. MANOVA and canonical correlation are used when there are multiple dependent variables. We might have two or more sets of jobs, such as first-level manager, middle manager, and executive, that we want to compare on multiple items from the Management Position Description Questionnaire. In such a case, we could use MANOVA to make the comparisons for us. Discriminant analysis is used when our dependent variable is categorical rather than continuous. If we were trying to predict whether a job was professional, managerial, white-collar, or blue-collar, we could use discriminant analysis. Multivariate techniques are described in references such as Flury (1997).

Consequential Validity

Recently, there has been a good bit of discussion about what validity means as applied to job analysis. Sanchez and Levine (2000) have argued that what is needed is an estimate of the degree of success we achieve when we use job analysis to help us carry out our purposes. For example, we need to compare the results of selecting employees using a test based on job analysis with selecting employees using another test that is not based on job analysis. Sanchez and Levine (2000) refer to this as "consequential validity," and they define it as "the extent to which the [job] analysis adds incrementally to the effectiveness or efficiency of individual or system-level interventions derived from it" (p. 13; see also Levine & Sanchez, 2000). In common language, the question is about how much value job analysis adds to our human resource programs. This is a very complex issue, which explains why we do not have a lot of good information or even good ways to address this question. But investments in job analyses do need to be evaluated for payoff. We hope to see more research on this in the future.

A Note About Accuracy in Job Analysis

It is essential that job analysis data exhibit adequate reliability and validity. Because virtually all job analysis data rely on human judgment, however, and such judgments have been shown to be fallible in a number of different ways, job analysis is potentially subject to various sources of inaccuracy or what some may prefer to call *bias*. Recognizing this, Morgeson and Campion (1997) identified 16 distinct potential sources of inaccuracy by drawing from basic research in social and cognitive psychology as well as more applied industrial/organizational psychology research.

The different sources of inaccuracy are shown in Table 9.4. The social sources of inaccuracy are created by normative pressures from the social environment, reflecting the fact that individuals exist within a social context. The social sources are subdivided into inaccuracy due to social influence versus self-presentation processes. For their part, cognitive sources reflect problems that result from the fact that people have distinct limitations when processing

Table 9.4 Sources of Job Analysis Inaccuracy and Potential Mitigation Strategies

Social Sources	Potential Mitigation Strategies
Social Influence Processes 1. Conformity pressures 2. Extremity shifts 3. Motivation loss	• Collect information before and after group discussion to check for social influence processes • Verify collected data from multiple sources (for example, incumbent, supervisor, analyst) • Use groups/committees composed of equal status members • Explore alternatives to unanimous decision rules (for example, anonymous responding, averaging decision rules) • Structure meetings to ensure full participation (for example, taking turns, collecting judgments individually, emphasizing importance of individual contributions)
Self-Presentation Processes 4. Impression management 5. Social desirability 6. Demand effects	• Collect data from different sources that are likely to vary in their motivation to self-present • Use objective measures (for example, archival records or counts of observable behaviors) • Communicate that job analysis results will be verified by others • Focus attention on the job and not people who perform the job
Cognitive Sources	
Limitations in Information Processing 7. Information overload 8. Heuristics 9. Categorization	• Reduce information-processing demands on respondents by using shorter questionnaires or dividing longer questionnaires into smaller parts that can be completed by different respondents • Ensure adequate time to complete survey and sufficient respondent motivation to respond carefully • Train raters on problems associated with common decision-making heuristics • Use fewer response scales

Cognitive Sources	
Biases in Information Processing	
10. Carelessness 11. Extraneous information 12. Inadequate information 13. Order and contrast effects 14. Halo 15. Leniency and severity 16. Method effects	• Develop simple and user-friendly instructions and questionnaire layout • Include a carelessness responding index • Ensure job analysis participants have adequate job knowledge • Employ training to ensure all participants have the same and correct frame of reference • Vary question order on surveys • Collect data from different sources

information. The cognitive sources are further subdivided into inaccuracy that results from limitations versus biases in individual information processing systems. Nested within these social and cognitive sources are 16 psychological processes that constitute the specific sources of inaccuracy.

By identifying these sources of inaccuracy, Morgeson and Campion (1997) called our attention to a number of different ways in which the job analysis data may be affected by factors that are unrelated to what is done on the job or the KSAOs needed to effectively perform on the job. Research is beginning to investigate how some of these processes operate in the job analysis context. For example, Morgeson, Delaney-Klinger, Mayfield, Ferrara, and Campion (2004) found that ability statements are more likely to be subject to self-presentation processes than task statements, potentially leading to inaccurate ability requirements. In addition, Conte, Dean, Ringenbach, Moran, and Landy (2005) found that different work attitudes (job satisfaction, organizational commitment, and job involvement) were related to task ratings, with stronger relationships with tasks that have higher levels of discretion.

In total, the conceptual and empirical research suggests that it is important to explicitly consider these sources of inaccuracy when designing, conducting, and summarizing the results of any job analysis study (see Morgeson & Campion, 1997, and Table 9.4 for more specific advice on what can be done to mitigate potential inaccuracy). It is important to recognize, however, that efforts aimed at determining inaccurate responses are complicated by the fact that there rarely exists a "gold standard" or "true score" in job analysis (Morgeson & Campion, 2000; Sanchez & Levine, 2000). Numerous alternatives have been proposed (for example, considering consequential validity, focusing on the validity of job analysis inferences), but little research has been conducted on the effectiveness of these strategies. Recently, Van Iddekinge,

Putka, Raymark, and Eidson (2005), in a study we summarized briefly in Chapter 4, employed variance components analysis to examine the extent to which different factors contribute to error variance in job analysis ratings. This offers one way to estimate how different sources of inaccuracy affect ratings of job experts. Clearly, additional research is needed both on the different sources of inaccuracy as well as methods for detecting such inaccuracy.

Chapter Summary

In this chapter, we described how to conduct a job analysis study and how to analyze data from such a study. As we are very fond of saying, the purpose of the study determines the nature of the job analysis. We began by looking at some purposes for job analysis and matching them up against various attributes of people and jobs, types of descriptors, methods of data collection, and units of analysis. Next we talked about selecting job analysis approaches for several applications, such as job classification, worker mobility, workforce planning, and efficiency/safety. We considered practical aspects of doing a job analysis study, including issues related to the job analysis methods per se and also to organizational issues such as keeping management happy and dealing with project staffing. We concluded the first section by offering practical tips and comments on conducting observations and interviews and in developing and administering questionnaire surveys.

The second half of the chapter concerned data analysis. We began this section by describing the contents of a typical report that would be generated based on a task inventory. Then we described estimating the reliability of job analysis data. We described two methods for estimating interjudge agreement: percentage agreement and $r(wg)$. Interjudge reliability estimates by intraclass correlation were then described. We discussed the ordinary correlation coefficient, the split-half, and alpha as methods that could be used to assess internal consistency and temporal stability of job analysis data. (One important caveat is in order: As Sanchez and Levine (2000) point out, lack of reliability may indicate not error but real differences in the way SMEs view the job. Studying these differences may produce big payoffs. For example, high performers may report different patterns of time spent on tasks than low performers.) Then we moved to techniques for examining the validity of job analysis information. We briefly described correlation and regression, factor and cluster analysis, and other multivariate techniques. We briefly mentioned the idea of assessing the value of job analysis by considering how it affects human resource programs. We closed with a discussion of potential sources of inaccuracy or bias in job analysis responding.

10

The Future of Job Analysis

N othing is more certain than change. The world of the future will be different from what our world is today. Although change is certain, predicting the form that change will take and especially what response people will make to change is very uncertain. Predictions are often wrong. Our task in this chapter is to talk about a future that is not far off, based on trends that we see today. We hope our guesses about what will happen will be right on target. We begin by describing societal, technological, and business changes that are likely to affect the way people work. We speculate on the changes in work that will occur and then, based on changes in work, describe what job analysis must do to fulfill its functions. We consider the future in terms of the building blocks of job analysis. In addition to the four that we have given the most attention, that is, the types of descriptors, the sources of information, the methods of collecting data, and the units of analysis, we add fifth and sixth concerns, namely, how roles come to be defined and redefined by workers and methods of information dissemination, storage, and retrieval.

Changing Conditions

CHANGES IN SOCIETY

The most profound changes in work may come from changes in societal values. For example, child labor laws and compulsory education forever changed the composition of factory workers in the United States. Values influence who is working, where they are working, and when they work. It is difficult to say with any confidence how such changes will affect work in the future. However, there are certain trends that are likely to prove influential. We mention several such trends, mainly applicable to the United States.

- Currently, the workforce is aging, or rather, the average age of workers is increasing. In 1984 the median age of the workforce was 35. In 2014 it is projected to be 42 years of age. The Baby Boom generation is now largely past middle age. Despite the fact that many are contemplating retirement seriously for the first time, the percentage of older workers in the labor force (age 55 and above) is projected to increase the most over the next 10 years (Toossi, 2005).
- Over the past 40 years, women have increasingly joined the workforce. In 1960, only 36 percent of women were in the workforce. By 2000, 58 percent of women were in the workforce. During that same time, the percentage of men in the workforce decreased from 80 percent to 71 percent (Clark & Weismantle, 2003). Some occupations have changed radically in the relative numbers of men and women during this time. Two examples that come to mind are lawyers and psychologists.
- The diversity of the workforce in the United States is expected to increase in the future. Hispanics in particular are expected to increase more rapidly than other groups. For example, Hispanics accounted for about 12.5 percent of the labor force in 2000 but are expected to account for more than 24 percent of the labor force in 2050 (U.S. Census Bureau, 2004).
- New generations are entering the workforce for the first time. Both Generation X (born between 1965 and 1976) and Generation Y (born between 1976 and 2000) are the most highly educated demographic groups in history. But not only do they bring enhanced skills, they also have different expectations compared to previous generations.

In addition to demographic changes, there may be changes in the role that work plays in life. The amount of education that the average person receives has steadily increased since the Industrial Revolution, and it appears that this trend will continue. One side effect of increasing education is that people who are well educated desire and expect work that they find meaningful. Such individuals often want work that either contributes to their own development (challenging or self-developing work) or contributes to the welfare of others in nontrivial ways (task identity and significance). In Sweden, for example, Volvo has trouble getting its highly educated workforce to come to work assembling automobiles. One of the main reasons for introducing autonomous work groups in Volvo's Kalmar factory was that such groups are less impeded by absences than is the traditional assembly line (Karlsson, 1976). Volvo also hoped that by having work groups and cross-training, workers would be less bored and more likely to come to work.

The cohort of workers labeled "Generation X" has been described as seeking balance between work and nonwork activities. In other words, they want to "get a life." Such individuals may set a lower priority on work than do Baby Boomers born after World War II. The cohort of workers labeled "Generation Y" (also called "Millennials") have been described as having strong technical skills, but lacking in other skills such as listening, communicating, and being a team player. In addition, Generation Y workers have been described as desiring instant gratification rather than long-range commitments of time and effort. The differences among the Baby Boomers, Generation X, and Generation Y are likely to prove challenging in designing and redesigning work to accommodate these differing viewpoints. With larger numbers of working women, dual-career couples have become increasingly common. Partners in such couples may be less willing to move or simply less willing to make sacrifices for an employer because of their partner's career.

What does all this mean? One possibility is that work will need to accommodate people more than people will need to accommodate work. For example, flexible work schedules or working at home (often called "telecommuting") may become increasingly well accepted as a way to allow a trailing spouse or a part-time worker to work at greater distances from the office. The Bureau of Labor Statistics reported (in 2004) that approximately 28 percent of workers had flexible work schedules that allowed them to vary the time they began or ended work (U.S Department of Labor, 2005a) and about 15 percent of workers did some work at home (U.S. Department of Labor, 2005b). Another possibility is that jobs will become increasingly complex to allow well-educated individuals to experience growth and challenge at work. Still another is that the nature and quality of interactions among employees with diverse backgrounds will become a more important issue at work.

CHANGES IN TECHNOLOGY

The advent of the computer and its transformation by the microchip have truly revolutionized many jobs. It is hard to imagine writing a book or an article without word processing (and this book is no exception) or conducting statistical analyses without computer-based statistical software. (Painfully, the authors learned how to do statistical analyses by hand. It wasn't fun; we're glad those days are over!) Most large machines such as jets, cars, and harvesters contain computers. Many other devices either contain computers or depend on them, especially communication devices such as telephones, e-mail, and the Internet. Although computers were initially developed for number-crunching problems in physics and mathematics, they are now used for a very broad array of purposes, including weather forecasting, generating images for movies, commercials, and Web sites, managing the engine in your favorite automobile, and receiving cell phone calls and wireless e-mails.

Computers continue to advance in speed and power, all the while decreasing in price and size. Computers are now ubiquitous in our lives and the world of work, ranging from large clusters of networked computers (often called "server farms") to the familiar desktop and laptop computers found in business, to those embedded in numerous devices such as cellular telephones and all manner of consumer and industrial equipment (Did you know that even some refrigerators now have Internet access?). The advent of the Internet and its proliferation (at least in its current, graphical form) starting in the mid-1990s has had a tremendous impact on industry and the world of work. What changes are likely to result from such a development? Probably the kind of change will depend on the type of work. Some jobs will be changed much more than will others.

In manufacturing, work that was once done by hand is now often done by machine. Industrial robots are now fairly common. Such a change has redefined the role that people play in manufacturing. Today, people supervise machines. People look for malfunctions. They attempt to diagnose the malfunction. What was the root cause? And of course, people correct the problems. People reconfigure the machines in order to change products. Thus, the job has changed from assembling something to setting up, monitoring, and solving problems. The worker's role in manufacturing has changed from working primarily with one's hands to working primarily with one's head.

Advanced manufacturing technology (AMT) includes computer-controlled manufacturing and processes (Wall & Jackson, 1995). In addition to robots, there are also computer-controlled machine tools and assembly machines. One of the main advantages of such machines is that they are reconfigured for new jobs through software rather than hardware such as cams and timers. As a consequence, the actions that people take to adjust machines are more likely to be completed through keyboards or other computer interfaces than through wrenches and screwdrivers. The machines that manufacture products can be extremely complex; the people monitoring such machines may not be able to sense mechanical functioning directly by sight, sound, or touch. They may instead have to infer what the machine is doing from data presented on a control board or a computer monitor. Power plant operation has always been like this (barring utter disaster, the operator never actually sees, hears, or feels the core of a nuclear reactor), but the manufacture of many other kinds of products increasingly fits such a description. Here again, the shift is from working with the hands to working with the head.

Where office work is concerned, authors have addressed the impact of modern technology on deskilling, control of the work (autonomy), and health issues (Coovert, 1995; Keita & Sauter, 1992). *Deskilling* refers to the loss of human skill as computers strip jobs of complexity, leaving them dull and routine. Some have argued that management has taken control of the process of work from workers by fragmenting jobs into small pieces that do not require thought (Braverman, 1974). Others have argued that the same technology can be implemented in different ways and that the implementation rather than the technology determines the kinds of skills required (Attewell, 1992).

Coovert (1995), as well as Wall and Jackson (1995), has noted that the control of the work is vital to understanding people's reactions to technology. If the introduction of computers or other technology takes control of the job away from the incumbent, the incumbent will typically find the introduction to be stressful. On the other hand, if the control of the work remains with the incumbent or increases due to the introduction of technology, then the new technology will be welcome. McInerney (1989) proposed a list of factors to be considered when assessing the impact of technology:

- An individual's control over others
- An individual's control by others
- An individual's control over work
- Planning and the uses of information
- Access to people and information in the organization

Several health issues have been associated with the introduction of computers into the office. Workers were worried about exposure to radiation from computer monitors, although research showed that the level of radiation coming from the monitors was minimal (Coovert, 1995). Current health issues are recurrent strain injuries and carpal tunnel syndrome, which result from repeated, limited movements such as those required by computer keyboards. Other researchers have investigated nonspecific somatic complaints due to work fragmentation caused by the introduction of computers (Linstrom, 1991).

It is quite difficult to predict accurately the uses to which people will put new technology. Before the personal computer was widely adopted, people thought that there would be a rather small market for them and that the amount of memory needed would be measured in kilobytes rather than megabytes or gigabytes. However, authors have speculated on what we can expect in the near future. Coovert (1995) mentions *computer-supported groups, augmented reality,* and *ubiquitous computing.*

Computer-supported groups use computers to work together. The computer may be the main interface for communication. In such cases, groups may use Internet bulletin boards to e-mail one another, or they may have computer connections that allow simultaneous video and audio presentations through multiple windows in real time. In the latter case, the experience approaches meeting face to face around a table, as most meetings are conducted today.

The computer may also use some type of data-sharing capability so that one member of the group can see and operate on another member's work. For example, many so-called productivity applications (such as Microsoft Word) allow one member to edit another member's document. The edits can be marked so that the original member can see each editorial change and either accept it, reject it, or accept it with modifications. There are also the electronic equivalents of blackboards that will accept and share handwritten characters, drawings, tables, and symbols that the user inserts with a device that is the electronic equivalent of chalk. Such devices are analogous to flip charts used in today's meetings. Technology-enabled groups have become more common in organizations today, as the competitive environment requires working across geographic and cultural boundaries. These "virtual teams" are likely to proliferate as technology becomes more sophisticated.

Augmented reality refers to devices that enhance the environment by providing additional information that is incorporated into mundane reality by the user. For example, the KARMA (knowledge-based augmented reality for maintenance assistance) system (Feiner, MacIntyre, & Seligmann, 1993) was developed for repairing laser printers. The technician using the system wears goggles that present visual information used in repairing the printer. The technician looks at the printer, and the computer recognizes it. The computer responds by (perhaps) showing the technician a schematic of the printer with the paper tray removed. The schematic would be overlaid on the actual printer, so the technician sees both the printer with the tray closed in real life and the tray open in the computer graphic at the same time. Thus, the instruction to remove the paper tray is intuitive to the technician.

Ubiquitous computing refers to the increasing number of computers that appear in the office. Weiser (1991, 1993) predicted the use of three different kinds of computers in the office of the future, predictions that have already been fulfilled in some measure. The smallest kind will be used to carry information about a project. It will fit in your pocket so you can take it from place to place like a diskette. USB flash drives have become commonplace and have effectively replaced floppy disks, in part because of the flash drive's much larger storage capacity and higher reliability. The next largest type of computer would look like a pad of paper and be used much like such a pad. Tablet computers, in which the screen can be used like a pad of paper, represent a relatively recent innovation that would fit in this category. Also in this category would be a variety of personal digital assistants (PDAs) that can be used for numerous purposes, including scheduling, browsing the Internet, and answering e-mail (BlackBerry, a popular device for wireless e-mail, has been dubbed "CrackBerry" for its addictive properties). These devices have proliferated in recent years and are here to stay. The largest would look something like a window and might appear on a desk surface or on a wall like a blackboard. Both the medium and large computers are expected to accept information from multiple sources, including pens and gestures. Although there may be many more computers in each person's office, the computers themselves may become psychologically invisible because they will be easy to use in natural ways.

As a result of the improvements in technology and the rapid pace of change, employee stress and how to cope with it will become more critical. The advent of wireless communication technologies has created an "always on" work environment, where it becomes increasingly difficult to get away from work, even in nonwork hours. This poses clear challenges to balancing work and nonwork life. In addition, person-machine interfaces and system features, including answers to the question of whether people or machines will complete certain tasks, will increasingly dominate the way work is organized.

CHANGES IN THE BUSINESS ENVIRONMENT

Several interrelated changes are expected to occur in the way many organizations function. The theoretical basis for the changes can be found in the literature on organizational design (for example, Huber, 1990; Mintzberg, 1979). The basic idea is that the most effective form of the organization will depend on the organization's environment, strategy, or technology. An analogy is that mammals with thick coats will do better in cold climates. According to several theorists, if the business environment is simple and stable, a bureaucratic form of organization is most effective. However, complex environments require decentralized authority, and dynamic environments require fewer written rules and regulations in favor of more flexible and rapid responses to changing environments (see Wexley & Yukl, 1984, pp. 271–301). Similar arguments have been made for technology (Davis, 1995). Technology can reduce or eliminate barriers and boundaries.

Organizations have adopted principles from the total quality management (TQM) movement and just-in-time inventory control (JIT; Wall & Jackson, 1995). TQM pushes customer service and quality control to the top of the organization's list of values. Steps are taken throughout the production process from start to finish to ensure that the customer receives the highest-quality products and services. A focus on the whole system is an integral part of this movement. JIT attempts to remove stockpiles of partially produced goods (that is, inventory) so that pieces are produced just as they are needed for the next step of the production processes. Along with advanced manufacturing technology (described earlier in the chapter), TQM and JIT provide the core of what has been called "integrated manufacturing" (Dean & Snell, 1991). Together, AMT, JIT, and TQM help manufacturers to respond quickly to changes in customer demands, to produce high-quality products, and to reduce the cost of production (Wall & Jackson, 1995).

The pressure to create more, better, and cheaper products has intensified, due in part to economic globalization, market deregulation, and the introduction of information technologies that have removed traditional competitive barriers (Friedman, 2005; Harvey & Novicevic, 2002). Global competition has increased radically in the past decade (Cascio, 1995; Kraut & Korman, 1999). In the 1960s, about 7 percent of the U.S. economy was subject to global competition. In the 1980s, that number had increased to about 70 percent, and it is expected to increase further (Gwynne, 1992). It seems clear that globalization has created a new competitive landscape that is here to stay. Some have gone so far to suggest that this represents a revolutionary (as opposed to evolutionary) change (Ireland & Hitt, 1999). The new competitive environment is one in which many organizations are struggling to compete.

Cascio (1995) listed several other trends that have implications for the way we will work in the future, including

1. Smaller companies. Although large companies have resources and achieve economies of scale, they are slow to adapt. On the other hand, Kraut and Korman (1999) point to an increase in mergers and acquisitions that create ever larger firms whose culture and work processes must be integrated.

2. Coordination by mutual adjustment or networks rather than formal hierarchies. Such a structure is helpful in a complex environment.

3. Technicians replacing machine operators as the worker elite.

4. Pay being tied to skills rather than positions. As people work in teams rather than at individual jobs, compensation systems that pay people for knowing more serve as an incentive to expand skills.

5. A move from making products to providing services.

6. A move from the job as a fixed set of tasks to work as a flexible set of behaviors that changes to meet changing demands.

With regard to the last point, a number of authors have questioned whether jobs will even exist in future organizations. Bridges (1994) referred to "the end of the job" as a fixed set of requirements.

Sanchez (1994) and Sanchez and Levine (1999) identified numerous emerging trends in business that have implications for job analysis. Several of these are related to those identified by Cascio (1995). Among issues identified were moves from

1. Simplified and predetermined job responsibilities to enlarged and cross-functional responsibilities

2. Adversarial relations between labor and management to a blurring between labor and management

3. Static jobs with fixed knowledge, skills, abilities, and other characteristics (KSAOs) to fluid work with dynamic KSAOs

4. Little competition and large market share to global competition and free trade

5. Isolated work stations and minimal worker contact to teamwork and self-managing teams

6. Selecting individuals for jobs to selecting individuals for teams, and

7. A hierarchical approach to performance appraisal to input from multiple constituents

Note that both Sanchez (1994) and Cascio (1995) identified increasing global competition, increasing flexibility in the assignment of tasks to jobs, and a reduction in hierarchy such that workers contact one another directly rather than through supervision.

Others have referred to "boundaryless" organizations (for example, Davis, 1995; Mohrman & Cohen, 1995). Such authors describe conventional organizations as possessing organizational charts in which jobs are depicted as little boxes that are connected with lines that indicate who works for whom. Mohrman and Cohen (1995) describe future organizations as what happens when people "come out of the box." Rather than doing the same thing every day, workers will respond to changes by doing what needs to be done to accomplish organizational objectives. To react swiftly, workers will have to be empowered to make decisions and carry out actions rather than getting permission from higher management. Cascio (1995) described a move from task-based toward process-based organization of work. A process is a work unit that has high task identity; that is, it involves the complete transformation of one or more kinds of input and creates an output of value to an internal or external customer.

In an extreme form, such an organization would be an interesting place to work. For example: "The new organization will rely on self-motivation. Managers will have to create motivating contexts—day-to-day supervision will be impossible. Evaluation will be based on results, which may be team or business unit phenomena" (Church, 1995, p. 54). Davis (1995) made a similar point with regard to telecommuters or others working at a distance from managers. Such individuals may need to be evaluated on the achievement of goals rather than on work processes.

As we mentioned earlier, it is likely that the content of work will influence the kind of changes that we will observe. For example, food preparation does not lend itself well to telecommuting. One cannot scrub the carrots or peel the potatoes and then upload them to the network so that they can be downloaded at the restaurant. Work that requires physical contact such as massage or surgery is constrained in similar ways, although in the future surgeons and masseurs could operate machines that actually contact the patient or client from a distance. Or consider police officers and firefighters. Although such jobs are unquestionably affected by changing technology, much of the content of such jobs is timeless.

With regard to management, it will be interesting to see how the need for speed and flexibility balances against the need for planning, deliberate coordination, and performance management. Although one can hire people, aim them at a goal, make payment contingent on goal attainment, and then turn them loose without supervision, this may not always be the most effective course of action. For example, one could hire professional athletes, place them on a soccer field, and tell them that they will get lots of money if they win soccer games. However, this is unlikely to be a winning strategy because (1) they have not been selected so as to fulfill specific positions such as goalkeeper and forward, and (2) there is no mechanism to coach them; planning, coordination, feedback, and so forth is all left up to the players. Although people will form organizational systems spontaneously, such organizations are unlikely to be the most efficient possible.

Put another way, the autonomous work group must still carry out all the management functions of its traditional counterpart, the hierarchical work group. Autonomous work groups are best suited to carrying out management functions when the work process is well understood and the work itself provides feedback about goal attainment (Neck, Stewart, & Manz, 1996). It is increasingly helpful to have a formal manager, therefore, when the work process is not well understood or when the work itself does not provide much feedback about goal attainment. In fact, Morgeson (2005) found that formal leaders were most helpful when teams encounter novel and disruptive events. Coordination by mutual adjustment becomes increasingly difficult as the organization or project group grows larger.

Some jobs of the future will be more flexible and less constrained by specific tasks than they are today. Some jobs will have less (or possibly no) direct supervision and will be evaluated by results rather than by process. On the other hand, we are pretty sure that people will still be working for a living whether or not their work is called a "job." And some people's work in the future will in large part be to structure the work of others (management).

Implications for Jobs and Job Analysis

We anticipate that, at least for some work, jobs will become flexible and contain boundaries that are vague or dynamic. Some authors have criticized job analysis because they view it as legalistic and serving to increase boundaries rather than to reduce them (Drucker, 1987; Olian & Rynes, 1991; Young, 1992). Others have responded that the culprit is not job analysis itself, but rather some of the purposes that job analysis serves, such as narrow job descriptions (Sanchez & Levine, 1999). In addition, some have suggested that the term *work analysis* should replace *job analysis* (Sanchez, 1994; Sanchez & Levine, 1999). Others have used the term *work profiling* to substitute for job analysis. As we said at the outset, we view work analysis as the more general term, with job analysis a subset of work analysis methods. But we have paid homage to tradition by continuing the use of the label job analysis.

What will the changes in society, business, and technology bring to job analysis, or if you prefer, work analysis? Doubtless there will be new challenges to supply the kinds of information needed to ensure the success of tomorrow's human resource programs. But there will also be new possibilities for producing, analyzing, and updating information due largely to changes in technology.

We consider likely developments in work analysis with regard to descriptors or types of data, the sources of information, the methods of data collection, and the units of analysis. As an extra added attraction we discuss the ins and outs of how the empowerment of workers offers them more discretion in defining what their role is in the organization. We end the chapter by introducing methods of data storage, retrieval, and dissemination.

DESCRIPTORS

Descriptors are the job features we examine during the job analysis. Generally, we are concerned with attributes of people and descriptions of the work itself. There are many more specific and concrete instances of each type, such as grip strength and the use of pliers. What features must we add to capture the essence of jobs that are increasingly flexible, complex, team oriented, and infused with new technology? One potentially effective response to these changes in modes of work and jobs themselves is the emergence of competency modeling. This approach has been described at some length in Chapter 5, and is not discussed further here, although we expect that competencies will continue to enjoy an expanding frequency of use in the future.

Flexibility

Jobs will possess fewer boundaries between workers and management, areas of expertise, and organizational function. Workers' tasks will change frequently. Job analysis can respond to such changes in a number of ways. One way is to simply define jobs more inclusively, so that a person's job is all that he or she might do in a given time period. For example, there are currently sets of jobs through which workers rotate to reduce boredom. The *Handbook for Analyzing Jobs* (U.S. Department of Labor, 1972) recommends treating all such jobs as a single job that contains tasks of all the constituent pieces. Such an approach really requires nothing new from job analysis except, perhaps, a more inclusive philosophy.

But suppose that tasks not only change rapidly but also change in ways that cannot be foreseen. In such a case, it would be virtually impossible to create a meaningful job description based on tasks. Of course, there are limits to the amount of change in tasks that people can manage. A master woodworker will not become a master glassblower in a short period of time and vice versa. Similar comments apply to a psychologist and a physicist. But back to the premise. If we cannot say in advance what the tasks are going to be, how can we proceed with job analysis?

One answer is to base the analysis on broad characteristics required by the work rather than more specific characteristics required by specific tasks (for example, Cunningham, 1996). The characteristics might focus on attributes that are important regardless of tasks, such as conscientiousness. Taken to an extreme, where we know only what is to be accomplished at work and nothing about how it is to be accomplished, there is little to do for job analysis beyond specifying virtually universal desirable qualities of work and workers. Suppose one's job is to make sure that a certain group of people gets from Tallahassee to Tucson. It matters from a job analysis standpoint whether one achieves this goal by acting as a travel agent or as a bus driver. However, consider a less extreme position where we have some ideas about how the work is done, even if we do not have all the details. For example, we have medical care (essentially nursing) teams where task assignments change depending on the team members. In such a case, we can still proceed.

Personality Characteristics

One type of descriptor likely to prove useful with flexible jobs is the personality characteristic. Recent progress has been made in using the Big Five theory of personality to serve as a theoretical basis for determining the personality requirements of jobs, or at least those dealing with broad characteristics. The Big Five theory organizes a multitude of personality characteristics into five overarching dimensions. There is a mnemonic device you can use to remember these (look that word up in your e-dictionary). It's OCEAN: Openness to new experience (curious, adventurous), Conscientiousness (dutiful, compliant), Extroversion (gregarious, dominant), Agreeableness (team player, collaborative), and Neuroticism (worried, negative). It is difficult to think of a job in which conscientiousness would not be an asset (although politics comes to mind). In fact, research has found that some occupations such as artist demand less conscientiousness, perhaps because of the conformity component. Agreeable people tend to function better as team members; neurotic ones tend to function worse as team members. You can imagine that openness to new experience could be helpful for some occupations, such as travel agent, and that extroversion could be helpful for other occupations, such as sales.

Raymark, Schmit, and Guion (1997) developed a scale called the Personality-Related Position Requirements Form (PPRF). This form helps us assess the personality requirements of jobs relative to the Big Five dimensions. Salgado (1999) reported a similar effort by Rolland and Mogenet (1994) in France that resulted in a job analysis system called "description in five dimensions." Finally, as you'll recall from Chapter 4 (didn't we tell you there'd be a quiz?), O*NET includes information on work styles, which includes a number of personality characteristics.

Although broad personality characteristics like those of the Big Five can be used for job analysis and have, especially in the case of conscientiousness, been shown to be modestly related to job performance, it is not clear that broad personality characteristics are the most useful for predicting job performance. Although it is still controversial because of a shortage of good data on the issue, it may turn out that more specific personality characteristics are more useful depending on the kind of work and the work context. If so, we may see other job analysis techniques based on more narrow and focused personality characteristics. We also note that elements of personality such as values, self-esteem, and locus of control overlap some with the Big Five but are not fully captured therein. Such characteristics may also be useful. Furthermore, when we wish to select people based on their fit with an organization rather than a particular job, various attributes such as values may become more important. One last challenge associated with collecting data on personality characteristics is that most of the descriptors are very socially desirable. In other words, they are almost always positive attributes or "virtues" everyone should possess. For example, O*NET includes such personality characteristics as dependability (being reliable, responsible, and fulfilling obligations) and integrity (being honest and ethical). It is difficult to imagine a situation where these characteristics are not rated as being very important for any job. Because of this, what can happen is that all of these characteristics will be rated very highly for every job. This limits their usefulness because there is little differentiation across jobs.

Interpersonal Relations

Traditional job analysis typically fails to capture the quality of interpersonal relations. Sanchez and Levine (1999) described an example where a major determinant of the performance of a pharmaceutical plant was the relations between plant operators and quality auditors. The quality of such relations is usually not captured well in lists of tasks. Interpersonal relations are important for teamwork, service industry work, and working with people from different backgrounds and cultures. Two general sets of descriptors may prove useful in the analysis of requirements for interpersonal relations, namely, personality characteristics and interpersonal skills. Personality characteristics such as agreeableness, sensitivity to others' needs, and preference for working with other people are examples of characteristics that may be of use. Ability to deal with other people in its many forms is another place in which to start. *Functional job analysis* provides a hierarchy of people functions. That is, the job may require any or all of the following: taking instructions, exchanging information, diverting, coaching, persuading, treating, instructing, consulting, supervising, negotiating, and mentoring. Such descriptors could form the bases for skills requirements. In addition, O*NET has several descriptor domains that concern interpersonal aspects of work. This includes social skills (for example, social perceptiveness, coordination, persuasion) and generalized work activities (GWAs; for example, communicating/interacting). Although the descriptors do not speak directly to the quality of relations, they could form the basis of rating scales or other approaches to judging the requirements for interpersonal aspects of jobs.

Teams. The defining features of teams are that they are composed of multiple members who have different roles and share joint responsibility for valued work outcomes. A tank crew, for example, usually has one member to drive, one to shoot, and one to decide what to do. They all want to eliminate the enemy and to survive, and they work together in service of these goals. Although the importance of other people at work is obvious, teams cause the importance of interpersonal relations to come to the forefront. Because team members depend on each other to carry out the work, interpersonal difficulties among any of the members are likely to cause problems for the entire group. As we discussed in Chapter 5, the job analysis for teams might focus on the dependencies among the team members, and even the understandings they share about each other's roles, which are called "shared mental models" (for example, Mathieu, Heffner, Goodwin, Salas, & Cannon-Bowers, 2000; Rasker, Post, & Schraagen, 2000). We say more about roles in the following section. (Bet you can't wait.)

Customer Service. Good customer service also depends on the quality of interpersonal relations. Such a quality is difficult to capture in a list of tasks. Gronroos (1982) described the *functional quality* of services, which concerns the manner in which services are delivered to the customer. Here we might be interested in characteristics such as service orientation or such skills as questioning with tact and diplomacy. Hogan, Hogan, and Busch (1984) found that emotional stability of caregivers was associated with the quality of customer service in a sample of health care workers.

Culture. With increasing global competition, companies have representatives in many parts of the world. Managers are often asked to work in foreign countries. In the United States, increasing use of teams means that people will increasingly be asked to work with people of different backgrounds and cultures. In such cases, dealing with people that seem quite different in appearance, values, and customs can be an issue. When we consider the increased number of people assigned to jobs in countries other than their own, their relationships with local people will likely require a slightly different set of KSAOs for success. Social and perceptual skills and characteristics such as flexibility and openness to new experience seem relevant for selecting people who will adjust well to exposure to people from different backgrounds. In this case of postings to foreign countries, knowledge of local customs may be relevant as a descriptor for a job requirement. Expatriate managers can then use this knowledge to adjust their behavior to the local cultural norms. Managers in foreign cultures need to understand the local requirements for *power distance*, for example (Sanchez & Levine, 1999). Power distance concerns the social distance appropriate given different jobs.

In some places, high-level employees can socialize with lower-level employees; in other places, they cannot. Consistent with this, Shin, Morgeson, and Campion (in press) found that expatriates in nations high in power distance tended to more frequently (1) perform administrative activities and (2) monitor and control resources. In addition, Shin et al. (2006) found strong evidence that expatriates working in collectivistic cultures focus more on behaviors related to relationship development because these cultures tend to emphasize the importance of interpersonal relationships (relative to individualistic cultures).

Roles

Another potentially useful approach is to examine the role requirements for jobs (Jackson & Schuler, 1990). A focus on roles leads more directly than traditional job analysis toward interpersonal and citizenship activities. A role is an expected pattern of behavior that is focused on specific positions in a group (McCormick & Ilgen, 1985). Similar to norms, roles indicate the types of behavior that are encouraged and discouraged in given situations. One example of such roles is Mintzberg's (1973) managerial roles. Mintzberg described three general types of roles. For each general type, he further described three specific roles within that general type. Each of these is briefly described below.

Interpersonal Roles. These roles involve the relations between the manager and other people. The three specific roles are the following:

1. *Figurehead.* This role allows the person to be an ambassador for the company. The president may tour the plant with foreign visitors; the first-line supervisor may attend a wedding; the middle manager may speak to a class of MBA students.

2. *Leader.* The role of the leader is what one ordinarily thinks of in terms of day-to-day management. Here we are talking about assigning tasks, determining training needs, and so forth. But it may also deal with "the vision thing."

3. *Liaison.* This role allows the manager to contact people outside his or her vertical chain of command. Here we are talking about work-related activity between units. Managers may spend as much time with peers as they do with superiors and subordinates (Mintzberg, 1973).

Informational Roles. Managers serve as the nerve center for organizations. They must be able to collect and disseminate information. The three specific roles are the following:

1. *Monitor.* This role involves scanning the environment for input.

2. *Disseminator.* This role involves sharing information with subordinates.

3. *Representative.* This role involves sharing information with people outside the work unit.

Decisional Roles. Once the manager has information, he or she ordinarily must do something with it (except if he or she is the CEO's son or daughter). The specific roles are the following:

1. *Entrepreneur.* This role involves scanning the environment for new opportunities and developing new projects, ideas, or products to benefit one's work group.

2. *Disturbance handler.* This role involves handling problems that come from staff but also from the broader environment, such as the threat of a strike or the bankruptcy of a major client.

3. *Resource allocator.* This role involves deciding who gets what. Doing this fairly is often a difficult business.

Although such roles do not directly provide descriptors for the quality of interpersonal relations, they are clearly related to dealing with other people. And so they provide another way in which to organize a job analysis.

Group Process Roles. Hersey and Blanchard (1993) described several roles related to individual behavior in groups. Such roles may be particularly important for understanding teams and teamwork. Their roles included the following:

1. *Establishing.* The purpose of this role involves helping the group get started on a task by defining issues and problems, suggesting roles for members, and generally providing structure. Such a role also includes setting goals and helping maintain direction or keeping the group on track.

2. *Persuading.* This role encompasses arguing for a particular course of action, but is much broader, including information gathering and encouraging others to provide full input. This role also includes supporting legitimate dissent.

3. *Committing.* This role involves summarizing group progress on an issue and synthesizing what is known. The role may allow one to create a concrete course of action for the group to decide on. It involves trying to get everyone to participate and then to buy into a decision.

4. *Attending.* This role involves being a good listener. This could mean, for example, taking time to draw others out and to be genuine in one's reaction to others. It does not necessarily mean agreeing with others, only paying proper attention to them.

Similar comments apply here as well as they did for Mintzberg's roles. However, Hersey and Blanchard (1993) did provide some behavioral descriptions of better and worse performance with regard to each of the roles, and these might be helpful in relating the descriptors to the quality of interpersonal interactions.

Job Design Features

Campion (1994) suggested that aspects of job design should be incorporated into future job analysis techniques. Campion's Multimethod Job Design Questionnaire was described in detail in Chapter 4 on hybrid methods. Here we remind you that his descriptors are organized by four schools of thought: mechanistic, motivational, perceptual/motor, and biological. Examples of descriptors taken from the respective schools include repetition, autonomy, lighting quality, and physical endurance requirements. Campion (1994) suggested that using such features as part of job analysis could show benefits through identifying (a) criteria for selection, (b) differences that could be used in selection, (c) the implications of job changes, or (d) the creation of new jobs.

Job design can also be used to improve system reliability. For example, a technique called *variance analysis* (Davis & Wacker, 1988) can be used to identify discrepancies between desired states and actual states in manufacturing processes and then to design changes in the work process so as to quickly detect, correct, or prevent such discrepancies. A similar logic can be brought to bear on project teams that appear to be the wave of the future. By analyzing the jobs in question, the project team may come to a better understanding of the problems that are likely to develop during the project and thus be better able to prevent them or at least to cope with them when they occur.

Connections

Traditional job analysis typically results in lists of tasks, human attributes, or both. On the task side, the job is a structure like a pyramid in which duties are at the top, and these are composed of tasks, which are composed of elements at the bottom. On the abilities side there are several types of "can do" and "will do" attributes. The connections among the tasks are typically ignored except for *time study* and *motion study* analyses. We expect to see further development of methods that show the connections among tasks, concepts, and people in the future.

Mental Representations. As working with the head increasingly takes over for working with the hands, the work itself becomes increasingly unobservable. Hypothesis generation, for example, is not easy to observe. A class of techniques called *cognitive task analysis* has been developed to better understand headwork (we described this initially in Chapter 3). More specifically, cognitive task analysis seeks to understand the mental representations that people have of their work, and how they use such representations to achieve work goals. For a simple example, suppose a pizza delivery person gets in a car to deliver a pizza. The car won't start. The driver has an understanding of what a car is that can be used to generate a hypothesis about why the car won't start. (Such a representation is called a *schema*. No, this is not a New Yorker who is constantly plotting.) Such hypotheses are useful in diagnosing and solving the problem. It might turn out, for example, that when the car was turned off, the transmission was left in drive rather than in park. For another example, the driver has a mental map of the city that is quite helpful in getting the pizza from the parlor to the customer in the shortest period of time.

A common form of cognitive task analysis requires subject matter experts (SMEs; usually incumbents) to provide information about the relatedness of various objects or ideas at work. The analyst uses this information to represent the relations among the total set of objects so that a structure or organization emerges. Such a structure is thought to represent a schema for the incumbents in question. For example, Prince (1999) had pilots sort flight problems into categories based on their similarity. Then, using a technique called *multidimensional scaling*, she created a map that showed the similarity of the problems in terms of distance, so that similar problems showed up close to one another and dissimilar problems showed up farther away from one another. By looking at such a map, she could tell something about the features of problems that differentiate them according to the pilots. In the case of the pilots' flight problems, the important attributes turned out to be such things as time pressure to produce a solution and whether other people needed to be part of the problem's solution.

Cognitive task analysis covers not only tasks but also concepts and their interrelationships. Thus, concept relations are described by the connectedness, contiguity, proximity or closeness of tasks, concepts, or actions to one another. In other words, cognitive task analysis provides quantitative data about what goes with what. Such an approach has been labeled concept mapping (see Seamster, Redding, & Kaempf, 1997, for more aviation examples).

Cognitive task analysis may provide a source of evidence for the validity of tests in selection as well as the content of training programs.

Flowcharts and Time Charts. Flowcharts present information on the relations among tasks. They may also present information about system states and decision points. Such flowcharts are sometimes called *process maps*. They show how the work is done to achieve specific goals (Galloway, 1994). We presented examples of flowcharts and time charts during our description of job analysis for teams (Chapter 5).

Considering job design at the group or team level can have dramatic benefits. Cascio (1995) described an intervention by Bell Atlantic in which a "case team" was developed to install high-speed digital service links. Case teams were composed of members who were needed in all phases of the installation. The teams were brought together from physically different locations and different departments. The typical installation time after the introduction of the teams dropped from 30 days to 3. Wellins, Byham, and Dixon (1994) described an analogous situation in Cape Coral Hospital. They examined the process involved in patient care, considered the entire set of tasks to be accomplished by a team, and bundled tasks to create new jobs and multiskilled teams of caregivers.

New Scales

The rating scales often employed in job analysis are things such as importance to the job, difficulty to learn, whether it is reasonable to expect applicants to perform the task without training, and so forth. As organizations strive to focus on their core competencies, that is, their unique competitive strengths, they also tend to shed (outsource) fringe operations. For example, a company might hire an external company to maintain its computers or to recruit its employees. Some companies are currently experimenting with having suppliers staff workstations in their assembly plants. Scales aimed at the degree to which tasks affect core functions or scales centered on how feasible it is to outsource the task may be useful in future job analyses (Sanchez & Levine, 1999). Similarly, if redesigning work with the goal of outsourcing certain functions, it might be useful to identify which tasks or other aspects are core to a particular job (see Morgeson & Campion, 2002). The job can be redesigned to retain only those aspects that are core to the mission of the job or organization. Other analyses might focus on the extent to which the job as a whole is important to the strategic mission of the organization (Huselid, Beatty, & Becker, 2005). Those that are deemed noncore might be candidates for outsourcing. Finally, when customer service is a primary goal of the organization, scales that assess the impact of the task on customer service might be used. Such scales help show the value of job analysis by linking the tasks to the core values of the organization, a problem that we mentioned during the description of competencies.

SOURCES OF INFORMATION

The most commonly used source of information for conventional job analysis is the incumbent. Particularly for the *task inventory,* the incumbent usually provides virtually all of the information gathered in the project. Other commonly used sources of information are the job analyst and the incumbent's supervisor. Other SMEs are used less often. We suspect that in the future, the incumbent will still be the most commonly used source of information (Sanchez & Levine, 1999). The reason is that the incumbent knows the job best and so is typically in the best position to provide high-quality information about the job. This is particularly true as more and more jobs involve knowledge work, where much of what is done on the job is not directly observable (because it involves mental processes) or involves virtual work arrangements where workers are geographically distributed. However, we suspect that other sources of information may also become increasingly important in the future.

Customers

As service becomes increasingly central to the economy, the relations between workers and customers or clients become increasingly important. Customers can provide valuable input about how a job should be designed as well as provide standards or measures of job performance. Customer focus groups can be used to provide input to the job analysis. For example, we recently worked on a project in which community groups were used to inform a police officer job analysis. In addition to using customer input, retailers use "mystery shoppers" to gather information about the quality of customer service. Mystery shoppers are employed by the company to act as customers. The employees providing service to the mystery shoppers do not know that the shoppers are also employees. The mystery shoppers are usually trained to make systematic observations of how they are treated. The mystery shoppers are also a good source of data for a job analysis for service jobs.

Both external and internal customers may provide a legitimate source of information (Bernardin, 1992). Internal customers are people whose jobs receive as input what other jobs produce as output. For example, in an auto dealership, the employees in the maintenance department (the mechanics who fix cars) are customers of the employees in the parts department (who stock the parts for cars). By considering a work process, we can form a panel of workers that jointly accomplishes the transformation of one or more inputs to a useful output. This work group may or may not be formally recognized as a team. However, such a group can often improve the work by discussing problems that the workers encounter with one another. Sanchez and Levine (1999) described such a project in a high-tech electronics company. They assembled panels of workers from multiple areas and locations. The panels were able to assess flaws in the current work processes and to recommend solutions.

Specialists

Incumbents are not always the best judges of their own jobs. Physical laborers are some of the people who are least likely to complain about their jobs being physically tiring, perhaps because they expect to be tired. Along the same lines, Sanchez and Levine (1999) reported a study of cruise line engine workers who reported that they were not subject to loud noises. However, job analysts found that the incumbents' engine rooms were very noisy indeed. Trainers or education specialists may provide more accurate judgments of difficulty to learn than do incumbents (Sanchez & Levine, 1999), probably because they teach people the different tasks and therefore know well what gives people trouble. Tolerance for stress may be best assessed by those with a background in psychology (Jones et al., 2001). There are doubtless other instances in which specialists provide better judgments about job features than do incumbents.

In addition to special expertise, panels may be assembled because they provide information quickly and relatively cheaply compared with large samples responding to task inventories or other structured questionnaires. A couple of issues with regard to such panels have been investigated. A main concern is whether such panels provide information that is equivalent to larger samples. Thus far, studies suggest that data from the panels are likely to be similar to data from the larger sample (Ash, Levine, Higbee, & Sistrunk, 1982). However, it remains to be seen whether the products resulting from job analysis using panels are equivalent to products resulting from job analyses using larger samples of respondents. A second issue regards the group dynamics caused by panel composition. In other words, do demographics influence the outcome of the panel? Levine and Sanchez (1998) examined group variables such as age, group size, gender, and racial diversity and their impact on scales applied to tasks and to KSAOs. They found no indication of the group-level variables on agreement or other indices of the quality of the data. Both sets of results are encouraging, but clearly further research is warranted on the use and composition of expert panels.

Computers

Computers are used routinely in the physical sciences to study the likely effects of changes in conditions. For example, there are models of global warming that forecast weather patterns around the world as the average temperature increases. Physiological and biological data about humans are now available in sufficient quantity to model judgments about the comfort of seats, perception of noise, and so forth. Although human responses to tasks and job context are more complex than judgments of sensation and perception, it may not be all that long before models of people (that is, simulated people) are used to test changes in work to examine the likely outcomes (Coovert, Craiger, & Cannon-Bowers, 1996). Polito and Pritsker (1988) described two different computer simulation systems for analyzing human operator performance. Thus, we expect computer models to become an additional source of job analytic data in the not-too-distant future.

METHODS OF COLLECTING DATA

The most commonly used conventional methods of collecting data include observing the work, interviews with individuals and panels, and responses to questionnaires. Less commonly used methods include diaries, mechanical recording devices, and records of work performed. As we found with sources of information, the methods that are commonly used today will continue to be used. However, we expect to see a major impact of technology on methods of collecting data, so that the relative frequency of methods of collecting data may change.

Computer Networks

The widespread use of networks such as the Internet (or its within-organization counterpart, the Intranet) is likely to have pervasive effects on data collection. Task inventories or other surveys that have typically been administered as paper-and-pencil surveys are now being administered over networks, particularly for jobs that require the use of computers (much as paper-and-pencil tests have given way to point-and-click tests). Because the survey respondents put the information directly into the computer, clerical work in terms of printing and mailing forms is eliminated (at least for the employer), as is the tedious and error-prone business of keypunch data entry needed to process completed surveys. Internet administration will have its own problems. Such problems will include the visual presentation of the survey (it will look different on different machines), assuring the anonymity of the respondent, potential over-surveying of respondents to the extent that they simply ignore the survey (imagine that!) and assuring the integrity of the data because of illegitimate respondents and hacking the database of responses. An unanswered question is whether Web-based surveys would yield the same results as paper-and-pencil surveys. Some research in a related area (the employee attitude of job satisfaction) has examined the comparability of paper-and-pencil and Web-based measurement methods (Donovan, Drasgow, & Probst, 2000). Donovan et al. found that responses across the two different methods were similar, suggesting that questionnaire type does not affect survey results. On the other hand Levine, Yang, Xu, and Lopez-Rivas (2006) found, in two separate studies, that response rates for Internet surveys were considerably lower than rates for hard copies. Although the overall trends in these results are promising, it is not clear that these results will generalize to the job analysis context, in part because job analysis questionnaires are much longer and more involved than short attitude questionnaires. For these reasons, the impact of computerized administration on the quality of data is an important issue to investigate.

Networks will also change the way in which expert panels meet. Rather than meeting face to face, panels will more and more often meet in virtual spaces created by computers connected through networks. As the technology improves, such meetings will appear increasingly natural to the participants. It will be much cheaper to convene panels of experts from distant places by network than by traveling to a meeting.

Electronic Performance Monitoring

Computers will fulfill the role of collecting data with increasing frequency in the future. Even today, truck leasing companies are installing computers that track the truck's speed, idle time, and even the physical location of the truck. Where the work requires the use of a computer, the computer itself can track every keystroke and mouse movement along with the current time. Such a capacity allows an extremely detailed analysis of work performance. It is possible to connect cameras to computer networks as well and to sample and transmit pictures of the current computer operator. With the current technology, computers can gather and store staggering amounts of information about work performance. They do not yet have much capacity for understanding what it is that they are recording, however. For example, a computer can take a picture of the person working at the keyboard once every 60 seconds and store the information in the file. However, the computer is not likely to know who it is recording or what the person is doing at work. However, that too will change in the not too distant future. Computers now monitor public spaces in some cities and can identify known criminals and alert police as to their presence. With a little programming, computers can tell whether a person is writing a letter, writing some code, developing a budget, or even downloading something from the Internet that does not, shall we say, appear to be job related. As computers become increasingly sophisticated in recognizing what people are doing, the possibilities for electronic performance monitoring will grow exponentially. A key issue in job analyses of the future is whether we should rely on human estimates of such factors as frequency of task performance or amount of time spent on tasks when the use of electronic performance monitoring can give us more reliable and valid data (Sanchez & Levine, 2001).

There are ethical issues that emerge from electronic performance monitoring, of course. It is commonplace today for companies to monitor service phone calls, for example, for credit card inquiries, to question a water bill, or to order cable service. However, customers are informed that they may be monitored, and in some cases, customers are allowed to refuse being monitored. Most people do not want to be videotaped at work. Employees find such monitoring invasive, and they are particularly offended if they are monitored without their knowledge by hidden cameras.

Forecasting

Incumbents cannot be observed, interviewed, or questioned when the focal job does not yet exist. In such cases, people have to make their best guess about what the job will be. One method for doing so involves asking a panel to make ratings of current and future tasks (see Arvey, Salas, & Gialluca, 1992; Sanchez & Fraser, 1994; Schneider & Konz, 1989). Although such procedures are systematic, little is known about their reliability and freedom from bias or consequential validity. Our raters must infer what the job will be like in the future and then base their ratings on a mental representation that was constructed in some manner or other.

Another method that can be used to forecast jobs and their requirements is the simulation. One type of simulation is the hypothetical scenario. The scenario provides information to the expert about such aspects as demographic, social, economic, political, and technological trends. For example, air traffic control is changing as technology improves. Many operations that had been completed in a control tower essentially by looking out the window are now moving to windowless rooms and are being completed by looking at a computer screen. Some jets are being designed so that there will be no direct view from the cockpit—during landings the pilots can only see the runway through video monitors. The scenario for experts could involve asking them to imagine that they are working in the new, windowless environment. They could be asked about what is different in the new job and how it might change communications and information processing (Sanchez & Levine, 1999).

Just recently we heard from a colleague that job analysis may look, not just to the future, but back to the past (Jone Papinchock, personal communication, 2005). What prompts this retrospective approach are court cases or Equal Employment Opportunity Commission investigations. Charges about potentially discriminatory selection programs or equal pay issues may include the problem that job analyses were not done or perhaps were done in ways that were not professionally acceptable, when the selection programs or pay plans were developed. This then calls for people to look back and recreate the jobs as they were at the time. Of course, the reliability and validity of these retrospective accounts would need to be carefully researched.

UNITS OF ANALYSIS

Time-and-motion studies used elemental motions as the primary units of analysis. Elemental motions are still important, but now they are often used in job analysis for robots (Nof, 1988). The philosophy of the engineering approach to jobs was embodied in the notion of "one best way." The trend today is to move from working with the hands to working with the head. Jobs are becoming more flexible, and the units of analysis appear to be broader. As noted earlier, use of "task clusters" (Cascio, 1995; Morgeson & Campion, 2002) may provide a useful level of analysis between the task and job levels.

As we mentioned earlier, we may expect broader characteristics that apply to multiple jobs to see increasing use. Personality characteristics such as the Big Five and competencies may become more common. However, there are still pressures to focus on tasks. First, without reference to tasks, systems based on broad characteristics may have trouble withstanding legal scrutiny (EEOC, "Uniform Guidelines on Employee Selection Procedures," 1978; Varca & Pattison, 1993). Second, without referring to tasks, it is difficult to understand the nature of the work itself, and so the information is of limited value for some applications. If a job is reported as a Position Analysis Questionnaire (PAQ) profile, for example, that information is useful in predicting salary, but it is not very helpful for job design. Third, due to scarcity of information, panels or others responsible for defining and listing competencies for an organization may be unable to do a better job than a single person visiting the business section of a library (Sanchez & Levine, 1999).

The closeness or connectedness of concepts is a relatively new unit of analysis. It has been used primarily for the representation of job knowledge possessed by workers. Research is needed to understand how to analyze connectedness data so that the data can be used for selection, training, job design, or other human resource programs. It could be, for example, that connectedness data are very useful for assessing expertise, and thus could be used as part of training certification, training evaluation, or standards for job performance. Or it could be that certain patterns of connections are associated with better and worse job designs.

ROLE DEFINITION AND REDEFINITION

In any job analysis effort, some level of variability is observed among workers who have the same job. This within-job variability has traditionally been viewed as measurement error to be eliminated, where the responses of multiple job incumbents are simply averaged. In many instances such variability is no doubt simply measurement error or a source of bias (see Chapter 9; also see Cranny & Doherty, 1988, for problems in interpreting correlations among items rated by experts). Yet there is reason to believe that some of this variability reflects true and meaningful differences among workers.

Role theory has long recognized that individuals with the same job will perform a somewhat different set of tasks and enact their roles in slightly different ways (Biddle, 1979; Katz & Kahn, 1978). This would suggest that workers are actively "crafting" or "sculpting" their jobs to fit their own needs and abilities (Staw & Boettger, 1990; Wrzesniewski & Dutton, 2001). Differences among workers are therefore potentially meaningful, particularly as organizations depend on discretionary behaviors that extend past formal job requirements (Sanchez & Levine, 2001). As a consequence, strategies focused on averaging across incumbents might obscure these differences.

Research has begun to investigate the circumstances under which workers expand their work roles. Hofmann, Morgeson, and Gerras (2003) found that the quality of relationships workers have with their supervisors is related to the performance of extra-role behaviors. Morgeson, Delaney-Klinger, and Hemingway (2005) found that job autonomy, cognitive ability, and job-related skill were positively related to the performance of additional work tasks, which, in turn, was related to higher supervisory evaluations of job performance. These findings suggest that job analysis research should not always treat within-job title differences as error to be eliminated. Rather, such differences should be viewed as potentially meaningful and efforts should be made to predict the differences. Doing so will enhance the validity of job analysis data. Additional research needs to be conducted to identify the range of factors that can lead to differential role definition.

DISSEMINATION, STORAGE, AND RETRIEVAL

When the job analysis project is finished, the project sponsor needs to be told (see Chapter 9 for discussion of the project sponsor). So may others, and thus the need for the dissemination of information. At the very least, job analysis data come in handy for legal reasons, and so the information has to be stored and retrieved if it is needed. However, job analysis data may prove useful in many other ways as well. If the information can be stored in such a way that it can be linked to other information, it has a greater potential for future use. For example, O*NET will provide a means of linking job-related human abilities to labor markets and wage surveys. The rest of this section of the chapter describes important aspects of dissemination, storage, and retrieval.

Written Copies of a Formal Report. The immediate product of a traditional job analysis has always been a written report. The report contains a description of the job analysis process (what was done) and a description of the products of the job analysis. The products might be such things as a job description or a list of tasks or a list of abilities and associated ratings of importance. Such reports will continue to be written in the future because they are so important for documenting the process. Job analysis reports establish the paper trail that leads from the study of the job to the human resources practice, whether it is personnel selection, job evaluation, or any other. Such reports are major weapons in legal battles.

Online Storage. With the advent of modern technology in the form of computer databases and the Internet, job analysis data can now be stored so that they can be used for multiple purposes. Consider O*NET, which is a database of job information that can be accessed in many ways for different purposes. By developing such databases, it may be possible for people to find uses for job analysis data that were not envisioned by the original gatherers of the data. Computer storage of written documents also allows users to find relatively obscure documents and to search the documents without having to read them. Several different systems are currently available for searching that range from sorting by keywords supplied by users to search engines that scan entire texts.

Key Recipients. Whether the job analysis information is a report or a database, it will certainly go to the project sponsor. Beyond that, job analysis information may or may not be widely disseminated. Business establishments may not want other businesses to know what they have discovered. In some cases, the job analysis may result in a publication in a scientific or trade journal. In such a case, the recipients of the report are a wide audience.

Periodic Retrieval. As we have mentioned several times, we expect the pace of change in jobs to increase in the future. If there is a systematic process of doing and documenting job analysis, then there ought to be a systematic means of reviewing the job analysis data after some meaningful period because the data become stale and increasingly obsolete. If the data are kept in a database such as O*NET, there may be a greater impetus to maintain the quality and currency of the data.

Chapter Summary

We began the chapter by describing three types of changes that are likely to influence work of the future and thus potentially to have an impact on job analysis. Although changes in societal values are likely to have some of the most profound effects, such changes are the most difficult to predict, and so we have not developed this topic much. Different authors have described many changes that are likely in the business climate. Commonly mentioned factors include increasing global competition, increasing flexibility in the assignment of tasks to jobs, and a reduction in hierarchy such that workers contact one another directly rather than through supervision. Such changes will allow organizations of the future to adapt quickly to changes in the business environment. On the other hand, such changes may cause problems in coordination of work and tend to reduce efficiency. On the technology front, we expect computers to be increasingly pervasive because of their continuing progress toward greater memory, speed, and affordability. In the short term, computers will make a great deal of information known about work processes. Further down the road, computers may analyze and even direct work processes.

We then turned to the building blocks of job analysis in order to examine the likely impact of the expected changes, particularly those due to business and technology factors. With regard to the descriptors, we expect several changes. First, we expect to see more use of broad-based human attributes such as personality characteristics and competencies. Second, we expect to see more attention to human relations, both from a customer service standpoint and from a teamwork standpoint. Descriptors that may apply include personality characteristics such as emotional stability and roles. We mentioned two different sets of roles, those of Mintzberg (1973; relational, informational, decisional) and the roles related to group process (establishing, persuading, committing, attending). Third, we described connections. The connections may represent means-ends relations in the pursuit of task accomplishment as shown in a work-flow diagram. The connections may illustrate sequence and simultaneity requirements as in a time-flow diagram. Or the connections may represent the closeness of concepts in a schema, as in a concept map. Finally, we mentioned new scales that might be used to gather information to make decisions about whether to accomplish a task using people inside or outside of the organization or to assess the impact that an activity has on customer service.

We turned from descriptors to sources of information. The incumbent is likely to remain the most important source of information because the incumbent usually knows the job best. However, we expect to see other sources of information with increasing frequency. We expect to see more input from internal and external customers, including mystery shoppers. Although incumbents usually know the job best, such is not always the case. Panels of specialists may be better suited to specific kinds of judgments such as stress, noise, or difficulty to learn either because the specialists have specific background and preparation or because the incumbents have adapted to the job and no longer notice its requirements. Finally, we mentioned computers as a source of information. There are currently available programs that simulate human operators of machines. As such programs grow in sophistication, it will be possible to learn a great deal about modifying jobs without having people experience the changes. Research is needed on the impact of the computer on the quality of job analysis data.

We then moved to methods of data collection. We discussed three main issues: computer networks, electronic performance monitoring, and forecasting. Our basic message in this section is that technology will influence how we collect data. We expect to see a shift away from paper-and-pencil questionnaire administration to administration through computer networks, particularly for jobs that ordinarily use computers. Because the respondents to a questionnaire input the data into the computer, lots of clerical work is saved. We expect panels to meet with increasing frequency through computer networks rather than face to face. Electronic performance monitoring uses computers and peripheral devices to monitor work processes. As computers become better at analyzing such data in addition to recording them, computers may in some sense take the place of supervisors. There are ethical issues involved with electronic performance monitoring. Forecasting is about predicting what jobs will be like in the future. Panels of experts can be used to provide such data.

We turned next to the units of analysis. We expect that broader units of analysis will become more popular. However, task information will still be useful when we want to defend the accuracy of the job analysis to people outside of the organization and when task information is useful for the purpose at hand, such as job design. We also expect to see the development of methods for the analysis of connections data. For example, both flowcharts and time charts are useful, but there is no rigorous way in which to analyze them or to determine if they are in some way optimal. Similarly, cognitive task analysis has provided ways to represent connections data (concept maps), but there has been little effort to relate such representations to the development of human resource programs.

Issues of role definition and redefinition were then discussed. The traditional approach in job analysis has been to assume that within job title variability is measurement error to be eliminated. It was suggested that such differences might be meaningful and could be predicted based on other factors such as leadership, job autonomy, ability, and skill. This represents an area where there is great potential for additional job analysis research.

Finally, we mentioned the dissemination, storage, and retrieval of job analysis information. Although the traditional job analysis report is likely to remain with us, there are exciting developments in the storage and retrieval of job analysis information that are likely to make job analysis information more widely available and more useful.

A Final Note

Sanchez and Levine (1999) asked whether job analysis was "dead, misunderstood, or both." They concluded that the objections to job analysis were really objections to some of the products of job analysis, such as the narrow job description. We believe that as long as people must organize to accomplish work, some understanding of what the work requires is necessary. Because job analysis is the process of understanding the requirements of work, some form of job analysis will be necessary whenever people form organizations to accomplish work. It should be clear from this chapter that although some form of job analysis will be needed, there will be changes in the descriptors, sources of data, methods of data collection, and units of analysis in the future. We also believe that job analysis will continue to be fun to do in the future, and we hope that you get a chance to do your fair share.

Glossary

Ability Requirements Scales (ARS) are related to a taxonomy of human abilities covering cognitive, perceptual, physical, and psychomotor areas. The abilities are each linked to one or more psychological tests. ARS are used to evaluate or judge the degree to which each of the generic human abilities is required by the job.

Adverse impact is a term used to describe a situation in which a test or hiring process results in disproportionate failure or rejection rates among protected categories of applicants such as racial or sex groups. *See also* "Uniform, Guidelines on Employee Selection Procedures" (1978).

AET (*Arbeitwissenschaftliches Erhebungsverfahren zur Tätigkeitsanalyse,* "ergonomic task analysis data collection procedure") is a job analysis method that comes from an ergonomics perspective, and attempts to minimize human stress and strain while maximizing performance quality and quantity.

Age Discrimination in Employment Act (1967) and later extensions or amendments prohibit discrimination in employment based on age. The act protects people 40 years of age and older.

Americans with Disabilities Act (ADA) (1990) prohibits employers from discriminating against qualified people with disabilities, or a history of disabilities, as well as those who are regarded as being disabled due to assumed disabilities such as disfigurement.

Behavioral observation scales (BOS) use behavioral statements to illustrate the meaning of a facet of job performance. They do so by having the rater respond to each item in terms of frequency of occurrence rather than to the category as a whole, as in behaviorally anchored rating scales (BARS).

Behaviorally anchored rating scales (BARS) are used in performance appraisal, where they assist raters by providing behavioral descriptions ("anchors") to help people understand what the points on a rating scale mean.

Building blocks of job analysis methods include descriptors, sources of data, methods of collecting data, and units of analysis. See Chapter 1 for details.

Civil Rights Acts (1964, 1972, and 1991) prohibit employers from discriminating on the basis of race, color, sex, religion, or national origin.

Cognitive task analysis is a collection of techniques all of which focus on understanding the mental processes involved in successful completion of a task.

Combination job analysis method (C-JAM) gives information about what gets done on the job and how, as well as information on the human attributes needed to do the job, which is information essential for legal, quasi-legal, and other purposes that relate to human resource management.

Competency models link the specific business strategy to attributes needed in people to pursue the strategy. For example, if an organization were to pursue a business strategy focused around innovation, the organization would want to hire, develop, and reward creative people.

Comprehensive Occupational Data Analysis Program (CODAP) is a computerized system developed originally in the U.S. Air Force for collecting and analyzing task inventory data.

Critical incidents are short stories about particular instances of either outstanding or poor performance in which the context, worker actions, and degree of worker responsibility for the outcome are specified.

Critical incident technique (CIT) is a job analysis method that helps to restrict the job analysis information by ignoring typical or ordinary job behavior. It requires that job experts recall specific incidents of either very good or very poor performance on the job.

Descriptors are the units or components of the job examined during the job analysis.

Dictionary of Occupational Titles (*DOT*) was developed by the U.S. Department of Labor to create a common set of job descriptions that would allow people in different agencies and geographic locations to communicate effectively about jobs. The latest version of the *DOT* contains more than 10,000 job descriptions.

Equal Pay Act (1963) requires employers to pay men and women the same salary for the same job, that is, equal pay for equal work.

Executive orders come from the U.S. president's authority to make rules and regulations for the federal government and also for those doing business with the federal government.

Forced-choice scales are a format for rating scales used in performance appraisal that aim to control for leniency on the part of the rater. The scales make it difficult for the rater to tell how favorable the rating is.

Functional job analysis (FJA) is a job analysis method that is based on tasks and the premise that whatever workers do, they do in relation to one of three aspects of work: data, people, or things.

Generalized work activity (GWA) is a task description that is written at a broad level so that it can apply to multiple occupations. These descriptors are part of the new Occupational Information Network (O*NET) that will replace the *Dictionary of Occupational Titles* (*DOT*).

Graphic rating scales are used for performance appraisal. The scales usually require the manager to make quantitative ratings of various, often generic, aspects of the worker's job performance such as quality of work or quantity of work.

J-coefficient, in the job element method (JEM), is an estimate of a validity coefficient that would result if a validation study were conducted using a job element for selecting employees.

Job classification is the process of placing one or more jobs into a cluster or family of like jobs.

Job Components Inventory (JCI) is a questionnaire that lists 220 items related to tools and equipment plus other information useful for vocational purposes.

Job description is a brief written description of work intended to communicate the essence of the job. It usually contains identifiers, a summary, and duties and tasks. Job description is the most common application of job analysis.

Job design is the process of bundling tasks or units of work into a collective called a job. It is intended to meet three kinds of organizational needs: production system needs, social-organizational needs, and individual worker needs.

Job element method (JEM) focuses on knowledge, skills, abilities, and other characteristics needed to perform work, and their degree of importance for selection or training.

Job evaluation is the process of establishing the worth of jobs to an employer.

Job redesign is the resorting or redistribution of tasks to replace old jobs with new ones.

Knowledge, skills, abilities, and other characteristics (KSAOs) are human attributes needed to perform work. Their definition and use varies somewhat by author (see the sections on job elements, e-JAM, and legal aspects (Table 6.1).

Machines, tools, equipment, and work aids (MTEWA) are tangible objects used by the worker to accomplish work goals.

Management Position Description Questionnaire (MPDQ) uses quantitative responses to standard items in a questionnaire for the analysis of the job. The MPDQ was designed to use managers' self-reports of their jobs.

Materials, products, subject matter, and services (MPSMS) are the work outputs, or immediate goals, of the job.

Multimethod Job Design Questionnaire (MJDQ) is a method of analyzing jobs based on four different approaches to job design. The approaches are biological, mechanistic, motivational, and perceptual/motor. Trade-offs in benefits are typically expected across the four areas.

Multiphase analysis of performance (MAP) system is a job analysis method that covers team mission and functions; team member tasks; and team member knowledge, skills, abilities, and other characteristics (KSAOs) needed to perform their tasks. The term *MAP* also conveys the idea that the method proceeds from a global picture of the team to the specific actions taken by the team as a whole and its members separately.

Occupational Information Network (O*NET) is an online occupational database organized around six sets of descriptors that serve as a content model. The information may be accessed at a general or specific level and can be used for numerous human resource applications. The network awaits refinements and updating based on sound research. The data can be accessed via the Internet: http://www.onetcenter.org/.

Occupational Reinforcer Pattern (ORP) is a worker-oriented method of job analysis. ORP traits are linked to human motives at work that can be used for vocational guidance purposes.

Performance appraisal is the formal process of evaluating the job performance of individuals (and teams) who have been working for some period.

Position Analysis Questionnaire (PAQ) is a questionnaire containing generic descriptors aimed at describing the basic nature of all jobs. The PAQ also notes that the environment and social setting play a role in job performance. Questionnaire responses are analyzed into job dimensions, which can be used in selection and job evaluation.

Professional standards are guidelines for job analysis proffered by organizations whose members conduct or evaluate job analysis. The *Principles for*

Validation and Use of Personnel Selection Procedures published by the Society for Industrial and Organizational Psychological Psychology, and the *Standards for Educational and Psychological Testing* published by the American Educational Research Association, the American Psychological Association, and the National Council on Measurement in Education are most relevant.

Purpose and **practicality** are the two primary influences on choice of job analysis methods.

Rehabilitation Act (1973) served as the foundation for the Americans with Disabilities Act. The law prohibits discrimination in employment based on handicap.

Reliability of job analysis data refers to the degree of consistency or agreement among raters using various scales and across time, which is referred to also as *stability* of data.

Role is an expected pattern of behavior that is focused on specific positions in a group.

Subject matter expert (SME) is an incumbent, his or her supervisors, or specialists who are considered to have in-depth knowledge about their own jobs or jobs with which they have substantial familiarity.

Task inventory is a listing of all the work activities performed to complete one or more jobs; each activity is commonly referred to as a *task*. A task inventory is presented to incumbents and supervisors in a survey format. Usually, the items are rated on scales such as time spent that serve to indicate task importance. The survey responses provide the data for the job analysis.

Task Inventory/Comprehensive Occupational Data Analysis Program (TI/CODAP) (*see* Comprehensive Occupational Data Analysis Program).

Threshold traits analysis (TTA) or **Threshold Traits Analysis System** (TTAS) is a job analysis method based on a standard set of 33 traits derived from a comprehensive database of work activities.

Time-and-motion study is a method of job analysis that evolved primarily from industrial engineering rather than from industrial psychology. Its descriptors are generally very small elements of work such as the timing of movements of the arms and fingers and/or their relationship to each other.

Training is the structured and systematic process by which workers learn what they need to know, think, or do to perform successfully on the job.

"Uniform Guidelines on Employee Selection Procedures" (1978) are instructions to employers that tell how to ensure the legality of employment tests. The Guidelines describe requirements for job analysis and validation when adverse impact occurs. They were issued jointly in 1978 by federal compliance agencies including the Equal Employment Opportunity Commission.

Validity of a job analysis can be inferred by the extent to which human resource programs developed from job analyses are noticeably and significantly improved relative to programs not developed from job analyses.

Work Performance Survey System (WPSS) is a computerized task inventory approach used in industry that descended directly from the Comprehensive Occupational Data Analysis Program (CODAP) system devised by the U.S. Air Force.

Worker mobility deals with how employees move into and through the organization and includes such movement as promotions, demotions, and transfers to different geographic locations. Organizations may provide career ladders and lattices to facilitate worker movement. Jobs in the ladders and lattices may be described by their needed experience; training; and knowledge, skills, abilities, and other characteristics (KSAOs).

Workforce planning involves the estimation of the supply of qualified employees and the demand for employees of various types. Action plans are developed to ensure that supply and demand match as closely as possible.

References

Adams, J. S. (1965). Inequity in social exchange. In L. Berkowitz (Ed.), *Advances in experimental social psychology* (pp. 276–299). New York: Academic Press.

Albemarle Paper Co. v. Moody. (1975). *Fair Employment Practices, 10,* 1181.

Amason, A. C. (1996). Distinguishing the effects of functional and dysfunctional conflict on strategic decision making: Resolving a paradox for top management teams. *Academy of Management Journal, 39,* 123–148.

Amason, A. C., Thompson, K. R., Hochwarter, W. A., & Harrison, A. W. (1995). An important dimension in successful management teams. *Organizational Dynamics, 24,* 20–35.

American Educational Research Association, American Psychological Association, and the National Council on Measurement in Education. (1999). *Standards for educational and psychological testing.* Washington DC: Author.

Amrine, H. T., Ritchey, J., & Hulley, O.S. (1975). *Manufacturing organization and management.* Englewood Cliffs, NJ: Prentice-Hall.

Arvey, R. D., & Faley, R. H. (1988). *Fairness in selecting employees* (2nd ed.). New York: Addison-Wesley.

Arvey, R. D., Salas, E., & Gialluca, K. A. (1992). Using task inventories to forecast skills and abilities. *Human Performance, 5,* 171–190.

Ash, R. A. (1988). Job analysis in the world of work. In S. Gael (Ed.), *The job analysis handbook for business, industry and government* (Vol. I, pp. 3–13). New York: Wiley.

Ash, R. A., & Levine, E. L. (1980). A framework for evaluating job analysis methods. *Personnel, 57,* 59.

Ash, R. A., Levine, E. L., Higbee, R. H., & Sistrunk, F. (1982, March). *Comparison of task ratings from subject matter experts vs. job incumbents.* Paper presented at the annual meeting of the Southeastern Psychological Association, New Orleans.

Ash, R. A., Levine, E. L., & Sistrunk, F. (1983). The role of job-based methods in personnel and human resources management. In K. M. Rowland and G. D. Ferris (Eds.), *Research in personnel and human resources management* (Vol. I). Greenwich, CT: JAI Press.

Astrand, P. O., & Rodahl, K. (1977). *Textbook of work physiology: Physiological bases of exercise* (2nd ed.). New York: McGraw-Hill.

Attewell, P. (1992). Skill and occupational changes in U.S. manufacturing. In P. S. Adler (Ed.), *Technology and the future of work.* New York: Oxford University Press.

Bailey, K. D. (1994). *Typologies and taxonomies: An introduction to classification techniques.* Thousand Oaks, CA: Sage.

Banks, M. H. (1988). Job components inventory. In S. Gael (Ed.), *The job analysis handbook for business, industry, and government* (Vol. II, pp. 960–990). New York: Wiley.

Banks, M. H., & Miller, R. L. (1984). Reliability and convergent validity of the Job Components Inventory. *Journal of Occupational Psychology, 57,* 181–184.

Barrett, G. V., & Depinet, R. L. (1991). A reconsideration of testing for competence rather than for intelligence. *American Psychologist, 46,* 1012–1024.

Bartram, D. (2005). The great eight competencies: A criterion-centric approach to validation. *Journal of Applied Psychology, 90,* 1185–1203.

Bartram, D., Robertson, I. T., & Callinan, M. (2002). Introduction: A framework for examining organizational effectiveness. In I. T. Robertson, M. Callinan, & D. Bartram (Eds.), *Organizational effectiveness: The role of psychology* (pp. 1–10). Chichester, UK: Wiley.

Bernardin, H. J. (1992). An analytic framework for customer-based performance content development and appraisal. *Human Resources Management Review, 2,* 81–102.

Bernardin, H. J., & Beatty, R. W. (1984). *Performance appraisal: Assessing human behavior at work.* Boston: Kent.

Biddle, B. J. (1979). *Role theory: Expectation, identities, and behaviors.* New York: Academic Press.

Borg, I., & Groenen, P. (1996). *Modern Multidimensional Scaling.* New York: Springer.

Borgen, F. H. (1988). Occupational Reinforcer Patterns. In S. Gael (Ed.), *The job analysis handbook for business, industry, and government* (Vol. II, pp. 902–916). New York: Wiley.

Borman, W. C., & Brush, D. H. (1993). More progress toward a taxonomy of managerial performance. *Human Performance, 6,* 1–21.

Borman, W. C., Dorsey, D., & Ackerman, L. (1992). Time-spent responses as time allocation strategies: Relations with sales performance in a stockbroker sample. *Personnel Psychology, 45,* 763–777.

Borman, W. C., & Vallon, W. R. (1974). A view of what can happen when behavioral expectation scales are developed in one setting and used in another. *Journal of Applied Psychology, 59,* 197–201.

Bownas, D. A., & Bernardin, H. J. (1988). Critical incident technique. In S. Gael (Ed.), *The job analysis handbook for business, industry, and government* (Vol. 2, pp. 1120–1140). New York: Wiley.

Boyatzis, R. E. (1982). *The competent manager: A model for effective performance.* New York: Wiley.

Brannick, M. T., Brannick, J. P., & Levine, E. L. (1992). Job analysis, personnel selection, and the ADA. *Human Resource Management Review, 2,* 171–182.

Brannick, M. T., Salas, E., & Prince, C. (1997). *Team performance assessment and measurement: Theory, methods, and applications.* Mahwah, NJ: Erlbaum.

Braverman, H. (1974). *Labor and monopoly capital.* New York: Monthly Review Press.

Bridges, W. (1994, Sept. 19). The end of the job. *Fortune,* 62–74.

Buster, M. A., Roth, P. L., & Bobko, P. (2005). A process for content validation of education and experience-based minimum qualifications: An approach resulting in Federal court approval. *Personnel Psychology, 58,* 771–799.

Butler, S. K., & Harvey, R. J. (1988). A comparison of holistic versus decomposed rating of Position Analysis Questionnaire work dimensions. *Personnel Psychology, 41,* 761–771.

Cain, P. S., & Green, B. F. (1983). Reliabilities of selected ratings available from the Dictionary of Occupational Titles. *Journal of Applied Psychology, 68,* 155–165.

Caldwell, D. F., & O'Reilly, C. A. (1982). Task perceptions and job satisfaction: A question of causality. *Journal of Applied Psychology, 67,* 361–369.

Campion, M. A. (1988). Interdisciplinary approaches to job design: A constructive replication with extensions. *Journal of Applied Psychology, 73,* 467–481.

Campion, M. A. (1989). Ability requirement implications of job design: An interdisciplinary perspective. *Personnel Psychology, 42,* 1–24.

Campion, M. A. (1994). Job analysis for the future. In M. G. Rumsey, C. B. Walker, & J. H. Harris (Eds.), *Personnel selection and classification* (pp. 1–12). Hillsdale, NJ: Erlbaum.

Campion, M. A., & Berger, C. J. (1990). Conceptual integration and empirical test of job design and compensation relationships. *Personnel Psychology, 43,* 525–553.

Campion, M. A., & McClelland, C. L. (1991). Interdisciplinary examination of the costs and benefits of enlarged jobs: A job design quasi-experiment. *Journal of Applied Psychology, 76,* 186–198.

Campion, M. A., & McClelland, C. L. (1993). Follow-up and extension of the interdisciplinary costs and benefits of enlarged jobs. *Journal of Applied Psychology, 78,* 339–351.

Campion, M. A., Medsker, G. J., & Higgs, A. C. (1993). Relations between work group characteristics and effectiveness: Implications for designing effective work groups. *Personnel Psychology, 46,* 823–850.

Campion, M. A., Mumford, T. V., Morgeson, F. P., & Nahrgang, J. D. (2005). Work redesign: Obstacles and opportunities. *Human Resource Management, 44,* 367–390.

Campion, M. A., Papper, E. M., & Medsker, G. J. (1996). Relations between work team characteristics and effectiveness: A replication and extension. *Personnel Psychology, 49,* 429–452.

Campion, M. A., & Thayer, P. W. (1985). Development and field evaluation of an interdisciplinary measure of job design. *Journal of Applied Psychology, 70,* 29–43.

Cascio, W. F. (1995). Whither industrial and organizational psychology in a changing world of work? *American Psychologist, 50,* 928–939.

Cascio, W. F., & Ramos, R. A. (1986). Development and application of a new method for assessing job performance in behavioral/economic terms. *Journal of Applied Psychology, 41,* 761–771.

Christal, R. E. (1971). *Stability of consolidated job descriptions based on task inventory survey information.* Lackland AFB, TX: USAF AFHRL, Personnel Research Division.

Christal, R. E., & Weissmuller, J. J. (1977). New Comprehensive Occupational Data Analysis Programs (CODAP) for analyzing task factor information. *JSAS Catalog of Selected Documents in Psychology, 7,* 24–25.

Christal, R. E., & Weissmuller, J. J. (1988). Job-task inventory analysis. In S. Gael (Ed.), *The job analysis handbook for business, industry, and government* (Vol. II, pp. 1036–1050). New York: Wiley.

Church, A. H. (1995). From both sides now: The changing of the job. *Industrial Organizational Psychologist, 33,* 52–61.

Clark, S. L., & Weismantle, M. (2003). *Employment status: 2000* (Publication No. C2KBR-18). Washington, DC: U.S. Department of Commerce.

Conley, P. R., & Sackett, P. R. (1987). Effects of using high- versus low-performing job incumbents as sources of job analysis information. *Journal of Applied Psychology, 72,* 434–437.

Conte, J. M., Dean, M. A., Ringenbach, K. L., Moran, S. K., & Landy, F. J. (2005). The relationship between work attitudes and job analysis ratings: Do rating scale type and task discretion matter? *Human Performance, 18,* 1–21.

Converse, P. D., Oswald, F. L., Gillespie, M. A., Field, K. A., & Bizot, E. B. (2004). Matching individuals to occupations using abilities and the O*NET: Issues and an application in career guidance. *Personnel Psychology, 57,* 451–487.

Coovert, M. D. (1995). Technological changes in office jobs. In A. Howard (Ed.), *The changing nature of work* (pp. 175–208). San Francisco: Jossey-Bass.

Coovert, M. D., Craiger, J. P., & Cannon-Bowers, J. A. (1996). Innovations in modeling and simulating team performance: Implications for decision making. In R. A. Guzzo, E. Salas, & Associates (Eds.), *Team effectiveness and decision making in organizations* (pp. 291–332). San Francisco: Jossey-Bass.

Cornelius, E. T. III. (1988). Analyzing job analysis data. In S. Gael (Ed.), *The job analysis handbook for business, industry, and government* (Vol. I, pp. 353–368). New York: Wiley.

Cornelius, E. T., DeNisi, A. S., & Blencoe, A. G. (1984). Expert and naive raters using the PAQ: Does it matter? *Personnel Psychology, 37,* 354–464.

Cornelius, E. T. III, & Lyness, K. S. (1980). A comparison of holistic and decomposed judgment strategies in job analyses by job incumbents. *Journal of Applied Psychology, 65,* 155–163.

Cornelius, E. T., Schmidt, F. L., & Carron, T. (1984). Job classification approaches and the implementation of validity generalization results. *Personnel Psychology, 37,* 247–260.

Cranny, C. J., & Doherty, M. E. (1988). Importance ratings in job analysis: Note on the misinterpretation of factor analyses. *Journal of Applied Psychology, 73,* 320–322.

Crocker, L. M., & Algina, J. (1986). *Introduction to classical and modern test theory.* New York: Holt, Rinehart & Winston.

Cronbach, L. J. (1951). Coefficient alpha and the internal structure of tests. *Psychometrika, 6,* 671–684.

Cronbach, L. J., Gleser, G. C., & Rajaratnam, N. (1963). *The dependability of behavioral measurements.* New York: Wiley.

Cunningham, J. W. (1996). Generic job descriptors: A likely direction in occupational analysis. *Military Psychology, 8,* 247–262.

Davis, D. D. (1995). Form, function, and strategy in boundaryless organizations. In A. Howard (Ed.), *The changing nature of work* (pp. 112–138). San Francisco: Jossey-Bass.

Davis, L. E., & Wacker, G. J. (1988). Job design. In S. Gael (Ed.), *The job analysis handbook for business, industry, and government* (Vol. I, pp. 157–172). New York: Wiley.

Davis, T. C., Fredrickson, D. D., Kennen, E. M., Arnold, C., Shoup, E., Sugar, M., et al. (2004). Childhood vaccine risk/benefit communication among public health clinics: A time-motion study. *Public Health Nursing, 21,* 228–236.

Dean, J. W., & Snell, S. A. (1991). Integrated manufacturing and job design: Moderating effects of organizational inertia. *Academy of Management Journal, 34,* 776–804.

DeNisi, A. S., Cornelius, E. T. III, & Blencoe, A. G. (1987). Further investigation of common knowledge effects on job analysis ratings. *Journal of Applied Psychology, 72,* 262–268.

Dickinson, T. L., & McIntyre, R. M. (1997). A conceptual framework for teamwork measurement. In M. Brannick, E. Salas, & C. Prince (Eds.), *Team performance assessment and measurement* (pp. 19–43). Mahwah, NJ: Erlbaum.

Dierdorff, E. C., & Wilson, M. A. (2003). A meta-analysis of job analysis reliability. *Journal of Applied Psychology, 88,* 635–646.

Dieterly, D. L. (1988). Team performance requirements. In S. Gael (Ed.), *The job analysis handbook for business, industry, and government* (Vol. I, pp. 766–777). New York: Wiley.

Donovan, M. A., Drasgow, F., & Probst, T. M. (2000). Does computerizing paper-and-pencil job attitude scales make a difference? New IRT analyses offer insight. *Journal of Applied Psychology, 85,* 305–313.

Droege, R. C. (1988). Department of Labor job analysis methodology. In S. Gael (Ed.), *The job analysis handbook for business, industry, and government* (Vol. II, pp. 993–1018). New York: Wiley.

Drucker, P. F. (1987, Aug. 2). Workers' hands bound by tradition. *Wall Street Journal,* 18.

DuBois, D. A., Shalin, V. L., Levi, K. R., & Borman, W. C. (1995). *A cognitively-oriented approach to task analysis and test design.* Office of Naval Research Technical Report.

Dunnette, M. D. (1966). *Personnel selection and placement.* Belmont, CA: Wadsworth.

Dunnette, M. D. (1999). Introduction. In N. G. Peterson, M. D. Mumford, W. C. Borman, P. R. Jeanneret, & E. A. Fleishman (Eds.), *An occupational information system for the 21st century: The development of O*NET* (pp. 3–7). Washington, DC: American Psychological Association.

Dye, D., & Silver, M. (1999). The origins of O*NET. In N. G. Peterson, M. D. Mumford, W. C. Borman, P. R. Jeanneret, & E. A. Fleishman (Eds.), *An occupational information system for the 21st century: The development of O*NET* (pp. 9–19). Washington, DC: American Psychological Association.

Edwards, J. R., Scully, J. A., & Brtek, M. D. (1999). The measurement of work: Hierarchical representation of the multimethod job design questionnaire. *Personnel Psychology, 52,* 305–334.

Edwards, J. R., Scully, J. A., & Brtek, M. D. (2000). The nature and outcomes of work: A replication and extension of interdisciplinary work-design research. *Journal of Applied Psychology, 85,* 860–868.

Eggerth, D. E., Bowles, S. M., Tunick, R. H., & Andrew, M. E. (2005). Convergent validity of O*NET Holland code classifications. *Journal of Career Assessment, 13,* 150–168.

Englestad, P. H. (1979). Sociotechnical approach to problems of process control. In L. E. Davis & J. C. Taylor (Eds.), *Design of jobs* (2nd ed.). Santa Monica, CA: Goodyear.

Equal Employment Opportunity Commission. (1978). Uniform guidelines on employee selection procedures. *Federal Register, 43,* 38290–38315.

Feiner, S., MacIntyre, B., & Seligmann, D. (1993). Knowledge-based augmented reality. *Communications of the ACM, 36,* 52–62.

Fine, S. (1988). Functional job analysis. In S. Gael (Ed.), *The job analysis handbook for business, industry, and government* (Vol. II, pp. 1019–1035). New York: Wiley.

Fine, S. A., & Cronshaw, S. F. (1999). *Functional job analysis: A foundation for human resources management.* Mahwah, NJ: Erlbaum.

Flanagan, J. C. (1954). The critical incident technique. *Psychological Bulletin, 51,* 327–358.

Fleishman, E. A. (1982). Systems for describing human tasks. *American Psychologist, 37,* 1–14.

Fleishman, E. A., & Mumford M. D. (1988). Ability requirements scales. In S. Gael (Ed.), *The job analysis handbook for business, industry, and government* (Vol. II, pp. 917–935). New York: Wiley.

Fleishman, E. A., Mumford, M. D., Zaccaro, S. J., Levin, K. Y., Korotkin, A. L., & Hein, M. B. (1991). Taxonomic efforts in the description of leader behavior: A synthesis and functional interpretation. *Leadership Quarterly, 2,* 245–287.

Fleishman, E. A., & Quaintance, M. K. (1984). *Taxonomies of human performance: The description of human tasks.* Orlando, FL: Academic Press.

Fleishman, E. A., & Reilly, M. E. (1992). *Handbook of human abilities: Definitions, measurements, and job task requirements.* Palo Alto, CA: Consulting Psychologists Press.

Fleishman, E. A., Wetrogan, L. I., Uhlman, C. E., & Marshall-Mies, J. C. (1995). In N. G. Peterson, M. D. Mumford, W. C. Borman, P. R. Jeanneret, & E. A. Fleishman (Eds.), *Development of prototype occupational information network content model* (pp. 10.1–10.39). Salt Lake City: Utah Department of Employment Security (Contract Number 94–542).

Fleishman, E. A., & Zaccaro, S. J. (1992). Toward a taxonomy of team performance functions. In R. W. Swezey & E. Salas (Eds.), *Teams: Their training and performance.* Norwood, NJ: Ablex.

Flury, B. (1997). *A first course in multivariate statistics.* New York: Springer.

Ford, R. N. (1969). *Motivation through the work itself.* New York: American Management Association.

Friedman, L., & Harvey, R. J. (1986). Can raters with reduced job descriptive information provide accurate Position Analysis Questionnaire (PAQ) ratings? *Personnel Psychology, 39,* 779–789.

Friedman, T. L. (2005). *The world is flat: A brief history of the twenty-first century.* New York: Farrar, Straus, and Giroux.

Gael, S. (1983). *Job analysis: A guide to assessing work activities.* San Francisco: Jossey-Bass.

Gael, S. (1988). Job descriptions. In S. Gael (Ed.), *The job analysis handbook for business, industry, and government* (Vol. I, pp. 71–89). New York: Wiley.

Gael, S., Cornelius, E. T. Levine, E. L. & Salvendy, G. (1988). *The job analysis handbook for business, industry, and government.* New York: Wiley.

Gagne, R. M., & Briggs, L. J. (1979). *Principles of instructional design* (2nd ed.). New York: Holt, Rinehart & Winston.

Galloway, D. (1994). *Mapping work processes.* Milwaukee, WI: ASQC Quality Press.

Gambardella, J. J. N., & Alvord, W. G. (1980). *TI-CODAP: A computerized method of job analysis for personnel management.* (City unknown), MD: Prince George's County.

Gatewood, R. D., & Feild, H. S. (1998). *Human resource selection* (4th ed.). Ft. Worth, TX: Dryden.

Geller, E. S. (2001). *The psychology of safety handbook.* Boca Raton, FL: Lewis Publishers.

Geyer, P. D., Hice, J., Hawk, Boese, R., & Brannon, Y. (1989). Reliabilities of ratings available from the Dictionary of Occupational Titles. *Personnel Psychology, 42,* 547–560.

Ghorpade, J. V. (1988). *Job analysis: A handbook for the human resource director.* Englewood Cliffs, NJ: Prentice-Hall.

Gilbert, T. F. (1978). *Human competence.* New York: McGraw-Hill.

Gilbreth, F. B. (1911). *Motion study: A method for increasing the efficiency of the workman.* New York: Van Nostrand.

Gladstein, D. L. (1984). Groups in context: A model of task group effectiveness. *Administrative Sciences Quarterly, 29,* 499–517.

Goldstein, I. L., & Ford, J. K. (2002). *Training in organizations: Needs assessment, development, and evaluation* (4th ed.). Belmont, CA: Wadsworth.

Green, P. C. (1999). *Building robust competencies: Linking human resource systems to organizational strategies.* San Francisco: Jossey-Bass.

Griggs v. Duke Power Company. (1971). *Fair Employment Practices, 3,* 175.

Gronroos, C. (1982). An applied service marketing strategy. *European Journal of Marketing, 16,* 30–41.

Guion, R. M. (1998). *Assessment, measurement, and prediction for personnel decisions.* Mahwah, NJ: Erlbaum.

Gutenberg, R. L., Arvey, R. D., Osburn, H. G., & Jeanneret, P. R. (1983). Moderating effects of decision-making/information-processing job dimensions on test validities. *Journal of Applied Psychology, 68,* 602–608.

Gutman, A. (2000). *EEO law and personnel practices* (2nd ed.). Thousand Oaks, CA: Sage.

Guzzo, R. A., & Shea, G. P. (1992). Group performance and intergroup relations in organizations. In M. D. Dunnette & L. M. Hough (Eds.), *Handbook of industrial and organizational psychology* (Vol. 3, pp. 269–313). Palo Alto, CA: Consulting Psychologists Press.

Gwynne, S. C. (1992, Sept. 28). The long haul. *Time,* pp. 34–38.

Hackman, J. R., & Oldham, G. R. (1975). Development of the job diagnostic survey. *Journal of Applied Psychology, 60,* 159–170.

Hackman, J. R., & Oldham, G. R. (1980). *Work redesign.* Reading, MA: Addison-Wesley.

Hadden, W. C., Kravets, N., & Muntaner, C. (2004). Descriptive dimensions of US occupations with data from the O*NET. *Social Science Research, 33,* 64–78.

Hakel, M. D., Stalder, B. K., & Van de Voort, D. M. (1988). Obtaining and maintaining acceptance of job analysis. In S. Gael (Ed.), *The job analysis handbook for business, industry, and government* (Vol. I, pp. 329–338). New York: Wiley.

Halpin, A. W., & Winer, B. J. (1957). A factorial study of the leader behavior description. In R. M. Stogdill & A. E. Coons (Eds.), *Leaders behavior: Its description and measurement.* Columbus: Ohio State University, Bureau of Business Research.

Hamilton, J. W., & Dickinson, T. L. (1987). Comparison of several procedures for generating J-Coefficients. *Journal of Applied Psychology, 72,* 49–54.

Harris, J., & Brannick, J. (1999). *Finding and keeping great employees.* New York: AMACOM.

Harvey, M., & Novicevic, M. M. (2002). The hypercompetitive global marketplace: The importance of intuition and creativity in expatriate managers. *Journal of World Business, 37,* 127–138.

Harvey, R. J. (1991). Job analysis. In M. D. Dunnette & L. M. Hough (Eds.), *Handbook of industrial and organizational psychology* (Vol. 2, pp. 71–163). Palo Alto, CA: Consulting Psychologists Press.

Harvey, R. J., & Hayes, T. L. (1986). Monte Carlo baselines for interrater reliability correlations using the Position Analysis Questionnaire. *Personnel Psychology, 39,* 345–357.

Hemphill, J. K. (1960). *Dimensions of executive positions.* Columbus: Ohio State University, Bureau of Business Research, Research Monograph 98.

Hemphill, J. K., & Coons, A. E. (1957). Development of the Leader Behavior Description Questionnaire. In R. M. Stogdill & A. E. Coons (Eds.), *Leaders behavior: Its description and measurement.* Columbus: Ohio State University, Bureau of Business Research.

Henderson, R. I. (1988). Job evaluation, classification, and pay. In S. Gael (Ed.), *The job analysis handbook for business, industry, and government* (Vol. I, pp. 90–118). New York: Wiley.

Heneman III, H. G., & Judge, T. A. (2003). *Staffing organizations* (4th ed.). Boston: McGraw-Hill Irwin.

Hersey, P., & Blanchard K. H. (1993). *Management of organizational behavior* (6th ed.). Englewood Cliffs, NJ: Prentice-Hall.

Herzberg, F. (1966). *Work and the nature of man.* Cleveland, OH: World.

Hofmann, D. A., Morgeson, F. P., & Gerras, S. (2003). Climate as a moderator of the relationship between LMX and content specific citizenship: Safety climate as an exemplar. *Journal of Applied Psychology, 88,* 170–178.

Hogan, J., Hogan, R. T., & Busch, C. (1984). How to measure a service orientation. *Journal of Applied Psychology, 69,* 167–173.

Horgen, T. H., Joroff, M. L., Porter, W. L., & Schon, D. A. (1999). *Excellence by design: Transforming workplace and work practice.* New York: Wiley.

How to be efficient with fewer violins. (1959). *American Association of University Professors Bulletin, 41,* 454–455.

Huber, G. P. (1990). A theory of the effects of advanced information technologies on organization design, intelligence, and decision making. *Academy of Management Review, 15,* 47–71.

Hughes, G. L., & Prien, E. P. (1989). Evaluation of task and job skill linkages judgments used to develop test specifications. *Personnel Psychology, 42,* 283–292.

Hunter, J. E., & Schmidt, F. L. (2004). *Methods of meta-analysis: Correcting error and bias in research findings* (2nd ed.). Newbury Park, CA: Sage.

Huselid, M. A., Beatty, R. W., & Becker, B. E. (2005, Dec.). "A players" or "A positions"? The strategic logic of workforce management. *Harvard Business Review,* 1–7.

Ilgen, D. R., Hollenbeck, J. R., Johnson, M. D., & Jundt, D. (2005). Teams in organizations: From I-P-O models to IMOI models. *Annual Review of Psychology, 56,* 517–543.

International Labour Organization. (1992). *Introduction to work study* (4th ed.). Geneva: Author.

Ireland, R. D., & Hitt, M. A. (1999). Achieving and maintaining strategic competitiveness in the 21st century: The role of strategic leadership. *Academy of Management Executive, 13,* 43–57.

Jackson, S. E., & Schuler, R. S. (1990). Human resource planning: Challenges for I/O psychologists. *American Psychologist, 45,* 223–239.

James, L. R., Demaree, R. G., & Wolf, G. (1984). Estimating within-group interrater reliability with and without response bias. *Journal of Applied Psychology, 69,* 85–98.

Jeanneret, P. R., Borman, W. C., Kubisiak, U. C., & Hanson, M. A. (1999). Generalized work activities. In N. G. Peterson, M. D. Mumford, W. C. Borman, P. R. Jeanneret, & E. A. Fleishman (Eds.), *An occupational information system for the 21st century: The development of O*NET* (pp. 105–125). Washington, DC: American Psychological Association.

Jeanneret, P. R., & Strong, M. H. (2003). Linking O*NET job analysis information to job requirement predictors: An O*NET application. *Personnel Psychology, 56,* 465–492.

Jones, A. P., Main, D. S., Butler, M. C., & Johnson, L. A. (1982). Narrative job descriptions as potential sources of job analysis ratings. *Personnel Psychology, 35,* 813–828.

Jones, R. G., Sanchez, J. I., Parameswaran, G., Phelps, J., Shoptaugh, C., Williams, M., & White, S. (2001). Selection or training? A two-fold test of the validity of job-analytic ratings of trainability. *Journal of Business and Psychology,* [AUS: add vol and page nos. in proof]

Jones, S. D., & Schilling, D. J. (2000). *Measuring team performance: A step-by-step, customizable approach for managers, facilitators, and team leaders.* San Francisco: Jossey-Bass.

Kane, M. T., Kingsbury, C., Colton, D., & Estes, C. (1989). Combining data on criticality and frequency in developing test plans for licensure and certification examinations. *Journal of Educational Measurement, 26,* 17–27.

Karlsson, A. H. (1976). *The Volvo Kalmar plant.* Stockholm: Rationalization Council SAF-LO.

Katz, D., & Kahn, R. L. (1978). *The social psychology of organizations* (2nd ed.). New York: Wiley.

Keita, G. P., & Sauter, S. L. (1992). *Work and well-being: An agenda for the 1990s.* Washington, DC: American Psychological Association.

Kirkpatrick, D. L. (1959). Techniques for evaluating training programs. *Journal of the American Society of Training Directors, 13,* 3–9, 21–26.

Kirkpatrick, D. L. (1960). Techniques for evaluating training programs. *Journal of the American Society of Training Directors, 14,* 13–18, 28–32.

Kleiman, L. S., & Faley, R. H. (1985). The implications of professional and legal guidelines for court decisions involving criterion-related validity: A review and analysis. *Personnel Psychology, 38,* 803–833.

Kline, P. (1994). *An easy guide to factor analysis.* London: Routledge.

Kluger, A. N., & DeNisi, A. (1996). The effects of feedback interventions on performance: A historical review, a meta-analysis, and a preliminary feedback intervention theory. *Psychological Bulletin, 119,* 254–284.

Kochhar, D. S., & Armstrong, T. J. (1988). Designing jobs for handicapped employees. In S. Gael (Ed.), *The job analysis handbook for business, industry, and government* (Vol. I, pp. 288–302). New York: Wiley.

Kraut, A. I., & Korman, A. K. (Eds.). (1999). *Evolving practices in human resource management: Responses to a changing world of work.* San Francisco: Jossey-Bass.

Kumar, S. (1999). *Biomechanics in ergonomics.* Philadelphia: Taylor & Francis.

Landy, F. J., & Farr, J. L. (1980). Performance rating. *Psychological Bulletin, 87,* 72–107.

Landy, F. J., & Trumbo, D. A. (1980). *The psychology of work behavior.* Homewood, IL: Dorsey Press.

Langdale, J. A., & Weitz, J. (1973). Estimating the influence of job information on interviewer agreement. *Journal of Applied Psychology, 57,* 23–27.

Latham, G. P., & Wexley, K. N. (1977). Behavioral observation scales for performance appraisal purposes. *Personnel Psychology, 30,* 355–368.

Latham, G. P., & Wexley, K. N. (1993). *Increasing productivity through performance appraisal* (2nd ed.). Reading, MA: Addison-Wesley.

Levine, E. L. (1983). *Everything you always wanted to know about job analysis.* Tampa, FL: Mariner.

Levine, E. L., Ash, R. A., & Bennett, N. (1980). Exploratory comparative study of four job analysis methods. *Journal of Applied Psychology, 65,* 524–535.

Levine, E. L., Ash, R. A., Hall, H., & Sistrunk, F. (1983). Evaluation of job analysis methods by experienced job analysts. *Academy of Management Journal, 26,* 339–348.

Levine, E. L., & Baker, C. V. (1990). *Team task analysis: A test of the multiphase analysis of performance (MAP) system.* Contract No DAAL03–86-D-001. Orlando, FL: Naval Training Systems Center.

Levine, E. L., Bennett, N., & Ash, R. A. (1979). Evaluation and use of four job analysis methods for personnel selection. *Public Personnel Management, 8,* 146–151.

Levine, E. L., Brannick, M. T., Coovert, M. D., & Llobet, J. M. (1988). *Job/task analysis methodologies for teams: A review and implications for team training.* Contract No. DAAL03–86-D-0001. Orlando, FL: Naval Training Systems Center.

Levine, E. L., & Dickey, T. (1990, August). *Measuring task importance: A replication and extension.* Paper presented at the annual convention of the American Psychological Association, Boston.

Levine, E. L., Maye, D. M., Ulm, R. A., & Gordon, T. R. (1997). A methodology for developing and validating minimum qualifications (MQs). *Personnel Psychology, 50,* 1009–1023.

Levine, E. L., & Sanchez, J. I. (1998, April). *Sources of inaccuracy in job analysis and suggestions for remediation.* Paper presented at the 13th Annual Society for Industrial and Organizational Psychology Conference, Dallas, TX.

Levine, E. L., & Sanchez, J. I. (2000, March). *Working with work analysis in the twenty first century.* Paper presented at the First Annual Conference of the National Business and Economics Society, San Diego.

Levine, E. L., Thomas, J. N., & Sistrunk, F. (1988). Selecting a job analysis approach. In S. Gael (Ed.), *The job analysis handbook for business, industry, and government* (Vol. I, pp. 339–352). New York: Wiley.

Levine, E. L., & Weitz, J. (1971). The relationship between task difficulty and the criterion: Should we measure early or late? *Journal of Applied Psychology, 55,* 512–520.

Levine, E. L., Yang, L., Xu, X., & Lopez-Rivas, G. (2006). *Surveying via the net vs. hard copy: A cautionary note.* Paper presented at the Annual Conference of the Academy of Management, Atlanta, August.

Lievens, F., Sanchez, J. I., & De Corte, W. (2004). Easing the inferential leap in competency modeling: The effects of task-related information and subject matter expertise. *Personnel Psychology, 57,* 881–904.

Linstrom, K. (1991). Well-being and computer-mediated work of various occupational groups in banking and insurance. *International Journal of Human-Computer Interaction, 3,* 339–361.

Lopez, F. M. (1986). *The threshold traits analysis technical manual.* Port Washington, NY: Lopez & Associates, 1986.

Lopez, F. M. (1988). Threshold traits analysis system. In S. Gael (Ed.), *The job analysis handbook for business, industry, and government* (Vol. II, pp. 880–901). New York: Wiley.

Lucia, A. D., & Lepsinger, R. (1999). *The art and science of competency models: Pinpointing critical success factors in organizations.* San Francisco: Jossey-Bass/Pfeiffer.

MacLeod, D. (2000). *The rules of work: A practical engineering guide to ergonomics.* New York: Taylor & Francis.

Mallamad, S. M., Levine, J. M., & Fleishman, E. A. (1980). Identifying ability requirements by decision flow diagrams. *Human Factors, 22,* 57–68.

Manson, T. M., Levine, E. L., & Brannick, M. T. (2000). The construct validity of task inventory ratings: A multitrait-multimethod analysis. *Human Performance, 13,* 1–22.

Martinko, M. J. (1988). Observing the work. In S. Gael (Ed.), The *job analysis handbook for business, industry, and government* (Vol. I, pp. 419–431). New York: Wiley.

Mathieu, J. E., Heffner, T. S., Goodwin, G. F., Salas, E., & Cannon-Bowers, J. A. (2000). The influence of shared mental models on team process and performance. *Journal of Applied Psychology, 85,* 273–283.

McClelland, D. C. (1973). Testing for competence rather than for "intelligence." *American Psychologist, 28*, 1–14.

McCormick, E. J. (1976). *Human factors in engineering and design* (4th ed.). New York: McGraw-Hill.

McCormick, E. J. (1979). *Job analysis: Methods and applications.* New York: AMACOM.

McCormick, E. J., & Ammerman, H. L. (1960). *Development of worker activity checklists for use in occupational analysis* (WADD-TR-60-77). Lackland AFB, TX: USAF, WADD, Personnel Laboratory.

McCormick, E. J., & Ilgen, D. R. (1985). *Industrial and organizational psychology* (8th ed.). Englewood Cliffs, NJ: Prentice-Hall.

McCormick, E. J., & Jeanneret, P. R. (1988). Position Analysis Questionnaire (PAQ). In S. Gael (Ed.), *The job analysis handbook for business, industry, and government* (Vol. II, pp. 825–824). New York: Wiley.

McCormick, E. J., Jeanneret, P. R., & Mecham R. C. (1972). A study of job characteristics and job dimensions as based on the position analysis questionnaire (PAQ). *Journal of Applied Psychology, 56*, 347–368.

McInerney, W. D. (1989). Social and organizational effects of educational computing. *Journal of Educational Computing Research, 5*, 487–506.

Meyer, H. H., Kay, E., & French, J. R., Jr. (1965). Split roles in performance appraisal. *Harvard Business Review, 43*, 123–129.

Mintzberg, H. (1973). *The nature of managerial work.* New York: Harper & Row.

Mintzberg, H. (1979). *The structuring of organizations.* Englewood Cliffs, NJ: Prentice-Hall.

Mirabile, R. J. (1997, Aug.). Everything you wanted to know about competency modeling. *Training and Development*, 73–77.

Mital, A., Kilbom, A., & Kumar, S. (2000). *Ergonomics guidelines and problem solving.* New York: Elsevier.

Mohrman, S. A., & Cohen, S. G. (1995). When people get out of the box: New relationships, new systems. In A. Howard (Ed.), *The changing nature of work* (pp. 365–410). San Francisco: Jossey-Bass.

Morgeson, F. P. (2005). The external leadership of self-managing teams: Intervening in the context of novel and disruptive events. *Journal of Applied Psychology, 90*, 497–508.

Morgeson, F. P., & Campion, M. A. (1997). Social and cognitive sources of potential inaccuracy in job analysis. *Journal of Applied Psychology, 82*, 627–655.

Morgeson, F. P., & Campion, M. A. (2000). Accuracy in job analysis: Toward an inference-based model. *Journal of Organizational Behavior, 21*, 819–827.

Morgeson, F. P., & Campion, M. A. (2002). Minimizing tradeoffs when redesigning work: Evidence from a longitudinal quasi-experiment. *Personnel Psychology, 55*, 589–612.

Morgeson, F. P., & Campion, M. A. (2003). Work design. In W. C. Borman, D. R. Ilgen, & R. J. Klimoski (Eds.), *Handbook of psychology: Industrial and organizational psychology* (Vol. 12, pp. 423–452). Hoboken, NJ: Wiley.

Morgeson, F. P., Delaney-Klinger, K. A., & Hemingway, M. A. (2005). The importance of job autonomy, cognitive ability, and job-related skill for predicting role breadth and job performance. *Journal of Applied Psychology, 90*, 399–406.

Morgeson, F. P., Delaney-Klinger, K. A., Mayfield, M. S., Ferrara, P., & Campion, M. A. (2004). Self-presentation processes in job analysis: A field experiment investigating inflation in abilities, tasks, and competencies. *Journal of Applied Psychology, 89*, 674–686.

Morgeson, F. P., & Humphrey, S. E. (2006). The Work Design Questionnaire (WDQ): Developing and validating a comprehensive measure for assessing job design and the nature of work. *Journal of Applied Psychology, 91,* 1321–1339.

Morgeson, F. P., Reider, M. H., & Campion, M. A. (2005). Selecting individuals in team settings: The importance of social skills, personality characteristics, and teamwork knowledge. *Personnel Psychology, 58, 583–611.*

Morsh, J. E., Madden, J. M., & Christal, R. E. (1961). *Job analysis in the United States Air Force.* (WADD-TR-61–113). Lackland AFB, TX: Wright Air Development Division, Personnel Laboratory.

Motowidlo, S. J. (2003). Job performance. In W. C. Borman, D. R. Ilgen, & R. J. Klimoski (Eds.), *Handbook of psychology: Industrial and organizational psychology* (Vol. 12, pp. 39–53). Hoboken, NJ: Wiley.

Mumford, M. D., Peterson, N. G., & Childs, R. A. (1999). Basic and cross-functional skills. In N. G. Peterson, M. D. Mumford, W. C. Borman, P. R. Jeanneret, & E. A. Fleishman (Eds.), *An occupational information system for the 21st century: The development of O*NET* (pp. 49–69). Washington, DC: American Psychological Association.

Mundel, M. E. (1988). Motion study methods. In S. Gael (Ed.), *The job analysis handbook for business, industry, and government* (Vol. I, pp. 469–497). New York: Wiley.

Mundel, M. E., & Danner, D. L. (1994). *Motion and time study: Improving productivity* (7th ed.). Englewood Cliffs, NJ: Prentice-Hall.

Murphy, K. R., & Cleveland, J. N. (1995). *Understanding performance appraisal: Social, organizational, and goal-based perspectives.* Thousand Oaks, CA: Sage.

Neck, C. P., Stewart, G. L., & Manz, C. C. (1996). Self-leaders within self-leading teams: Toward an optimal equilibrium. In M. M. Beyerlein, D. A. Johnson, & S. T. Beyerlein (Eds.), *Advances in interdisciplinary studies of work teams* (pp. 43–66). Greenwich, CT: JAI Press.

Nemeth, C. J. (1992). Minority dissent as a stimulant to group performance. In S. Worchel, W. Wood, & J. A. Simpson (Eds.), *Group process and productivity* (pp. 95–111). Thousand Oaks, CA: Sage.

Niebel, B. W. (1988). Time study methods. In S. Gael (Ed.), *The job analysis handbook for business, industry, and government* (Vol. I, pp. 498–517). New York: Wiley.

Nieva, V. F., Fleishman, E. A., & Reick, A. (1978). *Team dimensions: Their identity, their measurement and their relationships* (Contract No. DAHC19–78-C-0001). Washington, DC: Advanced Research Resources Organization.

Nof, S. Y. (1988). Job analysis for robots. In S. Gael (Ed.), *The job analysis handbook for business, industry, and government* (Vol. I, pp. 587–613). New York: Wiley.

Nunnally, J. C., & Bernstein, I. H. (1994). *Psychometric theory* (3rd ed.). New York: McGraw-Hill.

Olian, J. D., & Rynes, S. L. (1991). Making total quality work: Aligning organizational processes, performance measures, and stakeholders. *Human Resource Management, 30,* 303–333.

Page, R. C. (1988). Management Position Description Questionnaire. In S. Gael (Ed.), *The job analysis handbook for business, industry, and government* (Vol. II, pp. 861–879). New York: Wiley.

Parker, S., & Wall, T. (1998). *Job and work design: Organizing work to promote well-being and effectiveness.* Thousand Oaks, CA: Sage.

Parry, M. E. (1968). Ability of psychologists to estimate validities of personnel tests. *Personnel Psychology, 21,* 139–148.

Pasmore, W. A. (1988). *Designing effective organizations: The sociotechnical systems perspective.* New York: Wiley.

Pearlman, K. (1997, April). Competencies: Issues in their application. In R. C. Page (Chair), *Competency models: What are they and do they work?* Practitioner forum presented at the twelfth annual conference of the Society for Industrial and Organizational Psychology, St. Louis, MO.

Pedhazur, E. J. (1997). *Multiple regression in behavioral research* (3rd. ed.). Fort Worth, TX: Harcourt Brace.

Peterson, N. G., Mumford, M. D., Borman, W. C., Jeanneret, P. R., & Fleishman, E. A. (Eds.). (1999). *An occupational information system for the 21st century: The development of O*NET.* Washington, DC: American Psychological Association.

Peterson, N. G., Mumford, M. D., Borman, W. C., Jeanneret, P. R., Fleishman, E. A., Campion, M. A., Levin, K. Y., Mayfield, M. S., Morgeson, F. P., Pearlman, K., Gowing, M. K., Lancaster, A., & Dye, D. (2001). Understanding work using the occupational information network (O*NET): Implications for practice and research. *Personnel Psychology, 54,* 451–492.

Pheasant, S. (1996). Bodyspace: Anthropometry, ergonomics, and the design of work. Bristol, PA: Taylor & Francis.

Ployhart, R. E., Schneider, B., & Schmitt, N. W. (2006). *Staffing organizations: Contemporary research and theory* (3rd ed.). Mahwah, NJ: Erlbaum.

Polito, J., & Pritsker, A. A. B. (1988). Computer simulation and job analysis. In S. Gael (Ed.), *The job analysis handbook for business, industry, and government* (Vol. I, pp. 570–586). New York: Wiley.

Prahalad, C., & Hamel, G. (1990, May–June). The core competence of the corporation. *Harvard Business Review,* 79–91.

Prien, E. P., & Ronan, W. W. (1971). Job analysis: A review of research findings. *Personnel Psychology, 24,* 371–396.

Primoff, E. S. (1957). The J-coefficient approach to jobs and tests. *Personnel Administrator, 20,* 34–40.

Primoff, E. S., & Eyde, L. D. (1988). Job element analysis. In S. Gael (Ed.), *The job analysis handbook for business, industry, and government* (Vol. II, pp. 807–824). New York: Wiley.

Prince, A. (1999). *The effect of experience on the perceptions of decisions scenarios: A field study.* Unpublished doctoral dissertation, University of South Florida.

Rasker, P. C., Post, W. M., & Schraagen, J. M. C. (2000). Effects of two types of intra-team feedback on developing a shared mental model in Command & Control teams. *Ergonomics, 43,* 1167–1189.

Raymark, P. H., Schmit, M. J., & Guion, R. M. (1997). Identifying potentially useful personality constructs for employee selection. *Personnel Psychology, 50,* 723–736.

Rohmert, R. (1988). AET. In S. Gael (Ed.), *The job analysis handbook for business, industry, and government* (Vol. II, pp. 843–859). New York: Wiley.

Rousseau, D. M. (1977). Technological differences in job characteristics, employee satisfaction, and motivation: A synthesis of job design research and sociotechnical systems theory. *Organizational Behavior and Human Performance, 19,* 18–42.

Rynes, S. L., Gerhart, B., & Parks, L. (2005). Personnel psychology: Performance evaluation and pay for performance. In S. T. Fiske, A. E. Kazdin, & D. L. Schacter (Eds.), *Annual Review of Psychology, 56,* 571–600.

Salgado, J. F. (1999). Personnel selection methods. In C. L. Cooper & I. T. Robertson (Eds.), *International review of industrial and organizational psychology 1999*, (Vol. 14, pp. 1–54). Chichester, UK: Wiley.

Salvendy, G. (Ed.). (1982). *Handbook of industrial engineering*. New York: Wiley.

Sanchez, J. I. (1994). From documentation to innovation: Reshaping job analysis to meet emerging business needs. *Human Resource Management Review, 4,* 51–74.

Sanchez, J. I., & Fraser, S. L. (1992). On the choice of scales for task analysis. *Journal of Applied Psychology, 77,* 545–553.

Sanchez, J. I., & Fraser, S. L. (1994). An empirical procedures to identify job duty-skill linkages in managerial jobs: A case example. *Journal of Business and Psychology, 8,* 309–326.

Sanchez, J. I., & Levine, E. L. (1989). Determining important tasks within jobs: A policy-capturing approach. *Journal of Applied Psychology, 74,* 336–342.

Sanchez, J. I., & Levine, E. L. (1999). Is job analysis dead, misunderstood, or both? New forms of work analysis and design. In A. Kraut & A. Korman (Eds.), *Evolving practices in human resource management* (pp. 43–68). San Francisco: Jossey-Bass.

Sanchez, J. I., & Levine, E. L. (2000). Accuracy or consequential validity: Which is the better standard for job analysis data? *Journal of Organizational Behavior, 21,* 809–818.

Sanchez, J. I., & Levine, E. L. (2001). The analysis of work in the 20th and 21st centuries. In N. Anderson, D. S. Ones, H. K. Sinangil, & C. Viswesvaran (Eds.), *Handbook of industrial, work and organizational psychology* (Vol. 1, pp. 71–89). Thousand Oaks, CA: Sage.

Sanocki, T. (2001). *Student friendly statistics*. Upper Saddle River, NJ: Prentice-Hall.

Schmidt, F. L., Hunter, J. E., Croll, P.R., & McKenzie, R. C. (1983). Estimation of employment test validities by expert judgment. *Journal of Applied Psychology, 68,* 590–601.

Schmitt, N., & Borman, W. C. (1993). *Personnel selection in organizations*. San Francisco: Jossey-Bass.

Schmitt, N., & Cohen, S. A. (1987). *Internal analysis of task ratings by job incumbents*. Unpublished manuscript, Michigan State University.

Schmitt, N., & Cohen, S. A. (1989). Internal analysis of task ratings by job incumbents. *Journal of Applied Psychology, 74,* 96–104.

Schmitt, N., & Fine, S. A. (1983). Inter-rater reliability of judgments of functional levels and skill requirements of jobs based on written task statements. *Journal of Occupational Psychology, 56,* 121–127.

Schneider, B. (1987). The people make the place. *Personnel Psychology, 40,* 437–453.

Schneider, B., & Konz, A. M. (1989). Strategic job analysis. *Human Resources Management, 28,* 51–63.

Schneider, B., & Schmitt, N. (1986). *Staffing organizations*. Glenview, IL: Scott, Foresman.

Schultz, D. P., & Schultz, S. E. (1990). *Psychology and industry today* (5th ed.). New York: Macmillan.

Schwab, D. P., Heneman, H. G., III, & Decotiis, T. A. (1975). Behaviorally anchored rating scales: A review of the literature. *Personnel Psychology, 28,* 549–562.

Seamster, T. L., Redding, R. E., & Kaempf, G. L. (1997). *Applied cognitive task analysis in aviation*. Brookfield, VT: Ashgate.

Shavelson, R. J., & Webb, N. M. (1991). *Generalizability theory: A primer*. Newbury Park, CA: Sage.

Shiflett, S. E., Eisner, E. J., Price, S. J., & Schemmer, F. M. (1982). *The definition and measurement of team functions.* Final Report. Bethesda, MD: Arro.

Shin, S. J., Morgeson, F. P., & Campion, M. A. (in press). What you do depends on where you are: Understanding how domestic and expatriate work requirements depend upon the cultural context. *Journal of International Business Studies.*

Shippmann, J. S., Ash, R. A., Battista, M., Carr, L. Eyde, L. D., Hesketh, B., Kehoe, J., Pearlman, K., Prien, E. P., & Sanchez, J. I. (2000). The practice of competency modeling. *Personnel Psychology, 53,* 703–740.

Siegel, S., & Castellan, N. J. (1988). *Nonparametric statistics for the behavioral sciences.* New York: McGraw-Hill.

Silverman, S. B., Wexley, K. N., & Johnson, J. C. (1984). The effects of age and job experience on employee responses to a structured job analysis questionnaire. *Public Personnel Management Journal, 13,* 355–359.

Smith, J. E., & Hakel, M. D. (1979). Convergence among data sources, response bias, and reliability and validity of a structured job analysis questionnaire. *Personnel Psychology, 32,* 677–692.

Smither, J. W. (1998). *Performance appraisal: State of the art in practice.* San Francisco: Jossey-Bass.

Snelgar, R. J. (1982). The comparability of job evaluation methods in supplying approximately similar classifications in rating one job series. *South African Journal of Psychology, 12,* 38–40.

Snow, C. C., & Snell, A. A. (1992). Staffing as strategy. In N. Schmitt, W. C. Borman, & Associates (Eds.), *Personnel selection in organizations* (pp. 448–480). San Francisco: Jossey-Bass.

Society for Industrial and Organizational Psychology, Inc. (2003). *Principles for the Validation and Use of Personnel Selection Procedures* (4th ed.). Bowling Green, OH: Author.

Sparks, C. P. (1988). Legal basis for job analysis. In S. Gael (Ed.), *The job analysis handbook for business, industry, and government* (Vol. I, pp. 37–47). New York: Wiley.

Spector, P. E., Brannick, M. T., & Coovert, M. D. (1989). Job analysis. In C. L. Cooper and I. Robertson (Eds.), *International review of industrial and organizational psychology 1989* (pp. 281–328). New York: Wiley.

Spencer, L. M., & Spencer, S. M. (1993). *Competence at work: Models for superior performance.* New York: Wiley.

Staw, B. M., & Boettger, R. D. (1990). Task revision: A neglected form of work performance. *Academy of Management Journal, 33,* 534–559.

Stevens, M. J., & Campion, M. A. (1994). The knowledge, skill and ability requirements for teamwork: Implications for human resource management. *Journal of Management, 20,* 503–530.

Stevens, M. J., & Campion, M. A. (1999). Staffing work teams: Development and validation of a selection test for teamwork settings. *Journal of Management, 25,* 207–228.

Sundstrom, E., De Meuse, K. P., & Futrell, D. (1990). Work teams: Applications and effectiveness. *American Psychologist, 45,* 120–133.

Surette, M. A., Aamodt, M. G., & Johnson, D. L. (1990). Effects of analyst training and amount of available job related information on job analysis ratings. *Journal of Business and Psychology, 4,* 439–451.

Taylor, F. W. (1911). *The principles of scientific management.* New York: Norton.

Tett, R. P., Guterman, H. A., Bleier, A., & Murphy, P. J. (2000). Development and content validation of a hyper dimensional taxonomy of managerial competence. *Human Performance, 13,* 205–251.

Thompson, D. E., & Thompson, T. A. (1982). Court standards for job analysis in test validation. *Personnel Psychology, 35,* 865–874.

Toossi, M. (2005). Labor force projections to 2014: Retiring boomers. *Monthly Labor Review, 128,* 25–44.

Tornow, W. W., & Pinto, P. R. (1976). The development of a managerial taxonomy: A system for describing, classifying, and evaluating executive positions. *Journal of Applied Psychology, 61,* 410–418.

Trattner, M. H. (1982). Synthetic validity and its application to the uniform guidelines validation requirements. *Personnel Psychology, 35,* 383–397.

Trattner, M. H., Fine, S. A., & Kubis, J. F. (1955). A comparison of worker requirement ratings made by reading job descriptions and by direct job observation. *Personnel Psychology, 8,* 183–194.

Ulrich, D., Brockbank, W., Yeung, A. K., & Lake, D. G. (1995). Human resource competencies: An empirical assessment. *Human Resource Management, 34,* 473–495.

U.S. Census Bureau. (2004). *Projected population of the United States, by race and Hispanic origin: 2000 to 2050* [On-line]. Available: http://www.census.gov/ipc/www/usinterimproj/

U.S. Civil Service Commission. (1977). *Instructions for the Factor Evaluation System.* Washington, DC: U.S. Government Printing Office.

U.S. Department of Labor. (1939). *Dictionary of occupational titles.* Washington, DC: U.S. Government Printing Office.

U.S. Department of Labor. (1967). *Manual for the General Aptitude Test Battery, Section III: Development.* Washington, DC: U.S. Government Printing Office.

U.S. Department of Labor. (1972). *Handbook for analyzing jobs.* Washington, DC: U.S. Government Printing Office.

U.S. Department of Labor. (2005a). *Workers on flexible and shift schedules in May 2004* (Publication No. USDL 05–1198). Washington, DC: U.S. Government Printing Office.

U.S. Department of Labor. (2005b). *Work at home in 2004* (Publication No. USDL 05–1768). Washington, DC: U.S. Government Printing Office.

Van de Voort, D. M., & Stalder, B. K. (1988). Organizing for job analysis. In S. Gael (Ed.), *The job analysis handbook for business, industry, and government* (Vol. I, pp. 315–328). New York: Wiley.

Van Iddekinge, C. H., Putka, D. J., Raymark, P. H., & Eidson, C. E. (2005). Modeling error variance in job specification ratings: The influence of rater, job, and organization-level factors. *Journal of Applied Psychology, 90,* 323–334.

Varca, P. E., & Pattison, P. (1993). Evidentiary standards in employment discrimination: A view toward the future. *Personnel Psychology, 46,* 239–258.

Wagner, R. F. (1951). Using critical incidents to determine selection test weights. *Personnel Psychology, 4,* 373–381.

Wall, T. D., & Jackson, P. R. (1995). New manufacturing initiatives and shopfloor job design. In A. Howard (Ed.), *The changing nature of work* (pp. 139–174). San Francisco: Jossey-Bass.

Webb, N. M, Shavelson, R. J., Shea, J., & Morello, E. (1981). Generalizability of general education development ratings of job in the United States. *Journal of Applied Psychology, 6,* 186–192.

Weiser, M. (1991). The computer in the 21st century. *Scientific American, 265,* 94–104.

Weiser, M. (1993). Some computer science issues in ubiquitous computing. *Communications of the ACM, 36,* 74–84.

Wellins, R. S., Byham, W. C., & Dixon, G. R. (1994). *Inside teams.* San Francisco: Jossey-Bass.

Wernimont, P. F. (1988). Recruitment, selection, and placement. In S. Gael (Ed.), *The job analysis handbook for business, industry, and government* (Vol. I, pp. 193–204). New York: Wiley.

Wexley, K. N., & Silverman, S. B. (1978). An examination of differences between managerial effectiveness and response patterns on a structured job analysis questionnaire. *Journal of Applied Psychology, 63,* 646–649.

Wexley, K. N., & Yukl, G. A. (1984). *Organizational behavior and personnel psychology* (2nd ed.). Homewood, IL: Irwin.

Wheelan, S. A. (1999). *Creating effective teams: A guide for members and leaders.* Thousand Oaks, CA: Sage.

Wiersma, U., & Latham, G. P. (1986). The practicality of behavioral observation scales, behavioral expectation scales, and trait scales. *Personnel Psychology, 39,* 619–628.

Wrzesniewski, A., & Dutton, J. E. (2001). Crafting a job: Revisioning employees as active crafters of their work. *Academy of Management Review, 26,* 179–201.

Young, S. M. (1992). A framework for successful adoption and performance of Japanese manufacturing practices in the U.S. *Academy of Management Review, 17,* 677–700.

Zerga, J. E. (1943). Job analysis: A resume and bibliography. *Journal of Applied Psychology, 27,* 249–267.

Index

About the Authors

Michael T. Brannick earned his PhD in industrial and organizational psychology from Bowling Green State University in 1986. He is currently Professor in the Psychology Department at the University of South Florida. He teaches a graduate seminar in job analysis. His research interests include research methods and teams.

Edward L. Levine earned his PhD in industrial and organizational psychology from New York University in 1970. He is currently Professor in the Psychology Department at the University of South Florida and served as chair of the department from 1993 to 2001. His research interests include job analysis, personnel selection, control in organizations, and affect at work. He is certified as a diplomate in Industrial and Organizational Psychology by the American Board of Professional Psychology, and he is a Fellow of the Society for Industrial and Organizational Psychology and the American Psychological Association.

Frederick P. Morgeson earned his PhD in industrial and organizational psychology from Purdue University in 1998. He is currently an Associate Professor of Management at the Eli Broad College of Business at Michigan State University and is a recipient of the 2005 American Psychological Association Distinguished Scientific Award for Early Career Contribution to Psychology in Applied Psychology. His research involves attempting to understand the nature of work, which includes the design and measurement of work activities, including those assigned to teams. In addition, he studies the effectiveness of different staffing techniques and the role leadership plays in high-risk and team-based environments.